Nationalism, Capitalism, and Colonization in Nineteenth-Century Quebec

Nationalism, Capitalism, and Colonization in Nineteenth-Century Quebec

The Upper St Francis District

J.I. LITTLE

McGill-Queen's University Press
Kingston, Montreal, London

© McGill-Queen's University Press 1989
ISBN 0-7735-0699-3

Legal deposit 3rd quarter 1989
Bibliothèque nationale du Québec

Printed in Canada on acid-free paper

This book has been published with the help of a
grant from the Canadian Federation for the Humanities, using funds provided by the Social Sciences and
Humanities Research Council of Canada.

Canadian Cataloguing in Publication Data

Little, J. I. (John Irvine), 1947–
    Nationalism, capitalism and colonization in nine-
teenth century Quebec: the upper St. Francis district

    Includes index.
    ISBN 0-7735-0699-3

    1. Land settlement – Quebec (Province) – Wolfe
(Census division) – History – 19th century. 2. Land
settlement – Quebec (Province) – Saint-François River
Region (Yamaska) – History – 19th century. 3. Wolfe
(Quebec): Census division) – History. 4. Saint-Fran-
çois River Region (Yamaska, Quebec) – History. I.
Title.

FC2945.S226111L48 1989   971.4'573   C89-090037-X
F1054.S24L48 1989

61,075

To my mother and the memory of my father

Contents

Tables

Maps and Figures

FIGURES

Preface

French-Canadian settlement boundaries began to expand dramatically in the 1840s, after more than two centuries of incremental growth within the seigneuries of the St Lawrence River and its major tributaries. Rich land was brought under the plow in the Lac Saint-Jean region and in the Bois-Francs, but much of the newly colonized territory was of marginal agricultural potential at best. Indeed, the colonization movement did not arise in spontaneous fashion, but as a carefully orchestrated campaign to prevent emigration to the United States. Beginning in 1848 the French-Canadian élite, largely inspired by the Roman Catholic Church, mobilized itself to entice the province's surplus rural population onto a marginal rural hinterland at the very time that industrial capitalism was beginning to revolutionize North American society.

These are well-known historical facts, but social scientists have been too quick to conclude that the colonization movement was strictly a conservative, agrarian-inspired reaction to the perceived threats of a new social order. Such a deduction is based more on hindsight than on careful attention to the historical context of the mid-nineteenth century. Not only did Canada East's urban development remain too slow to absorb a large percentage of the habitants who left their home parishes, but the original American destinations were the midwestern frontier and rural or small-town communities in Vermont and Maine. Only in the early 1860s did the tide turn toward the southern New England mill towns.[1] Colonization propaganda inevitably acquired an anti-urban tone, but the reality behind the rhetoric was that proponents, including priests, did not hesitate to promote industries to attract a permanent population to the frontier. Finally, while the fundamental role played by the Church cannot be denied, the anticlerical Rouges and even the pragmatic Bleus were from the outset active spokesmen for the colonization movement.

There is no particular reason why the secular *petite bourgeoisie* should have favoured the preservation of a traditional peasant culture, but large-scale emigration did threaten to diminish its clientele and therefore to undermine its already rather precarious livelihood. From this point of view the colonization movement remains a French-Canadian nationalist reaction to the habitant exodus, but one motivated by the élite's desire to direct that exodus into channels where it could maintain and even strengthen its community-based socio-economic hegemony. In sum, the French-Canadian nationalists were not reacting against the rise of industrial capitalism so much as they were attempting to accommodate themselves to the challenges it presented.

The habitants were actually encouraged to continue the process of agricultural commercialization, with the mechanization and consolidation that this implied, since a subsistence-oriented peasantry would be of relatively little economic value to the merchant-professional class. Even on the settlement frontier the rapidly expanding lumber operations would provide markets for agricultural production until external communications links could be completed. The flaw in this strategy was that the agricultural potential of the province's hinterland was considerably poorer than seemed generally to be appreciated. The forests themselves offered the most dependable source of capital wealth, yet the nationalist élite failed to challenge the monopolization of crown timber by large-scale English-speaking entrepreneurs. The reason, in large part, was that they were slaves of the North American agrarian view of the forests as a temporary phenomena, an encumbrance to the natural process of population expansion. They simply could not envision a system such as that in Finland or northern Sweden whereby settlers themselves owned the timber resource, relying on agriculture only for their household subsistence. Yet that is in part the system of survival which the French-Canadian colonists practised, taking from company timber limits that which the miserly land-granting system legally denied them. Ironically then, the agrarianism of the French-Canadian colonization proponents was more antithetical to the survival of a peasant-oriented economy than it was to the rise of industrial capitalism.

During the past ten years Quebec historians have finally begun to pay serious attention to the nineteenth-century colonization movement.[2] Important new insights have emerged in intellectual-cultural studies as well as in regionally based, socio-economic analyses. Not surprisingly, however, such sharply differing focuses have resulted in conflicting interpretations. Based on a careful reading of their subjects' rhetoric, three recent ideological studies have put forward the revisionist theory that the colonization movement was a visionary, expansionist process in every sense of the term.[3] A different image emerges from the work of social historians who are less concerned with the motivation behind the expansion of the settlement frontier than with its results. For those who concentrate on the dynamics of population migration, the organization of the colonization movement was basically irrelevant, at least once the process had been set in motion.[4] For others, who have placed their local and regional studies within a theoretical economic framework, colonization contributed to the economic and social underdevelopment of the province.[5]

The following study takes a different methodological approach by examining the agents of colonization (basically church, state and capital, but also certain key individuals) as well as their impact on a specific Quebec frontier. The historical, geographical, and theoretical context is established in the first chapter, and each of the following chapters focuses on a particular project or enterprise which influenced the socio-economic development of the upper St Francis district. While that development is traced in a roughly chronological order, each chapter can be read as a self-contained study which contributes in a particular way to the overall analysis. That analysis claims that Quebec's nineteenth-century colonization movement was a dynamic but intrinsically flawed response on the part of the French-Canadian *petite bourgeoisie* to the rise of industrial capitalism. The flaw lay in the failure to take greater advantage of the potential for local development offered by the timber industry. Perhaps the opportunity for local control was weaker in districts less centrally located than the upper St Francis watershed, but the greatest limitation seems to have lain in the failure of the politicians and the colonization proponents to conceive of an alternative to the hegemony of large-scale capital. When the grip of the British American Land Company was removed from much of the St Francis Tract and the British government relinquished control of provincial crown lands, the local administration simply handed the timber over to large-scale lumber firms, even while it was launching the colonization movement. Normand Séguin, in *La Conquête du sol*, concluded that colonization was promoted essentially to advance the interests of the timber capitalists, and that the lumber industry was intrinsically inimical to agricultural progress. This volume will argue that there are two basic reasons why these aspects of Séguin's interpretation do not apply to the upper St Francis district. First, the major lumber companies had little to gain and much to lose from settlement in their timber berths; and, secondly, environmental limitations to agricultural commercialization dictated that a mixed agri-forestry economy was essential to the long-term survival of the settler community. A further analysis of that economy, and its socio-cultural impact, will appear in a forthcoming volume which will focus exclusively on the lives of the settlers themselves. It should be noted, finally, that this study quotes the settlers' spokesmen and government agents, among others, exactly as their words were written but without flagging missing accents and obvious errors with *sic*.

Acknowledgments

Research for this book was funded by the Social Sciences and Humanities Research Council of Canada, as well as by research grants from Simon Fraser University. Grateful acknowledgment is also made for courteous assistance by the archivists at the National Archives of Canada, the Archives nationales du Québec at Quebec and Sherbrooke, the Scottish Record Office, the Eastern Townships Historical Society, and the McCord Museum. The staffs at the Ministère d'Énergie, Mines, et Ressources and the Ministère des Terres et Forêts very kindly provided me with research space and unlimited access to their historical records. Access and assistance were also readily forthcoming from the regional registry offices, the Sherbrooke archdiocesan archives, the Séminaire de Saint-Hyacinthe, the presbytery of Piopolis, the St Andrew's Society of Montreal, the municipality of Winslow South, and various other ecclesiastical and private institutions.

Maps are reproduced with the kind permission of the Service arpentage of the Ministère d'Énergie, Mines et Ressources, the National Map Collection of the National Archives of Canada, and the Archives nationales du Québec. Several photographs were made available by the Eastern Townships Historical Society and the National Archives of Canada. Quotations from the R. G. Dun and Company collection are by authorization of the Baker Library, Harvard University. The editors of *Histoire sociale – Social History* and the *Revue d'histoire de l'Amérique française* kindly granted permission to republish revised versions of articles which appear as chapter 5 (*Hs – SH* XIX, 37 (1986): 9–37) and part of chapter 9 (*RHAF* XXXII (1978): 19–39), respectively. An earlier version of chapter 8 was published in the Canadian Historical Association, *Historical Papers*, 1977, 65–85.

Many individuals have been involved in the production of this volume. I wish to express my appreciation first to those who generously contributed their critical advice – Hugh Johnston, Graeme Wynn, Stephen Gray, Wendie Nelson, and the dedicated readers for the ssfc and McGill-Queen's University Press. I was also fortunate to work with an outstanding research assistant, Diane Couture. Finally, I wish to thank Anita Mahoney and Barbara Barnett for their patience in typing the manuscript, and the staff at Simon Fraser's Instructional Media Centre who drafted several of the maps, and editor Mary McDougall Maude for her prompt and careful reading. To my wife Andrea above all goes my gratitude for her patience and encouragement.

La Patrie. This photograph was taken around the turn of the century, long after the village had been moved to a more promising site than that of the repatriation colony. Some of the project's cabins can be seen in the centre of the village. In the background is Mount Megantic, one of the highest elevations in the Eastern Townships. (Collection of Aldage Rancourt, La Patrie)

Scotstown in the Year 1874. This painting illustrates the settlement headquarters of the Glasgow Canadian Land and Trust Company during its first year of operations. The sawmill had yet to be built. The artist noted that Isaac Pinkham occupied the company's two-storey, square-timber building – the fifth to the left – and claimed that he was the mail carrier and stage driver from Lennoxville. Next to it is the company's office and store, the only building with a foundation and white clapboard siding. A small girl can also be seen with her dog beside one of the worker's log cabins. (Collection of P. Sherman, Scotstown)

The Village of Robinson, Bury Township. The small size and rural nature of Robinson (today's Bury), thirty-five years after its founding by the British American Land Company, illustrates the lack of progress made in the St Francis Tract. In 1871 Robinson served essentially as a local service centre, with a model school, two churches, store, public house, and several artisans' shops and mills. Some additional growth was about to take place with the arrival of the St Francis and Megantic International Railway. (Charles P. de Volpi and P.H. Scowen, *The Eastern Townships. A Pictorial Record* [Montreal: Dev-Sco Publications 1962])

Notre-Dame-des-Bois. Chesham Township may have been the home of the rebellious repatriate Pierre Vaillant, but this thousand-pound statue donated by Jérome-Adolphe Chicoyne in 1876 symbolized where the ultimate authority lay. The name of Vaillant-bourg was changed to Notre-Dame-des-Bois, which was sanctioned as a pilgrimage site for the district's colonists. The church shown here had been converted from the original hostel built as a temporary shelter for the repatriation colonists, and the presbytery was erected in 1879–80. (Collection of the Eastern Townships Historical Society)

Townships Colonization – A Settler. A satirical, rather racist comment on the colonization efforts of the "Association pour l'établissement des Canadiens-français dans les Townships du Bas-Canada." (J.W. Bengough, *A Caricature History of Canadian Politics* [Toronto: The Grip Printing and Publishing Co. 1886; repr. Toronto: Peter Martin Associates 1974])

TOWNSHIPS COLONIZATION—A SETTLER.

YOUNG LITERARY LEADER.—HERE IS ONE SETTLER, SARE, FOR YOUR TOWNSHIP, SARE, ON YOUR FARM, SARE.
TOWNSHIPPER.—OH, THAT'S YOUR SETTLER, EH ? WHY THERE'S LOTS OF THEM CHAPS HERE ALREADY—IN THE MASHES !

PUNCH IN CANADA, 1849.

Bethléem – Two Views. Taken around 1882, these
two tin-types record the work accomplished by the
three Trappists from Meilleray, France. Note that
each of them holds a different implement to symbol-
ize the main tasks they faced. The log chapel originally built for the repatriation colony had been
moved to the Trappists' 800-acre site. The small
space overhead in the chapel served as living quar-
ters. When the abbott inspected the property in 1882,
he expressed great disappointment with the climate
and the condition of the roads in the area. The
project was soon liquidated at a substantial loss to the
religious order. (Collection of the Eastern Townships
Historical Society)

Residence of John Henry Pope, Cookshire, Quebec. Now a medical clinic, Pope's imposing house appears just as it did in a photograph published in the *History of Compton County* seven years after his death, in 1889. (Photo by author, 1988)

Jérome-Adolphe Chicoyne. Trained as a lawyer and journalist, Chicoyne did not allow his agrarian nationalism to interfere with the business side of his colonization projects in the upper St Francis district. (Collection of Eastern Townships Historical Society)

John Henry Pope, 1869. Though he would not be
elevated to the cabinet until 1871, Pope's stature as
one of the leading entrepreneurs and politicians
of the Eastern Townships is clearly reflected in this
photograph by Notman's Studio of Montreal. (NA
Photograph Division, *NA-25322*)

First House in Louise Township, 1899. The last
corner of the Eastern Townships to be settled was
remote and mountainous Louise Township which,
like Woburn further west, juts sharply into Maine as
part of the dividing line between the St Lawrence
and Atlantic watersheds. The Campagna family
– shown here with five of twelve offspring, the bishop of Sherbrooke, and two priests – lived alone in
the township for fourteen years. Their isolation was
ended to a degree when Mgr Larocque convinced the
government to build a colonization road along the
eastern side of Lake Megantic shortly after the visit
recorded in this photograph. (Bishop's University
Library, Eastern Townships Collection)

Woburn Timber Drive. The centre of Chicoyne's Nantes-financed colonization company was to be Woburn Township, south of Lake Megantic. Though few families ever settled in this remote and mountainous township, it did serve as the principal source of timber for the company's large mill at Lake Megantic. This photograph of a timber drive on the Arnold River, which flows north into Lake Megantic, was taken around the turn of the century. (Collection of the Eastern Townships Historical Society)

CANADIAN PACIFIC RAILWAY

(SHORT LINE.)

INTERNATIONAL RAILWAY COMPANY.

The direct route for Sportsmen from New York, Boston, Toronto, Montreal, and Quebec, to the Best Fishing and Hunting Grounds east of the Rocky Mountains.

Connecting with the Passumpsic, Vermont Central, Quebec Central, and Grand Trunk Railways, at Sherbrooke, P. Q., for

LAKE MEGANTIC,
SPIDER LAKE,
MOOSE RIVER,
DEAD RIVER REGION,
####### AND SEVEN PONDS,

Landing Passengers nearer these Famous Fish and Game Resorts than any other Railway or Stage Line.

DAILY PASSENGER TRAIN leaves Sherbrooke at 3.30 P. M., arriving at Lake Megantic at 6.55 P. M. Returning, leaves Megantic at 7.15 A. M., arriving in Sherbrooke at 11.15 A. M.

MIXED TRAIN leaves Sherbrooke daily at 7.00 A. M., connecting with the morning train from Boston and New York, over the Lowell system (B. & M. R. R.) at Lennoxville, arriving at Lake Megantic at 12.15 P. M. Returning, leaves Megantic at 2.10 P. M., arriving in Sherbrooke at 7.20 P. M., in time to take supper and connect with the evening trains for Boston and New York.

CONSTRUCTION TRAINS leave Megantic Village (Agnes) almost daily for Holeb Pond and the Moose River Region. Return tickets from Sherbrooke to Holeb issued to sportsmen at single fare.

For connections with other lines and steamers on Lake Megantic, see chapter on *routes, in this book.*

N. B. — SPECIAL REDUCED RATES given members of the Megantic Fish and Game Club, from Sherbrooke to Spider Lake and return, including coupons on steamer, upon presentation of requisition from the Secretary.

J. H. VAN ZILE, Supt., SHERBROOKE, P. Q.

20

Canadian Pacific Railway Advertisement. The International Railway may have been promoted originally as a colonization line, but it brought more American sportsmen to the district than it did settlers. The brochure in which this ad appeared was published by the Boston-based Megantic Fish and Game Corporation, which held exclusive fishing and hunting rights over a large tract in the Lake Megantic area as well as in northern Maine. (*Guide to the Megantic, Spider and Upper Dead River Regions of Quebec and Maine* [Boston: Heber Bishop, 1888], Bishop's University Library, Eastern Townships Collection)

(*Facing page*)
British American Land Company Advertisement. This rather misleading advertisement was printed at a time when the hard-pressed land company had ceased investing in what remained of its St Francis Tract. Note that the long-term credit scheme has replaced all attemps to assist immigrant settlers, and that only prospective purchasers of cleared farms were offered transportation assistance.

IN SEARCH OF

LANDS

FOR SETTLEMENT.

THE BRITISH AMERICAN LAND COMPANY, incorporated by Royal Charter, and Act of Parliament, offer for sale, a number of FARMS, partly cleared and cultivated, and ready for immediate occupation. TOWN LOTS, and MILL SITES, and seven hundred thousand acres of WILD LAND, in portions of any extent from fifty acres, upwards. These properties are situated in the District of Saint Francis, in the Eastern Townships on the SOUTH SIDE OF CANADA, one of the most beautiful, fertile, healthy portions of British America. They are held under the Soccage Tenure, direct from the Crown, and free of all Feudal burden whatsoever.

These Townships are centrally situated at a distance of from Fifty to Eighty miles, from Quebec and Montreal. They are well watered every where, possessed of excellent roads, and diversified with pretty lakes and fishy streams and rivers. The soil is equal in fertility to that of any part of the Continent, the appearance of the Country is highly picturesque, and the climate is eminently salubrious. There are Saw and Grist Mills, Mechanic's Shops, Smiths, Foundry, Woolen Manufactory, Academies, Schools, Churches of all denominations, and a College is being built. Every description of Grain and Root Crops cultivated in Great Britain is found to succeed well in this district, and Corn, Cattle, Horses, Sheep and Pigs, are raised with great advantage, as articles of export to the neighbouring sea port Towns.

The Company sell their lands at very reasonable prices, and on an indulgent credit, six years being allowed to pay up the annual instalments. To such persons as can prepay thirty dollars, the first instalment of a lot or farm of 100 acres, they grant A FREE TRANSPORT for their FAMILIES and LUGGAGE not (exceeding 8 cwt.,) from MONTREAL, QUEBEC, or the ST. LAWRENCE to SHERBROOKE; and, if on arrival there, they think they can do better than purchase from the Company, they will return them the money, retaining only the proportion of it actually expended on themselves. To such persons of respectable character as have come out under the present depression and have no money, they grant permission on credit to settle on new land, and to form at once an independent family home, in which case NO MONEY IS REQUIRED DOWN; they sell most excellent settling land at about ten shillings per acre, and when the price is paid, they give at the Company's expense, a warranted freehold Title, which, when enregistered, becomes the most free and sure holding under the Crown.

There is, generally, a fair demand for hired labour in these Townships, at good wages both for men and women, the Gosford road affords present employment for destitute emigrants; and parents blessed with large families, can generally subsist themselves and half their children by the hire of the other half, during the first winter, while they are clearing and preparing for crop, the lot which they may have selected, from the Company on Credit, as their future family home.

The Company's property is accessible by the roads from Quebec, Montreal and Sorel, but the route most easily travelled at present is that from Port Saint Francis through Drummondville to Melbourne and Sherbrooke, &c. The stage fare is about 3d. per mile, and the cartage of furniture is 3s. 9d. per cwt. to Sherbrooke or nearly a half-penny per mile for each cwt. The Company have Agents in the several sections of the District itself, as well as at the ports of landing, for the convenient local sale of land, and for the advice, protection, and encouragement of their settlers. Further particulars may be learned on application at the Company's head office in Sherbrooke, or to the Company's Agents, Mr. C. M. Hyndman, Quebec; Mr. James Court, Commissioner Street, Montreal; Mr. Hayden, Sorel; Mr. Smith Leith, Port St. Francis; Mr. G. L. Marler, Nicolet and Drummondville; Mr. Tait, Melbourne; Mr. Wood, Shefford; Mr. Lyman, Granby; Mr. Fee, Eaton; and Mr. Hubbard, Stanstead.

Quebec Emigrant Agency Office of
The British American Land Company,
·20th June, 1342·

Sawmill of C.S. Clark and Company, Brompton Falls. Said to be one of the largest sawmills in North America at the time of its construction in 1854, it employed eighty to one hundred men when operating at full capacity and produced as much as twenty million feet of lumber per year. Note that in this photograph the middle ventilator no longer boasts the elaborate weather-vane described by the *Canadian Times* in 1855. (Bishop's University Library, Eastern Townships Collection)

The Town of Lake Megantic. The stumps in the foreground suggest that this photo was taken when Lake Megantic was a young town. The head of the lake was essentially still wilderness before the arrival of the International Railway in 1879, but it rapidly became the site of the only significant urban centre east of Sherbrooke. The long wharf shown here must have served to hold log booms towed up the lake by steam vessels. (Bishop's University Library, Eastern Townships Collection)

Piopolis – Road Construction. This photograph was taken a considerable number of years after the original settlement of Piopolis, but it illustrates that the local priest (shown here at the right) continued to oversee work on colonization roads. The plow is presumably being used to improve drainage. (Collection of the Eastern Townships Historical Society)

*Nationalism, Capitalism, and Colonization in
Nineteenth-Century Quebec*

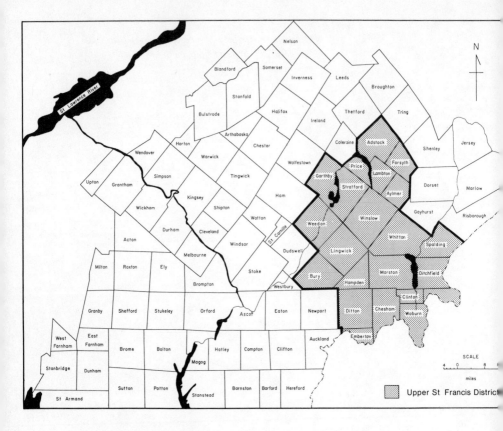

Map 1   The Eastern Townships (From "Map of Montreal and the Eastern
Townships" published by E.R. Smith & Sons, 1897)

The Colonization Movement and the Agri-Forestry Economy in the Upper St Francis District

> These few huts now scattered in the middle of the woods will be converted into elegant houses. We will have a village of several thousands. Who knows, perhaps a city. Stores, shops, workshops, mills will appear like magic. We will have a doctor, a lawyer and in the centre of the township a church, and behind it a school.
>
> Antoine Gérin-Lajoie, *Jean Rivard*

French-Canadian nationalism owes its origins and ongoing strength to a sense of resentment against the economic domination of Anglo-Protestant capital. After the Conquest, with access to high civil and military office cut off, and the "staple" trades in fur, timber, and wheat controlled by British merchants, the seigneurial élite atrophied and the middle class found its options essentially limited to local trade and the legal and medical professions. Men from these professions dominated the popularly elected House of Assembly after its institution in 1791, but found that basic political power, including the exercise of patronage, remained in the grip of the local British official and merchant clique. As a result, French Canada's middle class became receptive to the powerful twin doctrines of liberalism and nationalism then emanating from its neighbour to the south as well as from its former mother country.[1]

Radical ideology was crushed along with the Rebellions of 1837–38, and the birth of the united Province of Canada brought to the fore in the Legislative Assembly a more pragmatic group, willing to join forces with the moderate Reformers of Upper Canada in order to win "responsible government." Through the agency of double ministries, and by voting essentially as a bloc, French Canada ex-

ercised political self-government for most practical purposes after
1848.[2] Concurrently, the commercial "Empire of the St Lawrence"
was coming to a close as England took her final steps towards free
trade.[3] But, important as these developments were to the progress
of colonial independence, English-Protestant economic domination
became more entrenched than ever with the rise of industrial capitalism after mid-century. A leading politician such as George-
Étienne Cartier might well be satisfied with his role as Grand Trunk
solicitor, but more ardent nationalists remained concerned about the
inferior economic status of the French Canadians.[4] Not only did the
Rouges offspring of the Parti Patriote perpetuate its agrarian anti-
capitalist bias, but the reactionary ultramontane movement was fast
becoming the major nationalist force in the province. According to
its tenets, the vocation of French Canada was to perpetuate in a
godless, materialistic North America the untainted, orthodox Catholic religion and social values of pre-revolutionary France.[5]

The greatest immediate threat to French Canada's providential
mission was the draining of large numbers of its population south
to the United States where they would be directly exposed to the
forces of assimilation and secularization. The 1849 legislative inquiry
into the emigration problem claimed that 20,000 Lower Canadians
had left the province since 1844, the year the exodus first became
widespread.[6] The growth of the textile industry in New England
during the 1860s further stimulated the diaspora, which surpassed
200,000 by 1870 and 600,000 by the end of the century.[7] The Catholic Church, which was now taking a more active role in politics,
helped to define the response to what was perceived to be a major
national crisis. Thus the great ultramontane champion, Mgr Ignace
Bourget of Montreal, became instrumental in founding one of the
first colonization projects in Lower Canada, the "Association pour
l'établissement des Canadiens-français dans les townships du Bas-
Canada." Indeed the launching of this society was the last occasion
in which Bourget and the radical nationalists of the Institut Canadien
would collaborate with each other.[8]

Frontier settlement was ideally suited to the purposes of the ultramontanes because it meant that French Canadians would not only
remain in Canada East / Quebec, but on the land as well. Like the
concept of a providential mission, the colonization movement was
somewhat paradoxical, for what was basically a conservative defensive reflex also had its positive expansionist side. Furthermore, not
all colonization proponents were ideologues or idealists, ultramontanes or Rouges; the movement would have simply remained a utopian dream without the active support of the pragmatic and

moderate Bleu administration. Among their number were the authors of the first two novels to promote French-Canadian colonization, the future premier, Pierre-Joseph-Olivier Chauveau, and the legislative librarian, Antoine Gérin-Lajoie. The protagonists of *Charles Guérin* (serialized in 1846–47) and the two-volume *Jean Rivard* (1862 and 1864) may have established model parishes, but they were parishes where industry played a crucial role, and where Guérin and Rivard were able to reach the middle-class status they had originally been destined for in their overcrowded seigneurial homeland.[9]

The heroic Jean Rivard defended his promotion of industry by proclaiming that he aimed to "transpose all that is good in urban living, taking care to exclude the false, the exaggerated and the immoral."[10] Still, there was wealth to be made by Rivardville's *petite bourgeoisie*. The hard-working people might have been so healthy that the local doctor would have to do some farming on the side, but "exchanges, property sales, commercial transactions occurred from time to time, profiting individuals. The notary began to get rich from the fees he collected."[11] If the novels *Jean Rivard* and *Charles Guérin* are good representations of the mainstream nationalists' ideal colonization strategy, and there is no reason to feel that they are not, one must agree with geographer Christian Morissonneau when he suggests that their "ruralisme" was not a "refus catégorique" but rather a "rationalisation de l'échec de la bourgeoisie à entrer dans le monde des affaires continental dominé par le capital étranger."[12] During the mid-1870s, for example, Sherbrooke's *Le Pionnier* would proclaim that the English-speaking merchant class was preventing the implementation of protective tariffs and thereby causing the French-Canadian exodus: "La nation canadienne est essentiellement *colonisatrice* et *manufacturière*."[13]

After Confederation – as the exodus accelerated, as the ultramontane movement reached its apogee, and as the settlement frontier was stretched to its practicable outer limits – colonization propaganda took on more of the trappings of a utopian crusade. While the new province of Ontario reluctantly accepted the limitations of its settlement frontier, in Quebec the north became "la terre promise," and propagandists spoke of colonizing as far as the James Bay area and even the North Pole![14] But those actively involved in the movement, such as the famous Curé François-Xavier-Antoine Labelle, were generally forced to be pragmatic. Labelle not only was a strong advocate of agricultural commercialization through the dairy industry, he also did his best to attract French and Belgian capital for industrial development in the colonization zones.[15] As we shall see in this volume, Labelle's contemporary and counterpart in the Eastern Townships, Jérôme-Adolphe Chicoyne, was cut out of essentially the same ideological cloth.

Much of the colonization movement focused on the Laurentians and Lac Saint-Jean region, but the south shore, including the Eastern Townships, played a more important role than historians generally appear to realize. Morissonneau for one is wide of the mark when he states that "les Cantons de l'Est seront rapidement considérés comme un pis-aller, trop 'exposés' par la presence des Anglais, surtout des Loyalistes, ces sur-Anglais hostiles à la venue des Canadiens français."[16] First, few Loyalists ever settled the region, and its English-speaking residents were largely indifferent to those marginal townships which remained unsettled at mid-century.[17] Secondly, one of the reasons that the Eastern Townships became the first major focus of the colonization movement was the nationalistic desire to reclaim this section of the province for French Canadians.[18] It was no accident that Gérin-Lajoie explicitly located his two-part novel on the Townships' northern frontier (known as the Bois-Francs), where Jean Rivard had to acquire his land from an English absentee proprietor.[19] Furthermore, we shall see that when Confederation stimulated greater government involvement in the colonization movement, much of the initiative was focused on the region's upper St Francis district.

If one defines the Eastern Townships as including all the townships bordered by the seigneurial zone of the St Lawrence, Chaudière, and Yamaska-Richelieu valleys, the French-Canadian population of the region increased from 14,580 in 1844 (23 per cent of the total) to 97,041 in 1871 (58 per cent of the total). Approximately three-quarters of these francophones lived outside the traditionally English-speaking counties of Missisquoi, Brome, Stanstead, Richmond, and Compton. Within these older counties a disproportionate number of French Canadians occupied marginal land. During the following two decades about one-third of the French-Canadian expansion in the Eastern Townships took place in centrally located industrial centres such as Sherbrooke, Magog, and Coaticook. Nevertheless, by 1891, when the region's approximately 161,000 French Canadians were 69 per cent of the total population, the great majority lived in communities which had never been inhabited by anglophones.[20]

When nationalists such as Jules-Paul Tardivel spoke of "la conquête pacifique" of the Eastern Townships, they were referring to colonization rather than the displacement of English-speaking farmers, a process which would begin in earnest only after the turn of the century.[21] Nevertheless, the term "conquest" was in certain respects an appropriate one even in the nineteenth century. Not only were the English-speaking communities hemmed in, and their political power base challenged, but a contest did take place for control of the eastern frontier of the region, from the St Francis Valley above Sherbrooke to the Lake Megantic area.[22] The descendants of the American pioneers in the Townships may have shunned this isolated, mountainous district, but we shall see that during the 1830s and 1840s two land companies were established to attract British immigrants to this large area. The only permanent colonists introduced were a few families from southern England and the outer Hebrides, and most of the district reverted to the crown just as the local government was winning control over the province's public lands. Here it would focus its first major colonization roads programme at mid-century.

French Canadians would quickly assert their numerical dominance in the district, despite a continued influx of displaced Highlanders from the Isle of Lewis, but the British Protestant presence remained dominant in other less tangible ways. Thus the British American Land Company continued to hold some of the most accessible land from its original St Francis Tract; local speculators also gained significant blocks of the more arable land in certain townships; and, most significantly, large lumber companies leased timber berths which covered much of the district, placing them in direct and bitter conflict with the settlers who depended upon the sale of logs to supplement their agricultural income. The St Francis and Megantic International Railway was pushed through the district in the 1870s despite the protests of French-Canadian settlers who had to share the costs though it did not cross their settlements, and, finally, British-based colonization companies would reappear during the 1870s and 1880s to reserve large sections of unsettled land in one last futile attempt at introducing British settlers to the district.

The contest, which will be fully explored in the following chapters, was essentially between French-speaking settlers and English-speaking capitalists. The result was that the French Canadians won a demographic victory, but failed to gain complete control of the district's economic resources. This failure strikes at the heart of why French Canada's second great colonization movement has generally been perceived as a misguided effort of major proportions. Historians have tended to discount the colonization process on the grounds that it failed to absorb all the province's surplus population, surely an unrealistic expectation. Furthermore, in noting that Quebec had approximately 45,000 more land occupants in 1901 than in 1851, Hamelin and Roby jumped to the conclusion that ten people went to the United States for every one that became a colonist, thereby forgetting the wives and dependents who were part of each new occupant's family.[23] Much of the newly cleared land was certainly of marginal quality, but, given the incapacity of Quebec's urban centres to absorb her surplus population, colonization was the only alternative to increased emigration.[24] Where the colonization proponents truly fell short was their failure to demand freer access to the main source of wealth in the new communities – the timber resource. Like the small reservations designed to force western Indians into full-time agriculture, land sales to colonists were restricted in size to what a single family might be expected to exploit almost exclusively in an agricultural sense.[25] Two hundred acres per family was the official maximum allowed, and many colonists in the upper St Francis district made do, at least officially, with a fifty-acre free grant. The non-arable portion of each crown lot could include some maple trees for sugar production and provide lumber for farm buildings, fences, and firewood, but it would not have been large enough to bring much income from the marketing of logs. Indeed, for a limited time after each lot was granted, it actually remained within the timber lease of whatever lumber company happened to monopolize the local crown berth.

The irony is that although the colonization champions railed loudly and repeatedly against the lumber companies, it was almost always on the basis that they were starting fires, taking trees needed for local construction purposes, cheating settlers they hired as loggers, or seizing logs cut by settlers on their own lots. Henri Bourassa, for example, argued that the settler and the lumber company were compatible because the latter needed the hay and potatoes supplied by the former. The great nationalist spokesman simply demanded that companies be kept off the lots claimed by colonists.[26] The only influential nineteenth-century figure who seems to have come close to advocating a true agri-forestry economy for settlers was the combative missionary-priest, Father Charles Paradis. In 1887 he recommended that forest lands be divided into two zones, one totally unsuited to settlement, where lumber companies would enjoy full control, and one with arable land not yet needed for settlement, where the companies would have temporary access on the basis of annual licences. Once a township or group of townships was opened to colonization, public forest reserves would be established for careful, renewable use by the community. Paradis's ally, Premier Honoré Mercier, went part way by temporarily terminating the access of leaseholders to the timber on settled lots, by officially recognizing the right of colonists with no clear title to market wood from their farms, and by preserving as a future woodlot twenty acres in every hundred-acre crown lot.[27] But only in the post–World War I era was a flexible system of forest reserves introduced to the province, and the small areas set aside in the colonization zones were designed simply to serve the short-term fuel and lumber needs of the inhabitants.[28] The agri-forestry economy had been officially recognized to a limited degree in 1904 by an amendment which stated that as long as a licensee held timber rights to a colonist's lot, he should give the colonist an opportunity to cut the timber at the current local rates. The colonist in turn had to give the licensee the right to purchase timber chopped in the clearing of his land.[29] If the experience of the lower St Lawrence region during the 1930s was typical, lumber companies simply ignored these regulations, encouraging their subcontractors to chop logs at will. Even the threat of violence between settlers and non-resident labourers failed to move the government officials.[30]

Whether or not they were aware of it, the colonization promoters could have found a smoothly functioning model of a true agri-forestry economy in Finland and northern Sweden where the forest frontiers were opened to colonization during the nineteenth century. Through commons reserves and, later, direct grants of up to several hundred hectares per family, most of the timberland in these two countries was alienated to the resident peasant populations so that they could supplement their subsistence agricultural economies. When the sawmill companies began to threaten peasant ownership by widespread purchase of private "farms," prohibitive legislation was passed in Sweden in 1906 and Finland in 1915.[31]

Only during the past few years have such arrangements begun to be promoted in marginal regions of Quebec such as the Gaspé.[32] It is somewhat ironic, therefore, that A.R.M. Lower could declare that "in the history of Canada the settler has invariably had first place." While he admitted that "lumbermen rarely experienced difficulty in securing control of desirable 'limits' and that at prices which gave little returns to the public in comparison with the value of the timber sold," Lower maintained that settlers should have been kept out of territory where they did "more harm than good." His harshest words were for the "fraudulent" settler whose "'farm' was merely a lumber camp under another name," but he failed to mention that many of these individuals were actually on the payroll of the lumber companies.[33] Employees' names could be submitted to acquire location tickets for the best wooded lots in any given area.[34] Lower was reacting in part to the renaissance of colonization schemes during the depression era in which he was writing, but his attitude has survived among a younger generation of historians, as the following statement by Michael Cross illustrates: "Rarely were the timbermen able to prevent the penetration of settlers into *their* forests. And the results were always the same, reckless clearing, disastrous forest fires. For the farmer, the forest was the enemy, to be defeated, to be obliterated as rapidly as possible."[35] Douglas McCalla has recently demonstrated, however, that even on the rich frontier lands of south-central Upper Canada the sale of timber products was an important supplement to the agricultural economy.[36]

Lower assumed that "the small occupants ... would cut a good deal less prudently than the big firms," but subsequent research has shown that the major lumbermen remained indifferent to conservation until the 1880s, by which time clear-cut techniques were leading to the extermination of the white pine.[37] Furthermore, it appears that Ontario's small woodlot owners of the early twentieth century actually managed their resource with considerable care and expertise.[38] As Finnish historian Jussi Raumolin has pointed out, private ownership based on small peasant forests might in principle be inimical to all regulatory effort by the public power, but Finnish forests were well managed while the government-owned, corporate-leased forests of Canada were (and are) not.[39] The timber berths of the Eastern Townships were no exception to this rule, as we shall see.

Not all Canadian historians have viewed the colonization movement as an infringement on the vested rights of lumbermen, but those sympathetic to the settlers tend to argue that agriculture and forestry were not mutually compatible. Work in the woods simply took too much time and energy from the farmer and his horses, retarding clearing operations, delaying seeding, and so on.[40] Recently, however, Gérard Bouchard has found that the Saguenay lumber crews were composed largely of bachelors, with a small minority of young male spouses who needed cash to begin exploiting their land. Not only was forest revenue invested largely in the farm, but the logging and agricultural calendars were actually quite complementary, with woods work generally lasting only from November to March or even February.[41]

As Guy Gaudreau has pointed out, there are basically three different interpretations concerning the agriculture-forest relationship, epitomized above by Lower, Séguin, and Bouchard, respectively. Lower stresses the conflict between settler and lumber company to the detriment of the latter; Séguin stresses the economic link between the two to the detriment of the former; and Bouchard stresses the beneficial economic links between the two.[42] A fourth interpretation is necessary – at least as far as areas like the upper St Francis district are concerned – one that will account for the conflict between settler and timber monopoly, but not assume that there was a basic antipathy between farming and logging in marginal zones where physical conditions dictated that setters partake in both activities.[43] What explains the failure of a Scandinavian-type agri-forestry system even to be conceived of in Quebec, despite the strength of the province's nineteenth-century colonization movement and the physical similarities of the northern settlement frontiers? It is not enough to suggest, as H.V. Nelles has done, that: "Though there were scattered pockets of good land to be found there, the generally thin soil and rock of the bulk of the Shield precluded its being parcelled out to a permanent farming population. No amount of agrarian rhetoric could transform the wilderness Shield into the garden of the freehold farmer."[44] This statement does nevertheless identify the first of three major impediments to the concept of a mixed farm-forest economy – the North American agrarian myth.

Agrarianism was far from unique to Quebec.[45] As a matter of fact, exhaustive research by Lois Rock has revealed that agrarian propaganda was not a major literary genre in nineteenth-century French Canada, and that the message simply relied on a few well-worn moralistic platitudes.[46] It remains true, nevertheless, that a novel such as *Jean Rivard* was widely read, and that its hero did not simply reflect the idealist "pastoralism" of a Thomas Jefferson who was basically indifferent to economic questions.[47] While Jefferson failed to think of farms primarily as economic units, Gérin-Lajoie's hero – with his Ayrshire cows, South Down sheep, and Berkshire pigs – is obsessed with agricultural improvement. He echoes what appears to have been a common perception among the middle-class nationalists: educate the habitants to become progressive farmers and the province's economic problems will be solved.[48]

Jean Rivard might lament the "granting to poor settlers land that will never produce anything in spite of all their efforts," but, just as the agrarian promoters in the western dry belt argued that rain would follow the plow, French-Canadian advocates of colonization (supported, it must be said, by the reports of crown surveyors and land agents) tended to discount the physical impediments to agricultural expansion in Quebec.[49] Any concession that farmers might have to rely on the woods as a supplementary source of income would constitute an admission of doubt about an area's agricultural potential. On a more practical level, large land grants would theoretically limit the number of families who could be settled in any given area, though in practice most of the land in each township would remain in the hands of the crown to be leased to lumber companies. Finally, promoters of colonization in Canada East / Quebec had to compete with the frontier lands of the American Midwest where agriculture could indeed be a full-time occupation.[50]

Even when it became obvious that most French-Canadian colonists would remain dependent on the woods to some extent, "the Arcadian agrarian ideal of stability, ... and the solidity of the agricultural way of life" would mitigate against any notion that such a dual economy should be recognized and institutionalized.[51] Reflecting the North American agrarian bias, French-Canadian nationalists simply assumed that agriculture and logging were two distinct, indeed contradictory, ways of life; witness, for example, the following passage translated from Félix-Antoine Savard's *Menaud, maître-draveur*, published in 1937.

The men of the soil had learned from the land their slow, calm wisdom, their tenacious will to overcome, their patience of the slow flowering of its seed, their joy in its rich explosions of life. It was among the sheaves of the fruitful land that they learned their taste for cradles full of children.

The men of the forest had taken from the forest itself their daring in danger, their endurance of hardship, their ingenuity in all their needs. They had made their souls as the forest's own, fierce, watchful, drunk with freedom; they had cut themselves out a life suited to open spaces. All of them, beginning with the remotest of their marvelous wilderness treks in the past, possessed a pride of caste and a right of seniority over the settled men of the fields.[52]

Father Savard could safely eulogize a dying tradition, but ever since the days of the coureurs de bois the élite in French Canada had been particularly sensitive to anything which might promote a transient way of life. The colonists in *Jean Rivard* might labour in the village factories when they could spare some time from their farms, but the author studiously avoided mentioning work in the woods. In Sweden and Finland, of course, forest land was granted to encourage rural stability rather than the reverse, but one must remember that the official North American attitude tended to be that the forests were, for the most part, a temporary phenomenon of no lasting value. Thus, in attempting to explain Curé Labelle's failure to promote a French-Canadian–controlled lumber industry, his biographer writes: "son caractère essentiellement temporaire et transitoire dans les limites d'une localité la rend moins compatible avec le projet fondamental du peuplement que nourrit Labelle."[53] Because of their obsession with population stability, an obsession reinforced by the provincial exodus, colonization promoters such as

Gérin-Lajoie and Labelle were paradoxically more sympathetic to urban-based factories than to the more strictly rural-based lumber industry.

A second more tangible impediment to farmer control of the forest resource was the entrenched position of the monopolistic lumber companies. The power of the timber lords within the government was not unrelated to the state's dependency upon fees and duties from timber operations. At approximately 25 to 30 per cent of the total budget each year, these dues were second in importance only to the annual federal grant as a source of revenue and were a source which would have been much more difficult to tap if fragmented among large numbers of colonists.[54] The Finnish and Swedish governments had the advantage of the European tradition of taxing farmers, whereas even locally administered school and municipal levies were bitterly resisted when introduced to Canada East in the 1840s.[55] Such was the hard reality facing Curé Labelle when he became deputy minister of colonization, for in 1888 the Mercier government extended from less than a year to thirty months the companies' right to cut over any newly claimed lots within their reserves. An embarrassed Labelle could only rationalize that concessions had to be made to the lumber companies in order to raise sufficient revenue to pay for the new colonization railroads.[56]

Unlike Labelle, most colonization proponents did not have to concern themselves unduly with the government's fiscal problems, so political constraints do little to explain their failure to present a more radical programme. In fact, agrarianism was not the only ideological factor at work, for the nationalist spokesmen were members of the *petite bourgeoisie* with their own class interests to consider. This is not to agree with the social scientists who suggest that the colonization proponents feared "progress" for its threat to the traditional social structures as the basis of their authority. Rather, the colonization movement was basically a strategy of the French-Canadian élite to protect its economic status from the effects of large-scale emigration by its clientele. The leasehold system of the forest resource suited their purposes, in theory at least, because ultimate control remained in the hands of their provincial government rather than falling to the large-scale capitalists, as in the United States.[57] In Finland, farmers enjoyed the luxury of choosing between the Nationalist Party and the powerful Peasant Party, whereas in Quebec the title of "père des colons" would be given to long-time Conservative MLA, Jacques Picard, a merchant-notary who made his fortune on the backs of Wotton Township's impoverished settlers.[58] Picard was certainly critical of the lumber monopolists of the upper St Francis Valley, with whom he himself competed for a time, but his cautious business practices and his political affiliation served to temper that criticism.[59] The irony is that peasant proprietorship would have served the economic interests of the local *petite bourgeoisie*, and, in Sweden at least, even the large sawmill interests did not suffer unduly from such an arrangement.[60]

To a greater or lesser extent, each of the three aforementioned factors must be taken into account to explain why authorities resisted the development of a mixed agricultural and forestry economy for the settlers of the eastern-Canadian frontier.[61] Together, agrarianism, political-fiscal constraints, and self-perceived interests served to forge the middle-class consensus that settlers must at all costs be tied to a sedentary, agricultural livelihood. In spite of this consensus, however, an agri-forestry system – as defined by a subsistence-oriented agriculture and a dependency upon the forest economy – did develop in one form or another, and continue to operate in certain districts of Quebec up to World War II and beyond.[62] One need not assume, as Normand Séguin has done, that there was a tacit understanding between English-language lumber capitalists and French-Canadian colonization proponents to appreciate that each group effectively ensured that the colonists would be placed in a position of long-term economic dependency, and that the districts in which they lived would be subjected to economic underdevelopment.[63]

Séguin postulates that in isolated colonization zones there were two concurrent and mutually reinforcing forms of dependence by settlers upon lumbermen. First, the settler depended upon the timber monopolist to buy his surplus crops; secondly, because the price of farm produce could be suppressed in a captive market, the settler was forced to work for the company during the winter. With the settler raising his own food, wages could be kept to a bare minimum. The attraction of colonization for the timber companies therefore becomes apparent.[64] Whether or not Séguin's rather controversial theory can be applied to the north shore regions which he has researched, the lines of dependency he traces are not likely to be so strong in less-isolated districts. The upper St Francis district is an ideal one in which to observe the manifestation of the various forces behind the colonization movement, for it served as a testing ground for most, if not all, the various types of settlement projects attempted in the province during the nineteenth century. The area in question has never been populous enough to have a distinct political boundary, though much of it was included in the newly created constituency of Frontenac after the turn of the century. Part of Compton, Wolfe, and Beauce counties from 1853 to 1915, most of the twenty-two townships included in this study (see map 1) were drained by the upper half of the St Francis River, a crucial factor in their economic domination by a single lumber company. Several of the easternmost townships of the region have been included, even though they are drained by the Lake Megantic–Chaudière system (and were dominated by a Quebec-area lumber firm) because they were effectively part of the same settlement frontier.

As defined here, the upper St Francis district is approximately forty-five miles from east to west, and sixty miles from north to south. The international boundary defines its southern limits just where the line begins its sharp but erratic northward deviation from the forty-fifth parallel in an attempt to follow the divide between the St Lawrence and Atlantic watersheds. On the Canadian side of the border the Appalachian plateau tilts northeastward parallel to the course of the St Lawrence. Greatly worn down by glaciation and erosion, the district remains mountainous enough, with several peaks measuring over eight hundred metres, to force a southwestern deflection of the first forty miles of the St Francis River. Thus this river intercepts the streams running north from the international boundary before they can reach the St Lawrence, which explains why the upper St Francis district covers such a large area to the southwest of the valley itself.[65]

Although the Eastern Townships region was opened to settlement in the 1790s, much of the rather barren and isolated upper St Francis district remained unsurveyed and in the hands of the crown for another half century. In 1815 Surveyor General Joseph Bouchette pronounced many of these townships to be of moderately good soil, though he did point out their hilly nature, particularly as one drew further from the St Francis.[66] In 1835 the greatest part of the district was included in the British American Land Company's unsurveyed St Francis Tract, most of which was returned to the crown in 1841. In 1848, when preparations were being made to attract French-Canadian settlers to the district's crown land, a government surveyor submitted another basically favourable report:

The general features of the country are, a succession of gently sloping hills or broad undulating swells, lying between the different tributaries of the rivers Chaudière and the St. Francis; the soil being of an excellent quality, a brown loam resting on a firm subsoil called "hard pan"; the rock, slate and limestone; the timber a large and tall growth of maple, elm, basswood, ash, birch, and beech. Where the rock is sandstone, the land is generally flat, covered with a stunted growth of dark timber, spruce, fir, and cedar; the soil a shallow deposit of vegitable [*sic*] matter on the firm subsoil. At the bottom of the hardwood timbered slopes the soil is frequently a deep, black mould with cedar timber, which when cleared and drained, will produce good crops of grain and grass and the timber will be valuable for fencing etc. A mountain range crosses the westerly part of the block, which is in general too broken, rocky and stony for agricultural purposes: the timber is red and white pine, fir, spruce, larch, cedar, and white [sic], the rock granitic. The Megantic mountains lie in the easterly part of the block. The granite there is of a more limited extent, it covers only about one third of the summits of the range, the rest being a slate rock, the soil on which is of a good quality well adapted for grazing farms.[67]

The detailed descriptions submitted by provincial surveyors during the 1860s remained optimistic about the hardwood lands, though one made a revealing comment when referring to the north and south sides of Marston Township: "like all this part of the country, the ground is thickly covered with loose water-worn granite boulders, many of which are of considerable size, rendering it somewhat difficult of cultivation."[68] Although colonization was still being promoted in the Lake Megantic area during the 1880s, it had also begun to be advertised as a sportsman's paradise, with one of the country's first fish and game clubs reserving a large block of territory for its largely Boston-domiciled membership.[69]

The modern-day soil map shows well over half the district's surface to be totally unsuitable for agriculture, while the remainder consists almost entirely of class five soils, generally limited to use as forage and pasture.[70] Even where small pockets of reasonably rich land are to be found, the high altitude as one progresses southeastward from the upper St Francis River can reduce the growing season to a month shorter than in the Montreal region. There is danger of frost in early June and late August, and the snowfall averages 420 cm. at Milan, near Lake Megantic, as compared with 244 cm. at Sherbrooke.[71] Despite today's advantages of bulldozers, drainage pipes, improved seed, chemical fertilizers, and paved roads, or – more to the point – because farmers in marginal areas cannot afford the improvement expenses which would keep them competitive, many of the district's farms have been abandoned. In fact, the descendants of the original Scottish settlers dispersed decades ago. Those French Canadians who remain lead a precarious existence, for cheap-labour village factories appear to be replacing the forest industry as the main sources of non-agricultural income.

Table 1
Growth of the French-Speaking Population of the Upper St Francis District, 1844–91

Year	French-Canadian Population	District Population	Ratio to District %	Ratio to Eastern Townships %
1844	138	1418	9.7	0.9
1851	2064	3866	53.4	6.1
1861	4899	7709	63.5	7.4
1871	6738	10,507	64.1	6.9
1881	11,493	16,784	68.5	9.3
1891	15,379	20,889	73.6	9.5

Source: JLAC, v (1846), App. D; Canada, Census Reports, 1852–91.

The rapidity with which the isolated and mountainous upper St Francis district was populated by French Canadians is eloquent testimony to the population pressure in the seigneurial zone, and to the effectiveness of the colonization strategy organized by church and state. As we can see from table 1, the French-Canadian population multiplied from only 138 individuals in 1844 to 2064 in 1851 and 4899 in 1861. The growth rate levelled off in the 1860s, but increased rapidly again in the 1870s when government-sponsored colonization projects opened several new townships, and the construction of a rail link stimulated the local sawmill industry. Even during the following decade the French-Canadian population (and ratio) continued to climb, from 11,493 (69 per cent) in 1881 to 15,379 (74 per cent) in 1891 when the young railhead town of Lake Megantic boasted some 1400 people.[72] French-Canadian population expansion was a response not only to politically based incentives but to economic forces as well, yet it does not appear to have fluctuated greatly with the ups and downs of the timber and agricultural markets.

Although table 1 demonstrates that French Canadians quickly asserted their numerical dominance in the district, we can see from table 2 that most of the first settlers were British-born. In fact nearly all were English and Scottish families attracted by the British American Land Company during the 1830s. Their numbers increased only slowly from 1278 in 1844 to 2707 in 1861, by which time many of the English had departed leaving behind the Gaelic-speaking crofters from the Isle of Lewis and their Canadian-born offspring. Indeed most of the Eastern Townships' Scottish population was concentrated in this district, but few recruits would arrive to bolster their numbers during the following decades.

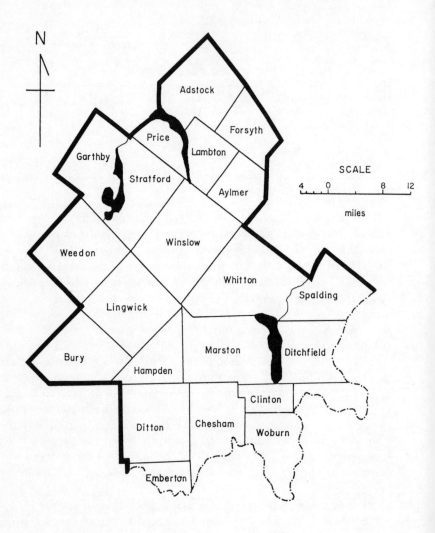

N

SCALE

4   0   8   12

miles

Adstock

Forsyth

Price

Lambton

Garthby

Aylmer

Stratford

Winslow

Weedon

Whitton

Spalding

Lingwick

Marston

Ditchfield

Bury

Hampden

Clinton

Ditton

Chesham

Woburn

Emberton

Map 2   The Upper St Francis District

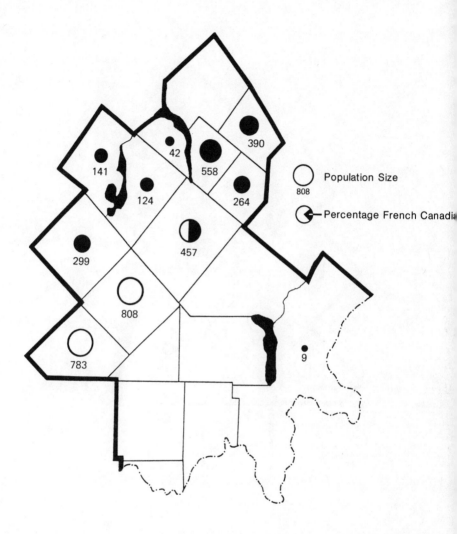

Map 3   Settlement in the Upper St Francis District, 1851

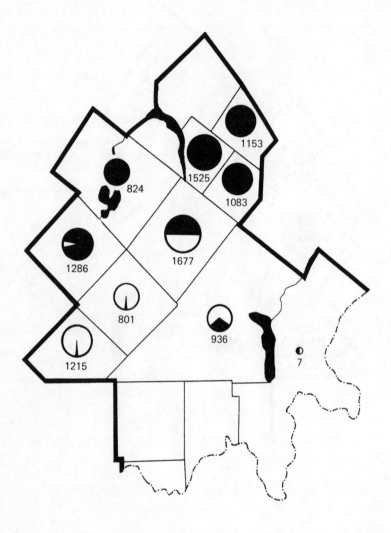

Map 4   Settlement in the Upper St Francis District, 1871

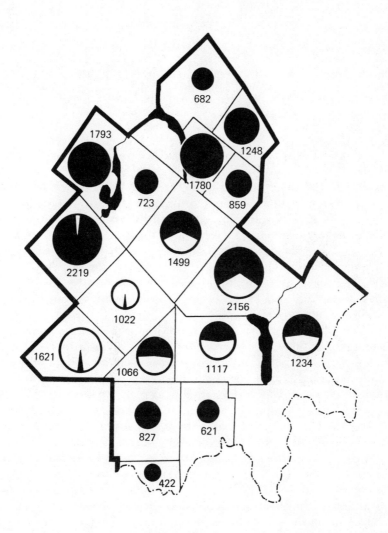

Map 5   Settlement in the Upper St Francis District, 1891

Table 2
English / Gaelic-Speaking Population by Birth Place, 1844–61
(Ratio to the Eastern Townships in Parentheses)

	Canada	England / Wales	Scotland	Ireland	U.S.A.	Total
1844	319 (1.1%)	473 (16.0%)	405 (18.1%)	66 (1.3%)	15 (0.2%)	1278 (2.7%)
1851	568 (1.6%)	201 (7.0%)	943 (32.0%)	55 (0.7%)	22 (0.3%)	1789 (3.0%)
1861	1277 (2.4%)	222 (7.6%)	1101 (35.0%)	61 (0.9%)	46 (0.5%)	2707 (3.6%)

Source: *JLAC*, v (1846), app. D; Canada, *Census Reports*, 1852–61.

Although the upper St Francis district covered approximately one-third of the Eastern Townships territory, table 1 reveals that even its French-Canadian population never reached 10 per cent of that group's regional total. Table 3 provides a clear indication of the district's relative poverty, for grain and livestock production here was consistently at a lower level than in the Eastern Townships as a whole. The available grain yield statistics, recorded in table 4, suggest that one reason was lower productivity per acre, particularly of oats, the major crop. But it is also noteworthy, as we can see in table 5, that cleared acreages in the upper St Francis district tended to be smaller than in the rest of the region.

Table 5 also indicates that despite the gradual increase in improved acreage over time, the average upper St Francis farmer did not become a commercial producer to any great degree. There was certainly a marked jump in production between 1851 and 1861, when the average farm yielded 168 bushels of cereal crops and 104 bushels of potatoes and turnips, and a recent study of late eighteenth-century Massachusetts does argue that 40 to 45 bushels of grain could feed the average family and its livestock for a year.[73] But the nineteenth-century consumption figures calculated by Frank Lewis and Marvin McInnis, among others, lead to a different conclusion. The average upper St Francis household of seven would have consumed the equivalent of the 96 bushels of potatoes and wheat, assuming a yearly diet of 30 bushels for two adults and half that for each of five children, as well as the 15 to 20 per cent of the harvest they would require for seed.[74] As for the 70 bushels of oats, the average farm's single horse would have consumed half that amount even if there had been an adequate supply of hay, which there was not. At 1.8 tons of hay per cow, the average of 4.8 tons per farm would not even have fed its five cattle adequately, though the 13.6 bushels of turnips would have helped to compensate. Furthermore, the equivalent of another 0.7 tons of hay and 13.8 bushels of oats would have

Table 3
Agricultural Progress in the Upper St Francis District, 1844–91
(Ratio to Eastern Townships in Parentheses)

Year	Occupier	Improved (acres)	Grain (bu.)[1]	Oats (bu.)	Livestock
1844	285 (2.6%)[2]	3871 (1.2%)	15,080 (1.7%)	4754 (1.0%)	1496 (0.9%)
1851	546 (4.3%)	8700 (2.0%)	41,494 (2.8%)	16,320 (2.1%)	5119 (2.3%)
1861	1123 (6.2%)	30,138 (4.3%)	188,326 (5.1%)	78,772 (3.6%)	13,953 (4.7%)
1871	1594 (6.2%)	60,596 (6.0%)	203,022 (6.3%)	93,695 (4.8%)	–
1881	2611 (9.6%)	89,285 (7.3%)	256,377 (6.3%)	113,268 (4.2%)	–
1891	3289 (9.2%)	143,341 (8.3%)	280,125 (6.9%)	157,545 (6.0%)	42,095 (8.0%)

Source: see table 1.
1 Also appears as minots
2 Proprietors, non-proprietors, and tenants

been required by the 4.6 sheep owned by the typical farmer. There were also two pigs, which would have consumed 30 of the 88 bushels of barley, rye, buckwheat, and peas produced on the average farm.[75]

Much of the remaining 58 bushels of grain were probably required by the farm family itself, for one can assume that some of the potato harvest was fed to the livestock to compensate for the lack of hay. Hay production increased substantially with the following three census enumerations, but there was a concurrent decline in the average turnip, oats, barley, and rye harvest, as well as in potatoes after 1871. The foregoing consumption estimates are obviously imprecise, especially as they cannot account for local variations in dietary levels, but they strongly suggest that cereal and root production was largely for home consumption. Certainly, that production failed to come close to the regional averages in oats, potatoes, and hay – the three crops most in demand by the lumber shanties.[76] The agricultural link between colonists and lumbermen – an intrinsic part of Séguin's agri-forestry theory of underdevelopment – was clearly weak in the upper St Francis district.

Another test for the role of the lumber shanty market is to compare the average production of hay, potatoes, and oats in the district with that in areas reported to be tightly integrated into the agri-forestry economy as defined by Normand Séguin. Table 6 reveals that in 1861 the upper St Francis colonists reaped comparable harvests of potatoes and hay to their counterparts in two Mauricie colonization parishes and two Ottawa Valley townships, but much less oats than in three out of these four areas. The latter is a telling point, given the large quantities of oats consumed by horses in the logging industry, and (as we shall see) the relatively high level of activity registered by the district's lumber monopoly in 1861. Admittedly,

Table 4
Crop Yields in the Upper St Francis District,
1851, 1861, 1891 (Eastern Townships Yields in
Parentheses)

Year	Grain Yield (bu./acre)	Oats Yield (bu./acre)
1851	12.4 (17.4)	16.2 (24.0)
1861	22.1 (23.8)	22.7 (28.0)
1891	–	9.8 (18.5)

Source: Canada, Census Reports, 1852, 1861, 1891.

settlement was still in its infancy in the upper St Francis district at this time, but we have already noted that the average harvest of oats would actually decline in the coming decades.

The gradual improvement of the transportation network would serve simply to facilitate the lumber companies' transportation of supplies from outside the district, with the result that local farmers continued to grow a more balanced variety of crops than did their counterparts in the region as a whole.[77] Despite their overall smaller harvests, the upper St Francis farms actually produced greater mean quantities of barley, buckwheat, and rye and comparable quantities of wheat, peas, and beans. The attention paid to buckwheat is particularly significant, for, to quote Paul Gates, it was "a hardy, fast-maturing cereal that was well adapted to high altitudes, short seasons, and poor soils."[78] Not a readily marketable crop, buckwheat was generally planted as a substitute for wheat to make flour for home consumption. In the upper St Francis district farmers harvested about five times as much buckwheat as wheat. Finally, the outstanding harvest of barley in 1861, 43 bushels per farmer, was concentrated among the recently arrived Hebrideans for whom it was the traditional crop staple, and therefore was not a response to the American brewery market.[79] The district's barley production actually declined after it gained railway access to distant markets in the 1870s.

The hilly and rock-strewn farms of the upper St Francis district were better suited to cattle grazing than to cereal crops, but an examination of the livestock sector of the economy further reinforces the impression of a general orientation towards self-sufficiency. Table 7 shows that livestock holdings consistently failed to match the regional average. Not surprisingly, given the isolation of most of the upper St Francis district farmers, they also failed to keep pace with the region's transition to dairy production for an international market.[80] Indeed, the average upper St Francis farmer would not

Table 5
Improved Acreage and Crop Production per Farm in the Upper St Francis
District, 1844–91 (Eastern Townships Production in Parentheses)

Year	Improved acres	Oats (bu.)	Wheat (bu.)	Barley (bu.)	Rye (bu.)	Buckwheat (bu.)
1844	13.6 (29.0)	16.7 (43.0)	9.6 (3.5)	15.8 (3.5)	0.5 (1.2)	9.7 (6.9)
1851	15.9 (34.2)	29.9 (62.2)	9.1 (21.3)	12.8 (3.3)	11.9 (4.0)	9.2 (12.2)
1861	26.8 (39.1)	70.1 (123.2)	5.8 (19.2)	43.1 (13.8)	17.6 (6.7)	26.9 (27.1)
1871	38.0 (39.2)	58.8 (76.0)	6.1 (9.7)	17.6 (5.5)	5.0 (1.2)	31.1 (18.9)
1881	34.2 (45.2)	43.4 (100.3)	6.2 (11.0)	12.2 (9.1)	3.7 (0.9)	30.8 (17.1)
1891	43.6 (48.2)	47.9 (73.7)	3.7 (7.0)	9.0 (11.9)	0.5 (0.1)	20.3 (12.5)

Year	Peas/Beans (bu.)	Corn (bu.)	Potatoes (bu.)	Turnips (bu.)	Hay (tons)	Maple Sugar (lb.)
1844	0.6 (2.4)[1]	0.1 (5.1)	144.0 (156.3)	–	–	32.2 (48.5)
1851	3.0 (3.9)	0.1 (9.7)	54.2 (50.2)	–	–	196.3 (129.2)
1861	4.1 (6.3)	0.0 (7.8)	90.8 (130.0)	13.6 (22.6)	4.8 (9.0)	186.7 (174.9)
1871	3.7 (4.9)	0.6 (8.8)	109.6 (125.6)	6.5 (9.5)	9.2 (12.0)	–
1881	4.0 (5.2)	0.1 (7.3)	43.7 (71.4)	8.9 (17.9)	9.0 (16.6)	–
1891	1.7 (2.8)	0.1 (5.4)	57.9 (74.6)	6.1 (16.1)[2]	10.4 (15.4)	–

Source: See table 1.
1 Peas only
2 Includes "other roots"

have been able to supply his own family's needs if each member
consumed close to the 24.8 pounds of butter and 5.6 pounds of
cheese calculated for farm residents of the northern United States
in 1861.[81] Dairy production for the region as a whole was greater
than table 7 suggests because butter factories were opening in the
more centrally located townships, but the census records only the
home-made product.[82]

The upper St Francis farmers were in a better position to market
meat than dairy products, since the typical woods worker consumed
seven pounds of salt pork a week.[83] During the late 1850s the C.S.
Clark lumber company's shanty crews numbered approximately four
hundred men, a large potential market for a district of less than a
thousand families.[84] Pork and beef production did increase markedly between 1851 and 1861, but there could have been little surplus
for sale given that the consumption per capita in the province was
upwards of one hundred pounds per year.[85] Presumably the local
farmers also faced the same sort of competition that Ottawa Valley
farmers did from pork imported via Cincinnati.[86] By 1891 the mean
number of pigs per district farmer had dropped from two to one.

Table 6
Mean Production of Potatoes, Oats, and Hay in the Upper St Francis, St Maurice,
and Ottawa Valleys, 1861

District	Potatoes (bu.)	Oats (bu.)	Hay (tons)
Upper St Francis	90.8	70.1	4.8
St Maurice			
St Tite	99.7	69.8	3.8
St Stanislas	80.7	180.8	6.5
Ottawa Valley			
Alfred	106.1	142.2	3.4
Caledonia	192.9	250.9	9.8

Source: Hardy and Séguin, Forêt et société, 163; Gaffield, Language, Schooling, 81–82.

Indeed the Clark company was, for a time at least, able to supply much of its own provisons from a thousand-acre farm it leased in fertile Ascot Township.[87] Perhaps beef found a market outside the district, given that cattle could be driven considerable distances to market, but the promise of a major regional industry was scotched with the collapse of Sherbrooke's new meat-packing plant during the depression of the mid-1870s.[88] By 1891 some of the major cattlemen in the Eastern Townships, including Senator Matthew H. Cochrane, had switched their operations to the ranch lands of the Alberta foothills.[89] Only 1.6 cattle per farm were reported as killed or sold that year in the upper St Francis district.

Local sheep and wool production had increased steadily while declining just as steadily in the region as a whole, but this is yet another sign of a mixed economy with a strong emphasis on self-sufficiency. Regional demand for wool may have expanded significantly during the 1860s due to the founding in Sherbrooke of the Paton woollen mills, the largest in Canada by 1872, but production of fulled cloth and flannel per household in Winslow Township multiplied three times between 1861 and 1871.[90] Recent research comparing domestic cloth production across Canada in 1871 has discovered an inverse relationship between that activity on the one hand and improved acreage and wheat production on the other.[91] Subsistence-oriented as the upper St Francis farmers may have been, complete autarky was impossible, and the production figures examined above suggest that many families would have actually had to buy some food in addition to the usual manufactured necessities. For them the forests must have been a particularly crucial source of income.

Table 7
Livestock and Animal Products per Farm in the
Upper St Francis District, 1844, 1851, 1861, and 1891
(Eastern Townships Production in Parentheses)

Year	Cattle	Horses	Sheep	Pigs	Wool (lb.)	Butter (lb.)	Cheese (lb.)
1844	2.5 (5.8)	0.3 (1.1)	1.9 (7.6)	0.5 (1.5)	2.5 (18.0)	–	–
1851	3.4 (7.3)	0.7 (1.4)	3.7 (7.1)	1.7 (1.7)	8.3 (17.9)	44.4 (146.1)	0.4 (39.7)
1861	4.9 (7.0)	0.9 (1.7)	4.6 (6.2)	2.0 (1.7)	11.5 (19.8)	96.2 (202.6)	0.2 (28.2)
1891	5.0 (6.9)	1.4 (1.9)	5.3 (4.3)	1.0 (1.6)	20.1 (16.8)	165.9 (211.7)	1.6 (93.3)

			Killed or Sold		
Year	Beef (lb.)	Pork (lb.)	Cattle	Pigs	Sheep
1844	–	–	–	–	–
1851	19.4 (204.0)	173.2 (477.6)	–	–	–
1861	53.8 (146.0)	270.0 (308.9)	–	–	–
1891	–	–	1.6 (1.8)	1.4 (1.7)	3.5 (3.0)

Source: See table 1.

The question remains as to whether there were essentially two
socio-economic levels in the district, one producing an agricultural
surplus and the other paying for some of that surplus with the
proceeds of its work in the woods. Certainly, colonists in the more
recently settled townships would depend for a time upon some food
supplies from the longer established families. But the question of
short-term agricultural dependency aside, a preliminary study of
Winslow Township reveals considerable socio-economic homogene-
ity provided one takes into account the waxing and waning of production with the various stages of each family's life cycle.[92] The major
dividing line in Winslow lay between the French Canadians concentrated in the northern half of the township and their more agricul-
turally productive Scots neighbours to the south. The French
Canadians generally exploited smaller farms than the Scots, and,
as we might expect, they were more intimately tied to the forest
industry.

As table 8 shows, the average French-Canadian farm family in
Winslow owned only 83 acres in 1871 – twenty years after the township was opened to settlement – as compared with 107 acres for the
Highlanders. The French Canadians had improved almost as much
land as the Scots – in fact their pastures were slightly larger – but
the latter owned considerably more cattle and sheep, and they produced one-third more butter. The French Canadians manufactured

Table 8
Mean Agricultural Production of French-Canadian and Scots Farmers in Winslow
Township, 1871[1]

	Acres Owned	Crop (bu.)	Pasture (acres)	Cattle	Horses	Sheep	Pigs	Butter (lb.)	Maple Sugar (lb.)
French Canadian	82.9	22.9	13.0	5.0	1.0	5.0	1.8	67.8	242.4
Scottish	106.7	27.4	12.2	7.7	0.7	11.1	2.0	106.5	34.0

Source: 1871 Manuscript Census.
1 The farm family is defined as living on at least 11 acres.

far more maple sugar than the Scots, and owned more pigs and
horses, all indicators of a closer association with an agri-forestry
economy. Indeed, the 1871 manuscript census records that while 42
of 127 French-Canadian farm families (33 per cent) cut logs, only
21 of their 105 Scots counterparts (20 per cent) did so. Furthermore,
the former reported an average of 60 logs per active family, and
the latter only 49 logs per active family. Finally, in contrast to the
Scots, 24 French-Canadian families cut square timber, bringing their
total involved in logging on their own account to 53 or 42 per cent
of all French-speaking households. Residents actually cut more timber in Winslow in 1871 than did C.S. Clark and Company – 4422
logs plus 1,600,000 square feet of tamarac versus 3500 logs, respectively – even though the company lease of 69 ¼ square miles
constituted virtually all the unsettled land in the township.

   According to the agrarian beliefs of the colonization advocates,
Winslow's French Canadians should have been in a considerably
more precarious position than the Scots. One would expect their
numbers to have begun diminishing once the forest was cut over,
yet it was the more "progressive" Scots who first began to lose their
population base. They declined from 120 to 116 families between
1871 and 1881, while the French-Canadian numbers continued to
increase from 149 to 181 families. As the generally declining mean
production figures from 1871 to 1881 and 1891 shown in table 5
suggest, agriculture became more tenuous after the railway network
reached into the upper St Francis district during the 1870s. Because
of the railway, the settler as food producer was inevitably drawn into
a more internationally integrated and competitive market, but the
settler as logger was able to take advantage of the small steam sawmills which sprang up to challenge C.S. Clark's monopoly.

Table 9
Timber Production in the Upper St Francis District, 1871

Township[1]	Pine Logs	Spruce & Other Logs	Other (cu.ft.)	Tan Bark (cords)	Staves
Winslow	526	7396	1,848,616	–	–
Bury	371	4857	6130	10	–
Lingwick	2030	3864	–	–	–
Garthby	1690	16,872	1200	–	–
Stratford	116	1422	5318	–	16,450
Weedon	256	2839	18,422	8	–
Lambton & Price	8343	15,562	143,190	109	–
Forsyth	873	2035	63,998	–	122,000
Whitton, Marston & Hampden	4343	9474	–	–	–
Totals	18,548	64,321	2,086,874	127	138,450

Source: 1871 Manuscript Census.
1 Aylmer was not included in the census. Adstock, Spalding, Ditchfield, Woburn, and Emberton were not inhabited. Ditton, Chesham and Clinton were included with the more populous Newport, which lies outside the upper St Francis district.

From table 9 we can gain some idea of how crucial a role the forest industry played in the economy of the upper St Francis district. Prices received by the colonists can only be guessed at, but they were probably somewhat less than the thirty-seven cents a log at which the Clark Company valued its raw material in 1871. Local sawmills reported a wide range for their logs, with twenty to twenty-five cents each being the most common averages.[93] At the latter price, the 82,869 logs cut by settlers in 1871 would be worth approximately $21,000, or $13 for each farm family in the district. In addition, there were over two million cubic feet of "other timber" – mostly tamarac – cut in 1871, about half of which was claimed by a single resident of Winslow Township. Other wood products were less impressive. The lucrative Montreal leather-tanning market for Eastern Townships hemlock bark had yet to make much impression on the district, perhaps because the railroad had still not arrived, and table 10 suggests that timber was too valuable for most colonists to market as ashes.[94]

The final link between company and colonist as outlined by Séguin's agri-forestry thesis is seasonal employment of the latter in the woods and mills of the former. Lumber companies supposedly favoured colonization because they needed not only a captive source

Table 10
Sawmill and Pearl-ash Production in the Upper St Francis District 1861, 1871
(Number of Mills in Parentheses)

Township	Lumber (ft.)					Logs Used 1871	Pearl-ash 1861[1]
	1861		1871				
Winslow	100,000[2]	(1)	103,000	(4)		2522	–
Bury	466,666[3]	(6)	760,000	(7)		7600	–
Lingwick	25,000[4]	(1)	270,000	(2)		2700	–
Garthby	?	(1)	15,000	(1)		150	–
Stratford	85,000[3]	(3)	18,000	(2)		205	$350
Weedon	50,000	(1)	297,000	(3)		2600	$1200
Lambton &							
Price	314,166[3&5]	(4)	372,000	(5)		7400	–
Forsyth	83,333[3&4]	(1)	171,333[3]	(4)		1280	–
Whitton, Marston							
& Hampden	–		60,000	(1)		600	–
Aylmer	25,000[3]	(1)	Not in census			Not in census	$728
Adstock	–		–			–	–
Totals	1,149,165		2,066,333			25,057	$2278

Source: 1861 and 1871 Manuscript Census.
1 No potash recorded.
2 Calculated from 1,000 logs raw material at 100 board feet per log
3 Calculated from dollar value of production, at $6.00 per 1000 feet
4 Whether saw- or grist mill not recorded
5 Includes production value of one joint saw- and grist mill operation.

of provisions, but a cheap supply of labour as well. As far as C.S. Clark and Company was concerned, however, a large percentage of its employees was based in the downstream company town of Brompton Falls where they worked in the mill during the off-season. This is not to deny that foremen and subcontractors hired colonists. For example, during the 1857–58 season Clark reported that twelve contractors supplied 6945 spruce logs while his own crews cut 27,200 pine.[95] The 1871 census records that Whitton colonists chopped 13,008 spruce and pine logs "under the orders of Dominick Morin of Lambton for Clark & Co.," and Morin also claimed another 3500 logs in neighbouring Winslow. This represents a significant chunk of the 80,000 logs processed by Clark that year. Table 11 also suggests that even after local sawmill production is subtracted, upper St Francis colonists could have supplied Clark with three-quarters of his logs for the 1870–71 season. The opportunity to tap a local supply of labour, or local sales of logs, may have added to the flexibility of the Clark Company's response to the rapidly fluctuating

Table 11
Lumber Production[1] in the Upper St Francis District and at
Brompton Falls, 1861, 1871

Year	Board Feet Spruce and Pine Cut by Colonists	Board Feet Sawed by Upper St Francis Mills	Board Feet Sawed by C.S. Clark and Co.
1861	–	1,149,165	14,000,000
1871	8,286,900	2,066,333	8,000,000

1 Calculated at 100 board feet per log

lumber market, but it seems likely that the company would have
preferred to seek its supplementary labour needs at some additional
cost outside the district rather than face the hostility and depredations of the local settler society. Subcontractors could have continued
to carry some of the risks even if they had been forced to go somewhat further afield for their labour.

The influential French geographer, Raoul Blanchard, was wrong
when he suggested that colonization followed the timber industry
up the St Francis Valley in a progressive and symbiotic fashion.[96]
On the contrary, lumbermen and settlers encountered each other
at the headwaters of the river during the initial stages of two mutually
independent and even antagonistic operations. Certainly an agri-
forestry system did exist in the upper St Francis and Lake Megantic
drainage basins, but one markedly different from that in the St
Maurice, Lac Saint-Jean, Ottawa, and Madawaska regions where the
major companies were apparently significant employers of colonist
manpower and important markets for local agricultural produce.[97]
Instead, many of the upper St Francis colonists, particularly the
French-Canadian majority, were actively involved in cutting timber
on their own behalf, much like the peasants of Finland and northern
Sweden. The extensive shore-line of the lakes, as well as the many
streams which fed these bodies of water, mitigated against monopoly
control to a certain extent, because they precluded the need for
lengthy logging roads.[98] The settlers' problem was that Clark still
dominated the market for this timber, but table 11 demonstrates
that the ratio sawed by local mills made a dramatic leap between
1861 and 1871. We shall see that the local challenge would become
overwhelming for Clark as the extension of the railway network into
the district provided access to alternate markets during the 1870s.

In the upper St Francis district the colonists would have to take
illegally what they considered to be legitimately theirs. Their problem was a lack of political clout, for even the nationalist champions
of colonization failed to demand full settler access to the forest re-

source. So-called colonist spokesmen such as Jacques Picard and his MLA successor, Jérôme-Adolphe Chicoyne, were too anxious to compete with the large timber monopolies to conceive of any radical challenges to the system. Chicoyne may have been less successful than Picard as a capitalist, but we shall see that he tended to confuse the ambitious colonization projects he was involved in with his personal business interests.

Far from being a retreat from the modern world, Quebec's colonization movement was essentially an attempt by members of the French-Canadian bourgeoisie to deal with the forces of industrial capitalism. They did not question the essence of the capitalist system, but they did wish to resist its offshoots – English-Protestant economic domination and massive emigration to New England. People forced to leave the overcrowded seigneuries therefore had to be channeled in such a way that the province's population base was not threatened and French Canadians could regain some control over the province's economy. Urbanization would fulfil the first requirement, but much of the necessary technical expertise and capital for manufacturing industries had to come from Britain and the United States. Montreal's French-Canadian entrepreneurs tended to focus instead on land development, an area of activity where they enjoyed a natural advantage over outsiders.[99] It should not be surprising that the same type of activity would be extended into the hinterland, particularly when the provincial government could be influenced in the name of national survival to provide much of the infrastructure.

The problem for French-language economic domination on the upper St Francis frontier was that the British American Land Company and the C.S. Clark and G.B. Hall lumber companies continued to control the lion's share of the most valuable local resource. There was little left for a French-Canadian bourgeoisie to exploit except the colonists themselves. As long as the state did not have to reconcile this inherent contradiction between French-Canadian nationalism and large-scale capitalism, it could continue the game of serving two masters at once. Attempts at British colonization in the district were certainly not exclusively motivated by economic considerations. Imperialist political sentiment played a role in the founding of the British American Land Company, and, as we shall see, in the construction of the Lambton Road into the district from the Chaudière Valley. But because the English, in contrast to the French Canadians, tended to operate through capitalistic corporations, it was inevitable that they would place profits first, even if this meant sacrificing population expansion. Indeed, once the French-Canadian majority began to show an interest in colonization during the 1840s, the mother country simply abandoned its responsibility for crown lands and ceased all efforts to anglicize the Eastern Townships region through land settlement. English-speaking capitalists from that point on would essentially confine their activities to the lumber industry, although in some cases under the guise of a colonization company.

None of the major theories pertaining to rural social and regional development in the era of industrial capitalism can be applied, at least without modification, to the upper St Francis district. Chayanov's populist concept of an enduring family-centred agricultural economy is certainly more relevant than the Marxist assumption that capitalist forces were causing peasant societies to polarize inevitably and rapidly into the bourgeois and proletarian classes.[100] It appears that there was no substantial socio-economic stratification among the farmers of the upper St Francis district, and that the terms proto-industrialization or semi-proletarianization do not apply here during the nineteenth century. Most settlers supplied the lumber companies with logs not as wage earners but as independent farmers, albeit farmers who did not own most of the local timber resource. Of course, the latter distinction is a crucial one, and Chayanov's exclusive focus on the internal dynamics of an essentially self-sufficient agricultural economy limits his theory's relevance for our purposes. In the words of Lise Pilon-Lé, "alors que Chayanov a surestimé l'indépendance des paysans par rapport au capitalisme, Lénine a, de son côté, sous-estimé sa capacité de survie dans le capitalisme et son importance sociale."[101]

An analytical framework for the upper St Francis district must take into account its frontier or hinterland status. As far as Turner's thesis is concerned, it is doubtful if such an independent frontier ever existed in Canada, much less as the product of a colonization movement strictly organized and controlled by metropolitan institutions.[102] The official goal was for the settlement frontier to follow the timber or "commercial" frontier, to use Michael Cross's phrase. According to him, "the order of penetration for much of the country was fairly uniform: first came the exploiting business pioneers, often operating on an itinerant basis; then the government, organizing the territory, assisting transportation; finally came the permanent – usually agricultural – settler."[103] This is not the way it happened in the upper St Francis district where the government issued timber licences at the same time as it was building colonization roads, causing settlers and lumbermen to meet and clash right from the start. The conflict and the frontier status – as defined by weak metropolitan linkages, isolation, and low population density – endured throughout much of the nineteenth century, if not beyond.[104]

External capitalist forces were inextricably linked with the development, or, perhaps more appropriately, the underdevelopment of nineteenth-century Quebec's settlement frontier. Indeed, the dilemma of the upper St Francis district was not unlike that of today's peripheral satellite economies as described by André Gunder Frank. To use Frank's terms, its development was dictated and distorted by the transfer of surplus to the metropolis, which inhibited industrialization and maintained the district's subordinate position as a primary export economy. But Frank also assumes that the satellite's domestic economy will quickly disintegrate under the influence of external capitalist forces, which, as we have seen, was not true of the upper St Francis district. Indeed it is possible, as other theorists of underdevelopment have argued for the Third World, that pre-capitalist relations of production were actually strengthened by the expansion of the external market on the Quebec frontier.[105] This is the implication of Gérard Bouchard's claim that in the Saguenay region of the nineteenth century, "le capital ne détruit pas la société paysanne mais contribue à la consolider, dans la mesure où le système familial nourrit des emplois et des revenues médiocres qu'il crée."[106] As far as the upper St Francis district is concerned, however, the lumber and land companies only detracted from the settlers' peasant-oriented strategy of combining agricultural self-sufficiency with a small yearly income from the forest.

As a corollary to their argument that metropolitan capitalist expansion has tended to perpetuate "feudal" institutions in peripheral zones, the neo-Marxist theorists of underdevelopment contend that capitalist forces benefit from the semi-independent economic status of the peasants. Thus Séguin's agri-forestry model assumes that Quebec's lumber industry encouraged the colonization of marginal lands for the basic reason that it required accessible provisions and seasonal labour. Because the settler community was essentially a captive market, the lumber companies could ensure that the lines of dependency remained rigidly in place. But, once again, as far as the upper St Francis district is concerned, it is the separation of the capitalist and the settler economies which is most striking. It would be hard to conceive of the C.S. Clark lumber company welcoming colonization, and we shall see that even the land companies were more interested in exploiting, or speculating upon, the timber resource than in promoting settlement.

In short, there were essentially two economies in the upper St Francis district, one externally controlled and one internally generated. The possibility that such economies might not be mutually dependent, but in open conflict with each other, is not taken into account either by the neo-Marxist theory of underdevelopment or by the orthodox "dualist" model of development, which assumes a clear-cut transition from feudal to capitalist society.[107] This is not to deny that external forces had a profound impact upon the district's population, if only by adding to its impoverishment, but the census statistics suggest that traditional socio-economic structures persisted throughout the latter half of the nineteenth century.

Feast or Famine: The British American Land Company and the Colonization of the St Francis Tract

The rich B.A.L. Company
Now takes their case in hand
Inducing all at prices small (?)
To settle on their land

Oscar Dhu (Angus MacKay), *Donald Morrison*

In contrast to its principal counterparts in Upper Canada and the Maritimes, Lower Canada's British American Land Company (BALC) still awaits comprehensive and detailed historical investigation.[1] The best overviews remain the brief sections in the classic works by O.D. Skelton, Norman Macdonald, and Helen Cowan, and a chapter in the doctoral dissertation of Philip Goldring. In addition, Ronald Rudin and Jean-Pierre Kesteman have written excellent analyses of the company's complex but crucial role in the development of Sherbrooke, the metropolis of the Eastern Townships.[2] But relatively little is known about its history as a land settlement agency beyond the fact that the directors made some serious mistakes and became the victim of considerable bad luck during their first few years of activity.

The BALC played a crucial role as developer and speculator in the older settled townships where it acquired all the crown reserves, much of the clergy reserves, and numerous privately owned lots.[3] It was, however, in the isolated and rugged block of land known as the St Francis Tract that the company first concentrated its energies and invested much of its capital, a policy which proved so disastrous that it would never fully recover. The remarkably similar and equally costly strategies of the Canada Company and the New Brunswick and Nova Scotia Land Company suggest that they represented something more fundamental than mistaken business judgements[4]. All three London-based companies were not only agencies of capitalism, but of imperialism as well, leaving them initially prone to the grand gesture of large-scale emigration and wilderness colonization projects. Once it had learned its lesson, however, the BALC never forgot it. As a result, those townships which remained in the company's hands after 1841 were neglected from that time onward. The BALC adopted a policy of long-term instalments, fixed-term leaseholds, and barter payments, but the result was simply a more effective exploitation of the settlers it had attracted in the late 1830s. Once the railway reached the Eastern Townships, the company focused its energies on the development of Sherbrooke, remaining content with the St Francis Tract's status as an increasingly valuable timber preserve.

The year 1825 saw the first concrete steps taken by British capitalists to monopolize the Eastern Townships' crown lands.[5] The Lower Canada Land Company was stillborn, due to the opposition of the governor, Lord Dalhousie, only to be reincarnated in 1832 in the guise of the BALC. Dalhousie's successor, Lord Aylmer, was initially sceptical as well, but he was driven by increasing necessity to escape the hostile House of Assembly's stranglehold over provincial tax revenues. In April, 1832, Aylmer wrote the colonial secretary, Lord Goderich, that the government had two choices to consider:

whether it will continue to dispose of the Crown Lands as has been the practice hitherto, having constantly to withstand the pretension of the House of Assembly, or whether by disposing of the whole of these lands it shall establish on the part of the House of Assembly, a *standing Grievance?* but which in that case will be without a remedy.

The first choice would lead to the inevitable victory of the assembly, the second to an eventual end to the complaints "unless supported by causes of real and well founded discontent in other matters." The assembly's refusal to grant a "very moderate" civil list demonstrated the necessity for the executive to have some pecuniary means at its disposal, the land and timber fund being of little value after managerial expenses and salaries were deducted.[6]

Assisted by John Galt, founder of the Canada Company, the BALC promoters convinced the Colonial Office and Aylmer that they would end "the monopolizing grasp of the Americans who threat-

ened to over-run the province," and curb the "extravagant preten-
sions" of the French Canadians who claimed "a prescriptive right to
all the waste lands of the Crown."[7] On 3 December 1833, the company received control of close to 850,000 acres of crown land, including all crown reserves and surveyed crown lots in Sherbrooke,
Shefford, and Stanstead counties, and a 596,000-acre unsurveyed
block comprising much of the upper St Francis district. The government had two years to withdraw up to 10,000 acres in town lots,
or sites already surveyed as such, while 90,000 acres of the St Francis
Tract was to be considered a margin for error pending a proper
survey. In setting a price, Lord Aylmer was instructed by Viscount
Goderich to:

bear in mind that while the advantages which may be anticipated from the
operations of the Company justly entitle them to every encouragement, the
value of so important and encreasing [sic] a source of Revenue as the Crown
Lands must not be overlooked in the contemplated arrangement with the
Company.[8]

Aylmer, however, did not go far above the company's initial offer
of three shillings per acre.[9] The price for the St Francis Tract was
£75,992 sterling or 3 s. (75¢) per acre, while for the much more
valuable 200-acre crown lots in the settled townships it was £44,008
or 3 ½ s. (87 ½¢) per acre. The total was payable in ten years at 4
per cent interest per annum.[10]

By the time the details of the crown purchase had been worked
out, in the spring of 1835, the BALC had acquired at auction an
additional 59,200 acres in clergy reserves as well as paying for 32,000
acres of privately owned land and holding options on 13,600 additional acres.[11] The original intention appears to have been to acquire improved land only from farmers who wished to trade for the
company's wild land, but many such purchases made in the years
1834–36 were clearly from families planning to leave the Townships.[12] The year 1836 brought 14.8 per cent more land than the
previous year, resulting in a 29.1 per cent augmentation over the
original purchase, at a cost of little more than four shillings per
acre.[13] A monopoly was essential, company directors argued, so that
they, rather than individual speculators, would reap the benefits
from the projected massive investments in the region's economic
development.[14]

The infusion of capital into the Eastern Townships was not actually
to be an extra charge to shareholders because the company was
allowed to direct half its payments towards officially sanctioned pub-

lic improvements. In fact the government even allowed the BALC to keep the "improvement moiety" in its own hands, thereby effectively surrendering its supervisory role.[15] In 1835 the company spent £9,841 on a mostly new 63 ½ mile road from Dudswell Township, at the limit of the judicial district of St Francis, through the small town of Sherbrooke to Shefford Township, thus forging quite a strong link to Montreal and a tenuous one to Quebec.[16] Another lengthy new road was constructed from Richmond, on the St Francis River north of Sherbrooke, to Port St Francis, on the St Lawrence, a short distance upstream from Trois-Rivières (see map 6). Here the company planned to develop its own port facility, while promoting industries in Sherbrooke where it had purchased 837 acres with most of the mill sites, at a reported cost of £8,044.[17] Bridges were built, streets surveyed, and shops, mills, and a woollen factory constructed in an attempt to establish the urban centre so crucial to the development of a market-oriented agricultural economy.[18]

It would have been prudent to reap some of the benefits of these sizeable investments in the heartland of the region before proceeding further, but the BALC overextended itself by simultaneously attempting to open its isolated unsurveyed tract to settlement. There was no shortage of British emigrants to North America, and the court of directors reasoned that little effort was needed to colonize company lands in the older townships because they would automatically increase in value.[19] It was clearly taken for granted that the chief role of monopolistic land companies was to colonize frontier territories by a large-scale infusion of capital and immigrants. The first townships to be developed would be Bury and Lingwick, northeast of Eaton, one of the oldest and most prosperous townships in the region. The company's first preoccupation was to purchase an 11,000-acre block of privately held land in Bury and a 12,000-acre block in Lingwick.[20] Originally granted by the crown to township "leaders and associates" early in the century, much of this undeveloped land, in Lingwick at least, had recently been snapped up by local speculators hoping to make a quick profit from the company.[21] Unfortunately for two of them, C.F.H. Goodhue and G.J. Goodhue of Sherbrooke, they overextended themselves, losing their extensive holdings by sheriff's sale in 1835. Curiously enough, however, the company failed to take advantage of this opportunity, allowing the Honourable Samuel Hatt, seigneur of Chambly, to demand and receive from it seventy-six cents an acre for the 11,000 acres of the Vondenvelden grant which he had acquired at twenty cents from the Goodhues a few weeks earlier.[22] Either one or more of the company agents was careless or perhaps was profiting surreptitiously

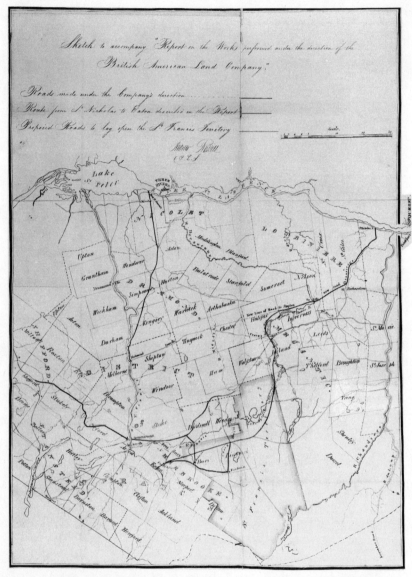

Map 6   Sketch to accompany "Report on the Works performed under the direction of the British American Land Company" (Archives nationales du Québec à Québec [ANQ-Q], B-307)

from the land flip. (For details on the transactions in Lingwick land up to the BALC purchase, see appendix A.) The local commissioners were certainly more fastidious insisting that the government cancel the location tickets (settlement permits) of three militia claimants in Bury, and in their haste to purchase the improvements of a fourth.[23]

With its acquisition of nearly all the privately held Lingwick block by 1835, the BALC had gained access to the St Francis River via its most important tributary in the St Francis Tract, the Salmon River. Captain R. Hayne, who was supervising the government surveyors, reported that from a point six miles up the Salmon River boats and batteaux could reach either Sherbrooke or, in the opposite direction, the outlet of Lake Aylmer and a possible nine-mile road link to Ireland Township and the Craig Road to Quebec.[24] In addition there was the projected Dudswell to Quebec road which would provide much shorter and more direct access to the St Francis Tract than the route via Port St Francis and Sherbrooke. A major problem with encouraging immigrants to take a steamboat to Port St Francis was that, once on board, they could easily be tempted to continue the voyage to Upper Canada.[25]

But rather than focus its energies on a trunk line to Quebec, the BALC chose to push a road from Cookshire in Eaton Township (linked to Sherbrooke by sixteen miles of "the best road in the Townships") to the "Great Falls" of the Salmon River, deep in the heart of the St Francis Tract.[26] The future village of Victoria was located nine miles upstream from the site favoured by Hayne, and in the surveyor's words, its water communication was "interrupted by a succession of strong Rapids and heavy Falls." Hayne's opinion was that the site was "too far in the back woods (considering the Land Company's operations are only yet in their infancy) to hold out any immediate prospect of success."[27] The BALC soon established a village, known as Gould, on the spot chosen by Hayne, but like Victoria it had to be linked by a new road southwest to Cookshire pending the construction of the Dudswell-Quebec route. The court of directors was quite aware of the advantages of having immigrants proceed to the Townships directly from Quebec, but much of this route lay far outside its territory and the government did not complete the road, named after Lord Gosford, until 1838.[28] Map 6 demonstrates that the company actually planned its own link from Gould to Ireland Township, but in the meantime it probably had little choice but to attempt to channel immigrants via the lower St Francis Valley. Whether or not Port St Francis could have become a viable outlet for Eastern Townships produce is probably impossible to know because its success demanded, at the very least, a surge in regional development which failed to materialize in the late 1830s.[29]

Given that the company was determined to open the St Francis Tract to settlement, then, it had to build roads towards Sherbrooke. Surveyors differed on the best route from Cookshire to the Great Falls, but it was clear from the start that not only distance but soil quality would be taken into account. Lennoxville agent John Moore declared that rather than incurring the expense of altering the existing grid survey in Bury Township, the Victoria Road should cut diagonally across the lots, as in the older townships. The rough Eastern Townships terrain precluded a regular, close-knit settlement pattern, so there was little advantage to having roads which adhered closely to the range lines.[30] Map 7 illustrates how the grid pattern could be adjusted to provide reasonably equitable lot sizes.

As far as the St Francis Tract was concerned, the year 1835 was devoted largely to the consolidation of landholdings in the company's hands, as well as to exploration and surveys, and the clearing of a rough path to the Great Falls where a cabin was built.[31] All was ready for a major colonization drive the following year, but immigrant response to the employment opportunities on the Dudswell-Sherbrooke-Shefford Township road did not augur well for the company. Of 12,297 arrivals reported at Quebec during the summer of 1835, approximately 9,800 proceeded to Upper Canada and only 200 (340 less than in 1834) to the Eastern Townships.[32] As of July, only 12 to 14 immigrants had actually sought employment on the company's projects, so it was eventually forced to employ French Canadians to complete the section which had not been subcontracted to local entrepreneurs.[33] The cause could not have been lack of awareness on the immigrants' part since a series of promotional pamphlets were printed, including enthusiastic letters from British settlers in the Townships, and company agents had been assigned to the U.K., Quebec, Montreal, and even Albany.[34] The case which would repeatedly be presented for the Eastern Townships was succinctly summarized in a brochure printed in 1833:

The district ... is ... reported to comprise some of the finest scenery and most healthy climate of America: where bilious and intermittent fevers and agues are unknown, and which even the cholera did not enter, with which the Canadas were so severely afflicted. The soil, too, is said to be inferior to none in Canada. And although the greater length of its winter may seem to operate against agriculture, its proximity to the grand markets and shipping ports of Montreal and Quebec, gives it a preponderating advantage over more distant localities.[35]

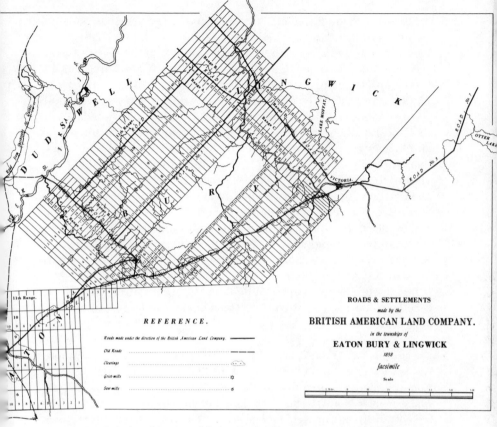

Map 7   Roads and settlements made by the British American Land Company in the townships of Eaton, Bury, and Lingwick, 1838 (Québec, Énergie, Mines, et Ressources, Service Arpentage, chemin SB)

Secretary Samuel Brooks of Sherbrooke suspected that potential clients were being intercepted in the seigneuries by "evilly-disposed persons" who persuaded them not to proceed to the Townships.[36] Quebec emigration agent, A.C. Buchanan Jr was also forced to defend himself against the company's charge that he was partial to Upper Canada.[37] His 1835 report nevertheless did express some reservations about the BALC's colonization strategy. He noted in July that the rate of wages was good, but that prospects of long-term employment or decent pay during the winter were not. He suggested that since labouring immigrants all wanted to acquire a little farm after their first or second year in America, the company should lease about a hundred log huts, each with an acre or two, for up to two years. The rent should be low and the tenants should be guaranteed preference to purchase at a moderate and fixed price – five pounds, for example. Employment offered the children by local farmers would further ensure that the labouring families would become permanent residents in the region.[38]

Buchanan's aim was apparently to create what H.C. Pentland has called a cottar class to provide seasonal labour for large-scale British agriculturalists:

There is no part of the Canadas, in my opinion, where a sober industrious body of emigrants from the United Kingdom accustomed to agricultural labour, is more required than in the eastern townships of Lower Canada. The general habits of the bulk of the present inhabitants of these townships are not strictly agricultural or calculated for laborious field drudgery; they are bent on pursuits that are less or more identified with traffic, such as the making of potash, horse breeding, dealing in cattle, manufactures, etc.[39]

Whether or not the company realized that few immigrants would be attracted by such a meagre homestead, the fact remained that its chief function was to sell farms, not garden plots.[40] Its commissioners insisted that even though road work could not proceed after the end of each season, demand for labour would remain high:

The preparation and marketing of grain, the drawing of other produce to market, the chopping and drawing of fuel, timber for export, and for supplying the sawmills, with many other employments, afford to the labourer the means, if not of adding to his funds, at least of supporting himself and his family in great comfort.[41]

Poor immigrants would have to pay only 6s. 3d. ($1.35) per acre for fifty-acre lots at the Great Falls, and the 20 per cent deposit could be paid off with twenty-five days of labour (at 2 ½s. or 50¢ per day). The subsequent six annual instalments of £2 1s. 8d. ($8.33) would be covered by only seventeen days' wages each year.[42]

The directors were initially cautious about recommending assistance with settlers' improvements, and they even counselled against providing transportation from Quebec or Trois-Rivières.[43] But the paucity of immigrants coming to the region in 1835 did lead the company to consider arrangements with agencies organizing pauper emigration from Britain. The first such opportunity arose after they learned that Dr James Marr Brydone had taken a quick tour of the Eastern Townships in the fall of 1835, travelling down the St Francis to Sherbrooke, then overland to Stanstead and Burlington, Vermont. He was actually en route to England from Upper Canada where he had delivered a group of immigrants for the Petworth Emigration Committee, organized in 1832 by the Earl of Egremont, lord lieutenant of the County of Sussex. By 1836 the committee, with funds from Egremont, other landlords, and a few parishes, would ship to Upper Canada more than 1,600 individuals, most of whom were farm labourers.[44] Meanwhile, hearing of Brydone's journey, the London directors of the BALC quickly approached the Petworth Committee, only to meet a cool reception. It had already begun negotiations with the Canada Company concerning 5,000 acres for a group settlement project, and Brydone had not been impressed with any advantages the Eastern Townships might offer for pauper emigrants.[45] He wrote to one of his colleagues:

was most pleased with the romantic pictoresque and (in many places) beautiful scenery on the banks of the river St Francis, and although I think favourably of these townships, as combining a certain proportion of the useful with the ornamental, to gentlemen already possessed of a moderate independence, I do not consider them of half the agricultural value of the Upper Province ... to the poor man − much inferior in climate and not superior in salubrity to the tract I have selected...[46]

To the company's deputy governor, Nathaniel Gould, Brydone was more brutally specific. He had been pleased with the scenery but had noticed much poor land, with crops still unharvested from the St Lawrence to Drummondville in mid-October. The region was clearly better suited for cattle and sheep pasture than for agriculture − for wealthy emigrants than for poor. Secretary Henry Bruyères protested that the soil and climate of the Eastern Townships were as good as those of Upper Canada, with cheaper wages and provisions, but all to no avail.[47]

The BALC would succeed, however, in attracting some of the arrivals from the southern counties of Hampshire, Norfolk, and Suffolk where parishes on their own initiative had been providing emigration subsidies since 1831.[48] No special arrangements appear to have been made for 1836, but the company clearly expected a large influx, for it reserved the entire eighteen-mile length of the Cookshire to Victoria road for immigrant labour and scoured the countryside for a large store of provisions.[49] The company's expectations were well founded, for not only did transatlantic immigration almost double to 27,728, but those assisted by parishes and landlords quadrupled to 4,625.[50]

Like Brydone, the organizers of the parish-assisted emigration preferred Upper Canada as a destination; however, some of them were willing to accept the Eastern Townships as an alternate choice. In April, for example, Buchanan was asked to forward twenty-five individuals to a light-soiled area of Upper Canada, but they had been provided with a letter to the BALC agent should they change their minds and should "you think it desirable for them to so engage themselves."[51] Buchanan did send eighteen people, along with £28, to the Eastern Townships late in May, and seventeen more in August when the £68 5s. provided for their settlement in Upper Canada failed to arrive with them.[52] The first group managed to plant a small crop, "which will enable them to pass the approaching winter in comparative comfort," while the second had been supplied with log houses and winter provisions.[53]

A much larger number of the pauper immigrants made their own way to the Eastern Townships. One not-unbiased source reported the natives of Norfolk and Suffolk to be "a set of fine able-bodied fellows with clean and cheerful looking families."[54] Commissioner Webster estimated that 6,000 individuals arrived in 1836, though this number included Americans, Upper Canadians, and Maritimers, as well as some 200 Swiss and Bavarian farmers originally destined for Ohio. The majority were seeking employment only, but 10,000 acres of company land were sold outside the St Francis Tract, and approximately 400 people settled in the Victoria area (see map 7).[55] The company's future seemed assured, but, even though sales values averaged three times the purchase price, the volume was not sufficient to offset the great expenses. In addition to extensive investments outside the block, the dam and mills at Victoria had cost £300, the Victoria Road £2000, and provisions £5400.[56] The company appears to have been more than generous with its food supplies, for local legend later had it that colonists used dough from the flour provided to plaster their cabin walls.[57] By the fall of 1838, expenses for the Victoria Road had escalated from the government-sanctioned £3378 to £7868, with the BALC attributing the blame to the high cost of local labour and provisions, as well as to the fact that immigrant labour rather than subcontractors had been employed.[58]

In order to cut expenses, no travelling agent would be employed in England in 1837, and those parishes from which the settlers had come were to be warned that the BALC would provide no assistance beyond employing labour:

doubtless many of the poorer class will proceed to the Townships by invitation from friends already there, but as these parties will be unsolicited on behalf of the Company they must be given clearly to understand that it will be incumbent on them to provide for the coming winter by their own exertions and prudence during the working season.[59]

In addition, the directors wished to have operations suspended "in all cases where practicable" during the summer of 1837, though they did sanction continued road construction and town improvements in the St Francis Tract. Up to one thousand pounds could be spent on the extension of the Victoria Road several miles northeastward into the wilderness towards a stream known as Otter Brook. The aim was ultimately to push twelve miles east to Lake Megantic and twelve miles west to Lake St Francis, but this the company was never able to do.[60]

During the summer of 1837 British immigration to the Eastern Townships slipped to about 1,500 from 6,000 the previous year, but more serious for the company's interests was the fact that some of the English settlers began to drift to the United States.[61] The crowning touch was the outbreak of rebellion in the fall, with its disastrous impact on the London capital market and the projected immigration for 1838.[62] As a result, the BALC won from the government a single year's suspension on its payments and accumulation of interest, as well as a provisional agreement to direct future instalments to the preparation of lands for immigrants.[63] Despite its unsatisfactory experience with the assisted English immigrants of 1836, the company clearly realized that some such programme would be needed to attract settlers in 1838, if not thereafter.

Attention turned north from the Sussex coast to the western Highlands and islands of Scotland where families were facing starvation due to the failure of the potato crop in 1836. Potatoes had become their staple diet after the turn of the century, when the growth of the kelp industry encouraged settlement on small, individually held, beach-front crofts. Here they gathered and processed seaweed to produce alkali salts, to the great but temporary profit of their land-lords. Alkali prices declined rapidly after the end of the Napoleonic Wars, so that by the 1830s much of the crofter population was of no economic benefit to the proprietors. The potato blight thus threatened to make them an intolerable burden, yet there was no parish system of poor relief to subsidize emigration.[64]

Interest in the potential of a Highland colonization scheme was initially aroused by Colonel Duncan McDougall, former inspecting field officer of the Nova Scotia militia, who had been competing with the BALC for wild land purchases adjacent to the St Francis Tract.[65] To prevent the "future destruction of the loyal, moral, peacefully suffering Highland peasantry," McDougall advocated the establishment of 5,000 families or 25,000 souls on 150,000 acres free of charge.[66] He claimed that all Canadian proprietors with whom he had conversed were ready to contribute land, but he was actually counting on the BALC as the sole initial participant. Because of the nature of "this great national undertaking," the Royal Navy would pick up the emigrants at small ports in the western Highlands and islands and carry them to Quebec. The company would then provide transportation to the 30-acre lots, where each family would find a log house, 5 acres prepared for cultivation, necessary implements, and sufficient provisions to last four months, when the potato and oat crops would be ready for harvesting. The BALC would be reimbursed by the government for the thirty-five pounds it invested in preparing a homestead for each family, and it was presumably meant to recoup its transportation expenses and the value of its land investments by the reservation of alternate 30-acre lots for sale to the immigrants. McDougall was no doubt familiar enough with the limitations of the Eastern Townships to realize that such a purchase would be essential if a family were to survive. The government and company would be further protected by obliging the settlers to clear and cultivate an additional 4 acres the following year, and by forbidding the sale of their farms for a fixed number of years.

The total cost to the British taxpayer, including £10 per emigrant family for the ocean voyage, would be £227,500. This sum was no more, McDougall claimed, than what was required annually to maintain the crofters as paupers in Scotland. Not only would they rapidly contribute to Britain's wealth "by acquiring the means of largely purchasing its woollen, cotton, and hardware manufactures," they could not fail, "under a judicious organization," to strengthen colonial defence. (In resubmitting his proposal in 1843, McDougall added that he had foreseen the rebellion and informed the government that Highland colonization was the remedy.)[67] A principal reason that no repayments should be required of the settlers was that it would not be wise to make them debtors to the government "when the political and geographical position of our North American Colonies is borne in mind." Finally, the colonel justified the expenditure by adding that the removal of protective duties on alkali made the destitution of the Highlanders as much a product of imperial legislation as had been the abolition of slavery. The results of free trade had been the destruction of an industry which had employed 60,000 people, and the near bankruptcy of most of the landlords involved. If £20 million could be voted for the West Indian proprietors, £2.5 million should not be withheld for the relief of their Highland counterparts.[68]

Thomas F. Elliot, agent general for emigration, agreed that mass removal from the Highlands seemed the obvious solution to their economic problems. Because of the great cost involved, however, parliamentary funds would have to be voted, and general principles laid down by the government.[69] Clearly no major project could be organized for the summer of 1837, but the possibility of such a scheme ironically increased with the recovery of the potato crop in the fall. The Highland Distress committees were left with some £20,000 which they wished to devote to promoting emigration. In a letter to the Colonial Office in January 1838 the Glasgow-based committee argued that assisted passages to Australia, as offered the previous summer, would not solve the population problem. It was desirable to move entire families, but only the able-bodied had been eligible for the Australian project. The elderly and disabled would have a greater chance to survive the voyage to "Canada," which was where most people preferred to go in any case because they had friends and relatives already there. But the Glasgow committee did not wish to commit its surplus funds unless the government organized the emigration, since only then could it be extensive enough "to cure or even greatly palliate the evils existing in the Highlands and Islands."[70]

Glasgow's Edinburgh and London counterparts supported her proposals, and a meeting of landed proprietors agreed to contribute, but once again T.F. Elliot effectively vetoed the project. At first his objection was that Ireland would expect the same kind of assistance, and later he argued on the grounds that emigration to the North American colonies was already "so large" that assisted passages were unnecessary.[71] Elliot obviously felt that emigration would recover without government prompting in 1838, but neither the Scottish proprietors nor the BALC had much reason to be optimistic. Having gained the tacit consent of the Colonial Office to direct all future instalments towards the preparation of homesteads for settlers, the company arranged with the Highland proprietor, Stewart Mac-kenzie, the immigration of 60 crofter families (200 individuals) to settle in the vicinity of the future village of Gould.[72] After a six-week delay, the emigrants boarded the 400-ton *Energy* at Stornoway, principal centre for Mackenzie's remote Isle of Lewis in the Outer Hebrides. A number had already been picked up at Lochbroom on the mainland, while those from Lewis were, for the most part, leaving the kelp-gathering parish of Uig on the west coast of the island. In 1841 the chamberlain of Lewis, recalled that three years earlier pro-prietor Mackenzie had provided the fares for fifteen families (sev-enty individuals) from the island. They had been forced to go because their farms were being converted to sheep-walks. The man-ager of the Lochbroom farm reported only that he had sent out "some families" who were "in arrear of their rents, and very desti-tute." The landlord had paid their passage to the "eastern townships of Lower Canada."[73]

The agent who organized the Lewis migration claimed that "they were probably the poorest crowd that ever left the Highlands," but Buchanan claimed that all were "in good health" when they arrived at Quebec in late September.[74] It was clearly too far advanced in the season for them to take much advantage of employment op-portunities on company projects, but in November a letter from Sherbrooke was printed in the Montreal *Gazette* reporting that the Scots had been "a good help to our farmers, raising potatoes, thrash-ing, mending roads, ditches, etc. I like to hear their Gaelic tongues here and there, and to see the robust hearty example of healthful field labour these Highland lasses give to our more effeminate Amer-ican house women." Some families had proceeded directly to their lots, while others were "hiring as servants for the winter season".[75]

Irish Catholics and French Canadians appear to have been doing much of the work in the St Francis Tract, where the company was determined to complete the economic infrastructure despite the fact that, as of February 1838, its expenditures and obligations outranked sales (two-thirds of which remained to be paid) by £176,636 to £4,500.[76] By autumn, the new villages of Robinson and Victoria boasted mills and schoolhouses, while Gould was awaiting devel-opment.[77] In addition to roads connecting the three sites, and the Otter Brook extension from Victoria, the company had also built a link from Robinson to the Dudswell (Gosford) Road and extended two others from Gould to the Lingwick-Weedon line (see map 7). Thus a total of some sixty miles of roads had been constructed in the St Francis Tract, but five major bridges (estimated at £2125) were still needed at various points on the St Francis and Salmon rivers to tie all the road links together.[78]

While development was still progressing in the summer of 1838, the new governor, Lord Durham, effectively pulled the rug out from under the BALC by recommending against any concessions. Outraged by the history of wasteful land grants his commission was uncovering, and suspicious of the company's sincerity, Durham suggested an offer to resume its land at the original price, including improvements at valuation.[79] As a result, the Colonial Office rescinded its approval of the homestead scheme, and presented a modified form of Durham's recommended ultimatum. The government would take back an amount of land equivalent in value to the company's remaining debt.[80] No further steps were taken as the company defaulted in its instalments during the following two years, but it was clearly in a poor position to continue promoting colonization. Total expenditure for assistance to all settlers up to the end of 1838 was said to be £17,798, and there were relatively few inhabitants in the St Francis Tract to account for it.[81]

As late as the spring of 1839, however, the BALC still had some reason to hope that the government would reconsider its rejection of the assistance scheme.[82] The directors were optimistic enough to attempt to reach an agreement with the Highland Association of the Mull district. Each family would receive a substantial log cabin and four cultivated acres, plus a cast-iron cauldron for manufacturing potash and maple sugar, a cast-iron baking pan, a grindstone, two axes, two grubbing hoes, and a spade and shovel, all valued at £33 10s. As for land, families would be settled on fifty acres and pay only 1s. in rent per year for seven years, commencing in the third year, then be eligible to purchase at $150, payable in five annual instalments with interest. Because the 1839 season would be well advanced before the immigrants could arrive, the company would employ two hundred families at $5 a week for each labourer. Most would receive their salaries for preparing their own homesteads.[83]

The company had also requested that government pay for the internal survey of the St Francis Tract, that half the expense of supporting the indigent immigrants be counted towards the purchase money, and that interest on unpaid instalments be cancelled, all concessions that were rejected out of hand. Possibly because it was considered part of the package, Lord Russell had also turned down the settlement proposal by the fall of 1839.[84] Consequently nothing appears to have developed from the Mull correspondence. While road work did continue in the St Francis Tract, it must certainly have been at a reduced scale. The Irish and French-Canadian numbers quickly diminished, but the small group of Lewis Scots appear to have remained intact.[85]

Channell claims that in addition to employment "grubbing out a road" from Gould to Robinson, the only assistance the Highlanders received was a sap kettle for each family and a supply of oatmeal at the price of five dollars per hundred pounds.[86] In the spring of 1839 the government inspector reported that the settlers were "succeeding well, having already cut down and burned off from two to three acres each family."[87] An observer in 1841 claimed that support for the first winter had brought a debt of £200, but that this had nearly all been repaid. Furthermore, within the first three years each family had cleared ten to fifteen acres and acquired one to three cows. "One of them told me the other day that he had raised this year more than would support his family for two years."[88] The success of the colony is further corroborated by the report of its Lewis organizer, who wrote in 1841 that "Providence blessed the work of their hands with outstanding blessing."[89] Despite their impoverished origins on a treeless island, the Lewis settlers did remain in the isolated and heavily forested Gould area, thus presenting a sharp and inexplicable contrast to the disastrous experience of their counterparts from Arisaig, Moydart, and Skye on the lands of the New Brunswick and Nova Scotia Land Company.[90]

The possibility of receiving subsidized reinforcements began to look promising again in 1840 when deteriorating conditions among the working classes of Britain were forcing the government to reconsider its laissez-faire policy. In addition to unemployed English labourers and dispossessed Irish small-holders, there were said to be 100,000 to 150,000 destitute Scots anxious to emigrate from the islands and northwest coast. Elliot's Land and Emigration Board recommended that the government co-ordinate the efforts of all agencies involved: parishes in England and Ireland, landed proprietors who wished to clear their estates, the colonies through their land funds, and the various land companies.[91]

Whether or not Russell would have changed his mind in 1840 concerning the BALC's settler-assistance scheme, it was too late as far as the company was concerned. Commissioner Fraser had pressed the proposal once again in March, but during the summer John Galt's twenty-three-year-old son, Alexander, succeeded in changing the focus of the company.[92] After a tour of inspection through the St Francis Tract, he reported that company roads were choked with bushes four feet high, and that the three villages were deserted by all but a handful of families, with their warehouses, mills, and pearl-asheries all in decay. The young Galt recommended that attention be shifted from helpless British pauper immigrants to Eastern Townships' residents, many of whom were looking for new opportunities. Furthermore, not only was the new governor, Charles Poulett Thomson, hostile to both the BALC and government assistance for pauper emigration, but the newly created municipal council of the County of Sherbrooke threatened a wild land tax of a penny per acre, which would amount to more than double the company's receipts.[93] As a result, the BALC dropped its colonization proposal to accept the government's offer, which had been renewed by Russell in 1839. The beleaguered company would rescind part of its holdings in order to cancel its burdensome debt of £72,000 sterling.[94]

After protracted negotiations, an agreement was finally reached in July, 1841 whereby the government would reclaim 511,237 acres of the St Francis Tract in exchange for the payments outstanding.[95] The BALC was thereby left with the most valuable part of the original purchase, including 85,000 acres in the Tract's most readily accessible townships – Bury, Lingwick, and Weedon. With the private acquisitions, company holdings still totalled over half a million acres. As commissioner, Alexander T. Galt was able to turn the company's fortunes around by mid-century, but at the cost of neglecting what was left of the St Francis Tract.

Meanwhile, because emigration accelerated again before the Land and Emigration Board's assistance project of 1840 could be implemented, the concern once more became what to do with the indigent families after they reached British North America. London had already pledged a grant for emigration purposes, but decided that its expenditure for 1841 should be limited to assisting families to proceed from the port of landing to districts where their services were needed.[96] The BALC followed suit by offering free transportation from Montreal to Sherbrooke to those with £7 10s. ($30) to spare for a down payment on land. For others, the only incentive would be several years' grace before the first payments came due.[97] A greater enticement was clearly required, since of the 28,000 immigrants who landed at Quebec in 1841 only about 400 were reported to have gone to the Eastern Townships.[98]

Over half this number was comprised of a contingent of Lewis crofters who had arrived in August. The 78 steerage passengers aboard the "Lady Hood" and the 145 aboard the "Charles" had endured crossings of seventy and fifty days, respectively. Buchanan reported that the members of the first group were "in great distress for want of provisions," having expended all their money in purchasing supplies from the ship's master during the voyage. The Quebec agent distributed two hundred pounds of oatmeal among them, and forwarded them to Port St Francis. From here they made their own way to Sherbrooke. The passengers of the "Charles," chiefly from Uig in western Lewis, were nearly as destitute. Letters from clergymen suggested of both groups that "in general, they had to leave their own land penniless, and that some of them owed to charity the balance that completed their passage money, and the half boll of meal on which they had endeavoured to subsist during the voyage."[99] Buchanan again provided a small amount of oatmeal before sending the immigrants on their way.[100] The BALC would be of little help, for it offered only seasonal employment to its settlers, and winter was fast approaching.[101]

The new arrivals were anticipating assistance from their predecessors of 1838, upon whose invitation they had come to the Eastern Townships. Admirable as the first contingent's progress may have been, however, there was certainly no chance that it could support such a large and sudden influx. For those men who could find work despite the lateness of the season and their lack of English, there remained the problem of finding shelter for wives and children. The inhabitants of Sherbrooke subscribed £70, but this was sufficient only to release the immigrants' baggage from the hands of carters, and to purchase immediate necessities. There was little alternative for most of them but to continue their journey to the St Francis Tract, there to rely on the help of others to see them through the winter.[102] In early September, the Emigration Association of St Francis petitioned the St Andrew's Society of Montreal for financial aid. The St Andrew's officials declared that relief grants did not lie within their society's constitution, but that in consideration of the "good character for industry and morality" of the immigrants in question, it would receive public donations on their behalf.[103] Montreal's emigration association had already exhausted its funds, but the popular colonization promoter, Dr Thomas Rolph, helped to arouse the general public to contribute approximately £250.[104]

Meanwhile, a dozen log cabins had to be built in the St Francis Tract, though their roofs presented a serious problem because there was still no sawmill in the Gould vicinity and spruce bark was of no use so late in the year. The settlers needed axes, kettles, and nails if they were to begin their new lives, but the scrupulous local emigration association was reluctant to purchase anything but oatmeal and potatoes, lest outsiders conclude that the gravity of the situation had been exaggerated.[105] The private donations nevertheless did enable most if not all of the newcomers to become settlers it would seem, since a petition circulated a year later – in 1842 – claimed that the population of Salmon River had reached 552. Of the 126 families listed, only the last 19 appear not to have been members of the Hebridean colony. The Church of Scotland's *Home and Foreign Missionary Record*, which published a petition requesting a Gaelic- and English-speaking minister, claimed that it issued from "by far the most numerous destitute congregation of Gaelic Presbyterians in Canada, or perhaps in any colony of Britain."[106] Destitute the settlers certainly were; though they again faced hunger during their second winter in Canada, the provincial government rejected their request for assistance on the grounds that it had "no funds applicable" to their relief.[107]

The lack of encouragement from both the BALC and the province no doubt explains why few of the 1,194 individuals who emigrated via Stornoway during the summer of 1842 seem to have made their way to the St Francis Tract.[108] The *Parliamentary Papers* do not mention their destination, but there is no record of a major influx to the Eastern Townships, and the 1844 census lists only 357 Scots-born in Lingwick Township and 44 in Bury.[109]

There would be no further large-scale migrations from Lewis until mid-century, by which time the BALC had demanded that the Lingwick settlers begin their payments of 10s. ($2.00) per acre of wild land.[110] Contracts called for annual interest, with the land to be repossessed if payments fell behind by two years. The company had actually taken a leaf from the book of the Crown Lands Office by issuing location tickets rather than deeds of sale prior to payment being received in full. These certificates were not transferable without special permission, and they specified that no trees could be cut except for clearing, fuel, fences, and buildings on the premises.[111] Small wonder that the company's investigator was able to report to his London superiors in 1853 that the form of contract employed had proven effective in the ejection of defaulters at little or no expense to the company.[112] O.D. Skelton clearly misses the point when he suggests that the absence of lawsuits against purchasers after 1843 "made clear the considerateness of the policy adopted."[113] To avoid losing its clients, however, the BALC allowed purchasers who had fallen into arrears to become tenants with a fixed-term leasehold. Thus, after some ten years of residence in Brookbury, six miles north of Robinson, English settler George Downes had to agree in 1846 to pay a rent of £3 6s. 6d. ($13.30) per year (6 per cent of the cash price) on a property of eighty-three acres. The same prohibition on cutting logs applied, the contract could be cancelled if rent was overdue by forty days, and the company could specify the number of acres to be cleared and cultivated each year. (In Downes' case these blanks in the contract were not filled in.) Then, after ten years of paying rent, Downes was to be given the privilege of meeting the full purchase price of £55 7s. 6d. ($221.50) in four annual instalments with 6 per cent interest.[114] The short-term leasehold system actually attracted a large number of immigrants to Upper Canada's Huron Tract in the 1840s, for the 6 per cent annual payment compared favourably with available mortgage rates, but the Canada Company appears to have charged no more for its fertile, advantageously located land than did the BALC for lots in the St Francis Tract.[115]

An additional feature of Galt's sales terms was the acceptance of payments in grain or stock. He claimed that the BALC was carrying on the most extensive system of barter known in the western world.[116] To take one example, between 1848 and 1856 George Downes delivered seven cattle to the company, valued at $96.00; from 1856 to 1860 he worked nineteen days on the company's account for approximately $17.50; and from 1860 to 1865 he contributed $176.00 in the form of eight cattle plus cash.[117] With a total of ten young cattle on his farm in 1861, it appears that Downes was delivering close to the equivalent of one fifth of his merchantable stock to the company during each of these six years. As of 1865 Downes disappears from the company's accounts, having failed to pay the full debt for his farm after almost thirty years of residence. The BALC's "Record of Deeds" volume includes no mention of him, though he may have obtained clear title after 1866, the last year for which such records survive. Certainly the manuscript census reveals that Downes and his family were still on the same farm in 1871.

The census also demonstrates the rewards that years of persistence and hard work could bring, even under the burden of debt. In 1861 Downes's farm was valued at $1000, his livestock at $450, and his implements and vehicles at $140. With the eldest daughter already outside the household, three sons aged sixteen and upward, and a twenty-one-year-old hired hand, the Downes family was probably near the peak of its productivity, as table 12 illustrates. But there were also six younger mouths to feed, and George and Jane Downes appear never to have been able to expand their relatively small holding to accommodate more than one of their heirs. Their first two sons were no longer in the household by 1871, and the third was about to move to New Hampshire where he would work for four years as a weaver before returning to farm, presumably on the family homestead.[118] In 1871, when father and mother had reached fifty-six and fifty-five years of age, respectively, they were clearly able to enjoy a certain freedom from want, but grain and root vegetable production had declined drastically even though there were

Table 12
Agricultural Profile of the George Downes Family, 1851–71

Date	Acres Owned	Crop (acres)	Pasture (acres)	Grain (bu.)	Root (bu.)	Hay (tons)	Horses	Cattle
1851	84	23	7	134	120	9	0	7
1861	83	25	25	470	310	12	1	14
1871	84	30	20	202	104	16	1	11

Date	Sheep	Pigs	Butter (lbs)	Sugar (lbs)	Wool (lbs)	Cloth (yds)	Garden & Orchard	Wood
1851	8	2	150	150	50	48	n.d.	n.d.
1861	26	3	400	300	50	50	$20	n.d.
1871	7	2	300	400	45	45	11 bu. fruit	75 logs/ 20 cords

Source: Canada Census, 1852, 1861, 1871
n.d. no data

still seven offspring aged seven to twenty-six remaining in the household. Of course, the fall of 1870 may simply have produced an unusually bad harvest, for the family actually had a greater acreage in crop than ten years earlier, but an aberration in weather would not explain the smaller pasturage and the drop from fourteen to eleven cattle, and twenty-six to seven sheep. Nor was the problem a lack of fodder, for the hay tonnage actually increased by 25 per cent. The relatively large number of logs cut by the family during the winter of 1870-71, and the marked increase in maple sugar production, suggests that it continued to rely quite heavily upon the woods to make ends meet.

A number of the Downes family's English neighbours were equally persistent in the relatively fertile Brookbury area, and in 1853 a recently arrived settler named Josiah Clarke wrote enthusiastically to his Suffolk County sister and her husband:

Here is them that left England 17 years back, and have got cows, oxen, and land of their own, and a horse to ride on, and when in England had not enough to eat, and many might be better of [*sic*] than they are if they would work, but they are too idle to. A man that will work can live here, but a lazy man cannot, as here is no parish to go to.[119]

Elsewhere in the township, however, the sacrifices called for by the BALC were simply too great. The 1852 census enumerator noted that the forty-five Highland families were living on poor soil, and that

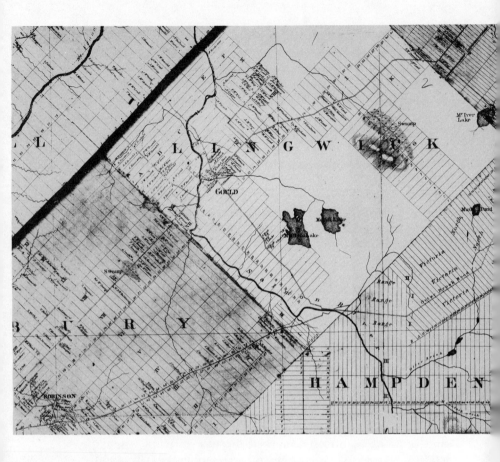

Map 8   Settlement pattern in Bury and Lingwick Townships, 1863. Section from
"Map of the District of St Francis, Canada East. From Survey ... under the
direction of O.W. Gray. Topographical engraving published by Putnam and Gray,
1863. D.E. Slack, Publishing Agent." (National Archives of Canada [NA], National
Map Collection [NMC]-13807)

many were planning to move north to the crown's free grants in Winslow, one of the townships relinquished by the BALC in 1841. Bury's population subsequently dropped from 835 in 1844 to 783 in 1852, reaching only 989 by 1861. Weedon's development would begin later, but, because it was part of the French-Canadian wave of expansion, its population grew more rapidly, from 279 in 1852 to 909 in 1861. As for Lingwick, despite the influx of Hebridean Scots to the region in 1851, its population actually declined from 808 in 1852 to 564 in 1861, many having moved north to neighbouring Winslow.[120] Land in the upper St Francis district was too marginal in quality for the majority of settlers to accept any form of tenant status.

Furthermore, the Highlanders had no reason to feel loyal towards a company which continued to offer them little if any encouragement. The former commissioner, John Fraser, had taken a certain paternal interest in the fate of his fellow Scots, as demonstrated by his request from Upper Canada in 1845 that the government provide aid to build a church.[121] But Fraser's young successor apparently had no such instincts, for Galt felt that the only suitable immigrant settlers would be small farmers and mechanics with eighty or ninety pounds to support them for the first year and a half.[122] He focused his energies on the development of Sherbrooke, on the construction of the St Lawrence and Atlantic Railroad, and on French-Canadian settlement in Shefford County, to the west of Sherbrooke. As a result of his reluctance to extend a short road link from Gould to the government colonization roads in Winslow, the latter township would remain cut off from Lingwick and Sherbrooke as late as 1855.[123]

Galt's successor of the following year, the Irish-born Richard W. Heneker, took a more lively interest in nurturing the British character of the Eastern Townships, though the first group he attracted was actually from Norway.[124] Some 90 Norwegians settled in Bury Township in 1857. By the end of 1858 25 families (126 persons) had purchased company land, and they were joined by another 15 families with "considerable sums of money" the following year, but all appear to have eventually joined their compatriots on less expensive land in the "western" United States.[125]

In 1859, Heneker arranged for a company agent named John S. Cummins to visit Ireland and England to promote emigration to the BALC's holdings. Cummins claimed to have extensive connections with landed proprietors in the County of Cork, and he hoped to rekindle interest on Lord Albermarle's estate in England where many of the company's first settlers had originated. The agent carried letters from some such families who had "attained an enviable position on the Company's territory."[126] He was also to investigate projects for group migration among some recent converts to Protestantism in western Ireland.[127]

Once in Britain, Cummins renewed the contact the BALC had made as early as 1833 with a number of London guilds which possessed estates in Londonderry. For those interested in reducing the number of flax-growing tenants, he offered to sell company land in Bury, either to the guilds themselves or directly to the emigrants.[128] Finally, Cummins attempted to arouse the interest of skilled farmers by distributing printed circulars among the previous ten years' graduates of the Agricultural Model School at Eglinton in Londonderry. The school's governor, who was the resident agent of the grocers' guild, could only lament that "the people here have such very unreasonable expectations on anything being proposed to them – that any overture of the kind is obliged to be made with considerable caution."[129] In fact, the London guilds themselves were not enthusiastic about the company's proposals, and, as for southern Ireland and Norfolk, emigration patterns seemed to be set for Pennsylvania and Australia, respectively. All that Cummins could report to Heneker, after his return in the fall of 1860, was the hope that the contacts he had made would be of future benefit to the land company.[130] His wishes were not destined to be fulfilled, for the British-born population of the Eastern Townships dropped from 12,500 in 1861 to 11,300 in 1871.[131]

Heneker's retrospective excuse for the failure of the BALC as a colonization agency was the government's colonization roads project at mid-century. He claimed that having paid 87 ½¢ per acre (in fact 75¢) for the St Francis Tract townships, it was impossible to compete with the free fifty-acre grants and 60¢ per acre sales offered by the Crown Lands Office. "The Company in doing their utmost to foster emigration, naturally avoided those parts of the Territory which adjoined the Government lands."[132] Heneker to the contrary, it is clear that the BALC did little to foster immigration to any part of the Townships after mid-century, and that the government's colonization projects had little to do with the slow development of the three remaining townships in the St Francis Tract. While a number of Scottish families certainly left Lingwick for Winslow in the early 1850s, the absence of colonists around Lake Aylmer and Lake St Francis would not necessarily have resulted in the settlement of company lands further south. The marginal free-grant townships were filled to capacity as early as 1860, thereby actually stimulating French-Canadian settlement in the adjacent township of Weedon.[133]

Admittedly, the Scots preferred to expand eastwards towards Lake Megantic, rather than settling in Lingwick, but there is no guarantee that they would not have simply left the region (as they ultimately did anyway), had not inexpensive government land become available. As for the English and Irish colonists of Bury, they clearly had no desire to move to the rocky and mountainous land made available by the crown.

The fact is that there was little or no reason for the BALC to promote colonization of the St Francis Tract once a railway link to Portland, Maine, opened the region's timber and mineral resources to the international market. In 1850, Charles Bischoff had cautioned against alienating large blocks of land for this reason, and, in 1853, the year the trunk line from Montreal to Portland was completed, the BALC launched its subsidiary British American Mining Association.[134] When 1137 acres in Lingwick were sold to Octavius Rooke, Esq., in 1859, the BALC was careful to preserve the mineral rights. As for lumber, impoverished settlers would simply be a thorn in the side of entrepreneurs such as Rooke, whose Lake Moffatt purchase (see map 9) at $3.48 per acre was at a considerably higher rate than what settlers had been paying. Unfortunately for both Rooke and the BALC, C.S. Clark and Company's large mill at Roxton Falls, near Sherbrooke, controlled upriver access to the Grand Trunk Railway, and it also monopolized the crown timber berths of the upper St Francis watershed. With no other outlet for his timber, Rooke had mortgaged his Lingwick property by 1863, only to lose it at a sheriff's sale five years later.

There were no further large sales in Lingwick until the 1870s when the arrival of the St Francis and Megantic International Railway promised to break the Clark monopoly. Small steam sawmills began to spring up throughout the district, and, as we shall see, the Glasgow Canadian Land and Trust Company invested a large sum in the new village of Scotstown, at the abandoned site of Victoria. Property values would clearly climb in Lingwick as well as in Weedon, through which the Quebec Central Railway was being constructed, but in 1872 the BALC suddenly sold nearly all its remaining land in the two townships (30,718 acres in Lingwick and 15,050 acres in Weedon) to Clark and Company for only $1.04 per acre (see map 9). The main reason seems to have been that, because of its crippling debt and ongoing failure to pay dividends, the land company had simply decided to alienate its remaining holdings as quickly as possible. In 1869, Heneker had recommended that even the Sherbrooke properties be sold and the share capital gradually liquidated, a policy which was embodied in the new charter issued in 1871.[135]

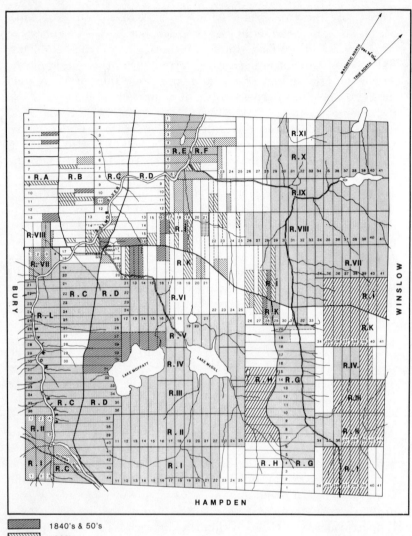

Map 9   British American Land Company sales in Lingwick Township (Québec, Énergie, Mines, et Ressources, Service Arpentage, L226, Lingwick; Sherbrooke and Cookshire Registry Offices; NA, BALC Papers, VIII, 1737–1813)

Table 13
BALC Sales in Lingwick Township, 1835–80

Dates	Acres	Receipts	Price per acre
1846–59	2,242	$6,772	$3.02
1860–69	1,848	$5,061	$2.74
1870–80[1]	34,755	$34,110	$1.24
Total	38,845	$54,943	$1.41

Source: Sherbrooke Registry Office, Lingwick Township, 1835–80; PAC, BALC Papers, VIII, 1757–1813
1 Statistics do not include land resold to Clark and Company in 1879 which had originally been sold in 1872.

Again the parallel with the New Brunswick and Nova Scotia Land Company is intriguing for it too began to wind up operations by selling large acreages to lumber entrepreneurs during the 1870s.[136] The land companies may have built mills and promoted railroad construction, but their consistent aim – no matter who the local commissioner happened to be – was simply to profit from their real estate holdings rather than to diversify operations.[137] If those profits could best be ensured by refusing to sell industrial sites in Sherbrooke, or by strengthening the deadly grip of a timber monopoly over the economic development of the upper St Francis district, then so be it.[138] The BALC may have continued its operations into the twentieth century, but by the 1870s it had long since lost any imperialist-inspired dreams it may once have held for a British-populated Eastern Townships, leaving the region with only the drawbacks of its colonial economic status.

Constructing the Lambton Road: Cul-de-sac for Imperial Expansion in Lower Canada

> it must henceforth be the first and steady purpose of the British Government to establish an English population, with English laws and language, in this Province.
>
> *Report of the Earl of Durham*, 212

The British American Land Company's 600,000 acre St Francis Tract, purchased in 1835, did not include all the unsurveyed land in the Eastern Townships. From the company tract's northern border at Lake St Francis to the Chaudière seigneuries there remained 220,000 acres of untouched wilderness in what was then known as Megantic County. Across this crown-owned block lay the shortest path between the settled townships near the Vermont border and the Chaudière Valley route to the port of Quebec. The government was in the process of constructing the Gosford Road from Lévis to Sherbrooke, but, to an even greater extent than the deteriorating old Craig Road to Richmond, this new trunk road would pass through thinly settled territory. There were sixty miles of uninviting wilderness between the Gosford Road's junction with the Craig Road in Halifax Township and the first settlements in Dudswell Township, north of Sherbrooke. Furthermore, the BALC was investing a great deal of money in pushing its Victoria colonization road to Lingwick Township in the heart of the St Francis Tract. If this route were extended a few miles to the tract's boundary at the tip of Lake St Francis, there would remain only some thirty miles to the privately owned land of Tring Township bordering the Chaudière seigneuries. In a sense, then, the BALC's role in opening the Eastern Townships to economic development would be incomplete without the colonization of the Megantic Territory. It appears to have been for this reason that the Quebec and Megantic Land Company was initially encouraged by the government, even though it would compete for British settlers with its hard-pressed London-based counterpart. The Quebec-based company would ultimately accomplish little, but its formation represented a temporary shift towards colonial capital's involvement in colonization, and its early demise signalled the origin of direct state control over land settlement projects. Finally, the failure of the government to attract a significant number of British settlers to the Megantic Tract marked the end of serious official attempts to anglicize the frontier of Lower Canada.

The Colonial Office never did officially sanction the Megantic project, but governors Aylmer and Durham both gave it unofficial encouragement. Lord Aylmer may have initially been unenthusiastic about the BALC, but political polarization had made him an ardent supporter of large-scale British colonization and French-Canadian assimilation.[1] As an equally unqualified proponent of the anglicization of Lower Canada, Durham was also naturally sympathetic to the new company, but his critical attitude towards absentee proprietors and the BALC led him to hedge on his commitment.

Without access to private correspondence it is impossible to state categorically what motivated the founders of the Quebec and Megantic Land Company. It would appear, however, that these major Quebec merchants were interested not so much in any direct profits to be made from such a speculative enterprise as in the extension of their town's metropolitian influence. To the limited degree that the Eastern Townships had access to an external market, it tended to lie to the west at the port of Montreal. Quebec was in a rather isolated position, with a marginal agricultural hinterland and tenuous communications links with American cities to the south. A good road to the Eastern Townships would not only help to bring this promising farming frontier into Quebec's orbit, it would also improve transportation ties to the New England states. At the same time, of course, it would add to the wealth and influence of the city's great merchants, and contribute to the extension of imperial authority and influence on the American-settled Townships frontier.[2]

The principal founders of the Quebec and Megantic Land Company were James Bell Forsyth, William Price, and Robert Hunter Gairdner. Forsyth, who acted as the company's attorney, was Quebec agent for Montreal's dominant trading firm, Forsyth, Richardson, and Company.[3] He was a major landholder, having acquired 10,000

acres from the crown according to the Durham Report.[4] Some of
his property was located in Megantic County, but in the vicinity of
the Craig Road, not the land company's projected Lake St Francis
– Chaudière artery.[5] Forsyth's Quebec partner, William Walker, was
a timber exporter, and by the 1840s Forsyth himself was primarily
interested in the timber trade.[6]

The land company's second partner, William Price, had been an
important Quebec timber merchant long before Forsyth, and by the
1830s he was beginning to acquire the sawmills and timber land that
would make him one of the province's largest lumber producers.
Price would actually encourage a French-Canadian colonization society to send squatters to the Saguenay during the early 1840s as a
first step to taking over the region from the Hudson's Bay Company.[7] There is little reason to suspect, however, that the Quebec
and Megantic Land Company was a timber operation in disguise. It
would focus its energies on townships drained by the upper St Francis watershed which ran in the opposite direction from Quebec towards Sherbrooke. The total distance to the St Lawrence at the
mouth of the St Francis was about 200 miles, presumably too far for
profitable exploitation of a district with no large stands of white
pine. During the late 1830s timber entrepreneurs petitioned for
licences in nearby Coleraine and Ireland, but these townships were
drained by the Bécancour River, a much more direct route to the
St Lawrence. As we shall see in chapter 4, lumber companies would
commence operations in the Lake St Francis area only after mid-
century when construction of the St Lawrence and Atlantic Railway
through the Eastern Townships opened a market for manufactured
spruce in Portland, Maine.

Price, nevertheless, did have a business link to the Eastern Townships. One of his two London partners was Nathaniel Gould, deputy
governor of the BALC.[8] The suspicion arises that the Quebec and
Megantic Land Company was a front for the BALC to complete its
monopoly over Eastern Townships crown land, but Lord Durham,
who was quick to criticize, does not appear to have expressed such
a fear, and the actual shareholders were all colonials. Gould and his
London partners in the BALC would begin to suspect that they were
overextended in the Eastern Townships before the Quebec-based
company had gone far beyond the planning stage.

Relatively little is known about the Quebec and Megantic Land
Company's third principal founder, R.H. Gairdner, but he was a
partner with Andrew Stuart in the most important law firm in Quebec. He would be appointed judge of the St Francis District in 1844,

and a Superior Court justice in 1850.[9] There is no evidence that he ever had any major interest in the timber industry. As for the possibility that Gairdner and his partners considered the company to be a potentially profitable land speculation, we shall see that they placed a strict limit on the number of shares one person could hold to deter just such a charge.

A tentative agreement was reached between Lord Aylmer and the Quebec and Megantic Land Company shortly before the end of the governor's term in late 1835. The conditions were almost the same as for the BALC. The unsurveyed block would be sold at three shillings per acre, and all the crown lots in the surveyed townships of Megantic County would be fixed at three and a half shillings per acre. The company would reserve the right to forego land unfit for cultivation. Half the purchase price would be invested in local public improvements, but initiative was to be taken by the government even though the Colonial Office had already virtually relinquished control over the BALC's improvement fund. Ten per cent of the purchase money was to be deposited within a year of the agreement's sanction by London, with the remainder paid within a decade at 4 per cent interest per year. As with the BALC arrangement, land titles would be issued only in proportion to each payment made. But the Quebec company also won an extra concession on the grounds that its land would be much less valuable than the more centrally located property of its sister company; the government agreed to take charge of the tract's outline survey. Furthermore, if the crown should eventually concede the BALC's request that it pay for the internal survey of the St Francis Tract, the same indulgence would be granted the Quebec-based company.[10]

The appointment of the Gosford Commission temporarily ended further progress in negotiations between state and company, but the project was renewed with the appointment of Lord Durham as governor after the Rebellion of 1837.[11] In April 1838 a prospectus was printed calling for a capital fund of £30,000 with shares valued at £50, payable in annual instalments. The company's endeavours, it claimed, would stimulate the economy of both the well-settled Chaudière seigneuries and the recently colonized northern Megantic townships. Still more significantly:

To every citizen in Quebec the prospect of settling 220,000 acres within a day's journey of the city cannot fail of being interesting, for not only will all the necessaries of life be abundant but all property will be enhanced in value, for sooner or later this must be the outlet of the Townships.[12]

Not all the fifteen names attached to the prospectus can be readily identified, but six (aside from Forsyth and Gairdner) have turned up in historical records as members of the town of Quebec's bourgeoisie.[13]

A preliminary meeting was to be held on 8 May, when stock subscription books would be opened. They would close on 1 June with the calling of a general public meeting to choose three commissioners and make necessary arrangements to complete the purchase upon Durham's arrival from England. In an attempt to demonstrate that the aim was not to launch a monopoly, the meeting of 8 May moved that if more stock were subscribed than necessary, the commissioners were to make an equitable distribution, taking only from shareholders with more than 2 shares.[14] The precautionary step proved to be unnecessary for only 426 of the 600 shares were called for. Once again, most of the thirteen subscribers who held the maximum 10 shares each appear to have been Quebec merchants, though the list also included the Upper Canadian entrepreneur-politician, William Hamilton Merritt, Postmaster General Thomas Allen Stayner, one of the largest landholders in the Canadas, and M. Bell, presumably the influential Matthew Bell, Forsyth's father-in-law and long-time lessee of the government-owned Forges de Saint-Maurice.[15] The shareholders were said to be "men of all shades of political opinion," and there was to be "no exclusion whatever of any class of Her Majesty's subjects, in the settlement of the tract, industry and sobriety being the requisites of those whom the Company will be anxious to encourage."[16] Nevertheless, the main body of settlers anticipated would be British immigrants. Only one French Canadian signed the prospectus and only eleven participated in the company (23 shares in total).

Two weeks after the 1 June meeting, the commissioners emphasized to Durham that they were not seeking an immediate confirmation of the sale, but they did want permission to complete an internal survey of the Megantic Tract and to commence a small settlement on Lake St Francis. The maximum expense would be £1500, which would ultimately be deducted from the company's debt to the government or reimbursed should the entire project fail to be sanctioned. The commissioners stressed that their aim was not to profit financially from the company. They would "cheerfully acquiesce" should the governor decide to deal directly with individual settlers, "our principal object being to open a fertile country and advance the prosperity of the Eastern Townships by facilitating the Communication between them and Quebec."[17]

Durham approved wholeheartedly of the company's aim to introduce an "emigrant" population to develop the country's natural resources and "contribute to its rapid advance in prosperity, and power," but he was in the process of devising a comprehensive system of land granting, "one main feature of which will be, that it is to be subject to no exceptions, on any pretence whatever." He therefore had to reject the provisional agreement entered into with Lord Aylmer. He would, however, support the company should it decide to complete the purchase according to the terms of his projected uniform system. In the meantime the governor accepted the commissioners' offer and terms for the internal survey, to be inspected and approved by a government-appointed officer. As for the experimental settlement, a detailed proposal would have to be examined and approved by Charles Buller, Durham's assistant investigating crown lands and emigration.[18]

Lord Durham's permission to proceed was rewarded by the company's decision to name both the road and projected settlement in his honour.[19] In August, Andrew Russell was employed to survey and clear a line of twelve feet in width, and to select a village site on or near the shore of Lake St Francis. Here a log house would be built to serve as a depot, and twenty acres cleared for seeding in the spring. Finally, Russell would survey the Megantic Tract townships, taking into account the natural features of the country and the quality of the soil. He was to exercise his judgement in laying off lots in the most convenient forms for farming. They would be reduced from the 200-acre standard to 120 acres, and some would face the projected trunk road while others would front on the lake and larger streams whose banks were of good quality soil. Rather than the regular size of ten miles in width and ten miles in depth, or 64,000 acres, each new township was to contain only 24,000 to 30,000 acres.[20] The result, as shown on Russell's map (map 10), was four small, irregularly shaped townships, Price, Lambton, Aylmer, and Forsyth, though the survey was essentially in the basic grid pattern.[21] Finally, Russell was instructed to report "on every minute particular" of each township surveyed in order to enable the government to proceed with settlement should the company purchase fail to transpire.[22]

In October Russell estimated that in addition to the approximately £400 allowed for road construction, £510 would be required to build four substantial bridges and twenty-eight others of smaller size.[23] Durham remarked that such an extension would be "objectionable in principle," but he would sanction it on the understanding that

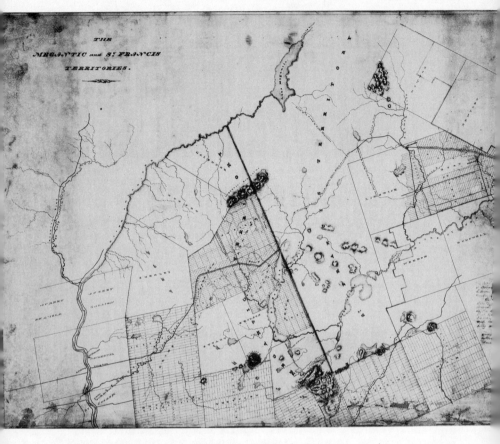

Map 10   The Megantic and St Francis Territories (NA, NMC-15197)

Table 14
Quebec and Megantic Land Company Expenses, Lambton Road,
17 August 1838–19 December 1839

Survey & road labour		£559.4.5
Clearing & building Lambton Depot		99.10.0
Surveyor & general superintendent (A. Russell)		328.17.8
Assistant surveyor (F.W. Blaiklock)		93.4.0
Works superintendent (W. Hargrave)		120.15.0
Wages	£1201.11.1	£1201.11.1
Provisions	467.7.0	
Hardware & miscellaneous items	38.8.5	
Cartage & transport	80.17.0	
Travel	33.14.8	
Procès-verbal of road	41.17.6	
Miscell. (horse hire, advertising, etc.)	20.1.7	
Interest	80.14.2	
	£1964.12.3	

Source: ANQ-Q, Terres et Forêts, Megantic Land Company.

this in no way signified a softening of his position towards the company's land claim.[24]

Russell pursued his task very actively for more than a year. His road line avoided the most direct but mountainous route through what would become Adstock Township (Neilson and Stuart on map 10), instead bisecting Forsyth before angling east towards the southern corner of Tring. The surveyor's carefully maintained accounts (see table 14) reveal that over £1900 (£54 per mile) was spent on the project, £1200 of which went to wages. Russell could certainly not be accused of extravagance with his labourers' salaries – their total bill only equalled that of the three men in charge of the work force. Whereas the BALC had paid two and a half shillings per day to unskilled immigrants in the St Francis Tract, his French-Canadian choppers were paid no more than one and a half shillings for a day's work.[25]

Surveyor General Bouchette was, for the most part, impressed with the documentation presented by the company. In December 1839 he reported to the commissioner of crown lands that the field notes, taken in "voluminous and minute detail," indicated that the survey had been completed in a "workmanlike and scientific manner." The various expenses reported all appeared to be reasonable, but Bouchette was critical of the small size of the townships and the unorthodox 120-acre lots, "an entire deviation" from the system authorized by the king's instructions of 1791. Such was the result of the "erroneous principle" of dispensing with "that control which the Surveyor General's department should properly possess."[26]

Meanwhile, in the spring of 1839, Commissioner Forsyth was enthusiastically claiming that the Megantic Tract had the capacity to support 12,000 people. As a start, he sought permission to establish one hundred families along the new road.[27] Durham refused to become further committed to the company at a time when its neighbouring counterpart was facing extreme financial embarrassment, but he was strongly advised that the road could not simply be left deserted. Andrew Russell warned of the danger of squatters moving in to escape the consequences of "their bad manner of cultivation and exhausted soil" in the Chaudière Valley. The French Canadians had "neither the habits nor the means" to bring the new territory into "a proper state of culture." As a temporary measure, the surveyor/supervisor recommended settling twenty "respectable families" who would hinder squatting, protect the timber, and keep the road open during the winter.[28] In accordance with Russell's advice, the commissioners suggested to the government that ten families be established near the half-way point, and another ten at the lake, on the understanding that the company would pay for the required 2700 acres at three shillings per acre should the pending purchase be completed. The company also sought permission to sell a mill site, with the same safeguards for the crown, so that a saw- and grist-mill could serve the settlement.[29]

The government accepted the first half of the proposal even though it implied free grants to settlers should the company fade from the scene.[30] Such grants ran directly counter to Durham's Wakefield-inspired colonization philosophy which favoured cash payments at high prices for crown land, but his principles remained quite safe because only ten families actually selected lots. Furthermore, all but two quickly abandoned the colony when the beleaguered BALC failed to extend its St Francis Tract road across the sixteen miles from Otter Brook to Lambton.[31]

Faced by the failure of British immigration to revive in 1839, the Quebec and Megantic commissioners decided in September that, "in the present state of the Country," it would be "utterly impossible" to accept a sales offer from the government.[32] In keeping, however, with its stated aim of opening a transportation link rather than profiting directly from colonization, the moribund company pursued its construction activities until December. By then the Lambton Road had been levelled with hoes and provided with more than a mile in causeways over swamps, as well as twenty-six small bridges and four larger ones averaging a substantial thirty-seven yards each. The road would now theoretically be passable for light cart loads during dry summer weather. But the narrow twelve-foot clearing meant that the pathway remained shaded and muddy, as well as being frequently blocked by fallen trees during storms.[33] Rather than becoming the principal thoroughfare between Quebec and Sherbrooke, the Lambton Road remained simply a dead-end trail into the wilderness.

Meanwhile, population pressure was becoming stronger than ever in the British Isles, and imperial sentiment toward the North American colonies was still a force to be reckoned with. In 1840, London's Land and Emigration Board observed that "there never was a period in which there seemed to prevail a greater anxiety for emigration throughout the three countries of the United Kingdom."[34] Furthermore, both the Canadas required labour and military strength, "and in one of them an immediate infusion of a British population has become a measure of the highest political expediency."[35] The board members felt that the time was ripe for "a large and systematic emigration," but they remained cautious about recommending a government grant to relieve particular areas, the only scope considered feasible, because this would bring charges of favouritism. Nor could they base their recommendation on the grounds that it would bring economic relief to the Canadas, because other colonies would demand equivalent assistance. There remained only "the consideration that a large increase of British population is essential to the security and tranquility of the province, and, as a consequence of that tranquility, ... the large saving of expense which will be effected by a diminution of the forces at present quartered there."[36] It was crucial, therefore, that some assurance be made that the emigrants would remain within the colonies rather than strengthening the potential enemy to the south, as so many had done in the past.

The board's military-defence rationale may have been inspired partly by William Lloyd of the Royal Navy when, a year earlier, he submitted his case for a mass emigration project to the Eastern Townships. According to Lloyd, this region's advantages over Upper Canada included its greater distance from the temptations of the United States:

As I presume a large proportion of the Emigrants would be Irish, it is a point worthy of consideration whether the Lower Order of that volatile, excitable and unthrifty people would not be liable to be inveigled away from the distant parts of the Upper Province to the American canals, railroads & other works by speculators & others ...[37]

The colonization of the Megantic Tract or the empty townships of the St Francis District would be of the utmost strategic importance, facilitating inland communication with the settled townships, "a highly important outwork of the Colony."[38] Lloyd also argued that, vis-à-vis Upper Canada, cheaper private land and more readily accessible blocks of crown land were available in the Townships, and the distance from the debarkation point at Quebec was much closer. Finally, he did not fail to point out one of the prime considerations in the minds of the Emigration Board members, the opportunity to check the preponderant influence of the French Canadians "by equalizing the Electoral interests in Lower Canada."[39]

Lloyd's proposals would have one major flaw in the minds of the Board members who were sufficiently influenced by Wakefield's theory that the colonies required a larger paid labour force to be unenthusiastic about isolated group settlements. They would prefer to direct the emigrants to public works projects, or in cases where no such employment could be found, to follow the Upper Canadian experiment of locating newly arrived families on five-acre allotments already provided with huts. Thus a dependable supply of wage labour would be encouraged to remain in the colony.[40] But such a scheme was simply not practicable for a large-scale emigration project which would have to be directed towards isolated blocks of wild land. As Upper Canada's chief emigration agent pointed out, no employment would be available to the settlers on their small lots once the roads were open unless "a better class of emigrants" settled in the area immediately afterward.[41] The new governor, Charles Poulett Thomson, recently created Baron Sydenham, realized that there could be no guarantee that such an influx of prosperous immigrants would ever be attracted by a colonization road. Furthermore, he did not share the Wakefield school's basic antipathy towards permitting poor immigrants to seek self-sufficiency on their own homesteads, and he was opposed to subsidizing emigration to the more thickly settled areas where much of the remaining wild land was in the hands of land companies and speculators.[42]

Even while the Colonial Office was considering the Land Board's 1840 report, Sydenham was proceeding with a scheme to build a colonization road in Upper Canada from Garafraxa Township to Owen Sound. Settlers were to be attracted by the offer of employment and free fifty-acre grants alongside the road. A somewhat reluctant Colonial Office agreed to the project for "political reasons," meaning the necessity to introduce British blood to an American-influenced region.[43] The political imperative would be at least as strong in French-speaking Lower Canada, and what better choice than the partially completed Lambton Road? Sydenham could not openly declare that he wished to block French-Canadian expansion, but he did state that there were many localities in Lower Canada where for political reasons it was important to encourage colonization, "and to which in ordinary circumstances settlers would not resort."[44] The settlers he was referring to were obviously not of French origin.

In the spring of 1841, the Emigration Association of the District of St Francis added support to the proponents of large-scale British colonization. Its petitions emphasized reasons of "internal policy" (a euphemism for the French-Canadian problem), the American boundary question, and the necessity to maintain a good road link to Quebec. And such a link was in turn necessary to attract British settlers:

Though other lines of communication have been opened to Montreal and to the St Lawrence by the valley of the Rivers St Francis and Nicolet in the hopes of improving the District, and, though the Land Company have for several years had, and do still maintain emigrant agents at Quebec, Montreal, and the St Lawrence, yet the experience of five years has proved [sic] that it is almost hopeless to expect any considerable or continued accession of emigrants here from any other quarter than direct by land from opposite the landing port of the British Shipping at Quebec ...[45]

A "direct natural Channel for immigration" was of crucial importance, and the Lambton Road offered "special facilities for another Garrafraxa [sic] Road and Settlement." Finally, the petitioners raised the issue of political support for the government, stressing that the Eastern Townships was being neglected while other districts of the Province of Canada were receiving liberal grants of public money for local works. "Under the present peculiar circumstances," the petitioners' loyalty disposed them "to strengthen the Government and to hope the best," but "nothing short of some such substantial liberal act as the opening of this road" would allay the public's feelings of resentment.[46]

Sydenham proceeded with the Lambton Road project confident that the French-Canadian members of the newly united assembly could not reject it because of their minority position. Walter Hargrave, who had acted as the Quebec and Megantic Company's supervisor, was hired to upgrade the colonization road. His first task was to spend £100 constructing causeways and levelling side hills on the eighteen-and-a-half-mile section between the Chaudière River and the Megantic Tract boundary at Tring. Then £500 would go towards widening the clearance from twelve feet to a much more practical sixty-six feet alongside the remaining sixteen-mile section. Selected British immigrants would be forwarded by the Quebec immigration agent, A.C. Buchanan. Canadians would not be expressly disqualified, but no one who had previously received a government land grant would be considered eligible. Prospective settlers were supposed to prove that they could support themselves until a crop could be raised, and to clear and plant one third of the fifty-acre grant as a settlement duty. Absenteeism was to be permitted only for short, specified periods with Hargrave's permission, and no private sales were to be allowed prior to the issuing of full title to the land.[47]

The road work, contracted in one-mile sections, was already completed by mid-November 1841. Hargrave reported that "the road is now so constructed that either an ox or horse cart can get along with safety after the freshets in Spring are over."[48] A saw- and grist-mill was operating in Tring Township, about twelve miles from the Lambton depot; there was a good road from Saint-François-de-Beauce to Quebec; and labour was plentiful in the Chaudière settlements. Once again, however, British immigrants demonstrated little interest in the area. At the time of Hargrave's report in February 1842, only three British families had joined the two remaining from 1839. Portentous for the future, however, twelve French-Canadian families had also settled on the Lambton Road. With only five acres in crop, the settlement was far from self-sufficient, producing about eighty bushels of grain and two hundred bushels of potatoes, and sustaining only three cows and one ox due to lack of fodder.

Hargrave claimed that the chief impediment to colonization was the eleven miles of narrow clearing on the section of the road located in Tring. Much of this township had long since been alienated to militia claimants, so the government presumably did not feel justified in expending large sums of money on the crucial section which intruded between the Megantic Tract and the Chaudière. Exclusive of the four major bridges, Hargrave had devoted close to fifty pounds to each mile in Forsyth and Lambton, but only half that amount in Tring.[49] He recommended that an additional seventy pounds be invested in widening the Tring section's clearance to one rod (sixteen and a half feet). The second major problem continued to be the eighteen-and-a-half-mile gap between the head of the Lambton Road and the Victoria Road to the south, a gap which the government could now close because it had regained control of much of the St Francis Tract. This it failed to do until more than ten years had passed.

Even if British colonization had not proven to be a failure, governors would no longer play a dominant role in crown land policy after 1841, and French-Canadian settlement would not assume priority status with the local administration until late in the decade. In the meantime, during the month of July 1842, Hargrave spent twenty-five and a half pounds sowing the Lambton Road with timothy and clover seed to preserve the roadway as well as to provide temporary pasture. Thirty new families arrived, but eleven of them soon abandoned their lots, leaving a total of only thirty-four resident households by the fall.[50] In the future it would not be British immigrants, but French Canadians who would populate this marginal district.

As early as 1844 the provincial census recorded 123 French Canadians, but only nine English Canadians and twenty-one British immigrants in Lambton and Forsyth. Table 15 indicates that the English-speaking settlers, who were all located in Lambton, were much more dependent upon potatoes than were the French Canadians. The larger cleared acreages of the latter, as well as their ties with the Chaudière parishes and their facility with woods work, were factors which would stand them in good stead during the coming years of potato blight, whereas the English-speaking settlers deserted the area altogether by mid-century. The Catholic Church would also act as an effective recruiting agency. In 1845 the first priest to visit Lambton asked himself: "comment se fait-il que tant de familles pauvres, tant de gens désoeuvrés, aiment mieux végéter dans nos villes et nos campagnes plutôt que de venir ici cultiver de belles terres qui les tireraient bien vite de la pauvreté et leur procuraient une honnête indépendance? Comment se fait-il que tant de personnes riches ne viennent pas faire ici des acquisitions de terres qui leur permettraient de faire des heureux, tout en augmentant leur capital?"[51]

In 1846, 221 petitioners from Forsyth, Lambton, Shenley, and Tring complained that the Lambton Road had never been completed, and that floods had since destroyed much of the original work. Twelve to fifteen miles remained too narrow, resulting in rapid deterioration, while rocks in other places made the route impracticable. The settlers had attempted repairs, but large sections were not inhabited and never would be due to the nature of the soil. An investment of seven thousand pounds would be needed, including the cost of a bridge across the Chaudière at Saint-François to provide access to the Kennebec Road, the only link to Quebec. Such a grant would provide essential wages for the settlers whose savings from the sale of their original properties had been exhausted owing to

Table 15
Agricultural Production per Family, Lambton and Forsyth Townships 1844

Township	Families	French-Canadian Population %	Acres Owned	Acres Improved	Potatoes (bu.)
Lambton	19	61	63.2	5.2	106.8
Forsyth	16	100	65.6	9.3	28.7

Township	Grain (bu.)	Cattle	Sheep	Pigs	Horses	Maple Sugar (lb.)
Lambton	16.3	1.2	1.3	0.1	0.3	31.1
Forsyth	44.6	0.8	0.9	0.9	0.8	54.7

Source: JLAC, v (1846), app. D.

crop failures. Finally, many of those families emigrating to the United States via the Kennebec Road would be attracted by the employment offered.[52]

The 1846 petition was rejected, but we shall see that the accelerating French-Canadian exodus would soon stimulate a renewed and intensified colonization-roads programme in the area to the immediate southeast.[53] Unfortunately for the Lambton Road settlers, the £5600 invested in 1848-50 all went towards the construction of a new route from the Craig Road in Shipton to Lake Aylmer. In the spring of 1850, several hundred petitioners complained that the Lambton Road remained impassable for several weeks in the spring and fall, and that the three main bridges were about to collapse. They argued that townships served by the road were the chief outlet for Dorchester and Bellechasse counties, which had provided over one hundred settler-families during the previous winter alone. Some French Canadians had even returned from Maine, and more would do so if the road were repaired.[54] Again in 1850, Lambton's missionary priest reported that the road was so dangerous that three horses had died in its mud holes during the previous five years. The result was that hunger remained a threat: "thirty families were under the deplorable necessity of subsisting on boiled herbs, raspberries, and bilberries, during the great part of the summer."[55] One settler later recalled that for a two-week period his family had been reduced to eating boiled leaves: "Rien n'avait pousée; nous étions écoeurrés du poisson."[56] In June 1851, the settlers, whose numbers had grown rapidly to 1254 in Lambton, Forsyth, Aylmer, and Price, petititoned for a road grant, threatening that if they were not heard there would be a mass migration "pour aller demander du pain à un pays étranger."[57]

The government finally responded in 1854 by directing £300 to the repair of the Lambton Road. Its aim was to recruit the active support of the settlers in order to forge a high-quality road link from the recently completed St Lawrence and Atlantic Railway at Richmond to the Chaudière seigneuries.[58] Given the enthusiastic response of the settlers, it appears likely that the Lambton Road was relatively well maintained after 1855 when municipal reform legislation encouraged local governments to tax wild land and assume responsibility for public works.[59] Nevertheless, it would never become a major trade route for the Eastern Townships region. By the fall of 1855 the Quebec and Richmond Railway provided a far superior link to the port city, which as an external market remained in the shadow of Montreal and Portland. Thus neither the metropolitan nor the imperialist aims of the Lambton Road's initial promoters came to fruition. Ironically, rather than contributing to the anglicization of Lower Canada, they had created an avenue for French-Canadian penetration into the frontier of what had been an almost exclusively English-speaking region. Furthermore, they had established a precedent for the nationalist-inspired, government-sponsored colonization projects which would continue the process of settling the upper St Francis district with French Canadians, a not insignificant step in the process of francisizing the Eastern Townships region as a whole.

CHAPTER FOUR

La Reconquête: The Church, the State and the Colonization Roads Project of 1848

Pour en faire à jamais une terre française,
C'est Dieu qui les poussait à peupler ces cantons.
Et malgré tous leurs noms à l'allure écossaise,
Nous les avons conquis et nous les habitons.

Adolphe Poisson, "Le Pionnier."

Lord Sydenham's decision to offer free fifty-acre grants along the upgraded Lambton Road represented a final attempt to direct British immigrants to Lower Canada's crown land. Jurisdiction over the public domain passed to the legislature of the newly united Province of Canada in 1841, and was followed by a hiatus of several years as far as colonization projects were concerned. The early 1840s was a period of heavy British immigration via the port of Quebec, and presumably neither the French-Canadian nor the Upper Canadian politicians wanted to do anything to interfere with the steady flow to points west.[1] At the same time, however, French-Canadian families were beginning to migrate in large numbers to the United States, a development which threatened the political strength of a people already on the defensive within the new provincial union. Inspired by missionary priests serving the Eastern Townships, the Catholic hierarchy and the young nationalists of the Institut Canadien combined forces in 1848 to establish two colonization societies. To prevent the constitutional separatists from gaining political advantage, the governing forces led by Louis-Hippolyte La Fontaine decided to co-opt the movement. Governor Lord Elgin provided valuable assistance by arranging for a large grant from the British government to be directed towards the construction of a number of access routes into the upper St Francis district. With free fifty-acre grants offered along the roads, the project would essentially be a larger-scale continuation of Sydenham's Lambton initiative. The crucial difference, of course, was that it was aimed at French Canadians rather than British immigrants. The result was that it succeeded in its aim of peopling a difficult frontier, but at the cost of great hardship and suffering on the part of the colonists themselves. Thus was the precedent set for the last great Franco-Catholic colonization movement in North America.

That movement was certainly stimulated by the Catholic Church's tendency to take a more active role in society and politics as it became increasingly ultramontane beginning in the 1840s.[2] But colonization beyond the seigneurial boundaries was not a new idea. As early as the 1820s the American-born convert to Catholicism, Father John Holmes, drew on his experience in the Drummondville mission to urge upon his young seminarians at Quebec the necessity of French-Canadian expansion into the Eastern Townships.[3] Holmes made a lasting impression on many members of the French-Canadian élite, but the geographic isolation of a region with no obstacle-free river artery to the St Lawrence ensured that few habitants would abandon their wheat-producing parishes. In almost every respect, the Eastern Townships remained foreign territory with its English system of laws, its Yankee and British settlers, and its livestock-oriented economy. Finally, with emigration to the United States becoming a focus of concern in the later 1840s, two missionary-priests succeeded in attracting widespread publicity to the plight of the small number of francophones in the Eastern Townships. During the winter of 1847–48, the Irish-born Father Bernard O'Reilly of Sherbrooke wrote a series of letters to Quebec's *Le Canadien* arguing that, to escape their poverty, local French Canadians would have to stop working for Americans and start acquiring property for themselves. He reported seeing young French-speaking families close to perishing from hunger and cold in the midst of a generally affluent population. The question of survival aside, they also faced the danger of assimilation because they had to speak the language of their employers. Placed in English-speaking families at the age of ten or twelve, French-Canadian children soon substituted the politeness of their fathers for the rude republican manners of their masters. The danger for their very souls was obvious:

Sans écoles où ils puissent s'instruire dans la connaissance de leur langue maternelle, sans églises où ils puissent recueillir même les éléments de l'ins-

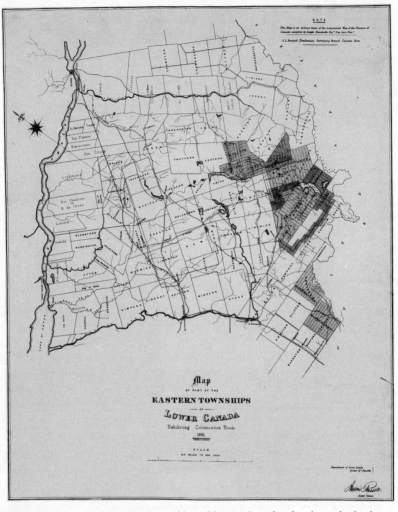

Map 11   Part of the Eastern Townships of Lower Canada, showing colonization roads, 1861 (NA, NMC-42925)

truction religieuse, il n'est point étonnant, si en cessant de parler français, une trop grande nombre, hélas! cessent d'être catholiques et canadiens.[4]

This picture of destitution and assimilation was painted in even more sombre hues by Father Pierre-Jacques Bédard of Kingsey. He claimed that for much of the year the French Canadians were forced to eat buckwheat or barley bread dipped in water or occasionally milk. Many families were actually reduced to wild herbs and roots for several weeks each year. Their clothing and furnishings were no better, and most lived in small log cabins with cedar shingles, earthen chimneys, and floors of rough split boards. Cold penetrated from everywhere, with the chimney hearth often the only source of heat. Like O'Reilly, Bédard did not forget the cultural and religious aspects:

il n'est pas rare de rencontrer des Canadiens qui ne lisent que l'anglais et des enfants qui ne parlent presque pas français. Qui le croirait? Je suis obligé de faire le catéchisme en anglais, à des enfants canadiens, et cela à Kingsey, à quatorze lieues du fleuve, à vingt lieues de Québec! Le mal se repand avec rapidité. Si on ne s'efforce de l'arrêter à sa source, une autre génération verra sa langue reléguée au petit cercle des gens instruits et des anciens qui auront survécu à leur siècle.[5]

Accounts such as these hardly seem designed to encourage French Canadians to flock to the Townships. It must be understood, however, that the two priests could see no benefit from an uncontrolled migration into the region. It had to be organized around the parish system so that Catholic churches and schools could be supported; otherwise the newcomers would simply be assimilated by the English-speaking Protestants.

The solution suggested by O'Reilly was a colonization society composed of both priests and laymen. It would evaluate unsettled land in the Townships, obtain grants for colonists under the most advantageous conditions possible, and direct families to well-organized communities rather than settling them in scattered groups.[6] In Montreal, the young men of the Institut Canadien became sufficiently interested in O'Reilly's proposals to call a meeting on the subject for 2 March, 1848. Here O'Reilly succeeded in convincing not only the Montreal institute members but also their Quebec counterparts to adopt his project.[7] The Montrealers launched the "Association du district de Montréal pour l'établissement des Canadiens-Français dans les Townships du Bas-Canada," using as an organizational model the Society for the Propagation of the Faith. Thus members were to contribute five sous a month, and join groups of ten which would in turn join groups of one hundred. Bishop Ignace Bourget of Montreal would be a member of the central committee, patron of the association, and chairman of the meetings. Finally, a provisional committee was formed, with the duty of completing the organization of the association in about thirty days.[8] On 16 March, the energetic young O'Reilly was already confident enough to proclaim: "Cette société, on peut le dire maintenant est formée; elle existe pleinement, elle embrasse dans ses ramifications tout le pays."[9]

O'Reilly's next step was to address mass meetings in Quebec and Montreal. At Quebec nearly three thousand were present to hear him proclaim that the colonization societies would save thousands of their generation alone from exile. Appealing to their sense of grievance against the absentee proprietors who held most of the Townships' wild land, he proclaimed:

Elle fermera une des plus profondes plaies faites à votre pays par une politique aveugle et jalouse. Elle réparera, autant du moins que cette réparation est maintenant possible, la longue injustice de plus d'un demi-siècle. Elle prouvera, par l'établissement des colonies qui se doivent former sous ses auspices, que les hommes qui ont morcelé, aliéné, vendu les terres incultes de la province pour qu'elles ne tombassent point entre les mains des Canadiens-Français, étaient non seulement les ennemis invétérés du sang français, mais les plus grands ennemis de tout le Canada.

He emphasized that not only would the French Canadians benefit by keeping their surplus population, but the Eastern Townships and Canada would prosper from the development of uninhabited territory. The Canadians might currently be in an inferior position in the Townships, but of all nationalities they were the most capable of succeeding in a new colony: "Mettez-les ensemble sur un sol fertile où ils aient des chemins, des écoles, une église et un missionnaire, et vous verrez si aucun établissement du même genre devancera le leur en progrès véritable."[10]

Inspired by O'Reilly's rhetoric, the public meeting passed resolutions endorsing the creation of a Quebec branch of the colonization society, under the patronage of the archbishop of Quebec. The assembly also chose a committee of forty members to organize the association. Because this committee included a number of priests, it was not completely dominated by the city's Institut Canadien members.[11]

Montreal's mass meeting took on a more political colouring for it was opened by Louis-Joseph Papineau, the famous rebel orator and idol of the young institute members. He wasted little time upon the subject of colonization itself, dwelling instead upon British crimes against the French Canadians, from the deportation of the Acadians to the union of the Canadas.[12] When O'Reilly's turn to speak finally came, he succeeded in moving the entire audience of seven thousand to pledge enrolment in the association. In contrast to Papineau's emphasis upon nationalist politics, O'Reilly stressed religion. He suggested that in each new township colonized by the association, the first blow of the axe should be delivered by the missionary, and that the first tree felled should be made into a cross, to be erected on Saint-Jean Baptiste Day to honour religion and nationality.[13]

Papineau's speech reinforced fears on the part of the ruling La Fontaine party that their critics were using the movement for their own political advancement. In Montreal the Institut Canadien, most of whose members were vocal supporters of the radical Rouge opposition party, gained complete control of the central committee, leaving only the honorary post of president open to a cleric, Mgr Bourget himself.[14] The same pattern developed in Quebec a few weeks later. Although the organizing committee had included some priests, Archbishop Joseph Signay as president was the only cleric to be appointed to the official executive body.[15]

With discontent brewing as a result of the typhus-plagued immigration of 1847, and with the danger of Irish and French revolutionary fervour sweeping the colony in 1848, Lord Elgin had no wish to see Papineau given a platform for his anti-British campaign.[16] When the Association des Townships asked the governor for support on 19 April, he personally donated £20, but his financially embarrassed administration could do nothing substantial for the time being.[17] Somewhat fortuitously, however, the Colonial Office had finally decided, four days earlier, to compensate the Canadian government for the expense of £20,000 it claimed to have incurred in fighting the typhus epidemic among the immigrants of 1847. This decision had been prodded by the province's threat to default on interest payments, and by its agreement to assume full responsibility for future immigration expenses, as well, no doubt, as by a general desire to soften anti-British sentiment in Canada.[18] It was for political purposes, then, that the La Fontaine–Baldwin ministry encouraged the mistaken belief that London had finally agreed to the grant only because Canada had declared that it would all be directed towards "the great object of settling and colonizing the vacant territory." Even though Canada West would obviously claim its share of the grant, the local government's official reply to the Association des Townships also implied that the entire £20,000 would be devoted to the colonization roads project in Canada East.[19]

The colonial secretary would not learn of the Association des Townships or of French-Canadian settlement until 26 April, and Elgin would not provide details until the end of June, nineteen days after the provincial government had publicly outlined its colonization programme.[20] The governor then openly admitted his political agenda:

I had but one of two courses to choose from ... either, on the one hand, to give the promoters of the scheme a cold shoulder – point out its objectionable features – to dwell upon difficulties of execution, – in which case, (use what tact I might) – I should have dismissed the Bishop and his friends discontented, and given Mr. P. an opportunity of asserting that I had lent a quasi sanction to his calumnies – or, on the other, to identify myself with the movement, put myself, in so far as might be, at its head, impart to it as salutary a direction as possible, and thus wrest from M[r] Papineau's hands a potent instrument of agitation –

But Elgin also argued that the project would strengthen the imperial connection because a French-Canadian population in the Eastern Townships would act as a security against annexation to the United States:

Was it, think you, love for England or hatred for those *sacrés Bostonais* which stirred the French Canadian mind in the Revolutionary war and again in 1812?

Nor does it matter when you are dealing with Frenchmen how near the Yankee line you locate them. An English man, Scotchman or Irishman when he is outwitted by his Yankee neighbour may be tempted to admire his superior sagacity, and to curse the Govt. and constitution of Great Britain for the consequences of his own stupidity or apathy. But it is not so with the Habitans. Contact with those precious specimens of Anglo Saxondom, who are ignorant of his language, despise his intellect, ridicule his customs, and swindle him in every transaction in which he is engaged with them, is by no means provocative of affection in his breast.

Echoing Governor Haldimand of the 1780s, Elgin claimed that the government should "fill up the Frontier country with French – and the lands to the rear with British, who may retain their love of home and its institutions at a distance from American influences."[21]

Bishop Bourget could not openly participate in the unseemly debate as to which political party had proven the greater champion of colonization, but his pastoral letter certainly suggested that Britain's generous grant was a direct reward for the French Canadians' loyalty. Because they had adopted some 250 Irish orphans, "la divine providence suscite une association dont l'unique but est de procurer à des milliers d'enfants de la patrie les moyens de se fixer sur le sol natal."[22] O'Reilly was much more direct in his support for La Fontaine, but even though Papineau's enemies succeeded in distancing his name from the colonization project, the fact remains that it was closely modelled on the original petition which he was reported to have drafted for the Association des Townships.[23]

The government document outlining its project acknowledged that the land-granting system and even seigneurial commutation had led to the monopolization of large tracts of land. The result was "the extraordinary and anomalous spectacle of an over crowded and emigrating agricultural population, in a country possessing wild uncultivated and at the same time fertile land, sufficient for the wants of the native inhabitants and of new comers for many years." The shift in emphasis from immigrants to French Canadians was explicit:

For while Canada offers a home to Emigrants from the United Kingdom, ... none, in the opinion of his Excellency, can have a better right to the benefits of that extension than the descendants of the ancient colonists whose patient and persevering industry in peace and whose gallantry in war have done so much for the improvement and defence of this portion of Her Majesty's dominions.

The evils which had arisen in the landholding system were essentially the result of the government having delegated its responsibilities to third parties. The aim of absentee proprietors was inevitably to raise the price of land, "and thus the object of the greatest public importance, namely the easy and rapid diffusion of the population, over the country, is sacrificed to the interests of speculation." Municipal taxation of wild land was alleviating the problem in Canada West, but the issue at hand was the disposal of land remaining in the hands of the crown.

Contrary to the recommendations of the Association des Townships, the government was not willing to sacrifice revenue from the Jesuits' Estates, designated as it was for a special fund, nor to launch immediately upon colonization programmes in the remote Saguenay and Ottawa regions, but it would invest in the million acres remaining at its disposal in the counties of Sherbrooke and Megantic.[24] The object would be to complete access routes from Quebec and Trois-Rivières, then build leading roads into the upper St Francis district. The Lambton Road would be extended nineteen miles from Lake

St Francis to the BALC's Otter Brook Road, and, crossing it at right angles, a forty-two-mile artery would link the Gosford Road with Lake Megantic at the furthest extremity of the territory. The roadways would be primitive, simply lines cleared of trees to a width of sixty-six feet, with cheaply constructed bridges and causeways where necessary. A few colonists might gain temporary employment, but, for the most part, they would be left to improve the roads after they had settled alongside them.

Because "the first occupants will labour under considerable disadvantages," to demand a price from them would simply be to take money which could best be employed by themselves. Therefore, every male of twenty-one years or over would be entitled to a free grant of fifty acres from the double line of lots which would extend along both sides of the roads. A resident land agent would ensure that all such grants went to bona fide settlers. Before assigning a lot to anyone, the agent would be expected to confirm that he had sufficient means to support himself over the short term. For this purpose each prospective settler was supposed to carry a certificate from the Association des Townships. As in Canada West, full title would not be issued unless sixteen acres had been readied for cultivation within four years. (At the request of the association this stipulation was later modified to twelve acres.)[25] Meanwhile, if the lot was abandoned at any time, the settler's location ticket would be cancelled.

To ensure that some individuals of means would be attracted, settlers could also purchase up to three adjoining lots (150 acres), either with cash or land scrip, at four shillings (80¢) per acre. Once the leading lines of communication had been settled, land in adjoining ranges would be sold at the same fixed price. In contrast to private landholders, the government did not intend to profit financially from the labour of pioneer settlers by making it increasingly difficult for others, including descendants, to afford land in the neighbourhood. "Increase in the numbers of the people of the province, and the consequent rapid increase in the public strength and resources, are objects of more value than the price which can be derived from sale of territory of the Crown."[26] Low crown land prices would, it was hoped, discourage the current trend of farm subdivision from recurring. In fact, the government anticipated that once a considerable portion of each lot was brought under cultivation, "the more wealthy class" would begin a consolidation process, while a semi-permanent group of frontiersmen would invest the proceeds of its sales in new and enlarged acreages of wild land.

Although no distinction as to nationality was to be entertained, and the government refused to share its authority over the local land agent with the Association des Townships, it was fully aware that the success of its project depended upon a large and rapid influx of settlers, an influx which the colonization society would help to ensure. Thus Bourget was assured that if any aspect of English property law was found to deter French-Canadian colonization, the legislature would speedily amend the situation. (Although historians have long assumed that the Church remained indifferent to colonizing the Townships prior to gaining civil sanction for tithe collections in the region in 1850, the association's petition mentioned only inheritance and road laws.)[27] The colonization society's role would be limited to supporting missionaries and teachers; financing the construction of churches, presbyteries, and schools; and acting as a guardian for the colonists' moral interests: "The advice, encouragement, the benevolent exertions of Your Lordship and Your Excellent associates will do more in promoting the happiness and moral condition of the future inhabitants of the settlement, than any interference of Government can accomplish."

By the time the government's proposal had been drafted, the Montreal branch of the Association des Townships had already begun a settlement project on BALC land in Roxton Township. The group would dissolve in political acrimony before long, leaving the upper St Francis district to its Quebec counterpart.[28] Particular impetus was given to the Quebec project by the depressed economic conditions prevalent in that city. The suffering which followed Britain's abandonment of preferential trade had been compounded by fires which caused two million dollars in damages, and left 16,000 homeless in 1845.[29] The effects were still being felt in 1848. At a July meeting of the association, Pierre-Joseph-Olivier Chauveau (who was then chairing a committee of the Legislative Assembly to investigate emigration from the province) moved that the lack of work and famine which threatened the coming winter made it essential to send the surplus labouring population to the Townships as colonists.[30] Mgr Signay's pastoral letter in support of the association proclaimed that one of its goals was to prevent farmers from coming to town where there was no work available.[31]

In early August notices appeared in the press advertising fifty-acre lots to settlers eighteen years and older. The age limit had obviously been dropped from twenty-one to attract families with maturing sons, for the settlement conditions required only that residence be taken up in the vicinity of a claimant's lot. "Particularly

invited" were "Canadians who cannot now obtain lands in the Seig-
niories." They would report to the resident agent who was a fifty-
five-year-old surveyor and former MLA from Yamaska named Jean-
Olivier Arcand. A fervent Patriote during the Rebellions of 1837–
38, Arcand exulted in the knowledge that "devant Lord Elgin et son
administration Canadienne, il n'est plus nécessaire d'être puissant
ou flatteur pour obtenir un octroi gratuit de terres ... C'est donc un
sisteme [sic] d'égalité et de liberté."[32] During the following four years
both his commitment and his capabilities would be tested to the limit.

Arcand's first task was to attempt to improve the Gosford Road
from Quebec. In late July he complained that carters were charging
settlers exorbitant prices because of the barely passable condition of
this principal access route.[33] Even the recent repairs had quickly
deteriorated because the county-based municipal system did not
function in the thinly settled, vast constituency of Megantic. Toll
gates were recommended as a solution by one government engineer,
but, in the meantime, Arcand was authorized to sink another £175
into the road.[34] Closer inspection during the winter led him to reject
the assignment on the grounds that proprietors of adjacent lands
were resisting the legal establishment of the Gosford Road as a public
thoroughfare. To avoid responsibility for its maintenance, settlers
(most of whom were British immigrants) were purposefully boycot-
ting attempts to constitute a council quorum. Rather than maintaining their road frontages "chacun semble conspirer à le détruire en
détruisant les ponts et les égouts." Settlers were removing construction materials to their side roads in the expectation that the government would repair the damages, and Arcand was determined not
to "confirm them in their ridiculous opinion."[35] In response, the
government agreed that its repair money should be withheld until
the Gosford Road was "verbalized" as a public responsibility.[36]

Unfortunately for the settlement project, the other two access
routes, the Lambton Road from the Chaudière and the St Francis
Road from Robinson, were in even worse condition. Owing to the
BALC's neglect, eight to ten miles of the St Francis link to Sherbrooke
were not even passable by horse. There would be little use in connecting these two roads in Winslow Township as long as each failed
to provide access to a market outlet. Meanwhile, settlers simply could
not afford to pay the three to four shillings which carters charged
for each pound of freight.[37]

Although Arcand also complained that the disillusioned British
immigrants attracted by the BALC had given the district a bad rep-
utation, his chief problem would not be a lack of settlers. Land
pressure in the seigneuries was great enough to force a dozen claim-

ants to begin clearances even before surveys were completed in September.[38] By October the Association des Townships was complaining that the shortage of available lots was forcing disappointed families to return to Quebec.[39] Road work had begun in mid-August, but little had been accomplished during the first month because Arcand had only been able to hire a score of carpenters from Quebec, many of whom deserted their jobs within a few days. Once the harvest season had ended, he replaced them with about forty "habitants de campagne" who cleared twelve miles from the Gosford Road to Lake Aylmer, and eighteen miles linking the Craig and Gosford roads through Wotton Township. The cost had been £1088, or slightly more than £36 per mile, with the labourers' salaries and provisions taking only half the total. (Their wages of 1s. 6d. per day equalled that of tree choppers on the Lambton Road in 1838.) But there was an additional investment of £1521 in draught animals, foodstuffs, and a wide variety of equipment such as stoves, axes, and picks, and Arcand's headquarters at Ward's Bay on Lake Aylmer had cost £85 for house, outbuildings and a clearing of twenty arpents. He had not been able to locate upon a water-power site, as instructed, because such sites were confined to the river between Lake Aylmer and Lake St Francis "au milieu de rochers incultivables."[40] With pun intended, he christened the property Malmaison: "Car au lieu des superbes lambris de la résidence de Joséphine, on ne trouve ici que planches brutes, et murs qui n'ont d'autre poli que celui de la hache de charpentiers à l'entreprise."[41] Arcand was provided with the services of a servant and a clerk, but he was dissatisfied with his salary of £112 10s. for 180 days of work, and with delays in payroll delivery which he claimed were placing him in debt.[42]

During the winter Arcand spent much of his time accumulating a large store of supplies for the following season's road work, while settlers continued arriving to begin working on their lots.[43] As of December there were 230 families, half of whom were in Wotton which lay northwest of the upper St Francis district, and the other half spread out thinly within four of the district's northern townships.[44] Those in Ham (22), Garthby (26), and Stratford (53) could only watch while parties from far and wide depleted the Lake Aylmer fish stocks which they depended upon for sustenance. In February Arcand claimed that one Quebec innkeeper had made three trips, taking enough fish to sustain at least ten families for a year.[45] By the spring Arcand was forced to devote the limited funds provided by the colonization society to seed grain rather than the construction of chapels.[46] His second major problem was the delay in the transmission of location tickets from the Surveyor General's Office. In fact Arcand had overstepped his authority in promising free grants of back lots to about half the families in Wotton.[47]

The strategy for the 1849 season was to improve the Wotton and Megantic roads to Lake Aylmer with another 5000 man-days of labour (2650 man-days had been expended in 1848), and to employ 7500 man-days on new roads. The budgeted cost would be £2617. Arcand had therefore altered the original strategy of simply clearing long road lines, claiming that this method had added to expenses by placing workers far ahead of where provisions could be transported by carts.[48] The fact that the government raised no objection suggests that in contrast to what some historians have claimed for the colonization roads project of the Canadian Shield, that of the upper St Francis district was not designed primarily to provide winter roads for lumber companies.[49] As it turned out, the agent had greatly underestimated the labour required to upgrade the previous year's work, and no time or money would be devoted to road extensions in 1849. Despite the improved quality of the roads to Lake Aylmer, settlement became still more strongly focused on Wotton, the most accessible and the most fertile of the free-grant townships. But even there the number of locations declined slightly from those reported the previous year.[50] In November 1848, the vicar of Saint-Grégoire had delivered 137 certificates for individuals planning to settle in Stratford, across the lake from the road terminus, but most of their claims remained untouched.[51] Father Calixte Marquis had joked about the opposition raised by girls to the departure of potential husbands, and Arcand himself claimed that the young men hesitated to forsake the paternal hearth for fear of "l'ennui." "Mais travaillons; occupons nous avec courage et persévérance, comme firent nos ancêtres, quand ils vinrent à douze cents lieues de leur patrie, mettre les premiers, la hache dans les immenses forets du Canada, et nous ne nous ennuirons pas." The urgency of the situation was underlined, Arcand felt, by the fact that 60 of Winslow's best lots had fallen in October to Scottish immigrants.[52]

It was as well for Arcand that more colonists were not wintering over because many of those who did so became dependent upon the store of provisions he was accumulating for the 1850 season's road work. They had not been able to clear enough land for seeding until June, with the result that a late August frost had destroyed all the crops. By the following March, Arcand found himself "incapable d'en refuser à des familles qui éprouvent les horreurs de la fa-mine."[53] Nevertheless, enough food remained in June to support another 12,000 man-days of labour (one hundred men for about four months). Arcand optimistically anticipated doubling the twenty-

Table 16
Settlement in Jean-Olivier Arcand's Agency, October 1850

Townships	Resident Claimants	Houses	Average Family	Average Age	Average Acres Cleared	Average Grain (min.)	Average Potatoes (min.)	Average Turnips (min.)
Wotton	107	83	3.7	33.7	5.3	33.0	39.9	24.7
Ham S.	9	10	5.0	34.4	10.7	97.3	75.6	14.2
Garthby[1]	18	17	5.4	37.2	7.1	58.3	124.7	2.3
Stratford	15	14	5.1	32.3	5.2	30.2	59.3	3.5
Winslow	5	4	5.2	39.8	3.2	0.6	25.0	0
Totals	154	128	4.1	34.2	5.7	38.7	54.1	18.6

Source: AC, Correspondance, 1850, no. 1453. The document does not indicate whether volume
    is measured in bushels or minots.
1 Excluding government farm

nine miles of colonization roads, but by the end of the season the
Megantic Road had been extended only twelve-and-a-half miles
through Garthby and Stratford into Winslow. Bad weather and
mountainous, marshy terrain had greatly increased construction expenses to £151 per mile.[54]

The time had arrived to take stock of the project. The previous
three years had resulted in the construction of forty-one-and-a-half
miles of good roads at the cost of approximately £5600. The £135
invested in each mile was considerably higher than the £104 per
mile which the Megantic Land Company and the government had
spent on the Lambton Road, but no one could deny that settlers
were being attracted to the free grants. Arcand submitted a detailed
census in October listing 154 claimants (see table 16), two-thirds of
whom remained in Wotton. Most of the Wotton and Stratford settlers
had come from south shore parishes in the Trois-Rivières district,
and the 1852 manuscript census indicates that Garthby's settlers were
born in rural parts of the Quebec district, though it appears that
most had actually been dock workers in the city.[55] Aside from the
few families living in Ham South, nearly all were recorded with only
the fifty-acre free grants. A few names from Arcand's list of residents
do reappear as land purchasers on his separate list of 202 absentees,
but the great majority of non-residents were also simply claiming
the fifty free acres. As figure 1 illustrates, many settler-claimants
were young men, often single, who claimed lots adjacent to next of
kin, thus the small average family size of 4.1 recorded in table 16 is
a rather meaningless figure, though it does suggest that the low
family crop averages were not so disastrous as might appear at first

Figure 1   Settlement pattern on range 2 and 3 (AC, Correspondence 11850, no. 1453)

Lot	R3		R2	
H			Boisvert	(?,1)
G	Beaudette	(56,2)	Ricard	(30,3)
F	Beaudette	(33,4)	Beaudette	(34,3)
E	Gendreau	(25,1)	Beaudette	(21,1)
D	Legendre	(19,1)	Michel	(42,8)
C			Ditto	(P)
B	Legendre	(54,12)		
A	Legendre	(23,1)	Larivière	(23,1)
1	Legendre	(25,1)	Larivière	(19,1)
2	Touton	(37-A,P)	Bertrand	(34,4)
3	Touton	(37,9)	Bertrand	(40-A)
4	Panneton	(19,1)		
5	Charland	(18,1)	Charland	(19,1)
6	Charland	(19-A)	Charland	(24,1)
7	Poisson	(31-A)	Morin	(24,1)
8	Poisson	(29-A)	Morin	(19,1)
9	Gauthier	(24,1)	Janelle	(24,1)
10	Gauthier	(20,1)	Janelle	(21,1)
11	Paquin	(36,7)	Faucher	(28,4)
12	Gagnon	(44,8)		
13	Gagnon	(19-A)	Faucher	(30,1)
14	Martel	(23,1)	Faucher	(28-A,P)
15	Martel	(24-A)	Filteau	(40,7)
16			Labonté	(50,11)
17	Filteau	(29-A,P)	Labonté	(21,1)
18	Ditto		Perron	(34-A,P)
19			Gauthier	(27-A)
20			Richer	(44-A)
21				
22			Forest	(30-A)
23			Jannelle	(45-A,P)

Source: AC, Correspondance, 1850, no. 1453.

A   Absentee
P   Purchased

sight. The Association des Townships had been accurate in its pre-diction that habitants would move to the frontier to maintain ex-tended family ties.

The relatively high number of absentees suggests a considerable amount of coming and going; indeed Arcand had difficulty keeping his records up to date, though he did not oppose the sale of claims because he felt that they usually fell into the hands of better-endowed colonists. Record-linkage for Winslow Township from 1851 to 1881 actually reveals an extraordinarily stable population once the settle-ment had been established. Arcand found that the resident families had made good progress in improving their land despite the fact that many had also laboured on the colonization roads. In fact, an average of 3.4 acres had been cleared by those who had claimed their lots only the preceding spring, though some of them would have gained a head start during the winter months.[56]

The question remained, nonetheless, as to whether the settlements were sufficiently advanced to progress without further investment by the government. As local agent, Arcand was not only the liaison with the Crown Lands Office, he remained the only community leader for the widely scattered settlements, aside from the resident priest who was appointed to Garthby in 1851 and moved to Wotton in 1852.[57] Arcand's residence, with its thirty cultivated acres, rep-resented the equivalent of a model farm, and it may have been at his instigation that so many turnips were grown during this period of potato blight (see table 16). Malmaison produced 600 bushels of turnips and only 400 bushels of potatoes in 1850. But more impor-tant to the settlers' future would be the income and superior market outlets provided by further road construction under Arcand's sur-veillance. He estimated that fifty-seven miles of construction would complete the original plan – eighteen miles to continue the Megantic Road eastward to Lake Megantic, eighteen miles to link the Lambton and St Francis roads, and twenty-one miles from the end of the Otter Brook Road to the other two roads in Winslow. At the same rate per mile as the previous season, the additional cost would be £8627 for three more years of road work.[58] The total investment of £14,227 would still be well below the original £20,000 which had supposedly been set aside for the colonization roads project.

The silence of the records for 1851 suggests, however, that no further road work was undertaken that year. In mid-July, after an on-the-spot investigation for the government, W.L. Felton of Sher-brooke suggested that to stop at that point would be to ruin the whole project. He recommended a yearly expenditure of £1500 as a means of fostering continued settlement.[59] Certainly the 1851 harvest brought little reason for optimism. In Garthby, where there were still only twenty-six families in the spring of 1852, rust and frost had reduced grain crop yields to nine bushels per acre. The average family of 5.4 members produced only forty-five bushels of grain and forty-eight bushels of potatoes and turnips, a portion of which would be needed for seed, milling costs, and other essential expenses. Some of the oats also undoubtedly went to feed the township's seven horses, but there may still have been enough food for the average family to survive on, provided some wild game was available to compensate for the fact that there were only seventeen cattle (nine cows), fourteen sheep, and thirty-one pigs in the township. Nevertheless, some families inevitably fell below the subsistence line, either because they planted less or were harder struck by frost or disease. The situation across the lake in Stratford was no better. The twenty resident families had a few more cattle, but fewer sheep and pigs, and a grain crop yield of only seven bushels per acre.[60]

A dispirited Arcand wrote in April:

La misère est à son comble, et l'affreux spectacle que je prévoyais et que je voulais éviter en résignant ma place profite des conditions qu'on m'a imposer pour m'affliger journellement. Quelles sont donc les vues de la Providence en m'éprouvant par tant des contradictions?[61]

The picture painted by the local curé was equally gloomy:

De toute ma dîme réunie de Garthby et de Stratford, dont la somme pour le blé peut s'élever à douze minots, pour l'avoine neuf minots et le reste en diminuant, c'est à peine si je pourrai sauver de naufrage de l'envahissement assez de farine pour deux mois; le reste est absorbé par des suppliants affamés ...[62]

By early May, the situation as described by a third witness had clearly become critical:

On Monday the 5th instant, a family of 8, named Ramsay, had had for four days preceding only half a minot of bad potatoes to eat. It was a sight to behold in what a state these unfortunates were. Two infants extended on a bed, where they were kept by sickness brought on by their enforced fast, and near them on a miserable couch their poor mother, a hideous skeleton, with an infant of two months in her arms, having no milk to give it, the source being dried by privation and suffering. Farther on there was a poor family named Houle, without nourishment, money, or provisions of any kind, reduced by famine to mendicity, and their neighbours so poor themselves, obliged to relieve them for three months, and now so poor themselves as to be on the point of soliciting aid from others just a little less indigent. Another family have lived for weeks and weeks on glue made of frozen wheat, and are reduced to such a state of physical weakness as to be incapable of labour. At this moment, too there are, in another family, four poor children extending the hand for bread to enable them to live until the return of their father, who is absent and uncertain about coming back.[63]

An urgent petition had been sent to the archbishop of Quebec asking for aid to tide the colonists over until the opening of navigation allowed them to seek work on the docks.[64] The Quebec branch of the Association des Townships had long since disintegrated due to lack of public support, but Mgr Turgeon did manage to collect some twenty-eight pounds from religious communities and clergy.[65] The money was spent on provisions which were sent to Richmond by rail in April, but the desperate colonists actually did not have the means to transport the food the remaining distance to their homes. The archbishop promised to approach laymen for the extra funds needed, but he was pessimistic concerning the results: "j'aurais peu d'espérances de succès, si j'en juge par l'impossibilité où s'est trouvé la société de Colonisation de recueillir parmi les citoyens toute la somme que j'avais été obliger d'avancer, il y a 2 ans, pour fournir de la semence à vos colons."[66]

When or how the rations finally reached Lake Aylmer is not known, and it appears that the government again devoted little if any money to the colonization roads during the summer of 1852. Arcand and the curé had both quit their posts, and the institutional focal point of the free-grant settlements soon shifted to the peripheral but heavily settled Wotton Township.[67] In 1853 the government finally came to the rescue with a £5000 grant "for continuing and perfecting the improvements commenced under Mr. Arcand," and the following year it inaugurated a system of annual grants for colonization roads throughout the province.[68] The long-suffering Winslow Township settlers at last gained access to Sherbrooke via the St Francis Road in 1855, while the Megantic Road was linked more directly to the Craig Road in Chester Township. By 1857 it had also reached its eastern terminus in the wilderness at Lake Megantic.[69] For many of the original settlers, the improved transportation arteries came too late. The former vicar of Saint-Grégoire noted in 1859 that "un bon nombre d'entre eux, découragés par les fatigues d'un voyage de 30 à 36 lieues à travers les forêts et les savanes ont abandonné la partie pour aller aux États-Unis . . . Qui pourrait les blâmer?[70]

The future of the settlements was secure, but they were destined to remain isolated pockets of rural poverty. In 1856 local crown land agent J.T. Le Bel recommended that the government encourage settlers to produce potash by supplying the necessary cauldrons. This would permit them to work on their own land and pay closer attention to their crops, rather than being forced to "aller s'engager dans les chantiers, ou ailleurs, pour se mettre à l'abrie des premiers besoins."[71] Le Bel also reported that he was awaiting instructions on the enforcement of regulations "car je n'osais prendre sur moi, de forcer ces personnes à payer ce qu'ils doivent au gouvernement surtout lorsque je voyais autant de misère autour de moi." Because of the bad crops, which suffered from consistently early frosts in August and September, he had pressed no further than to deliver proclamations at the door of each chapel. He expressed faith that the area "sera un lieu, où Ce brave Colon Canadien, pourra vivre heureux et content," but in 1871 the curé of Ham North and Garthby claimed that his mission was the poorest in the Eastern Townships, with the forty families "vivant avec beaucoup de misère des revenus de leurs chantiers d'hiver."[72] Indeed, as we saw in chapter one, the federal census taken that spring had already revealed how widespread in the upper St Francis district was the reliance on income from family-based wood-cutting operations.

Again in 1871, the remaining original settlers of Garthby and Stratford protested that they would never be able to repay the provisions they had long ago received from Arcand. The crown lands agent estimated that no more than nine of the original forty-seven accounts, valued at $1037 plus interest, were redeemable. His list indicated that most of the delinquents were absent (primarily in the United States), dead, or "very poor." Quebec had little choice but to write off their debts.[73] The government also moved to liquidate the 122-acre Malmaison property, most of which had been subdivided in anticipation of a town site that never developed. The buildings were in bad repair, the land subject to floods from C.S. Clark and Company's Weedon dam, and the parish church had been moved to a more central location.[74]

Somewhat ironically, the new provincial regime was at this point funding a second large-scale, Church-sponsored colonization programme further east within the upper St Francis district. The reason was simply that the province's emigration flow had only increased since mid-century. The Association des Townships may have failed to provide substantial institutional underpinnings for the free-grants settlements, but at least it had played a role in stimulating migration to the townships involved. Only 35 grants were ultimately patented in Garthby and Stratford, but there were also 263 free titles issued in Wotton (including St Camille), 15 in Ham South (aside from the earlier Gosford Road grants), 144 in Winslow, and 13 in Whitton, for a total of 470.[75] As of 1861 the census reported 660 families living in these six townships, and this number would grow slowly but steadily thereafter.

The question remains as to whether the entire scheme was wrong-headed given the considerable public expense at a time when the province was near bankruptcy, and given the undeniable poverty and suffering endured within the new communities.[76] Historian Norman Macdonald characterizes as "grossly defective" a land policy "that made grants indiscriminately to poor settlers without making adequate preparations for their material welfare."[77] But even though the governing authorities were certainly irresponsible in not providing some local employment in 1851 and 1852, the resident agent did arrange for the construction of mills, and he did provide emergency rations from the government store.[78] Echoing the Wake-field school, Macdonald is very critical of colonization by impover-ished, inexperienced families, but there is no evidence to suggest that the difficulties experienced on the colonization roads could be attributed to failings on the part of the settlers themselves. Finally, Macdonald is perhaps too hasty in attributing to land policy the existence of a basically self-sufficient, peasant-style agricultural econ-omy:

In the back townships ... settlers were not much better than squatters, em-ployed no hired labour, cultivated only so much land as they required for mere subsistence, and consumed what they produced. They amassed little or no capital and contributed little or nothing to the immediate development of the country.[79]

According to one recent historical interpretation, such was essentially the nature of agriculture prior to the 1840s in even the oldest and most accessible of rural communities in the Canadas, if not North America as a whole.[80]

The basic flaw in the colonization roads project of 1848 was not the concept of free grants per se, for they actually ensured immediate and permanent settlement. This project, however, was designed to draw settlers into the most isolated and barren district of the Eastern Townships, while large quantities of more promising land remained in the hands of absentee proprietors. The Roxton colony of the association's Montreal branch would enjoy far more prosperity than would its Quebec-sponsored counterpart in the upper St Francis district, even though its land had to be purchased from the BALC. The absentee-proprietor obstacle would finally be tackled in 1855 with the reform of the municipal system. In the meantime, given the political pressure being exerted by ultramontanes and Rouges – as well as the agricultural and commercial crisis of the period – La Fontaine probably had little choice but to concentrate upon the land at his immediate disposal. Perhaps it would have been more rational to advance colonization in a more compact, densely populated fashion, rather than stringing it out along lengthy, straight roads, regardless of terrain, in an attempt to open up a large territory in one fell swoop.[81] By 1848, however, the settlement frontier was already closing in on the headwaters of the St Francis from north, south and west, and the scattered pockets of arable soil precluded a dense settlement pattern in any case. Less defensible was the decision to limit the free grants to a miserly fifty acres when it should have been obvious even to those unfamiliar with the nature of the district's soil that such isolated colonies would long remain dependent upon the forest as their chief source of outside income. During the 1850s, settlers in Canada West's Shield country were at least offered hundred-acre grants, but as of 1848 the local government was obviously unwilling to transgress to any greater degree the prevailing Wakefieldian dogma, particularly when this would cut into one of its most important potential sources of revenue. Thus inspector general Francis Hincks claimed that free grants of up to fifty acres should be made only in areas where they would increase the value of the remaining crown lands, thereby making the public domain "a good security for borrowed capital."[82] As we shall see in the following chapter, the government would quickly turn to an alternate source of revenue from the crown lands of the upper St Francis district, one which would only add to the impoverishment of the local settlers.

Public Policy and Private Interest in the Lumber Industry of the Upper St Francis: The Role of C.S. Clark and Company

Defending only one's own little property inside its fences, and shutting one's eyes to all the encroachments of the stranger, meant betrayal and self-condemnation to being soon nothing more than a race of slaves.

Félix-Antoine Savard, *Master of the River*

The development of forest policy in Lower Canada and Quebec is well known in its essential outline. Perhaps the most striking feature is that, in contrast to the United States, most timber lands in British North America were not alienated into private hands. H.V. Nelles credits the Canadian system largely to the strength and longevity of the conservative "monarchical" principle, but adds that it can also be attributed to its "functional" role within the geographic context of the Canadian Shield.[1] Once this thin-soiled country was cut over, there was no reason to continue controlling it because the land was of no resale value for farming. Furthermore, properly constituted licences were just as usable for loan collateral as were deeds of ownership, and they offered the added advantage that little capital was required to obtain them.[2] The result of the Canadian policy was that the state played an active role in the administration of the forest resources, if only because it became so reliant on the revenues generated. The official aim was to ensure a high annual level of timber exploitation by encouraging large, well-capitalized enterprises while resisting the inevitable tendency towards monopoly control.

As of 1842 government regulation stipulated a minimum annual harvest on a maximum lease area, but the state rescinded much of its control within the next several years when it sanctioned the principle of lease renewals and transfers to third parties. The lumberman's security of tenure was solidified in 1851 when the requirement for a minimum annual cut was replaced by the ground rent system.[3] Observers have long suspected that the regulatory balance was tipped so radically towards monopolistic control that the public treasury suffered. The stronger the timber barons' position became, the more pressure they could bring to bear on politicians, not only as legislators, but as interpreters and enforcers of that legislation. But historians have not produced the case studies which would allow them to examine in detail the ongoing relationship between state and capital within the context of the lumber industry. Only at the level of the individual enterprise can one observe in concrete terms the conflicting forces to which governments were subject, and begin to analyse their responses in terms of benefits and costs to the public interest.

Hints of the pressures brought to bear on government can be found in the printed reports of the commissioners of crown lands,[4] but one must turn to the unpublished correspondence of the Crown Lands Office to follow the intricacies of the long-term relationship between particular companies and successive administrations. These records are not the place to find direct references to behind-the-scenes political deals, but they do help to explain how C.S. Clark and Company could hold a monopoly position for so many years in such a heavily settled, marginal timber-producing region as the Eastern Townships.

THE RISE AND FALL OF A
LUMBER MONOPOLY

Famous for its forests of sugar maples, the Eastern Townships was never an important centre for the square timber trade to Liverpool. The region did hold enough white pine and black spruce, however, to make it a pioneering centre for the sawn lumber trade to the United States.[5] American demand was only beginning to develop in the early 1830s, but by 1838 timber operators were petitioning for licences to cut spruce and pine saw-logs near the source of the Bécancour River, in Ireland and Coleraine townships.[6] The neighbouring headwaters of the St Francis were controlled by the BALC, but its large Sherbrooke sawmill was located on the Magog River and it exploited the timber lands to the south, drained by Lake Memphramagog.[7] By the time the government had reclaimed much of the St Francis Tract in 1841, the American market had begun to

decline, actually closing temporarily with a tariff imposed in 1846.[8]
It is unlikely, therefore, that the colonization roads built into the
upper St Francis district by the government during the late 1840s
had anything to do with providing access for lumbermen.

In 1853, however, the completion of the St Lawrence and Atlantic
Railway from Montreal through Sherbrooke to Portland, Maine,
opened up vast new market opportunities for lumber, especially after
the signing of the Reciprocity Treaty in 1854. A year earlier, entrepreneurs from Montreal, Quebec, New York, and Maine had suddenly begun to compete for berths on Lake Aylmer, which drains
into the St Francis River.[9] Portland offered a ready outlet, for in
the early 1850s it was the chief port for the 40 million board feet
per year being shipped in the form of sugar boxes from Maine to
Cuba, and it was also an important supplier of building materials to
the coastal states.[10] With local supplies beginning to dwindle, it is
not surprising that Maine merchants dominated the upper St Francis
timber lands from the start. In the fall of 1853, Cyrus S. Clark of
Bangor was reported to have contracted with others to deliver from
Sherbrooke to Portland 6 million feet of lumber in 1854, and 17
million feet in 1855.[11] In fact, his crews cut over 12 million feet the
first year, all within five of the uppermost St Francis Valley townships.[12] By 1860, the St Francis Timber Agency, which incorporated
nearly all of the Eastern Townships (see map 12), was the second
most important source of timber in Canada East, though this status
would not last long.[13]

C.S. Clark, categorized by R.G. Dun's credit investigator as
"shrewd" and "enterprising," quickly became the largest licence
holder in the region.[14] Regulations might limit the size of each berth
to 25 square miles in a surveyed township, but by 1856 Clark held
410 of the St Francis Agency's 825 square miles in timber limits (see
map 13).[15] In addition to acquiring licences directly from the crown,
Clark had purchased the sizeable limits of Pierce and Flowers, as
well as the smaller berths of G.B. Hall, the Pemberton Brothers,
Adolphus Aylmer, and other private parties.[16] Clark and Company
also owned 145,500 arpents of land adjoining Lake Temiscouata and
the Madawaska River, 19 licences on the St Maurice, and a town lot
fronting the river and railway in Sherbrooke.[17]

Facing a double duty after 1851 on the export of unfinished logs
to the United States, Clark and Company built a large sawmill in
1854 at Brompton Falls, several miles below Sherbrooke on the St
Francis River.[18] The mill, "renowned, as well in Europe as in America, for the superior adaptation of the machinery," was 333 feet long
by 70 feet wide, and it contained ten single saws and two gangs of

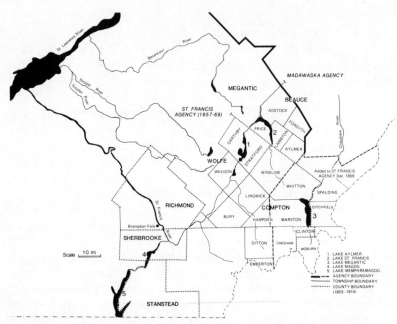

Map 12   Eastern Townships drainage arteries and timber agency boundaries,
1857–69 (From "Map of Montreal and the Eastern Townships" published by E.R.
Smith & Sons, 1897)

twenty-two saws each, plus "the usual circulars to edge with." The
saws were driven by a 600-force water-power, and the expected
production capacity was 50,000 feet in twelve hours. The operation,
lighted by locally produced gas, was to run day and night for eight
to nine months a year, employing 80 to 100 men and producing 20
million feet of lumber. With booms, piers, and other improvements,
including a large boarding-house, the cost for what was claimed to
be the largest sawmill in North America was about $70,000. As a
fitting symbol of the company's achievement and its status in the
region, the middle roof ventilator was topped with a weather vane:

composed of six pairs of golden oxen, drawing a "logging sled," upon which
is an immense golden log. A brilliant teamster is standing by. The oxen
make evident exertions to move their precious load, but do not succeed in
meeting the approval of the teamster, who raises high above them a golden
whip.[19]

Timber would be supplied by ten shanties, employing about 225
men.[20] By 1855 the company's property included fifty yoke of oxen,

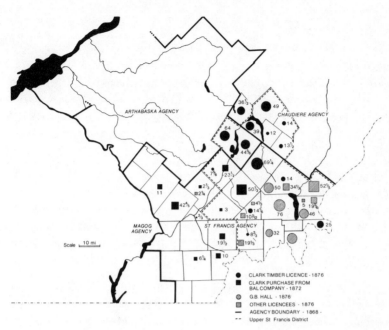

Map 13 Logging operations (sq. mi.) of C.S. Clark and Company. Limits of other lumbermen are shown in the St Francis Agency as well as in those outside townships where Clark held licences. (Quebec, *Sessional Papers*, 1876, no. 18, État des limites à bois; Cookshire Registry Office, reg. B., vol. 2, pp. 556–60, no. 818)

one pair of horses and 5 million feet of logs in the St Francis and adjoining waters.[21] When the decennial census was taken in 1861, C.S. Clark and Company reported that their mills consumed 9 million feet of pine logs, worth $90,000, and 5 million feet of spruce, worth $25,000. The following list of wood products was manufactured:

Boards	9 million feet	$90,000
Sugar boxes	675,000	42,000
Spruce deals	2 million	14,000
Clapboards	800,000 feet	9,000
Doors	1,500	1,200
Shingles	400,000	600
Blind slats	100,000	400
Pine laths	300,000	400
Curtain rods	25,000	100
		$157,700[22]

Without the company's financial statements, profits are difficult to estimate, but calculations based on 1861 census information suggest a value added of $52,000, which would produce a profit of $17,000 once wages were deducted.[23] The company would thus realize a healthy return of 8.5 per cent on its $200,000 capital investment, but difficult times lay ahead because of a restricted market in the war-torn United States. The company had, in fact, been in financial difficulty almost from the start. As early as the fall of 1855 it had been unable to meet payments to the Bank of Montreal on a debt of $81,250, or to the City Bank for $55,420. As a result, Clark and McCrillis, then in partnership with Thomas Howe of Dorchester, Massachusetts, transferred all their Canadian property and licences to the two banks in trust.[24] But the banks would be entitled to sell the property or take over operations only if, after sixty days notice, the company failed to meet the agreed payments of one pound for each thousand feet of lumber manufactured and sold.[25]

Clark survived the 1857 crisis of overproduction in the American market, but the banks decided to cut their losses in the spring of 1859.[26] The result was simply to write off a large proportion of the company's debt, for the highest bidder at the Montreal auction was John Henry Pope at only $30,000. A Cookshire farmer and politician who would soon become one of the dominant capitalists in the region, Pope had probably been an associate of Clark's almost from the beginning of his Eastern Townships operations.[27] Certainly Clark would remain an unofficial partner of Pope's during the next twelve years. Although supposedly only a company agent, paid to sell lumber in Portland, Clark continued to sign all transactions. For reasons that can only be surmised, official ownership shifted back to Clark in 1869 for the $30,000 still owed to the Montreal banks.[28] Even while in receivership, the company had experienced little difficulty in raising capital for its annual operations, but its margin of manoeuvrability was very narrow.[29] An obvious source of additional capital was the Eastern Townships Bank, of which Pope was a director, but in 1869 he was attempting to finance his local railway project and there was a $10,000 limit on individual loans. Indeed, he had been asked by the bank as early as 1860 to reduce his debt from $13,000 to the allowed maximum.[30] Not surprisingly, after the transfer to Clark in 1869, Pope remained the chief spokesman for the company.

Pope was probably reducing his own commitment to the company because it had begun to run out of timber supplies in the later 1860s, but the transfer to Clark would also facilitate large-scale borrowing to purchase privately held timber lands. While American demand was only temporarily cut by the onset of the Civil War, and the company's lumber could be exported via Portland in bond after the abrogation of the Reciprocity Treaty, the St Francis Agency never again produced as much lumber as it had in the late 1850s.[31] By the time of the 1871 census, the Brompton mill was processing logs valued at only $29,600, as compared to $115,000 ten years earlier. According to the census statistics, the profit for 1871 could only have been about $7200, though this did represent 18 per cent of the declared fixed capital of $40,000. And even if the company was deeply mortgaged to the Montreal banks, regional production was about to follow the provincial trend sharply upward for the next two or three years (see figure 2 and appendix B). The company's main concern was to keep up the supply of timber, particularly when, as we shall see, colonization societies and companies were reserving large quantities of land in eastern Compton County. Clark began to purchase scattered wood lots throughout the region (totalling close to $30,000 in price by 1875), and he also made a major acquisition from the BALC in the spring of 1872.[32] The latter purchase comprised 99,833 acres in eight townships, three of which lay in the upper St Francis district, and the remainder not far downstream. The price was $102,748, of which $23,555 was paid down in the form of 110 shares in the land company. The balance was to be distributed over the next four years, at 6 per cent interest per annum, with the option to pay in BALC stock either at par or at $214 per share.[33] The following fall, in two separate transactions, the land company sold Clark another 7,901 acres in the upper St Francis Valley. The total price was $17,321 with only $2,374 paid down.[34] All the private purchases together brought over two hundred square miles into the hands of C.S. Clark and Company, about half the area of their crown timber limits.

The company's expansionary phase was to be short-lived, for the general depression in wood commerce which began in 1874 saw the quantity of timber reported by all operators in the region plummet throughout the remainder of the decade.[35] As early as January 1874, Clark and Company transferred 87 ⅔ square miles from Spalding and Whitton Townships to a Quebec City merchant.[36] Clark's growing financial difficulties are reflected in the notary records from the Sherbrooke-Richmond area. In December 1874, the company mortgaged 12,533 acres, plus a Sherbrooke lot and mill property, to the Eastern Townships Bank for $58,000.[37] The fall of 1875 brought the sale of 5560 acres in Ditton, while, at the same time, employees and others began to register with notaries a long series of protests against Clark's failure to fulfil the terms of his promissory notes.[38] In fact,

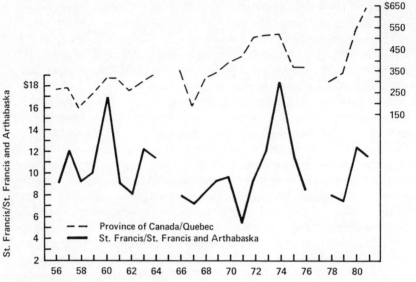

Figure 2   Dollars (thousands) accrued by crown in St Francis (1855–69)/St Francis and Arthabaska (1868–81) timber agencies and in province of Canada/Quebec.

workers had apparently begun to be paid in store scrip as business languished in 1876.[39] As early as the fall of 1875, Brompton Falls inhabitants had assembled to consider taking advantage of the government's colonization projects in Compton County. On 29 October, Sherbrooke's *Le Pionnier* pointed out the moral lesson:

La crise commerciale que nous traversons actuellement, tout déplorable qu'elle soit, a eu cependant pour les habitants de ce beau et coquet petit village de bons résultats.

Ils ont compris que s'appuyer purement et simplement sur l'industrie qui leur fournit tous les jours de si beaux salaires, n'est pas toujours le plus sûr moyen d'existence. Ils sentent le besoin de se faire un avenir plus solide tant pour eux que pour leurs enfants.

In the autumn of 1876, Clark was forced to mortgage the mill property itself to the Eastern Townships Bank for only $2,000.[40] The company managed to hang on for another two years without further major commitments, but in December 1878 all of the BALC purchases were forfeited to avoid seizure for back taxes.[41] It appears that little of the principal had been paid after the initial instalment.

In March 1878, $84,953 had still been owing, though this sum did include an additional $5,000 purchase made in January 1875.[42]

Meanwhile the company struggled on, raising capital by making short-term business deals with entrepreneurs involved in the timber trade. In the spring of 1877 Clark sold Pope all the logs cut that winter for $5,000, delivered to the Brompton mill. The agreement openly stated that the purpose of the sale was to allow Clark to pay off arrears in wages and to meet expenses in preparing the lumber. In fact, Pope was to advance more money if necessary, then reimburse himself after the lumber had been sold.[43] In February 1879, to raise enough money to pay back wages and process the winter's cut, Clark mortgaged all 6 million feet of timber for $9,000 cash to Weston F. Milliken, a prominent Portland merchant.[44] Milliken demanded reimbursement only for the sum he had advanced, his condition being that the market "insofar as the same can be made advantageous and profitable shall be at the said City of Portland."[45] In other words, Milliken would act as the middleman between the company and the ultimate purchasers of its wood products. In 1891, he was still "handling the productions of the C.S. Clark Mills," having apparently become at least part owner of the operation.[46]

International conditions finally began to improve during the 1879–80 season, a development reflected by increased production in the Eastern Townships' crown timber limits.[47] Clark was actually able to purchase back part of the land given up to the BALC – 42,745 acres in Lingwick and Weedon Townships for $40,000 in cash.[48] But he still was in debt to the Eastern Townships Bank. In fact, he mortgaged the new purchase for only $9,258 because he owed the bank $60,000 from loans advanced in 1874 and 1876. The mortgage is not recorded as having been discharged.[49] Clark died in 1880, leaving his son to take over direction of the mill.[50] Within a few years it was sold to Royal Paper Mills (directed by Pope's son, Rufus), which closed it in 1893. Fire ended the mill's existence in 1900.[51]

LOCAL REACTION AGAINST MONOPOLY CONTROL

The Clark Company's financial record may not have been a brilliant one, but its survival in a marginal timber-producing region says much about the link between government and capitalists in the nineteenth century. We have seen how state regulations set the stage for a considerable degree of monopoly control, but the manner in which those regulations were interpreted and enforced was equally crucial to the fortunes of C.S. Clark and Company. Ruthless management techniques, made possible in large part by either the government's ineffectiveness or its passive complicity, go a long way to explain the domination of the upper St Francis district by the Brompton-based company.

Clark not only trespassed on rivals' timber limits, but insisted on dominating the river itself.[52] As early as the spring of 1855, another American company – the Holyokes of Portland – complained that Clark's drive had swept its logs past its mill on the St Francis.[53] The fall of the same year saw Clark and Company notifying the Holyokes that they should remove logs which had become lodged in the booms at Brompton Falls.[54] Further conflict was eventually prevented by Clark's takeover of the Holyokes' Garthby limits, but the Brompton company was also aggravating lumber producers downstream from its mill.[55] In 1858 three entrepreneurs from Grantham Township, and two from Wendover, served a notice of protest against Clark's "constant and invariable practise habit [sic] of throwing into the said River Saint Francis all the Edgings of boards and other refuse lumber cut in the said Mills." The result was not only that booms downstream "have been many times heretofore broken and carried away and the logs and lumber therein lost," but farms on the river banks were flooded, and edgings penetrated the flooms and interfered with the wheels of the protestors' mills. To the warning that in future he would be held liable for all damages incurred, Clark simply replied: "I conceive that the parties suffer no damage and I believe that their object in protesting against me is to make a speculative [sic] out of me."[56]

Even public corporations, such as the municipal councils of Orford and Brompton townships and the Town of Sherbrooke, would prove to be powerless against Clark and Company. In 1858 they expressed their opposition to the company's projected dam across the St Francis "unless provision is made to secure the rights of the inhabitants."[57] Clark, in asking for the right to use of the river for a distance of three miles above the site of his mill, found support in the Legislative Assembly from J.H. Pope, the future purchaser of his company.[58] A.T. Galt, also a local MLA, proposed an amendment to Pope's bill which would have required Clark to deposit a security of £1,500 to £2,000 with the Town of Sherbrooke to ensure against damage to local bridges. The amendment was defeated, however, leaving Clark with an unencumbered guarantee that his dam and booms were inviolable.[59]

Aside from periodic flooding, an indication of the problems the dam would cause is to be found in the protests submitted by Sherbrooke manufacturers. In 1879, for example, Sherbrooke millwright Robert N. Arkley complained that the St Francis was choked with logs in many places within the townships of Ascot, Orford, Brompton, and Stoke. He demanded that the Clark Company open "a clear and unobstructed Channel of at least 100 feet in width" throughout the entire length of the river. Clark's only reply was "I am not ready to reply." In 1880, when the brewer James W. Wiggett registered essentially the same protest, the answer was, "I have no answer to make."[60]

The municipal councils of the Sherbrooke area had been joined in their protests against construction of the company's Brompton dam in 1858 by recently settled inhabitants in the upper St Francis district. They pointed out that those living in the Lake Aylmer area had already faced spring floods from company dams at the headwaters of the St Francis.[61] Roads had been washed out, making it impossible for some families to reach town for weeks at a time.[62] The settlers had a strong legal case, if they could have afforded the court costs, but the problem persisted.[63] In 1877 Garthby's council was forced to replace a one-and-a-half-mile section of road permanently flooded by Clark and Company dams, and in 1879 the government was still refusing to intervene against the company's ongoing dam construction projects along the upper St Francis.[64]

Successive administrations were placed in a rather embarrassing position by ongoing friction between lumber company and settlers because of the important ideological role played by French-Canadian colonization.[65] That friction had been made inevitable after 1849 when the state decided that settlement lots would be granted within licensed timber berths without immediately cancelling the licensees' cutting privileges on these lots when location tickets were issued. At the same time, settlers themselves could exploit commercial timber without possessing full title (letters patent) to their lots, if they purchased a timber permit from the government. This privilege was apparently dropped in the 1852 legislation,[66] but it remained standard government practice to grant timber permits to residents or their representatives for lots held only by location ticket. In fact, by 1858, even squatters were considered eligible to obtain cutting permits for crown lots they occupied.[67] On the other hand, even though company licences might not normally be renewed on lots for which location tickets had been issued, there was actually little to prevent a timber entrepreneur who faced the threat of local competition from quickly stripping a township of its best trees.[68] In 1856 J.T. Le Bel, the government colonization agent for the Lake Aylmer – Lake St Francis area, reported that timber reserves were une des principales raisons qui retarde le plus la colonisation, et décourage le colon, qui voit des spéculateurs étrangers enlever presque tous les bois de services, qui dans plusieurs cas, n'épargnent pas plus les terres habitées, que celles qui sont vacantes, et il est à craindre que plusieurs localitées aient avant longtemps, à souffrir du manquent de Bois de construction.[69]

Settler opposition to Clark and Company was focused in Lambton Township where the village of Saint-Vital acted as the local district's major service centre. In 1856 three "habitants" of Lambton complained that an American-owned chantier had been operating in the township for three years, taking "toutes les bois de construction même sur les terre consédé [sic]." The local municipal council petitioned the government "de bien Vouloir discontinué les chantier des amériquain [sic] dans les townships de l'est."[70] Two years later, in 1858, Doctor Louis Labrecque from Saint-Vital submitted a petition on behalf of the settlers of Lambton and four neighbouring townships: "On se plaint, avec raison, que beaucoup de nos compatriotes abandonnent le sol de la patrie pour émigrer aux États voisines. On en cherche les causes, ou plutôt on fait semblant de les chercher, car jamais on ne va plus loin."

According to Labrecque, the real cause for retarded development of the area was that Clark and McCrillis were cutting timber on the settlers' colonization road grants, and on other occupied and non-occupied lands for which individuals held location tickets in their own names and in those of their children: "si quelque pauvre malheureux veulent les empêcher de piller leurs bois, ils se moquent d'eux, quand ils ne font pas plus." Furthermore, company employees "font des embarras terribles sur nos terres," and properties were threatened by carelessness with fire. The interests of French-Canadian settlers were being sacrificed for the sake of foreign capitalists who sent all of the wood out of the country: "Pour un écu que donnent au Gouvernement tous ces étrangers, vous ruinez les townships, et vous feriez les enfants du sol à haïr et détester un Gouvernement qui doit les protéger."[71]

The county's MLA, Dunbar Ross, supported the petition, and the Crown Lands Office promised to take "new measures" to prevent licensees from cutting on colonists' lots.[72] Several months later, however, Labrecque was still complaining of "un vrai pillage" on non-patented lands.[73] The Crown Lands Office could only reply that particular care had been taken to remove from timber licences those lots for which location tickets had been issued, "et si les commercants de bois se permettent d'entrer sur ces lots et d'enlever le bois, ils le font sans autorité quelconque et se rendent passibles d'amende pour débit."[74] With the spring of 1859 the system was tightened up further when the local crown timber agent was instructed to obtain monthly reports of all crown lots sold, and all purchases paid in full.[75]

In spite of the precautions taken by government, relations between company and settlers continued to deteriorate. In May, inhabitants of Lambton and Aylmer demanded that Clark's permit be suspended pending the presentation of evidence "why said licence should be totally discontinued." They claimed that habitants working for the company "have been many times outraged and robbed by them," and charged that the company had "extensively defrauded the government by concealing the true quantity of timber cut." The petitioners hoped to produce affidavits from some of the foremen stating that over one million pine logs had not been accounted for during the previous four years.[76]

As we shall see in the next section, these charges were not without foundation. Nevertheless, the populist rhetoric of such appeals should not blind us to the fact that they were drafted by members of the *petite bourgeoisie* with their own class interests to defend. The conflict between Clark and the Lambton merchant, Romain Dallaire, illustrates how small local entrepreneurs operated in a region dominated by monopolists. In February 1859, Dallaire obtained a county court order allowing him to seize about 2,500 logs reportedly cut by Clark and Company men on five lots for which he held location tickets in Aylmer Township.[77] The following April, with the spring drive about to commence, Dallaire's eighteen guardians prevented Clark's men from "rolling in" not only the logs cut in trespass, but apparently others from the vicinity as well. The poorly defined boundary lines certainly aggravated the situation.[78]

Clark asked the crown timber agent, G.J. Nagle, to intervene because the company was "unwilling to lose driving time by arrest of men in case of forcibly putting out timber."[79] Nagle's solution was to appoint a representative, Michel Godette, to seize and sell the logs cut on Dallaire's lots, directing the proceeds towards the payment of the remaining four instalments on those lots.[80] This was a clever way of foiling Dallaire who presumably had intended to obtain cutting permits without acquiring full title to the land. Godette, who lived near Dallaire, felt that the latter had "purchased these lands more with a view to speculation on Clark & Co. than to settlement."[81] Dallaire himself had been involved in a trespass in Lambton the previous spring. Nagle agreed with his agent:

Dallaire if wished to [sic] protect only his property, should have stopped Clark & Co.'s people from cutting on or drawing Timber from the lands he claimed; but if on the contrary his object was speculation and that he wished to take utmost advantage of his man, his course would be to delay action until driving time when from the importance of time and the danger of delay he would be most likely to coerce Clark & Co. into his terms.[82]

Weak though his legal position was, Dallaire did not accept Nagle's decision without resistance. His lawyers petitioned that the logs not be removed until the courts had time to resolve the issue: "sans cela, il en résultera infailliblement un conflit dont les suites pourraient être très lamentables."[83] The threat was not an idle one, for in May Pope telegraphed Nagle: "Dalieu [Dallaire] threatened to forcibly remove logs your deputy guarded, and kill any one (1) that removes the logs or arrest him."[84] Three of Dallaire's sons and an employee were subsequently arrested by the Sherbrooke constable and condemned to prison by the local justice of the peace.[85] Their case was still before the courts nine years later.[86]

Meanwhile, in 1860, the mayor of Aylmer Township complained that Dominique Morin, the justice of the peace who had seized Dallaire's logs and sentenced the four men, was a paid agent of Clark and Company. Morin was said to have used intimidation and violence to drive away Dallaire's guards, and to have convened the court behind the closed doors of a tavern without giving the defendants a chance to speak.[87] Aylmer's councillors and fifty-eight other inhabitants petitioned for Morin's dismissal on the additional grounds that he was an illiterate alcoholic. The government demanded stronger evidence, but Morin eventually did resign two years later.[88]

Perhaps the defiance shown by Dallaire strengthened local resolve, for petitions against Clark and Company grew in numbers of signatures and charges laid. In the spring of 1860, 102 names were appended to those of Dr Labrecque and Aylmer Township's priest, notary, mayor, and four councillors. In addition to the old allegations of company trespass on private lots and fraud against the government, the petition labelled Nagle's assistant, Michel Godette, a co-conspirator, and claimed that the "compagnie d'Étrangers *Americaines*" was building roads which were destroying survey lines, and erecting dams which caused irreparable damage to colonists located by lakes and rivers. Once the company had finished with a lot, even the firewood was gone, making it useless for colonization.[89]

By the summer of 1862 the government had actually begun to waver on the issue of renewing timber licences for settled areas. In response to cries such as that of the Beauce County mayors that "nos forêts se ruinent entièrement," the Crown Lands Office asked Nagle to identify townships where licences might not be reissued in the interest of present and future settlers. Nagle presumably resisted this threat to his salary, for all permits were renewed as usual the following season.[90]

The settlers did have an ally in William Farwell, crown lands agent for the St Francis district, as well as forest ranger under Nagle's authority.[91] Farwell suggested in the fall of 1863 that licences not be reissued for Ditton, Chesham, and Emberton townships. They had already been cut over by the BALC, while briefly in its possession as part of the original St Francis Tract, and again by Clark and Company, "which has left no more than is wanted for local purposes to be used by the Inhabitants for building on their farms." Sawmills were about to be built in Ditton and Hampden to supply the needs of settlers.[92] But Nagle, himself a former timber entrepreneur, failed to support Farwell's position.[93] Ignoring the fact that logged-over land quickly produced thick brush and dangerous wind-falls, he argued that "lumbering in place of deterring the sale and settlement of Bush Land very frequently ... stimulates them," provided that sugaries and cedar timber were preserved. According to Nagle, the only alternative to the operations of large logging companies in isolated areas was usually fire because settlers simply were unable to market the timber, an argument which is belied by the timber schedules of the 1871 manuscript census. Nagle even argued that "however closely a Forest Country may be lumbered there will still remain Lumber Woods which will have to be burned off before a local demand for them arises." He was not willing to consider that the townships listed by Farwell presented a special case because he felt that conditions were similar enough throughout the region as a whole that any cancellation of licences would be considered a precedent. Nagle's clincher was that $65,000 in timber had been shipped from the Eastern Townships to Portland during the current year: "It would be well for Mr. Farwell to consider the effect the stoppage of this trade alone would produce in the Townships."[94]

Despite Nagle's arguments, the government did declare in 1864 that licences would not be renewed for townships which were two-thirds settled. In fact, this was not much of a concession because timber monopolists would hardly have been very active in such thickly populated areas. The list for 1864–65 did not include one township in the upper St Francis district.[95] Furthermore, the government even reneged on this minor reform the following year, "owing to the state of money matters just now."[96]

Although the provincial authorities were willing to turn a blind eye to the trespasses of needy colonists who could not afford to pay for timber permits, little was done to control the activities of Clark and Company.[97] Consequently, the inhabitants of the upper St Francis district continued their attacks throughout the 1860s. In 1864 J.F. Bérubé, curé of Forsyth and Shenley, went so far as to hire a lawyer to force Nagle to provide him with the names and residences of all parties constituting C.S. Clark and Company, however it is unlikely that local residents could have afforded to take effective legal action.[98] In 1868 a potentially more effective tactic was again resorted to. No doubt because the government could be expected to react most decisively when its own interests were at stake, the mayor of Lambton submitted an affidavit proclaiming that the Clark Company was instructing loggers to declare that the trees they chopped were from private land, and to report only half the wood actually cut. A Lambton farmer swore that during the twelve years he had worked for the company, employees had been ordered not to declare the correct amount of wood cut.[99]

Such testimony was grist for the Crown Lands Office's mill, for, as we shall see, Confederation was bringing to a head a protracted struggle with Clark and Company concerning unpaid fees. The new provincial regime was not only less tolerant than the old towards the company, but the upper St Francis Valley had been carved into three timber agencies (see map 13), thereby providing more effective supervision, especially for the vociferous Lake St Francis townships which were placed in the Chaudière agency. Not only had the whole district been distant from Nagle's headquarters in Saint-Hyacinthe, but Lambton and surrounding area had also been quite removed from the Bury home of his wood ranger, William Farwell. Under the new regime colonization took on a greater urgency, and the stream of protest petitions dried to a trickle.

As we shall see, the Quebec government actively promoted colonization in the upper St Francis district during the boom years of the early 1870s by reserving large chunks of crown land for parish-sponsored colonization societies and European-financed colonization companies. Most of this activity took place in the unsettled townships of the Lake Megantic drainage basin, but where it impinged on Clark's territory in Hampden and Ditton townships, Horace Sawyer, a barely disguised surrogate for the company, was able to lease all the unreserved lots.[100]

A greater threat to the lumber company than the short-lived colonization ventures came from local entrepreneurs as the railway network extended northeastwards during the 1870s. In 1873, for example, the Compton County registrar inquired about buying for cash, without settlement duties, all the crown lots in Chesham and

Woburn.[101] The same year, Flavien Paquette, sawmill operator and founder of a French-Canadian colony in Hereford Township, applied to purchase all the crown land in seven of eastern Compton County's townships. He was informed that the land would have to be sold at auction.[102]

The more usual practice was simply to trespass on licensed timber lots. This grew so prevalent during the 1870s that the government became concerned about its revenues. If the companies could not protect their berths, how were the timber agents to collect fees from logs cut thereon?[103] One solution was to appoint bush rangers on a permanent basis in settled townships, for "it requires more care to watch the inhabitants than the limit holders."[104] And, in cases where the competence of the bush rangers fell into doubt, crown timber agents were authorized to appoint secret inspectors to investigate suspected depredations. These rangers could in effect act as spies for the companies, reporting trespasses on their berths.[105]

Such defensive measures could not reverse the economic transformation introduced by the Quebec Central Railway and Pope's own International line. Even if Clark and Company were in fact able to protect their timber limits in the face of growing demand and shrinking supply, their mill could not survive the competition from smaller, more efficient steam sawmills springing up along the rail lines close to the timber sources.[106] As we shall see, the Glasgow-Canadian Land and Trust Company founded the sawmill centre of Scotstown on the Salmon River, after purchasing shares to attract the International Railway to the site. Only a few miles away another sawmill community known as Bown's Mills was born soon after.[107] On the Quebec Central line a new steam mill was reported at Lake Weedon in 1880, and the construction of two more soon followed at Black Creek (Disraeli) on Lake Aylmer.[108] In Compton County between 1871 and 1881 the number of mills increased only from fifty-six to sixty-three, but hands employed almost doubled (120 to 218), logs processed multiplied about two and a half times (182,381 to 417,849), and the value of production jumped from $79,080 to $185,496.[109]

Pope's son and son-in-law would maintain a strong position in the region's timber industry, but the upper St Francis district apparently enjoyed at least a mild measure of relief from monopoly control during the 1870s and 1880s.[110] With economic benefits somewhat more widely distributed, it is presumably no coincidence that local protests had declined. However any improvement in the residents' economic situation was short-lived because the best supplies of lumber had been exhausted. Such was the grounds for a petition in 1877 by some 400 inhabitants of six upper Beauce townships who faced judicial proceedings for arrears in crown lands payments:

Que la coupe des bois qui s'est faite depuis vingt cinq ans en nos Townships en profit du gouvernement mais par des étrangers, ayant completement dévasté nos forêts, nous ayant enlevé les dernières moyens sur lesquels les colons pouvaient compter pour faire leurs paiements sur le prix de leur terre.[111]

These colonists were not disinterested observers, but an 1885 report to the government on the nature of the timber on each unpatented lot in sparsely settled Winslow Township was filled with comments such as "culled," "dark stunted balsam, spruce, cedar," and "soft, scrubby timber, partly burnt."[112]

The inquiry was obviously commissioned because of the emergence of the pulp and paper industry in the region. The sudden demand for young, low-quality softwood would give a shot in the arm to the local economy, but once again monopolists would dominate. Clark's Brompton sawmill was replaced by a pulp mill, consuming 40,000 cords of spruce and fir a year from the same upper St Francis townships.[113] The only way the local inhabitants could resist was to continue their tradition of trespassing, as the commissioner of the BALC lamented in 1897:

The expense of watching has been increased, and in cases of trespass the costs of survey to prove trespass, together with the legal proceedings, almost invariably exceed the value of the timber stolen. We do not let any matter pass; it would be a premium for the poacher. In most cases the trespasser is himself without means, and can always dispose of the stolen property to the lumber dealers or the country storekeeper who has advanced money and provender for the work, and as in the case of smuggling, no dishonour seems to attach to this class of stealing.[114]

RELATIONS WITH THE CROWN LANDS OFFICE

While French-Canadian colonization remained an official priority throughout the last half of the nineteenth century, successive governments were clearly unwilling to heed colonists' complaints that the lumber monopoly was adding to their impoverishment. As a general rule, cash-starved administrations could not afford to diminish their chief source of income, but, in the case of C.S. Clark and Company, the timber revenue collected was far from impressive.

Problems with Clark developed as early as the spring of 1854 when S.V. Larue, crown timber agent for the Chaudière district, inspected the logs chopped in the Eastern Townships. When he reached the operations of Clark and Brown at the end of April, they asked for a nine- or ten-day delay on the grounds that they had not measured their cut. Larue was skeptical:

Il n'y a pas d'hommes plus attentifs à suivre leurs affaires. D'ailleurs ayant Contracté pour des bourgeois Américains, il va sans dire qu'ils avaient Compté le bois qu'ils faisaient couper. Le Foremen de Clark Brown et Cie ont dit qu'ils avaient Coupé au moins 50 Millions de pieds de bois, pendant que ces Messieurs en ont déclaré n'en avoir coupé que 17 Millions.[115]

Clark and Brown at first reported that they had cut 38,289 logs, but Larue protested that this was too few since they had employed 300 to 350 men. He felt the figure should be closer to 100,000. Five days later the company altered its claim to 44,368 seventeen-foot pine logs, equivalent to 62,854 of standard twelve-foot length. But after J.H. Pope returned from an inspection, the tally of twelve-foot logs was dropped again to 48,380, amounting to a mere 12 million feet "among which are many old dry trees and top logs which never were worth drawing from the woods." Pope actually deducted 10 per cent for useless logs, leaving a total of 43,542.[116] The deduction of substandard trees became a yearly ploy of the company, even though its mill was designed to process generally non-marketable wood by manufacturing boxes and laths, etc.[117]

At the end of May Larue sent a merchant from Saint-Vital-de-Lambton to inspect the Clark and Brown cut, but he was not able to obtain a "résultat définitif." Consequently, Larue himself interviewed "plusieurs Personnes qui me paraissaient bien informées," but with no success. He concluded that it would always be impossible for the government to determine how much wood was cut "par la règle actuellement existante de Compter et faire payer Chaque billot." The charge should instead be for each tree, as it would be easier to count fresh stumps at Lakes St Francis and Aylmer, than logs in "les Beaumes [booms] de MM Clark Brown et Cie." Larue had been forced to hurry in the enumeration of logs because they would soon be passing to the American side of the border.[118] The problem of tallying each year's cut would not be completely solved by the Crown Lands Office even after Confederation when it appointed special bush rangers. During the winter of 1873–74, for example, snow and river ice covered a large portion of the logs making accurate counting impossible. The province's timber agents were almost unanimous in declaring that the system was of very limited use in checking limit holders.[119]

For the 1856–57 season, Nagle appointed a crown surveyor, George Austin, to undertake the inspection of the upper St Francis area. Austin was informed that because "the lumbermen of the Saint Francis are in the habit of keeping no account of what they consider cull wood," he was to regard the company scalers' bills as only an approximate indicator of the quantity of timber cut at each camp. The surveyor was to report the force of teams and men in each camp, the date of commencement, when they intended to close operations, weekly progress, quality of wood, locations where wood cut, and the general character of the land.[120] He apparently reported that Clark and Company were indeed underestimating their cut, for on 9 April Nagle informed them that Austin was being instructed to re-examine the operations "of certain accessible camps," using his findings there as "a rule of charge" for all the company's operations.[121]

Unfortunately no account for 1856–57 can be found in the departmental documents, but a report for the following winter listed 36,338 pine, 3,053 spruce, and 400 cedar ties, with an estimated 2,491 additional trees to be cut by thirty-three company camps before the season ended.[122] The company, on the other hand, claimed that only 27,220 pine logs had been cut by its crews (an absurdly small number for approximately 400 men) and another 484 pine and 6,011 spruce by contractors.[123] Nagle's explanation for the discrepancy between the two reports was that Clark's return had been made from scalers' books, and "their rule is not to include culls or what they term *scoots*." The agent's duty was to count all logs cut, therefore 10 per cent should be added to the Clark estimate.[124]

By the winter of 1860 Clark and Company owed the government $9,834, but the new owner, Pope, asked for a credit of $11,238. His grounds were that part of the logs had been rotten and worthless, half had been swept past the mill to be lost in the spring of 1854 (resulting in the expense of $20,000 to improve the stream), and dues levied for some seasons were for more logs than had actually been taken out.[125] Nagle's reply was that the charges for the seasons 1854 to 1856 and 1857 to 1860 were based on the company's own returns, the only adjustments being in the number of twelve-foot logs computed from the number of full-length logs reported.[126]

However Nagle ultimately softened his stand, reporting to the superintendent of woods and forests that, for six of the seven seasons, one-third of the logs charged against the company "were bad, cull and worthless." This was a rather surprising reversal considering that the government's estimates were based on the company's own deflated reports, but Superintendent P.M. Partridge concluded that "there are strong grounds for making the allowance to the extent recommended by Mr. Nagle."[127] His superior, the commissioner of crown lands, observed that the regulations stated clearly that no distinctions could be made as to the quality of logs, but he admitted that "the claim is somewhat new to the Department." Consideration had been taken in one previous case of the small diameter of the logs, but a similar case in 1858 had been rejected:

If Messrs Clark & Co. had not cut the trees which they now claim a deduction for as having produced worthless logs, those Trees would no doubt, have been of some use at a later date to parties taking up the Lands for settlement. On the other hand if Clark & Co. manufactured their logs as the greater number of Saw Mill Owners do, cutting them up in the Woods into regular lengths, and not hauling and driving the trees nearly whole—much of what they claim deduction for, as worthless, would have been left in the Woods, as is done to a wasteful extent in many instances, by other Saw Mill owners ... However Clark & Co. were under no necessity to cut these trees down. They appear to have cut indiscriminately and wastefully.

After this vacillating preamble, Commissioner Vankoughnet suggested that dues on the wood found to be useless be reduced by half, on the understanding that no such consideration would be shown the company in future.[128] Nagle's concession that one-third of the wood was defective should have meant a one-sixth reduction in fees, but, typically enough, a full $5,286 was written off by order in council, leaving only $5,190 owing.[129]

Still Pope was not satisfied. He claimed that when he had purchased the company from the banks in 1859, Nagle had informed him that only $3,555 was owed to the government. This he had paid, understanding it to be the final settlement.[130] Pope almost won by default in the end, for in 1867 Partridge submitted a report crediting the company with $10,283, supposedly based on the 1861 order in council. Thus, in effect, the total debt for 1854 to 1860 had been eliminated. In 1871, however, the issue was reopened by Nagle whose agency was being closed, forcing him to collect back accounts. He had apparently received no instructions authorizing the more

generous interpretation of the 1861 decision.[131] Counting the
$5,190 owing as of 1860, the total debt amounted to $13,326 in
1871. Pope, who had become federal minister of agriculture in 1869,
had officially sold the company back to Clark that same year, but it
was he who protested that the earlier debt had been written off. In
an attempt to flex his political muscle, he asked that his cabinet
colleagues, George-Étienne Cartier and Alexander T. Galt, be chosen as arbitrators on the grounds that they had been part of the
administration which had made the original decision. Pope also
claimed a $4,500 deduction (6,000 pine logs at seventy-five cents)
for the "authorized" trespass of timber entrepreneur Charles King
on the Clark and Company's Coleraine berth. After Clark had been
paying ground rent for years to conserve "some of our best Pine,"
the lands had been declared fit for settlement. This had given King
the opportunity to take the timber upon payment of a trespass fee
to the government.[132] Finally, Pope claimed a $3,000 deduction for
the loss of limits in Garthby. On the latter two points he offered to
accept the decision of two arbitrators, one to be chosen by the Crown
Lands Office and one by the company, the arbitrators to pick an
umpire in case of disagreement. In sum, Pope was asking for a
$12,690 deduction, leaving a total debt of only $636.[133]

The crown lands commissioner declared his rejection of Pope's
claim within the week. He not only stuck to the initial interpretation
of the 1861 order in council, he also refused to accept responsibility
for King's trespass in Coleraine, stating that certain lots were removed from Pope's licence "parce qu'ils étaient demandés par des
colons supposé de bonne foi." Pope's suggestion of arbitration was
also vetoed, signifying that his move to the House of Commons after
Confederation had considerably diminished his political influence
over the Crown Lands Office.[134]

The new provincial administration soon began to take a closer
look at the company's ongoing operations. In August 1870 Pope was
reminded by Eugène Taché, the assistant commissioner of crown
lands, that because his company had, for many years past, been in
the habit of reporting only a small portion of its annual cut, the
department had made a careful inspection in the woods the previous
winter. The result had confirmed that less than half the quantity of
logs had been declared. The new timber agent for the Chaudière
division had refrained from seizing lumber at Brompton Falls in
lieu of unpaid fees only because the foreman had been absent. Pope
was again informed that his claim to exemption for rotten logs would
not be accepted, and that he could not refuse to pay the travelling
expenses of the agent who had discovered his trespass in Coleraine.

Finally, the Crown Lands Office was even taking a new and tougher stand on the 1861 order in council, which had granted a 50 per cent remission. Pope was told that he could not reasonably demand this when his petition had asked for only one-third off. The assistant commissioner intimated that if Clark and Company did not promptly close all back accounts, their request for a permit to export 3.5 million feet of lumber would not be forthcoming.[135]

Upon Pope's protest, Taché assured him that he had not suggested that intentional fraud had been perpetrated. Nonetheless, several serious charges had been made by influential persons, "which, through a sense of moderation, were not acted upon at the time, but on your late refusal to come to an agreement to the just requirements of our agent, the Commissioner could no more remain silent." Enclosed was a letter from a member of the Legislative Assembly, with five affidavits, which "will give you sufficient proofs, that there existed ample reason for adopting the course which has been pursued." Taché concluded that the form of the letter addressed to Clark's firm "could not in any way render justifiable the impropriety of the language used in your reply."[136]

After years of vacillation and remarkable lethargy, the Crown Lands Office was finally willing to back its words with action.[137] When Clark paid $444 in October for the season's ground rent in eight townships, he and Pope were informed that the licences had been forfeited, and the payment deposited in account for arrears due. The St Francis agent, Farwell, was also warned to ensure that the company made no trespass on its former limits.[138] The colour of the language in Pope's response will have to be left to the imagination, but he was probably forced to co-operate at last, for within a month all licences were renewed and a permit issued to export the season's lumber.[139]

There would be few clashes in the ensuing decade. Historian Marcel Hamelin condemns the Crown Lands Office of the 1870s for corruption and incompetency, but in fact the provincial government's growing dependence upon the public domain as a source of revenue seems to have made it less tolerant of lumbermen's abuses.[140] To take one example, bush rangers, appointed in 1874, were instructed to ascertain the quantity of logs left in the woods by limit owners so that stumpage dues could be collected.[141] The government's hardened attitude may be one reason why C.S. Clark and Company purchased so much land during the early 1870s. But they would be discouraged from making false claims that any logs cut on their crown leases had been acquired from privately owned land because bush rangers were instructed to keep an eye on such activities. In fact, the government demanded that affidavits be produced identifying the lot locations of all timber so obtained.[142] As far as the upper St Francis district was concerned, however, the government's awakened vigilance came too late for it to benefit from the best years of lumbering. Revenues soared briefly in the early 1870s, but, even when the market again re-established itself after the 1875–79 recession, the region's response would be a faltering one (see figure 2.)

Clark and Company contributed little to either the colonists of the upper St Francis district or the provincial treasury. Government revenue from all crown timber taken from the Eastern Townships prior to 1881 rarely exceeded fifteen thousand dollars a year, from which the costs of maintaining timber agents, woods rangers, and a portion of the Crown Lands Office bureaucracy had to be subtracted. J.E. Hodgetts' theory that the reason governments were lenient was to avoid killing the goose that laid the golden egg simply does not apply in this case[143]. A careful economic analysis would be necessary to test Michael Cross's claim that small firms were "doomed in a necessarily large-scale industry," but, even without direct evidence in the form of company records or private papers, one can conclude with some certainty that the history of C.S. Clark and Company had as much to do with political power as it did with market-place imperatives.[144] Pope's influence over the Crown Lands Office may have declined after Confederation, but the links between the federal and provincial Conservatives remained strong enough to ensure that Clark and Company's timber berths would not be disturbed, provided it conformed to the existing regulations. Nor did the Liberals' accession to power in both Ottawa and Quebec pose any danger because a provincial regulation passed in 1868 had guaranteed that all timber limits would be renewed automatically each year until 1889.

Thus a system which may have been essential for the conditions of the remote northern operations was imposed upon the relatively accessible upper St Francis district. Here it would only discourage the expansion of small-scale capital and make life more difficult for local farmers who relied upon the woods for economic survival. Because of the nineteenth-century North American attitude that the forest was basically a temporary obstacle to agricultural expansion, government would not recognize the ongoing necessity for settlers in marginal areas to supplement farm production with income from the woods. The fiction was even perpetuated in the colonists' protest petitions which focused upon the companies' illegal cutting of trees

required for construction purposes rather than upon local dependence on a mixed economy. Presumably it would have been folly
for the petitioners to admit that they were forced to trespass on
crown timber limits. Ironically, then, the lumber barons had little
reason to challenge the agrarian bias of government, since prior to
the 1880s the timber lords themselves generally perceived the pine
and spruce forests to be a non-renewable resource.[145] The consequence was that settlers would be seen as little more than a nuisance
provided that trespass could be forestalled and licence holders could
continue to enjoy cutting privileges on colonists' non-patented lots.
But, when Pope began to promote European settlement in eastern
Compton County during the early 1870s, settlers were becoming
serious competitors because of his own railroad's penetration into
the upper St Francis district. With most of the timber leases cut over
by this time, and the post-Confederation provincial regime dedicat-
ing large chunks of the district to various colonization experiments,
Pope simply removed himself a step or two from the lumber business.
Clark and Company survived a few years longer only by turning
increasingly to their private holdings.

CHAPTER SIX

"The Pope's Own Parish": Nationalism and Conflict at Piopolis, 1871–81

La vie du colon, c'est la vie du soldat, combattant sur un autre champ contre les ronces et les épines que Dieu a désignées comme devant être arrachées à la sueur de notre front. Cette victoire gagnée à la pointe du soc est digne de l'ambition d'un zouave du Pape; car c'est la conquête, par le travail, du sol encore inhabité et sa mise en valeur.

Benjamin-Antoine-Testard de Montigny,
Bulletin de l'Union Allet, juin et juillet 1880

Commenting on the French-Canadian anxiety about their minority status in North America, Fernand Ouellet has noted that "before 1837, the demographic peril unleashed an aggressive action against the English and an attempted conquest of political power; after 1840, it was channelled towards the conquest of new areas."[1] By the 1870s, in Arthur Silver's words, "colonizers spoke of sending out detachments of settlers as if they were units of soldiers on military campaigns."[2] The vocabulary and images of armed conflict were not surprising choices for spokesmen who wished to communicate forcefulness and determination of purpose. Furthermore, the terminology of slogans such as "Emparons-nous du sol" would strike a responsive chord in the North American context where the wilderness was widely viewed as both enemy and plunder. The interpretations of most historians, including Ouellet and Silver, is that the aggressive language chosen by advocates of French-Canadian colonization was aimed essentially at inspiring habitants to face the difficult challenges of Quebec's inhospitable frontier. Fundamentally, the rhetoric reflected not an aggressive expansionism but rather a defensive reaction; it was a cry to erect barricades against the encroachment of a modern, individualistic, and secularizing society.

Researchers more sensitive to the role of myth have begun to challenge this widely held view. Thus, religious sociologist Gabriel Dussault argues that colonization proponents were calling for nothing less than the "reconquête" of French Canada's dominant North American role in every sense of the term; geographer Christian Morissonneau declares that the "myth of the North" was "une réaction dynamique et optimiste de l'élite à un défi vital"; and literary historian Bernard Proulx stresses the fact that early novelists promoted industrialization and urbanization as necessary components of their idealized colonization centres.[3] These authors present convincing evidence for their case that the promotional message of the colonization movement was in many respects pragmatic and affirmative in nature, even though they fail to explain the paradox of its inspirational, utopian tone. The overblown rhetoric probably reflected insecurity rather than optimism – after all, the reality of impoverished settlers struggling on the Laurentian and Appalachian frontiers must have been difficult to ignore. Furthermore, the colonization movement did originate in response to a perceived social threat, even though that threat was not the modern, industrial world per se, but rather the attraction held by its New England manifestation for the impoverished habitants of Quebec.[4] Because the annual emigration of thousands of French-Canadian families was perceived to imperil "la survivance," the nationalist élite could only respond by urging a collective assault on Quebec's vast untapped wilderness. Their militaristic terminology represents neither empty posturing on the one hand, nor a sudden surge of aggressive optimism on the other, but rather a grim determination to survive by gradually expanding the traditional frontiers of their society. The peculiar combination of defensiveness and defiance underlying the colonization movement is effectively expressed in the words of Labelle's Laurentian colleague, Abbé T.S. Provost:

Qui sait si le peuple canadien ne sera pas trop heureux un jour d'aller chercher un asile dans ces montagnes ou de cacher derrière elles les restes de sa nationalité? Les guerres et les persécutions font monter les hommes vers les haut lieux. Et puis quelles populations ont plus d'énergie et de force que celles des montagnes? ... Il y a du roc dans les âmes comme dans la nature.[5]

The enemy was not simply the thickly forested, rocky, upland soil, but the absentee proprietors, timber merchants, and immigrant settlers from Britain who either controlled or threatened to control that soil. As a source of inspiration the imagery of war was particularly appropriate to the promotion of Piopolis, a colony originally founded for the papal Zouaves returning from military duty in Italy.

In fact that imagery would take on more than a symbolic value as the young veterans and their fellow French-speaking colonists came into conflict with G.B. Hall's lumber company, the Highland Scots settlers, and English-speaking land speculators. The French-Canadian colonizers and colonists were aggressive enough to cause a concerted regional backlash, but the Catholic Church was too respectful of authority to permit the situation to develop into one of physical violence against the local Scots, and the nationalist bourgeoisie was too respectful of property to challenge effectively a system which entrenched externally owned landholding and lumbering corporations.

Just as Britain's concession of responsible government was followed by an ambitious colonization roads programme in 1848, so the creation of a separate Quebec legislature in 1867 led to a renewed emphasis on French-Canadian expansion into back townships. In the words of one newspaper editor:

Parmi les rares attributions laissés aux gouvernements locaux, se trouve le contrôle exclusif des terres publiques. C'est une épave qui reste au milieu de naufrage de l'ancienne constitution, et si nous devons être sauvés, ce sera sur cette planche de salut que nous le serons ... Emparons-nous du sol, si nous voulons conserver notre nationalité.[6]

The new provincial regime may have placed most of its faith in railways and industries as agencies to counteract the accelerating exodus to New England's mill towns, but it nevertheless responded to nationalist pressure by introducing the Colonization Societies Act of 1869.[7] Blocks of crown land, located for the most part in the Lake Megantic area, would be reserved for societies whose aim was to organize and subsidize settlement by residents of their parishes. The size of each society's reserve depended upon the number of occupants it wished to establish, with the maximum set at 12,000 acres. The regular crown land fee of sixty cents per acre had to be paid, but colonization societies could receive a government grant based on the sum contributed by their members, up to six hundred dollars in some cases. The societies in turn would distribute their funds according to the amount of clearing each of their settlers had made. The programme was initially to last three years, but its life-span was later extended to April 1875.[8]

The only group to attract a significant number of settlers was the Société Générale de Colonisation de Montréal which eventually amalgamated eight city-based associations.[9] The driving force behind its activities was Abbé Edmond Moreau, dedicated ultramontane and chaplain of the province's papal Zouaves. His aim was to direct the

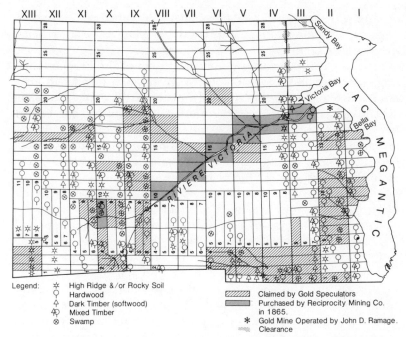

Legend:
☼ High Ridge &/or Rocky Soil
♀ Hardwood
♀ Dark Timber (softwood)
♀♀ Mixed Timber
⊗ Swamp

▨ Claimed by Gold Speculators
▪ Purchased by Reciprocity Mining Co. in 1865.
✳ Gold Mine Operated by John D. Ramage.
▨ Clearance

Map 14   Marston Township. Physical characteristics and gold speculation, to 1865 (ANQ-Q, NC 82–5–3, D-320, Frontenac, s.d., Section de la carte: canton Marston, Qué.; Qué. Énergie, Mines, et Ressources, Service Arpentage, Canton M.13B, Plan of the survey of the Residue of the Township of Marston by F.W. Blaiklock, 1862; Ch.29, Plan of an Exploratory Road Line from the US Boundary ... to the Megantic Road, Sept. 1861; Qué., Agriculture et Colonisation, adj. 4117, 4279; Sherbrooke Registry Office, Reg. B., vol. 18, p. 474, no. 347)

idealistic young returnees to an organized colony in Marston Township on the western shore of Lake Megantic.[10]

They would not be the first settlers at the lake for during the 1850s Hebridean Scots had crossed thirty miles of intervening frontier to take advantage of the plentiful supplies of fish and perhaps also the Chaudière River outlet to the Quebec timber market.[11] The Megantic Road did not come within two miles of the lake until 1858, but by 1861 there were one hundred Scots in Marston.[12] Three years later a short-lived gold rush in the Chaudière headwaters caused the government to modify its land-grant conditions to promote the local industry. All royalties and gold and silver reservations were dropped, but the price of crown lots purchased for mining purposes was increased from sixty cents to two dollars an acre.[13] Two separate groups of mining speculators took out location tickets on eighty lots (15,600 acres) scattered throughout Marston Township (see map 14). The larger group saw its lots reclaimed by the crown in 1870, after only the initial down payment had been met, and the Reciprocity Mining Company of New York lost its location tickets shortly thereafter.[14]

The speed of the cancellations was a result of the new post-Confederation provincial regime's active colonization policy. After exploring the old BALC line from Otter Brook Road in Hampden Township to the southern shore of Lake Megantic, the local crown lands agent had reported in 1868 that the fifteen-mile route would open the best block of wild land in his agency.[15] By 1870 construction had begun on what ultimately became known as the Bury and Megantic Road, and the St Francis and Megantic International Railway was projected to run from Sherbrooke to Lake Megantic, thereby ensuring that the newly formed colonization societies would take an active interest in Marston Township.[16]

Although the colonization societies project was clearly designed to stimulate French-Canadian colonization exclusively, the government had to consider the sensibilities of the English- (and Gaelic-) speaking population in the region. Consequently, the largest reserve in Marston, over 23,000 acres, was made by the province's three English-speaking societies, based in the towns of Quebec and Sherbrooke, as well as in Compton County (see appendix C and map 15.) Their aim was to attract British immigration, but together they managed to settle only seven Scots families before becoming moribund in 1872.[17] Meanwhile, the later-established but much more active Montreal societies were restricted to 12,000 acres in Marston, having received the bulk of their reserves across the lake in the less accessible township of Ditchfield. The resulting land pressure would contribute to perhaps the most serious cultural clash in the history of the Eastern Townships.

The Montreal societies did not begin their activities in Marston until the spring of 1871 when Abbé Moreau asked Bishop Louis-François Laflèche of Trois-Rivières to appoint one of his priests to accompany fifteen to twenty recently returned Zouaves to Lake Megantic, "car une bande de jeunes gens réunis se gâte vite, comme vous le savez, sans une forte surveillance."[18] Each Zouave veteran was to receive five dollars per month for two years, in addition to sharing access to the society's large "chantier," its two teams of oxen, and its store of supplies at cost. To gain the same privileges, other colonists would have to pay fifty dollars to the colonization society, but apparently only seven ex-Zouaves accompanied Father Alphonse Séguin, the priest chosen, in April.[19] As a group, the inexperienced young men would play an essentially symbolic role in the colony, just as they indeed had by going to Rome in the first place.[20] It appears that no more than a dozen of the close to four hundred

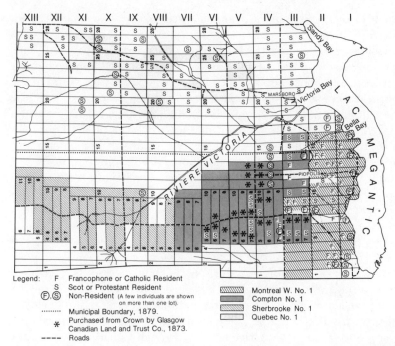

Map 15   Colonization Society reserves (to 1875) and settlement in Marston Township, 1876 (ANQ-Q, NC 82–5–3, D-320, Frontenac, s.d., Section de la carte: canton Marston, Qué., Qué., Agriculture et Colonisation, Branche Est, O.C. 940, 953, 954, 959, 982; Section Ouest, adj. 4474; Cookshire Registry Office, Reg. B., vol. 8, pp. 73–100, no. 4361–83)

papal recruits actually ever lived in what became the parish of Saint-Zenon-de-Piopolis, christened in honour of Pope Pius IX as well as a saint who was being credited with miracles throughout the province.[21]

The Montreal societies had no difficulty, however, in filling their Marston lots with settlers. During the colony's first year of operations (1871–72) they invested $2596, most of which went to hire labour and purchase provisions. The following year they distributed an additional $1023 among their colonists, reportedly 130 in number by July 1873.[22] Piopolis appeared to be well on the way to self-sufficiency, with one small sawmill in operation, a second under construction, and a large steam-operated mill planned by an American entrepreneur in anticipation of the railroad's arrival.[23] Luck was not with the settlers, however, for late spring rains had delayed their slash-burning operations and fall crops were destroyed by two nights of frost.[24]

To make matters worse, G.B. Hall and Company of Montmorency Falls had taken out a seventy-six-square-mile timber lease in Marston the previous year.[25] In the dramatic words of the Zouave publication, the *Bulletin de l'Union-Allet*: "un beau jour, un étranger arrive dans la Colonie pour engager les bucherons. Mais pour où travailler? Dans Piopolis même; c'était ça qui était commode? M.Hall faisait chantier sur les terres de nos Zouaves, et leur offrait de l'ouvrage pour l'hiver, sans presque se déranger, à la porte de leurs cabanes!" The article concluded bitterly that "le gouvernment avait deux cordes à son arc, ... il vendait au riche marchand de Québec, la coupe des bois, mais il *réservait* le fonds ruiné pour le pauvre colon."[26] The colony protested vigorously but to little avail as no lot in a colonization reserve could be removed from a crown timber berth until a settler had taken out a location ticket: "Et voilà comment il se fait, que nos pauvres colons, vont avoir de l'ouvrage à leur portes, en aidant à piller et à ruiner leurs terres. Ils auront toujours la consolation de dire à leurs enfants, *qu'il y avait autrefois de bien belles sucreries sur le sol qui les aura vus naître, et qu'ils les ont mêmes vues.*"[27]

It was small comfort for the settlers that any lots they claimed before the fall renewal of Hall's licence would legally be removed from the lease, for the Quebec-based timber company would clearly destroy any hopes that a major local sawmilling industry might develop once the railway arrived.[28] The French-Canadian community continued to grow, however, supported as it was by generous grants from the Montreal colonization society. Over $2000 was distributed in Piopolis in the fiscal year 1873–74, and another $4970 went towards operations in Marston and Ditchfield in 1874–75, the last year before termination of the Colonization Societies Act.[29]

The colony continued to be promoted in the most romantic and nationalist of terms. The heroic settlers were said to be "heureux, contents, leur santé florissante" despite the hardships they faced. "On se doute fort, peu même dans notre pays, encore moins en Europe, des misères endurées par ces hardis colons qui, la hache à la main, se frayent les premiers un chemin à travers la forêt." The use of alcoholic beverages might be widespread, but it did not lead to drunkeness in the midst of the forest. And the few Zouaves who remained at Piopolis were enough to add a special spiritual quality to the colony: "Que dirions-nous, que pouvons-nous penser de ceux qui ont été bénis par la main de l'auguste Pie IX; que ne pouvons-nous espérer des oeuvres de ces jeunes gens, oeuvres faits non dans l'espoir d'un lucre impatient, avide et rapide, mais ainsi que nous le disait l'un d'entre eux, oeuvres faites pour l'honneur du régiment béni par Pie IX."[30] To ensure and to demonstrate that in Piopolis man did not live by bread alone, the colony's promoters decided to open a popular library in 1875. Week-old newspapers would be forwarded by the Zouaves' "casino," and the public was invited to contribute books and brochures. By 1878 the collection held approximately two hundred volumes, including the complete fifteen-volume illustrated works of Jules Verne. The curé, however, never reported more than sixteen readers.[31]

When Canon Moreau inspected the fruits of his colonization societies' Marston investments in the fall of 1875, he found fifty-nine resident families with three hundred acres under improvement, two schools, a chapel, a post-office, a steam-powered saw- and grist-mill, thirty homes, and only sixty-eight cattle.[32] The colony's growth had been restricted by a land shortage ever since its origins, with the result that a series of expropriations had already taken place before 1875 when relations with the neighbouring Scots came close to the fighting point.

With the arable lots in its 4817-acre reserve all spoken for as early as the fall of 1871, the society known as Montréal-Ouest no 1 had asked three Scottish immigrants to drop their claims to land within the reserve.[33] John Hume, the region's inspector of crown land agencies, outlined the background to the situation:

It cannot be denied that on the first establishment of the French settlers in that locality there was some feeling of hostility between the two nationalities. The Scotch settlers looked with a degree of jealously [sic] upon the possession of the lands in their immediate vicinity by a class of people who spoke French instead of Gaelic, and more especially as the reserve above mentioned was composed in whole or in part, of lands the previous sales of which had been cancelled; while on the other hand the Scotch were styled "des colons etrangers."[34]

The Scottish claimants refused to budge, which quickly led to an open confrontation. Abbé Moreau claimed that the Scots were being encouraged by some unseen hand to drive the French Canadians out of the township:

la forme de leur raisonnement est qu'ils sont les premiers rendues et les premiers occupants, que ce township a commencé à être défriché par eux et qu'il leur appartient; et ils sont bien décidés, disent-ils, à ne pas laisser établir dans cette partie, les Canadiens qui finiraient par les chasser.

The Canadiens' answer to the Scots' obstinacy was: "Nous ne vous craignons pas, vous n'avez que de rateux [sic] et nous nous [sic] avons de bonne carabines." Moreau, fearing that the situation would deteriorate into armed conflict, asked for protection.[35]

The government's initial response was to assign John Hume to investigate. He recommended that one of the three Scottish claimants lose his lot on the grounds that he had made no improvements, but the other two individuals posed a more complex problem. Each had cleared about one and a half acres, and both were residing in log houses. They spoke English poorly, having come the previous year from a western island of Scotland (presumably Lewis). Their statement that William Farwell, the local crown lands agent, had given them permission to take the lots was corroborated by him. He justified his action by stating that he had not been told that the area was to become a colonization society reserve. Nevertheless, Hume warned the two settlers that, regardless of Farwell's word, their claim was not strictly legal because they had failed to make a cash deposit.[36] Still they stubbornly refused to accept the Montreal society's offer to pay them one hundred dollars for their improvements. A solution was reached only when pressure was brought to bear on the society through another land dispute.

In March the dormant English-Canadian Compton Colonization Society had given permission to the Montreal society to settle 1200 acres of its Marston reserve. There was one condition–that the Montreal society inform the Compton president before any of the lots were granted. Because Montreal's local agent failed to do this, the Compton society insisted upon cancelling the grants he had made from its reserve. When the curé of Piopolis begged that the settlers not be forced to suffer because of the oversights of others, the Compton society president suggested that if the two Highland settlers were allowed to remain on their lots, he would permit at least an equal number of French Canadians to do the same. Upon Hume's recommendation that a compromise along these lines be accepted, the controversy was finally resolved.[37]

This did not solve the Montreal society's land problem, so its members petitioned the government to rescind those grants in Marston upon which settlement conditions were not being fulfilled. Not all the French-Canadian settlers agreed with the society's tactics. In a letter to *Le Pionnier*, "Un colon de l'Est" accused the Zouaves of encouraging the government to drive the "anglais" from the Eastern Townships. He claimed that upon his arrival in Marston his neighbours had created jobs for him and kept him from begging. He chastized the Zouaves:

Vous voulez chasser mon voisin, faites-le. Je lui dois mon morceau de terre; moi, ma femme et mes enfants lui devons la petite aisance que nous possédons. ... Au lieu de nous revenir tels que vous nous aviez quittés, vous nous revenez plus guerriers que jamais. Vous ne pouvez pas endurer vos voisins. En conséquence, je vous conseille de retourner en Italie ... De nouveau, en présence du Grand Pontife, je vous prie d'ouvrir les yeux et les oreilles; étudiez sa conduite et tâchez de l'imiter tant soit peu.[38]

It was easy to sympathize with the local Scots, but, as Inspector Hume soon learned, they were not the only non–French-Canadian land claimants. Only fourteen of thirty-seven location tickets issued for the first three ranges were in the hands of residents. The gold speculators had lost their claims only to be replaced in part by a second group who had anticipated the railway's construction through Marston. Hume recommended cancellations, but only after sufficient time had elapsed to prove that each claimant was not acting in good faith. He also advised caution with regard to the older location tickets of those who lived in or near the township and who had paid the full instalments: "I would most respectfully take the liberty to remark that unless it can be considered as a common practice to cancel such sales, the doing of it in a settlement, composed of two different nationalities cannot fail to excite hostile feelings."[39]

Hume's warnings were timely because trouble had already developed in June when a Major William McMinn had threatened a French-speaking colonist with forceable removal from one of the lots he claimed. The colonist wrote to the press that "il me semble que le méfait dont cet individu s'est rendu coupable est d'autant plus grave que notre isolement nous met plus à le merci des vauriens de ce genre."[40] Faced with growing nationalist pressure, the government ignored Hume's advice by cancelling nine location tickets in September 1872, even though four had been issued since 1870 and three had been paid in full. The only local resident to lose land, however, was Major McMinn who quickly regained his 177 acres because he had met all five payments.[41]

There was no public outcry against the limited confiscations of 1872, but in 1875 the Montreal society's relentless demands for more land led to a second series of twenty cancellations in Marston and one in Ditchfield, which caused a furor throughout the Gaelic- and English-speaking communities of Compton County. The flames were fanned by none other than the bellicose major, who had lost two and a half lots this time. McMinn was one of the more colourful characters among the pioneers of Lake Megantic. Although he was a Scottish immigrant, his status was far from that of the poor Lewis crofters whose spokesman he claimed to be, for he had been educated in law at Edinburgh, and he remained a member of the Church of Scotland rather than the evangelistic Free Kirk. "A man of somewhat peculiar appearance" with a marked squint to one eye, McMinn had gained his military rank by fighting for the Confederacy in the Civil War. Forty-seven years old in 1875, the confirmed bachelor lived alone in a log cabin at Lake Megantic. He was no hermit, however, for he could frequently be found in local drinking establishments; he made lengthy visits to Montreal; and he did not shrink from involvement in local political squabbles.[42]

McMinn, who appears to have needed no visible means of financial support, was in an ideal position to organize a local branch of the Protestant Defence Alliance of Canada, and to publicize the protest in the pages of Montreal's rabidly anti-Catholic *Daily Witness*.[43] The first public meeting, held at the Winslow village of Stornoway in January 1876, included representatives from seven local townships. As secretary, McMinn described the audience's militant mood to the sympathetic readers of the *Witness*:

The crowd entered the building and seated themselves with the same decorous quietness that congregations do in the House of God, and no shuffling or noise of feet was made by the large proportion that had to stand during the whole proceedings. No need to call them to order when a Chairman and Secretary were nominated. Simultaneously they rose and reverently inclined themselves, while the Chairman invoked the divine blessing on their counsels. It was easy to see that these men met for no common purpose. Can it be possible that they met to demand civil and religious liberty – equal rights to all, irrespective of creed or nationality? Can it be possible that such a demand can be necessary within the Imperial British Empire in this nineteenth century? ... Would that you all had been present like myself to see the quiet, determined attitude of these men as they unanimously raised their right hands in token of their approval of each resolution – to my eye it seemed as if each hand held a shining glave ... Pause, Ultramontanes before my imaginary glave becomes a real one!

The chairman, a local Presbyterian minister, opened the meeting with a rousing condemnation of the land sale cancellations, not only of Protestants, but of two Irish Catholics "who cannot be led by Ultramontanes as sheep like French-Canadians." The mayor of Marston moved, seconded by the mayor of Whitton:

That whereas that liberty, which is the birthright of every British subject is endangered, as appears by the conduct of the Local Government in its cancelling lands held by Protestant and Irish Roman Catholics at Lake Megantic for the purposes of forming a compact French Canadian parish, thus stirring up national feelings, this meeting solemnly and emphatically protests against such conduct, and resolves to use all legitimate means for obtaining equal justice to all.

Motions were also passed protesting the repatriation colony, recently founded in nearby Ditton, Chesham, and Emberton townships, as well as the government's decision to freeze funding for south-shore railway construction. The mayor of Bury lamented that "there was no doubt but we were thoroughly ignored by the present Local Government, and treated as if we had no right to live in this section of the country, as if we were aliens and not British subjects." J.H. Pope, whose struggling International Railway stood to benefit from any pressure that would encourage the province to increase its construction subsidy, stated that "they were real grievances, such as no government should tolerate, far less perpetuate." He promised to do his utmost to see that the land title cancellations were put to a stop. Finally, whether or not Pope supported the motion, the meeting concluded by forming a branch of the Protestant Defence Alliance.[44]

McMinn himself charged that Protestant land was being seized "to make compact the Pope's own parish, Piopolis ... It only requires the establishment of the Inquisition to fill their cup of folly to the overflow."[45] But the tone of a letter written by "A Conservative of the Eastern Townships," was still more belligerent. This correspondent conceded that in many cases the settlers had failed to fulfil official conditions to the letter, but he complained that the government, traditionally careless in collecting payments, was now oppressing settlers not of the "favored nationality":

The unfortunate settler who is in arrears, no matter how much money and labour he may have expended in the endeavour to make a home for himself and his family in these back woods – perhaps seventy miles from Sherbrooke and ten miles from the nearest railway station – can expect no mercy if he is not a French Canadian. His lands are cancelled. His improvements lost ...

The "schemers" had better beware, for as sure as they are born, if they rouse the old Gaelic blood in those back settlements, there will be such a "tempest in a tea-pot" that it will require a stronger power than the Quebec Government to stop it. The farce if continued may end in tragedy and the scenes of '37 be played over – as the play-bills put it – with an "entire change of characters and programme!"[46]

The bombastic rhetoric, exaggerated though it was, sprang from a genuine concern for the future of the Scottish community in eastern Compton County. The ultramontane-oriented ministry of Charles-

Eugène Boucher de Boucherville was, after all, systematically settling the frontier with French Canadians, thereby choking off expansion by succeeding generations of Scots. But, most important, several of those who had lost their Marston lands did have legitimate cause for complaint, as investigator John Hume soon learned.[47]

According to Hume, Malcolm McLean's case was one of those which excited the greatest indignation. In 1871 he had purchased three half-lots (two in his sons' names), cleared thirty acres on two of them, and built two houses. All the payments were faithfully made, yet the government seized one of his half-lots with four acres cleared and one to one and a half acres in crop. There was no dwelling place upon it because he and his sons lived nearby. (Since 1859 several members of one family could live in the same house while holding more than one lot.)[48] Even the Montreal society's local agent, Father J.B.A. Cousineau of Piopolis, conceded that this cancellation was too severe, and Hume advised strongly that the land be returned.

To be fair to the Crown Lands Office, the McLean cancellation, as well as several others, was based upon the report of an inexperienced surveyor named Wright who rather consistently underestimated the amount of clearing done.[49] Thus J.F. McIver had lost his lot on the grounds that he had chopped only two acres of trees and built no house, but he had actually cleared six acres and he lived nearby. Hume felt that McIver too should regain his lot.

Another alleged victim was the Catholic Henry Ryan who in 1874 acquired 2149 acres of crown land by borrowing the names of people in his native Ireland. Not only was his plan to settle Irish families on these holdings greeted with enthusiasm by government officials, but the Montreal colonization society itself allowed him to purchase lots from its reserve.[50] Ryan, however, concentrated his efforts upon the 313 acres which he had bought in his own name. On one lot he chopped over an area of 50 acres (25 of which he cleared completely), as well as investing $400 in buildings and an equal amount on a mile and a half of road. On another lot he chopped 2 treed acres and cleared for cultivation 2 more. When, eighteen months after the sale, all but his 313-acre tract was taken back by the government, Ryan was said to have forfeited not only the $220 in cancelled sales, but $700 to $800 in improvements. The cancellations had followed demands by Canon Moreau, which in turn were a result of a disagreement between Ryan and Father Cousineau. Hume recommended that Ryan be given back some of his lost land, and that he be credited for the amount paid on the remainder.

The fourth case involved the Glasgow Canadian Land and Trust Company, a private colonization enterprise which lost four lots in

Marston. Because he had made no inspection, the surveyor had mistakenly reported that there were no improvements upon three of the lots. Furthermore, there was already a house built and an acre slashed of underbrush on one of the company's lots when a colonist named François Ladriarche took possession. Though asked to leave, he refused to do so. When Father Cousineau rejected the request to intervene on the part of the company manager, Aeneas McMaster, Ladriarche was taken to court. He was condemned for trespassing, but to prevent his going to jail, McMaster paid the thirty dollars in costs. In spite of this act of generosity, Cousineau complained to the Crown Lands Department concerning McMaster's behaviour. He claimed that there had been only "une espèce de chantier" on the lot. When the department refused to act, he "again and again asked for the cancellation of the sale of this lot." He accused the company of overcharging the settlers, criticized the method of slashing used, and stated that the company houses were less than five feet between floor and ceiling. Hume contradicted all of these charges. He also remarked that no colonization company could be expected to settle every lot of 10,000 acres within two years, and concluded that it was unfair to cancel sales when actual clearing was taking place, and when only half the time allotted for the performance of settlement duties had elapsed.

The final complainant dealt with in Hume's report was Major McMinn himself. His one and a half lots in Marston had been paid in full even before their first cancellation in 1872, and improvements had been made since that time. Hume argued that "the Revenue of the Province is suffering severely from the great majority of settlers, and others purchasing Crown Lands, neglecting or refusing to pay more than the first installment thereon, or occupying lands without making any payment at all upon them." Therefore those who made prompt payment warranted some consideration, "and they should be seriously warned to perform the conditions of settlement, and even some extra delay given them to do so, before the sale of their lands are cancelled and the money paid thereon forfeited."

But the real controversy centered around McMinn's Ditchfield lot. According to colonist Cyprien Beaudoin's own statement, he took possession of the lot upon finding it unoccupied. Soon after beginning his clearing operations, he found a paper fixed to a tree stating that the land belonged to McMinn. It ordered that he cease work, and asked him to go to McMinn's residence for payment on what he had accomplished. The note was ignored, but a month later McMinn's men also began to clear the lot and build a house on it. Beaudoin and six or seven armed men subsequently ordered them away, "and commenced falling trees all over the place they had cleared." McMinn's crew did leave, but soon returned to resume their work. Beaudoin and his men then chopped the house logs in half, and threw brush and trees over the site where the house was being erected. McMinn asked Father Cousineau to intervene, again promising to pay Beaudoin for the work he had done. Cousineau later told Hume that he had done what McMinn had asked, and that Beaudoin had agreed to place the value of improvements before arbitration. But Hume deduced that even if Beaudoin had been willing to reach such an agreement, this had not been made clear to McMinn. Hume's report concluded that "a greater outrage, in connection with the unauthorized occupation of land I have never known committed." Beaudoin could not even claim the right of possession because he had only been on the land for a month. "The news of the outrage excited as may be naturally supposed, strong feelings of indignation amongst the Scotch settlers, and their extreme moderation in not resenting it in a manner which might have produced unfortunate results, is to me, a matter of both surprise and admiration." The government had cancelled the sale of the lot, though McMinn had used every legitimate means to obtain redress. Furthermore, he was told that he could not purchase it again, even by again paying the full amount of the purchase money he had forfeited. On Cousineau's recommendation to the Department of Crown Lands, Beaudoin was to get the lot.

In Hume's general conclusions, he wrote that many people had told him that no serious complaints would have been made

had the sale of all lands in the locality, in the same situation been cancelled, and had all classes been permitted to repurchase them. But they cannot understand why the Directors of the Montreal Society claim the exclusive privilege of purchasing all lands the sale of which is cancelled, no matter of what origin the first purchasers are, and that in a Township where the first settlers were, and three fourths of the present actual residents are, of British origin.

The reply might be that it was departmental practice to permit the person who applied for cancellation of the sale of a lot to become the purchaser. But if this rule were to be invariably acted upon, English-speaking settlers could make the same requests for French-settled lands whose conditions were not fulfilled. As an example of the Montreal society's overzealousness, Hume cited the formal demand of Canon Moreau for cancellation of three lots in the Compton society reserve, although on each of them two instalments had been paid, a house erected, and one acre rough-cleared.

Hume's recommendations were subsequently approved by the commissioner of crown lands, and the dissolution of the colonization societies eased the pressure for collective cancellations of location tickets.[51] A state of peaceful, if not always harmonious, coexistence developed between Marston's French-Canadian and Scottish populations. When the township was divided into two municipalities in 1879, the few Scottish settlers remaining in the south reportedly moved north to settle among their compatriots.[52] Rather than selling farms to French Canadians, however, they simply abandoned lots which had been transferred from the Compton Colonization Society to the Glasgow Canadian Company in 1873 (see map 15). The company's purchase of twenty-three crown lots alongside the access roads to Piopolis remained a long-standing irritant to the French Canadians for it seriously hindered their expansion.[53]

The company would at least be required legally to contribute taxes to the Catholic schools of Marston South, which became a distinct school district at the time of the municipal division.[54] The Catholics had declared dissident status for one of the township's five schools in 1876, but because of difficulty in maintaining the legally required number of elected syndics, it appears to have seldom been open.[55] School assessments were apparently sacrificed to other financial obligations on the part of the Piopolis colonists, for, in addition to the annual municipal levy, they were obliged to support their church (see table 17).[56] Although permission was required from their elected parish council before parish property could be improved, the bishop was not inclined to accept excuses for delays.[57] Based on the cash value of the 1877 church collections, it appears that each family contributed the equivalent of approximately four dollars per year. This may seem little enough, but during the late 1870s the colonists remained isolated and impoverished. A traveller noted in 1877 that "most of all the buildings are of the roughest materials covered with shingles, boards, bark, and some with straw."[58] When the long-anticipated International Railway did reach Lake Megantic in 1879, it skirted Marston Township almost entirely with the result that by 1882 the local American-owned mill had been pushed out of business by its competitors at the foot of the lake.[59]

Poor as Piopolis remained, however, as far as the Catholic Church was concerned, it represented a model parish. Prior to 1881, at least, the curé had no disturbances to complain of in his annual reports, and the only "pecheur scandaleux" was a concubine mentioned in

Table 17
Population and Church Taxes for Saint-Zenon-de-Piopolis, 1872–81
(includes Marston, Ditchfield, Whitton, and Hampden Townships)

Date	Pop.	Families	Commun-icants	Fabrique Receipts[1]	Tithe (minots grain & $)	Supplement (tons hay, minots potatoes)
1872	130	–	90	–	–	–
1875	–	–	–	$167	–	–
1876	293	72	197	$199	–	–
1877[2]	383	82	244	$200	78m., $76	½t., 15m. & 20 lb.
1878	505[3]	106	322	$231	225m., $79	2.3t., 84m.
1879	600	123	388	$210	222m., $53	2.5t., 50m.
1880	439[4]	97	285	$144	216m., $67	$46 hay, 66m.
1881	473	100	292	$142	158m., $96	6.2t., 45m.

Source: AAS, Rapports sur les paroisses et missions, Saint-Zenon-de-Piopolis; Presbytère de Pio-
    polis, Cahiers de comptes pour la chapelle; Cahier de délibérations.
1 The curé's annual report does not always agree with the fabrique's accounts. The latter are
    given where there are discrepancies. A small portion of these funds is gifts from outsiders.
2 The cash value of $129 for the tithe and supplement is given for this year.
3 Statistics also recorded for Marston alone: 291 individuals, 58 families, 183 communicants.
4 Population must reflect a division of the parish, for the curé reported that eleven new families
    had arrived and only three had departed for the U.S.

1880. Religious observance continued to be faithful, with no more
than one or two individuals failing to make their Easter confes-
sions.[60] The religio-nationalist idealism of the colony's founders continued to be cultivated by the small local élite, whose numbers
included a couple of remaining Zouaves and the ultramontane Premier Boucherville's nephew.[61] Their ideological unity was strong
enough to dampen the customary internal dissension concerning
ecclesiastial building projects. No liquor licence had been issued in
the parish as of 1896, and a local militia unit did its best to maintain
the Zouave tradition.[62] Members presented arms to the bishop each
evening during his three-day visit in 1876, and the following year,
on 3 June, they saluted the pope's fiftieth jubilee with an early morning rifle volley.[63]

Such displays of arms on religious occasions were symbolic acts of
defiance by a local minority (39 per cent of Marston's population in
1881) hemmed in alongside Lake Megantic by the Scots of northeastern Compton County and the English Canadians of the Eastern
Townships as a whole. In many respects the situation in Marston
had been ripe for a violent conflict between the two ethnic groups.
Not only did they speak different languages, they also came from

radically different backgrounds, each with its own deep-rooted, traditional values and strong sense of historical grievance. The Free-Kirk Highlanders harboured a profound antipathy towards Catholicism, and the ultramontane-influenced French Canadians certainly had no sympathy for Protestantism. To the anti-episcopal Scots, no church within the British Empire should hold the right to interfere in secular, governmental affairs; to the French Canadians the line between church and state was unclear. Each group could forward its own historical justification for local dominance: the Scots as the first settlers in the district, the French Canadians as the original colonists in the province. The Scots felt they were not welcomed by the French-controlled provincial administration; the French Canadians resented the federal government's encouragement of British colonization in Quebec.[64] Finally, both French Canadians and Scots were in Marston not simply to improve their economic status, but to avoid breaking the link with their respective cultural communities and heritages.

At the pioneering stage it was no doubt inevitable that each group would tacitly stake out its territorial claim, for future survival as a community depended upon neighbours who would support schools, churches, and other social institutions. Yet, the fact remains that despite dire threats and considerable bravado on both sides, no blows were ever actually struck. What explains the sharp contrast between Marston and a frontier such as Kansas where during the 1850s Yankee and Missourian pioneers labelled each other with the most derogatory epithets imaginable, then engaged in barbarous acts of mutual slaughter during the Civil War?[65] Of course there was no war to trigger strife in the Lake Megantic area, but to understand why violence never erupted there one must appreciate the internal social dynamics of both communities. To begin with, neither shared the victorious revolutionary tradition which fuelled the aggressive sense of moral purpose to be found among both northerners and southerners in Kansas.[66] The French-Canadian Patriotes had suffered a decisive defeat in 1837–38, and the battle of Culloden had dampened the defiant spirit of the Scottish Celts. Both groups were small minorities in the North American context, and it was no doubt becoming evident to the Highlanders as early as the 1870s that their cultural hegemony in northeastern Compton County was on the wane. As they became assimilated to the English-speaking world through schools, employment in the United States, and contacts with neighbouring settlements, the Scots began to disperse towards more promising economic frontiers. The upper St Francis district was certainly no Kansas breadbasket, and by 1881 their numbers were already declining in the original Highland stronghold of Winslow. Within a few years their bards would sing the bitter Gaelic lament:

Is it not sad how the Catholics
Have upset this place.
The homes of the Gaelic speakers
Belong to the Roman Catholics.
This is what has distressed me,
And has hurt my nature.
That I see only Frenchmen
In the glen where I was young.

....

Winslow is now a wilderness
Where the brave men grew up
Those plagues have taken Whitton,
And part of Marston itself.
They have Ben-Ness, and Ben-Barvas,
And also the town of Tolsta.
There is a priest in Lingwick,
And they've claimed Hampden.

....

Today I do not hear the Gaelic
Where the heroes were raised.
Sallow, dirty faces
I see instead of Clan MacLeod.
Not much longer will God of the Sabbath
Be in this place
With the offspring of the Catholics
The place is teaming alive.

....

The sallow French are plentiful
With them re-producing at such speed.
It was not by the strength of their arm
That they settled in the north bens.
But the Gaels were leaving them
And the Catholics taking over.

That's what brought them to the corries
And gave them the rights to the red hills.

....

Since those dirty, grumpy ones
Grabbed all the land
The deer and hares have deserted it,
And every animal of clean habit.
But the skunk of the wastelands stayed there,
He is of a similar nature.
And the toad did not move away,
It is a Catholic itself.[67]

"Oran na Frangaich" or "The French People's Song" expresses contempt, but not defiance. And Angus MacKay (Oscar Dhu), the only published local poet, wrote of his French-Canadian neighbours in the affectionate if condescending style of William Henry Drummond.[68] The failure of the Scots to resort to violence was certainly not due to a profound respect for authority, as the "Megantic Outlaw" incident would reveal in 1888–89.[69] But, in sharp contrast to their original exile from Lewis, rather than being driven off the land by a landlord's stewards, they were selling their farms of their own free will. The Scots may have been among the first settlers in the upper St Francis district, but they – not the French Canadians – were the uprooted ones. They formed strong attachments to their adopted home, as the nostalgic laments of Angus MacKay living in Seattle will attest, but it would be much easier for an English-speaking generation of Scots to abandon "dear old Compton County" than it had been for their parents and grandparents to leave their ancestral island.[70]

It is also important to remember that the Scots' anger was channelled, at least briefly, into an organized protest movement, and that the inspector of crown lands agencies ultimately defused their protests by redressing specific grievances. And even if some of them had been dissatisfied with his decisions, they would have realized that he, or the department he represented, controlled their fate on the crown lands. Marston was not located on a distant, western frontier, but in a long-settled province where institutions of social control were becoming ever more firmly entrenched.

The strength and assertiveness of the French Canadians lay in their organizational base and in their urgent sense of national mission, both of which were implanted by the Catholic Church. But the concomitant hierarchical control over the colony of Piopolis also explains why the francophones pulled back from violence when facing Hall's lumber company and speculators such as McMinn. Sympathetic as the colonization society and the local curé were with their cause, no official representative of the Catholic Church could condone violence in the face of constituted authority. While the French-Canadian colonists were encouraged to think of themselves as frontline soldiers in a war for cultural survival and Christian civilization, their élite's message was also that victory would be won by patience, perseverance, and suffering.

Constructing a "Colonization" Railway: The St Francis and Megantic International, 1869–79

And C.P.R.! undreamt of then –
  Great system yet to be,
Its rumbling thunders echoed not
  As now from sea to sea.
No rails from Sherbrooke to the "Lake"
  Invaded hill or glen –
John Henry Pope (old Compton's hope),
  Was but a stripling then.

Oscar Dhu (Angus MacKay), *Donald Morrison*

By the time of Confederation, as envious promoters of north-shore railway construction frequently pointed out, the southwestern corner of the Eastern Townships was well served by rail lines running from Montreal to the United States.[1] Further north, there were also two branches of the Grand Trunk linking Richmond and Arthabaskaville to Quebec and Trois-Rivières, respectively, but the entire eastern half of the region remained untouched by tracks. These townships were neither situated on the most direct routes between Montreal and the American seaboard, nor blessed with deep-rooted and prosperous agricultural communities which could lobby for local connectors or tempt capitalists with the potential of a market-based economy. The chances for state assistance increased, however, with the creation of the federal system of government in 1867. Susceptible to nationalist pressures in favour of French-Canadian colonization, the provincial regime favoured projects which would open new territory to economic development. But even though the provincially subsidized colonization societies focused their activities on the upper St Francis district, a disappointed Eastern Townships would ultimately find railway assistance limited by the priority given to construction on the north shore in a period of economic recession.

Fortunately for them, the British North American union had added a second arrow to the quiver of the south-shore entrepreneurs – national unity required a commercial rail connection between central Canada and the disgruntled Maritimes.[2] The shortest and therefore presumably the most viable path for such a link lay through Compton County and across northern Maine to Saint John, New Brunswick. Considerable political pressure would nevertheless be required to finance a rail line through some eighty miles of thinly settled and uninviting wilderness in Compton alone, especially when the federal government was preoccupied with building the transcontinental in the opposite direction. No one was better equipped to exert such pressure at all three levels of government than the Honourable John Henry Pope, federal minister of agriculture and acting minister of railroads.

The idea of a rail link from Lennoxville to Lake Megantic was first seriously broached by Pope in the spring and summer of 1868.[3] It was probably understood from the start that the BALC would lend support, since it still held much of its original grant in Bury, Lingwick, and Weedon townships. As for Pope, he owned valuable properties in Eaton Township, he operated a small gold mine in frontier Ditton Township, and he may have wished to tap new sources of timber for C.S. Clark and Company.[4] In the final analysis, however, Pope probably was driven primarily by the entrepreneur-politician's instinctive urge to promote economic development in his own constituency.

That urge was temporarily compromised when the railroad had to be incorporated to bypass much of Compton County by running to Lake St Francis and the lower Chaudière Valley, rather than to Lake Megantic as originally planned. The change of direction for what became known as the St Francis Valley and Kennebec project was a strategic necessity forced by rivalry from the Sherbrooke, Eastern Townships, and Kennebec Company, founded by Sherbrooke MLA Joseph Gibb Robertson. Incorporated on the same day in April 1869, the two companies were competing for a subsidy offered by the province to so-called colonization railways.[5] The aid was clearly designed to encourage the use of wooden rails, for it was limited to only $1,500 per mile, but Pope realized the importance of having one foot lodged in the government's doorway. Robertson's decision to link with the projected Lévis and Kennebec Railway, thus promising Quebec City an improved connection to the American seaboard, had given the Sherbrooke project an important advantage in the campaign for financial aid. To ensure that his political constituency was not bypassed entirely, Pope had simply devised a route

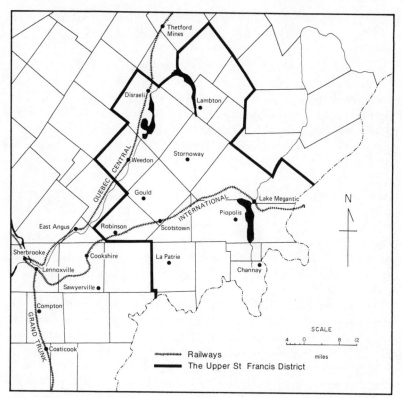

Map 16   Railway links to the Upper St Francis District to 1885 (From "Map of Montreal and the Eastern Townships" published by E.R. Smith & Sons, 1897)

which traversed Eaton, Westbury, and Bury townships before duplicating the Sherbrooke-Kennebec route by crossing to the northwestern shore of the St Francis River in Dudswell.[6]

Behind Robertson's Sherbrooke, Eastern Townships, and Kennebec project lay the Grand Trunk (GTR). Superintendent C.J. Brydges was a director of the company as was his friend A.T. Galt, though the latter no longer had a formal connection with the GTR.[7] Since it already operated a reasonably direct line between Quebec and Sherbrooke, the suspicion arises that the primary aim of the GTR was to block Pope's project. The GTR terminus, after all, was at Portland, while the St Francis railroad would gain access to Boston and New York via the Missawippi Valley Railway's headquarters at Lennoxville.[8] Our hypothesis is strengthened by the fact that the Robertson group had originally proposed three lines of hardwood rails from Sherbrooke to Weedon, Lake St Francis, and Lake Megantic, respectively.[9] Impractical as the scheme may have been, it was ideally suited to impeding the construction of any potential rival to the GTR.

Robertson's own motivation is less clear. As a citizen of Sherbrooke, and an elected representative who had to be sensitive to the demands of his constituency's largest population centre, he may have been resisting competition from the neighbouring village of Lennoxville. He had been an outspoken critic of the BALC which was tied to Pope's project through Commissioner Heneker, and there is always the possibility that he was secretly on the GTR's payroll.[10] Certainly the railway issue allowed Robertson to diminish the land company's political influence in his city, for he effectively took over the role of mayor from Heneker when the latter refused to support the Sherbrooke project.[11] According to Senator J.S. Sanborn, future vice-president of Pope's St Francis and Kennebec Company, Heneker was essentially powerless in this matter because "the prejudice against the Land Company renders anything coming from that quarter unavailing."[12]

The two railways could obviously not be built along essentially the same route, but, rather than making a choice between rival groups of Conservative party supporters, the provincial government offered half the regular subsidy to each.[13] Like Solomon, the administration realized that neither side could proceed unless the other backed down, or the two joined forces. The Sherbrooke-Kennebec Company quickly gained a head start by taking advantage of recent provincial legislation which encouraged municipal subsidization of railways.[14] The town of Sherbrooke subscribed $50,000 in stocks, and Dudswell and Weedon took $25,000 each.[15] Without a penny being directly invested by a private individual, Robertson's company had subscribed the one-sixth of its shares required before a board of directors could be elected.[16] Still stalled at the gate in 1870, the St Francis–Kennebec Company suffered the humiliation of seeing its rival claim the government's full subsidy.[17]

Rather than give up, however, the tenacious Pope rechristened his company the St Francis and Megantic International (know simply as the International after 1877), signifying a return to the original idea of laying track across Compton County to Lake Megantic. At the same time, Pope had somehow persuaded Galt to join his camp, for both men began to lobby the State of Maine to charter the Penobscot and Lake Megantic Railway Company as an eventual link to the Maritimes.[18] Their plan was clearly to make the International part of the projected transcontinental railroad, but the immediate reality was that a large amount of local capital would have to be raised before the project could move from the drawing board.

Support would be available from the Eastern Townships Bank, with two of its leading figures being Pope and Heneker, the railway company's president and secretary-treasurer, respectively. Furthermore, bank president Benjamin Pomroy was also on the railway's board of directors, but it was he who insisted on the conservative rule that no individual or firm could borrow more than $10,000. Heneker lifted this restriction when he became bank president in 1874, but despite the prominent role he played in the railway project, there is no evidence that his BALC became a major investor.[19] With few individuals willing to risk their capital in the International, it could not avoid emulating the Sherbrooke-Kennebec Company by seeking municipal subsidization. The problem was that most of Compton's townships were in the upper St Francis district and inhabited only by small numbers of poor settler-farmers. Of the two reasonably fertile and prosperous townships in the county, Compton and Eaton, the former was already served by the GTR and it would lie to the south of any reasonably direct line to Lake Megantic. Fortunately for the International's supporters, the county municipality rather anachronistically included the constituency of Sherbrooke – that is, Ascot and Orford townships as well as the town of Sherbrooke. The strategy therefore became one of gaining a subsidy from the county municipality rather than from individual townships.[20]

The first step was to organize opposition in Sherbrooke to Robertson's project. In the spring of 1870 a petition signed by forty-eight prominent city residents, whose collective property value was $126,000, protested the presence of the mayor and two councillors on the Sherbrooke-Kennebec Company's board, as well as the fact that no private parties had purchased stock. City council simply replied that the railway was not an ordinary commercial speculation, but an instrument to develop both town and countryside, and therefore it was only natural that ratepayers should finance it and that elected councillors should control it.[21] With Robertson et al. standing firm on the city's $50,000 stock purchase, Sherbrooke ratepayers soon found themselves faced with a new $45,000 tax bill – their share of the $225,540 in debentures (payable in twenty-five years at 6 per cent interest) voted by the county council for the International Railway. Robertson was sufficiently intimidated to suggest a compromise whereby a joint venture would ascend the St Francis twelve miles from Sherbrooke before turning eastwards into Compton

County, but Pope would accept no proposal that would bypass most of his home township of Eaton.[22]

The Compton MP's victory was not yet assured, however, for the ratepayers in nine of the county's fifteen local municipalities rejected his railway by-law. Not surprisingly, the opposition was centred in the Sherbrooke area – Sherbrooke Town, Ascot, Orford, Compton, Westbury – and in the peripheral colonization townships of Hereford, Auckland, and Clifton to the south and Saint-Romain-de-Winslow to the north.[23] On voting day the French Canadians of the latter parish had resisted the liberal dispensation of whiskey, as well as the pledge that a branch line would link Lake Megantic to the Lévis-Kennebec Railway via a rather circuitous route through Winslow. They had a right to be suspicious, for it was later charged that Pope had forged the signatures of Heneker and Sanborn to this pledge, read to the public only on the day of the vote.[24]

Still Pope refused to accept the Sherbrooke-Weedon deviation, and in the fall the International by-law was once again pushed through county council.[25] Persistence paid off, for a vigorous campaign resulted in the public's ratification of by-law 37 by the slim margin of eight local municipalities to seven. The French-Canadian municipalities had once again voted no, despite the advice of Fathers P.E. Gendreau of Cookshire and Jean-Baptiste Chartier of Coaticook, but the town of Sherbrooke had narrowly and surprisingly voted yes.[26] An outraged opposition charged that 1969 of the county's voters, representing $2,011,313 in property, were being subordinated to 1170 voters, representing only $918,609.[27]

The validity of the referendum was challenged in Sherbrooke's Superior Court in the name of the provincial attorney general, though costs were pledged by two local merchants, one of whom (R.D. Morkill) was vice-president of the Sherbrooke-Kennebec Railway. The plaintiff's case was based on the grounds that an identical by-law had already been defeated; that a county council was not a corporate body; that the assessment imposed (five mills on the dollar)[28] was in excess of the amount required to pay interest on the debentures and provide for the sinking fund; that the mayor of Ascot had voted for the by-law at the county council meeting in September (where the vote was six to four) even though his township had voted against it in June; that the town of Sherbrooke and the townships of Ascot and Orford were not part of Compton County; that, even if they were, the new obligation imposed on Sherbrooke would raise her public-works debts ($182,200) to more than 20 per cent of the aggregate value of her property ($870,000); that the by-law had not been published within fifteen days of the council meeting; that the election notice was not published in time; that the notice called for town meetings on two consecutive days, but in ten townships the poll was closed after the first day; and, finally, that in the swing municipalities of Sherbrooke and Westbury corruption and bribery had been widely practiced. The defence responded that a second vote had been necessary because a majority of the electors in Sherbrooke and Westbury had signed a petition in favour of the International Railway. As for the other charges, it simply denied both their validity and their relevance. The attorney general insisted that many who had signed the Sherbrooke and Westbury petition had been tricked "by representations that the said petition was for a totally different purpose." His point was weakened, however, by the fact that a majority in the two municipalities had subsequently voted for the by-law. Rightly or wrongly, the court found that the only allegation serious enough to render the ratification null and void was the one concerning notice given to the electors. The outcome of the proceedings thereby became a foregone conclusion, since the defence attorney had no trouble finding witnesses to testify that the county had discussed little else since the spring. Despite their high-handed dealings, Pope and his allies were completely exonerated when the case was dismissed with costs on 10 December 1870.[29]

A protest petition gathered 1770 signatures – half the ratepayers of the county – but again to no avail.[30] The disenchanted and effectively disenfranchised townships of Ascot, Orford, and Compton did attain separate municipal status with the sharply divided town of Sherbrooke, but this was a puerile victory as far as their obligations to the International Railway Company were concerned.[31]

The most plausible explanation for the International's surprisingly strong showing in Sherbrooke (apart from the influence of the BALC, the Eastern Townships Bank, and residents such as Sanborn) was the structural problems faced by the rival project. Thirty to thirty-five thousand dollars had been invested by the Sherbrooke-Kennebec Company in wooden rails before experience elsewhere in the province proved conclusively that such a method of construction was simply not viable.[32] To enable the American contractor, J.B. Hulburt, to switch to iron, Robertson arranged that Sherbrooke's $50,000 in stocks be handed over for the token sum of $20.[33]

A shortage of capital would stall progress on the Sherbrooke railway for another two years, but, in the meantime, Robertson ceased his efforts to block the International.[34] In the fall of 1871 the provincial government, whose treasurer Robertson had been for two years, offered Pope's company 10,000 acres of St Maurice woodland per mile of construction.[35] At the same time, Galt not only arranged a loan from the Bank of Montreal to meet advances on Compton's bonds, he also lobbied the City of Montreal, albeit without success, for a $260,000 subsidy to purchase iron rails.[36]

Work on the International advanced rapidly, with twenty miles of winding road-bed completed by December 1872.[37] At this point, however, the capital fund was close to exhaustion, and there would be no access to the government subsidy until twenty-five miles of the railway were in operation.[38] To make matters worse, in the spring of 1873 the price of iron rails skyrocketed due to heavy demand, and municipalities such as Compton Township refused to enforce the railway levy on local taxpayers.[39] In April the contractors had to launch a suit against the county to collect the previous eighteen months' interest, worth $9,000, on the $100,000 in debentures they had been paid with.[40]

By June Pope was contemplating his own suit against the county for the interest on the $125,000 debenture issue still held by his company.[41] He was, however, able to borrow some money locally on the strength of bonds he had sold in England, even though the subscribers' first instalments would not be called until 1883. As a result, the International could finally purchase its rails in New York, and take advantage of the government's relaxed subsidy requirements early in 1875.[42] The new regulation not only stipulated that no more than ten miles needed to be constructed to qualify for a portion of the grant, it permitted companies to exchange their land allotments for $4,000 cash per mile.[43] With approximately twenty miles of track already laid, the International qualified for $68,000, enabling it to complete its first twenty-seven-mile section to the village of Robinson (Bury) by July 1875.[44]

As for the longer run to Lake Megantic, the future looked ominous because of the impending bankruptcy of the two north-shore projects. The province announced its takeover of these two lines in September, followed in December by a budget which proposed to float over $4 million in railway bonds – without a cent promised for the south shore![45] The Conservative *Sherbrooke News* had already warned that if $4 to $5 million could go to north-shore lines, a minimum of $750,000 must be found for the south: "to refuse it, would be to inflict on this section of the country, a calamity almost above calculation. ... If this partiality be perpetuated we defy any ministry to hold office beyond a few weeks, perhaps days."[46] Owned by the Bélanger brothers of Sherbrooke, the *News* was not simply a mouthpiece for Anglo-Protestant capital.[47] Like Conservative MLA Jacques Picard of Richmond-Wolfe, the *News* argued that the first and most potent claim to aid for the International and the Sherbrooke-Kennebec (renamed the Quebec Central) projects was their potential as colonization roads.[48]

To maintain pressure on the government, a public protest meeting was held at the Sherbrooke town hall, where speakers reiterated the theme that the abandoned south-shore railways were designed to develop the "vastes étendues de nos terres publiques."[49] A few days later a deputation of mayors, wardens, and "private gentlemen of high social positions" travelled to Quebec, but they were apparently received with "very scant courtesy" by Premier Boucherville.[50] With Robertson's local political influence evaporating in the face of the government's obdurate stand towards the south shore, the Sherbrooke MLA resigned from the ministry in January. Emotions ran so high in the Eastern Townships that two branches of the Protestant Defence Alliance were formed to protest the government's colonization and railway policies. The president of the Sherbrooke branch was R.D. Morkill, ex-mayor and member of the Quebec Central's board of directors, and among the alliance's supporters was said to be another ex-mayor, R.W. Heneker.[51] The ethnic/religious aspect of the anti-Boucherville campaign reached national proportions when Galt published his controversial manifesto on civil liberties, and federal minister L.S. Huntington (another Townships railway promoter) attacked the ultramontane ascendancy in his widely publicized address to the electors of Argenteuil.[52]

Meanwhile, even without government support, the personal pledges of Pope and his allies allowed work on the International to proceed. The company was able to invest $40,000 in construction during the 1876 season, then, with the opening of the fall legislative session, the administration announced that it would subsidize all railways which had already undertaken considerable works.[53] In fact, an additional $2,000 per mile was to be made available for the completion of sections already under construction, though the money was to be subtracted from the subsidy on future mileage extensions. This apparent act of generosity ensured that construction on the remaining fifty-three miles of the International would drag on for several more years.[54] The *Sherbrooke News* again threatened rebellion from the party, but the south-shore promoters were presumably satisfied because the Eastern Townships protest movement quickly fizzled.[55]

Stimulated by a $70,000 stock purchase on the part of the Glasgow Canadian Land and Trust Company, by the end of 1877 the International had stretched an additional thirteen miles from Robinson to the colonization company's headquarters at Scotstown.[56] From here it proceeded northeast, swinging well into Whitton Township and paralleling the Megantic Road farmsteads for a few miles, before descending to the northern tip of Lake Megantic. Tracks finally crossed the Chaudière River outlet in the fall of 1879.[57]

As of September 1885, when the International had reached its full eighty-two-mile length to the Maine border, construction costs had absorbed a total of $1,227,841, or $15,000 per mile, of which $395,316 was a provincial subsidy.[58] Two years later, as had long been anticipated, the Canadian Pacific Railway (CPR) acquired it as part of the projected "Short Line" to the Maritimes. Compton County was paid only fifty cents on the dollar ($112,500) for its stocks, but the sale was a great relief to Pope who was said to have been all but ruined "both in health and purse" by the project.[59] In fact, Pope's close friend, CPR President Sir George Stephen, would later write: "but for my desire to relieve Pope from his load in connection with the International I doubt if [the 'Short Line'] would ever have been built."[60] The crucial support given to the CPR by the acting minister of railways during that company's darkest days certainly does not appear to have come cheaply. Stephen claimed that during the seven years prior to Pope's death in 1889 he delivered over $1 million to ensure electoral victories in Compton County. As for the state of Pope's purse after he sold the International, Stephen claimed that the CPR had paid him more than double his investment cost.[61]

If the "uncrowned king of several counties" needed such a rich political slush fund, it was largely because of the International Railway's lack of popularity in certain sectors of his constituency.[62] In 1896 the local historian and journalist, L.S. Channell, wrote:

Down to the present day this bitter feeling against the well-known by-law, No. 37 remains in some cases unabated. During the rest of the political life of the late Hon. John Henry Pope, his opponents used this as their only weapon against him, while some attempt at the present day to use it as an argument against his son, R.H. Pope, M.P[63]

While the average burden for municipalities which contributed to Quebec railways was only 4 ½ per cent of costs during the nineteenth century,[64] the ratepayers of Compton County had paid for a full 18 per cent of the International's construction expenses, though they eventually recuperated half their investment. In Winslow South, one of a number of impoverished municipalities in the county, the resulting tax was close to five dollars (eight mills on the dollar) for an average family in the single year of 1880.[65]

Ratepayers were helping to support a railway that added primarily to the fortunes of promoters and municipal councillors who held considerable assets in the county. It was no accident that among the company's directors were Eaton Township's Cyrus A. Baily, brother of Pope's wife and for twenty-seven years the county's secretary-treasurer; Colin Noble, the long-time mayor of Winslow South whose daughter married Pope's only son; and Lemuel Pope, Jr, cousin to John Henry and mayor of Bury Township.[66] As for the county's farmers, they had to face a reduction in the province's colonization roads budget[67] and, presumably, a deflation in prices caused by increased agricultural imports, but they did gain a measure of freedom from the lumber monopolies. Between 1881 and 1891, the greatest increase in the number of farm families was in Garthby (86 to 290) on the Quebec Central, and in the frontier townships close to the railway town of Lake Megantic. Even though some of the townships located south and north of the line actually saw their farms decline in number, for the upper St Francis district as a whole the number of farm families increased by 11 per cent during the 1880s. They clearly remained dependent upon the woods to some degree, for grain production actually declined by the same ratio, and the average farmer in 1891 had no more cattle than he had owned thirty years earlier (see tables 3 and 7.) Home butter production per farm did increase from 96 to 166 pounds between 1861 and 1891, but the rapidly expanding factory system would soon undercut all farmers without ready access to large efficiently operated plants, just as it had with the cheese industry since the 1860s.[68] However, the proponents of French-Canadian colonization had a broader aim than the expansion of the agricultural frontier, and they would welcome the fact that the largely French-speaking village of Lake Megantic sprang from the wilderness to a population of 1,200 individuals by 1891. Also to their liking must have been the 30 per cent decline in Winslow Township's Scots' population during the 1880s. Within several more decades the French Canadians would have the district almost entirely to themselves. Such a result would hardly have been foreseen or welcomed by railway promoters such as Pope and his family clique, but they could seek consolation in the added wealth and power the International brought them.

CHAPTER EIGHT

La Patrie:
The Repatriation Colony,
1875–80

Partant pour la Patrie
Un char plein de colons
Pour faire de l'abattie
Dans ce vaste Canton
Ils ont mangé des croutes,
Ne faut pas en douter
En regrettant sans doute
Les jobs qu'ils ont quittés.

Le Jean-Baptiste (Northampton, Mass.)[1]

The disappointing results of the colonization societies project did little to relieve the provincial administration from pressure to stimulate French-Canadian settlement on crown lands, particularly after the ultramontane Charles-Eugène Boucher de Boucherville became premier in 1874. Pressure caused by the sight of emigrating familes may have been declining due to the depression, which was closing many New England textile factories, but the nationalists simply switched their attention to the goal of repatriating the exiles to Quebec's colonization frontier. The upper St Francis district, for all its drawbacks, was an obvious place to begin because of its proximity to the American border, the size of its uninhabited territory, the effort already made by the colonization societies on the local crown lands, and the so-called colonization railway which Pope was gradually pushing to completion.

Quebec had first started promoting repatriation in a small way as early as 1870, when it appointed Father Jean-Baptiste Chartier of Coaticook in Stanstead County to be a colonization agent. One of his duties was to travel to New England to address potential returnees. In 1871 he published a pamphlet entitled *La Colonisation dans les Cantons de l'Est*, and distributed a third of its three thousand copies in the United States. Chartier's propaganda seems to have had some effect for in 1871 he claimed that he was able to spend only ten days south of the border owing to the large numbers of prospective colonists (765) arriving in Coaticook from the old parishes and New England. Most of the visitors were directed to the nearby townships of Barnston, Barford, Hereford, Clifton, Ditton, Chesham, and Stoke. Those from within the province tended to buy already cleared farms, but the Franco-Americans posed a problem. While repatriates generally returned to Quebec out of desperation for money, they refused to become servants or farm labourers. Since buying cleared land was out of the question, they insisted upon settling in the wilderness against the advice of Chartier, who felt that they lacked the qualities required of successful colonists.[2] Such reticence on Chartier's part may have hampered his effectiveness in the eyes of the Department of Agriculture and Public Works, for assistant commissioner Siméon Le Sage was not satisfied with his work.[3] The agency was subsequently terminated in December 1873.[4]

Although Chartier's campaign brought relatively few Franco-Americans back to Quebec and did little to stem French-Canadian emigration, it does seem to have aroused some interest in New England. Repatriation was on the agenda of the sixth annual convention of Franco-Americans held at Worcester, Massachusetts, in 1871. Two years later, with the cotton textile industry hit by depression, the Biddeford, Maine, convention passed a resolution asking the Quebec government for material support.[5] As federal minister of agriculture, Pope took advantage of this climate of expectation in 1873 to appoint Father P.E. Gendreau of Cookshire as special visiting agent to the New England French Canadians, as well as to make suggestions on what Ottawa could do to encourage repatriation. In his report, Gendreau claimed that the money used to encourage Europeans to immigrate to Canada would be much better spent if diverted to a programme for the thousands of Franco-Americans eager to return to their homeland. By the time the report was presented, however, the Conservatives were no longer in power, so Gendreau's suggestions were ignored.[6]

Because crown lands were a provincial responsibility, any hope for a sustained programme of this nature lay with the Quebec government. Already in 1872 assistant commissioner Le Sage had been ordered to design such a project.[7] He sent immigration agent Jérôme-Adolphe Chicoyne to New England on a study mission the following year. Chicoyne and Father Chartier each presented proposals, but Le Sage drew up his own instead, perhaps because he was sceptical of the practicality of any repatriation scheme.[8] He advised that European immigrants, and even Quebec inhabitants, should enjoy the same advantages as those Canadians who returned from the United States, but he also suggested the appointment of a full-time agent in New England for the first time. Le Sage presented his proposals to the provincial cabinet in the autumn of 1873, but no immediate action was taken. Then, on 24 June 1874, more than ten thousand Franco-American delegates attended the Saint-Jean-Baptiste day celebrations in Montreal where they fervently proclaimed themselves in favour of repatriation.[9] With the formation of the Boucherville ministry that September, the project finally moved beyond the talking stage. A modified version of Le Sage's report became a ministerial measure, and on 23 February 1875, the Repatriation Act was passed. To concentrate resources more effectively, overseas immigration was placed exclusively in the hands of the federal government for five years, and all of Quebec's agents but one were withdrawn.[10]

Under the Repatriation Act, the settler would be provided with a home and small cleared acreage with easy payment terms. Every head of family could select a hundred acres, with a dwelling house, and four acres ready for seeding, at the regular price of sixty cents per acre, plus $140 for the improvements. This sum was to be repaid within ten years: the lot itself during the first five, and the $140 (interest-free) during the last five. As what proved to be a more attractive alternative, the colonist could clear the first four acres himself, build his dwelling and receive the $140 as a loan which he would repay in the same manner. No letters patent (clear title) would be issued until all payments were completed. As the site of the original colony, the department chose the virtually unsettled townships of Ditton, Chesham, and Emberton in Compton County, all recent centres of road work and land clearing by colonization societies. Should the new scheme prove successful, the government hoped to extend it throughout the province.[11]

In charge of the repatriation colony was Jérôme-Adolphe Chicoyne, who, as we have seen, had submitted a report on the question a couple of years earlier.[12] Clearly wishing to avoid further involvement with intermediary bodies, the government made Chicoyne directly responsible to the Department of Agriculture and Public Works. Even the Catholic clergy, who had provided much of the local leadership for the colonization societies, was bypassed when Chicoyne decided to move from Sherbrooke to the site of the colony itself. However, this layman posed no real threat to clerical authority because he himself was a staunchly conservative Catholic. Born on a farm near Saint-Hyacinthe in 1844, at the age of three Chicoyne moved to town to live with his childless godparents. In 1856 he entered the local classical college, but he seems to have been too solitary and too independent to adjust to his new environment. He became so dissatisfied that, after putting in his year at the college, he ran off to New England with visions of making his fortune. The thirteen-year-old youth worked for a year and a half in a Connecticut factory, and then went to school for a year in Vermont. By this time he had become completely disillusioned with his adventure – in his memoirs he reports that he barely avoided contamination in "cet ocean de dissolution."

In October 1859 the young Chicoyne returned to his home, and to the fervently ultramontane Collège de Saint-Hyacinthe.[13] Suddenly attracted to academic life, he became a successful student. He studied philosophy during the 1864–65 school term, and law during the summers. At the same time he began to publish articles in the local Bleu mouthpiece, Le Courrier de Saint-Hyacinthe. His evolution from a democrat and revolutionary (to use his own words) to a confirmed conservative was now complete. In the fall of 1865, the sudden death of a fellow classmate, his most intimate friend, pushed Chicoyne towards religion. In December he became a novice with the Oblates in Montreal. His strong-willed temperament was not suited for the rigorous community life, however, and in May he returned to his legal studies in Saint-Hyacinthe, where he practised law from 1868 to 1872.[14] In 1870 he became secretary-treasurer of the newly formed Société de Colonisation de Saint-Hyacinthe. Two years later Chicoyne's interest in land settlement led to his appointment as provincial immigration agent in Montreal. In 1873, as we have seen, his duties were extended to promoting repatriation of French Canadians from the United Sates, and, in 1875, he was placed in direct charge of the repatriation colony.[15] It was at this point that he wrote his memoirs, apparently under the assumption that he was being guided by providence to accomplish a great national task.[16]

At the other end of the repatriation line was Ferdinand Gagnon, editor of the Worcester, Massachusetts, Travailleur. He was "entrusted with the care of making known and popularizing among our fellow citizens in the United States the law passed in their behalf."[17] Born in Saint-Hyacinthe in 1849, Gagnon had left the province in 1868 to become New England's foremost French-language journalist. He proved to be an excellent choice as American agent, for his influential newspaper published a steady stream of articles promoting the movement, and he travelled extensively among the Franco-American communities to recruit colonists.[18]

Each family head who wished to go to the colony from the United States was supposed to present Gagnon with a character reference from his parish priest. He would then receive a certificate which entitled him to a reduced train fare. Although the Department of Agriculture and Public Works asked Gagnon to enlist only those settlers who had some capital, he did not always follow this rule.[19] Anyway, the certificate actually meant little, for even those who went entirely on their own initiative were not turned away.

Chicoyne was optimistic about the finances of the colonists, for he attempted to make arrangements whereby some of them could purchase the cleared lots of the Bagot and Saint-Hyacinthe colonization societies rather than the forested crown lands. The Bagot society offered its lots for the sum invested plus interest (about ten dollars above the regular sixty cents per acre for wild land).[20] When Chicoyne argued that demanding interest constituted speculation, its secretary replied that some compensation had to be made for the time sacrificed by the members, not to mention the travel expenses which amounted to two or three dollars per year for six years. Unconvinced, Chicoyne charged that even his fellow Saint-Hyacinthe society members were motivated by ambition and self-interest.[21]

Meanwhile, Chicoyne's hands were full with more serious problems. In early April, assistant commissioner Le Sage informed him that repatriated families were already waiting in Sherbrooke and becoming impatient. When sixteen of these individuals left for La Patrie a week later, they had to walk for two days because of the poor condition of the roads.[22] Gagnon had forwarded over sixty people before he was told to delay the movement until 15 May. Even that date still found snow in Chesham and Ditton, with the Salmon and Ditton rivers flooding and causing widespread road and bridge damage. Because construction of the large house to shelter the new arrivals in Chesham could not begin until 1 June, the settlers had to be placed in camps and private homes.[23] By 22 May, although almost all the available Ditton lots had been claimed, many could not be touched because the government had not completed requisitioning uncleared lots from the colonization societies. Another annoying obstacle was the absence of roads – Chicoyne was so desperate that he offered to oversee construction himself, at no additional salary.[24] Taken together, the particularly inclement weather and the land and road problems resulted in the American agent again being asked to halt the movement for fifteen to thirty days. On 7 June, a frustrated Gagnon informed Le Sage that discouraged colonists were returning to New England. Repatriation would be easy, he said, but "vous n'êtes pas organisés, vous n'allez pas assez vites."[25]

Throughout the summer Chicoyne continued to bombard Le Sage with requests that the cancellation of earlier land claims be speeded up.[26] Not surprisingly, the strongest opposition to the proposed expropriations came from English-speaking interests, many of whom had been hostile to the project from the beginning. On 12 January, 1876 the Montreal *Daily Witness* charged that:

In the estimates of last year a sum of $50,000 was appropriated for the ostensible purpose of bringing back home from the United States, Canadians who had left their country. This has turned out to be simply a plot for the purpose of populating the Eastern Townships, etc. with French Canadians, to the exclusion of English-speaking settlers. Instead of taking English or French indiscriminately from the United States, ... the immigrants are taken from the North Shore from the old settlements and induced to take up land on the South Shore ... No English, Irish, Scotch or German need apply.[27]

Glasgow Canadian Land and Trust, a Scottish-owned colonization company, seems to have been the principal complainant. Chicoyne replied to the company's mouthpiece, local MLA William Sawyer, that had he visited the establishment after the special invitation personally extended to him, he would have realized that certain interested parties were attempting to arouse national and religious prejudices. Not only anglophones, but French Canadians as well, would lose their land claims.[28] Chicoyne eventually had his way, for in September the lots were cancelled.

This action was defended after an investigation by the regional inspector of colonization agencies, but, as we saw in chapter 5, it was accompanied by a number of less defensible expropriations from Highland Scots in nearby Marston Township.[29] As a result, the repatriation project was added to a list of grievances (which included the province's freeze on subsidies to south-shore railway construction) proclaimed at a meeting of settlers from seven local townships. In the opening address, the chairman, a local Presbyterian minister, complained of the:

partiality shown to French-Canadians above all other nationalities, whether Protestants or Roman Catholics, as manifested by the iniquitous working out of the grand repatriation scheme of the hierarchy alias the Quebec Legislature.[30]

As we have seen, the angry Scots decided to form a branch of the Protestant Defence Alliance, with one section of their local charter proclaiming that the so-called repatriation colony was operated by "the Church of Rome for French Canadians solely."[31] Nevertheless, the repatriation colony remained a peripheral issue in the minds of the local population; the agitation died quickly once the Marston colonists were given back their land.

Meanwhile, in spite of the endless summer rain which reduced the roads to all but impassible muddy trails, one hundred lots had been granted and eighty families settled by 1 July. Only half were repatriates – ten were Europeans, and the others were French Canadians from the old parishes.[32] With the Chesham house finally ready to accept newly arrived colonists, the future looked brighter. Even the harassed Gagnon grew more optimistic after his August tour. The American colonists appeared so satisfied with their lot that he decided to send his elderly father to live in the colony.[33] Nor was life in the colony all drudgery, since Chicoyne never missed an opportunity to organize a religious and patriotic celebration. To him, "une petite fête de temps à autre est loin de nier aux progrès de la colonie." On Corpus Christi day there was a high mass during which Chicoyne presented the colonists with the numerous loaves of holy bread donated by the commissioner of agriculture himself. The visit of Bishop Antoine Racine of Sherbrooke to the colony a couple of weeks later offered still another occasion for a religious demonstration.[34]

By November, when the influx of colonists had stopped for the winter, 240 families (1100 people) had settled in Ditton and Chesham. Ninety-two families were from the United States, 102 from within the province, and 36 from Europe.[35] The expenses were $10,838, with $3,442 going towards organization and labour for the colony itself, and the remainder towards local roads, bridges, and advances to colonists.[36] Technically the advances could not be counted as repatriation expenses, but in fact few colonists would ever pay them back.

To maintain close control over the winter operations, Chicoyne bought land near the Ditton headquarters, appropriately christened La Patrie, and moved his family there from Saint-Hyacinthe.[37] By this time he was concerned with attracting professionals and industries to give stability to his colony. Unfortunately, neither endeavour met with much success. In his fruitless search for a doctor Chicoyne's standards may have been too high, for he carefully checked into the history of all applicants.[38] After two years with no results, Chicoyne still insisted that the candidate be a good citizen, which appears to have meant a staunch Catholic and loyal Conservative: "Nous avons déjà malheureusement une élément libéral et anti-religieux très-prononcé, il nous faut des soldats pour le combattre."[39] The lack of professionals may not have been entirely to Chicoyne's distaste, since it left him, like the fictional Jean Rivard, in unchallenged control of his colony. In addition to being the government agent, he was mayor of the municipal council, justice of the peace, emergency doctor, pharmacist, merchant, and an important landowner.[40] But Chicoyne's ambitions did not prevent him from launching a determined, and successful, attempt to have a curé appointed to La Patrie. As the colonists were too poor to support one by themselves, Chicoyne suggested to the Department of Agriculture and Public Works that a priest be appointed as his assistant colonization agent. The government would pay half his salary, permitting him to fulfil the additional parish functions. The department accepted Chicoyne's proposal, authorizing the Bishop of Sherbrooke to appoint Victor Chartier, younger brother of the former repatriation agent, Reverend Jean-Baptiste Chartier of Coaticook.[41]

In view of the articles he published in the *Pionnier* expounding upon the evils of the New England factories, one might have expected Chicoyne to be reticent about attracting manufacturing industries. But much of this rhetoric seems to have been stimulated by the fact that agriculture was still the major attraction Quebec had to offer its growing population. It certainly did not prevent Chicoyne, again like Jean Rivard, from attempting to set up factories several times throughout his career.[42] In 1875 he did his best to lure a shoe company to La Patrie. In addition to two years of free waterpower, he offered free buildings, free land, and free construction of roads to the plant. He also promised that labour would be 20 per cent cheaper than in the larger towns, and that within a few months Pope's International Railway would be only eight miles away.[43] Not surprisingly, given the colony's isolated location, Chicoyne's offer fell on deaf ears.

In a less ambitious direction, Chicoyne reasoned that because a market for the ashes produced in clearing land would be a valuable source of income for the colonists, the government should finance the operation of a pearl-ashery. The colonists would keep it in repair, and use it for a nominal fee. Chicoyne also wished to establish a model and industrial farm for the poor of the municipality, but nothing seems to have resulted from either project.[44] As for the potentially more lucrative enterprises of manufacturing lumber and operating a general store, Chicoyne was willing to invest the necessary capital himself. He quickly raised $10,000 by selling shares at $100 each. His store opened its doors in the spring of 1876, and by August his steam sawmill was ready for business.[45] The enterprising colonization agent was certainly not exaggerating when he proclaimed: "J'ai fini par assimiler mes intérets à ceux de cette colonie; son succès fera mon succès, de même que sa déchéance pourrait me compromettre."[46]

Unfortunately for him, the mingling of public duties with private interest left Chicoyne vulnerable to suspicion of profiteering. Soon after his store opened, one colonist complained that its prices were double those in a neighbouring township, and that Chicoyne sold only to settlers with cash.[47] The opposition Liberal Party did not fail to take notice of these accusations. It proclaimed publicly that Chicoyne was benefiting from his official position at the expense of the colonists.[48] The hostile Sherbrooke *Progrès* also charged that Chicoyne sold his own goods as merchant to himself as government agent.[49] It is impossible to determine how much truth there was in these allegations, but the government maintained its confidence in Chicoyne for the time being at least.

Other early criticisms of Chicoyne were of a less serious nature. In January 1876, the *Progrès* attacked him for hiring two local English-Canadian contractors to clear one hundred acres and build fifty houses. To Chicoyne's reply that none of the colonists had the means to direct the operation, and that they would gain needed employment from it, the *Progrès* countered that a Franco-American could have been found to handle the contract.[50] When the *Progrès* reported that there was a lack of work for the colonists, Chicoyne replied that all those not employed by the two contractors were either labouring on their own land, or bringing logs to his sawmill.[51] Bishop Racine was convinced that the opposition to Chicoyne was stirred up by those who resented his blocking of a liquor licence for the colony. (They even spread the rumour that Chicoyne was selling liquor under the counter.)[52] The source of much of the animosity towards Chicoyne was Pierre Vaillant, a peripatetic Franco-American journalist who, before it came under the 1875 legislation, had planned to start his own repatriation colony in Chesham Township.[53] To the extent that Chicoyne was playing the heroic role of a Jean Rivard, Vaillant was cast as the villainous Gendreau the Quibbler: "perversity incarnate – the spirit of opposition in the flesh."[54] Vaillant's hostility became overt when he began to suspect that Chicoyne had interfered with his appointment as postmaster for Chesham. He was also upset because Bishop Racine and many colonists opposed the use of his name for the new village.[55] Chicoyne attempted to make peace by recommending Vaillantbourg as the name for the village post office, and Notre-Dame-des-Bois (the bishop's choice) for all other purposes. In addition, Vaillant replaced the original postmaster.[56] Chicoyne thereby won a temporary reprieve, but a year later Vaillant was again attacking him in a series of letters to the accommodating *Progrès*.[57]

On the surface at least, Chicoyne met the many reprovals philosophically. He wrote to Gagnon in the spring of 1876:

Tu me demandes les nouvelles de tes colons. C'est toujours la vieille et antique histoire: les uns trouvent le pays excellent et sont enchantés que tu les aies dirigés ici, les autres ne disent pas grand chose, mais on voit qu'ils regrettent un peu les oignons d'Egypte. Bûcher du matin au soir, vivre au lard, à la soupe aux poies [sic], c'est si dur pour des gens habitués à weaver et à spinner et dont l'estomac ne digère que des puddings et des boston-crackers depuis des années. D'autres sont en diable et permettent de te dénoncer dans les journaux.[58]

He rationalized that a certain amount of grumbling was inevitable among such a mixed population, especially with most of them having been pushed into the colony by straitened circumstances. In fact, Chicoyne had little reason to be discouraged in the spring of 1876. As table 18 demonstrates, by 30 June the repatriation colony had made significant progress, with 1871 people occupying 3095 cleared acres. Indeed, far from being disillusioned, Chicoyne's idealism waxed stronger than ever. He planned to start a newspaper called La Patrie which would ignore the burning issues of the day; its only aim would be to strengthen the people morally. He still felt that the colony would become "un foyer d'où rayonnera sur le peuple canadian-français en général le flambeau du patriotisme et des vertus civiques."[59] Religious and patriotic ceremonies continued to be held. On 24 June, both Saint-Jean-Baptiste day and the anniversary of the first mass in Chesham were celebrated with a long procession (led by a statue of Notre-Dame-de-Lourdes and French Canada's flag) from La Patrie to Vaillantbourg. Along the way, fourteen crosses were erected, with the curé reciting an invocation to the Virgin Mary at each one. Near Vaillantbourg he unveiled a thousand pound statue (donated by Chicoyne) of Notre-Dame-des-Bois standing on a huge rock. This spot subsequently became a pilgrimage shrine for the area's colonists, inspiring Chicoyne to write a long poem in its honour.[60]

Despite the optimistic atmosphere of the early summer, the colony's problems were far from over. Settlers arriving from New England were disappointed to find that they were not eligible for the $140 loan when they settled on lots already cleared by the contractors.[61] Moreover, not only was the government planning to reduce its injection of money into winter programmes, but autumn rain and snow hampered the harvesting of potatoes and other crops. In October, 102 residents signed a petition demanding government aid.[62] They were not supported by Chicoyne who, as late as December,

Table 18
Colonization in Ditton, Chesham, and Emberton Townships, June 1876

Township	Families	People	Buildings	Acres Cleared
Ditton	198	921	278	2055
Chesham	142	636	177	713
Emberton	69	314	66	327
Totals	409	1871	521	3095

Source: SPQ, x (1876), 8.

requested only strict necessities for a few families in exceptional straits.[63] Although Father Chartier reported that four families had eaten nothing but potatoes for several days, and that there was no longer enough food in Chesham to feed half the population, Chicoyne insisted that he personally could assist the colonists by buying logs from them for his sawmill.[64] He asked permission to have all of the wood which was collected from the clearings delivered to him tax free. Also he wanted wood taken from outside the clearings to be subject to a five cent tax only, though he realized that regulations of the Crown Lands Department officially forbade colonists to cut timber outside their clearing limits until they had received their letters patent. Tacit approval would satisfy him, for he felt that no court would condemn a colonist for cutting a few trees to maintain his family.[65] Of course, Chicoyne himself would be the chief beneficiary of such an arrangement. It was beginning to appear as though he were trying to profit from the settlers' poverty by forcing them to work for him, rather than receiving government assistance.

In late January the Department of Agriculture, no longer able to ignore reports of misery among the colonists, asked Chartier to report on the situation and for advice on how to help.[66] Chartier, like Chicoyne, claimed that the root of the problem lay with the colonists' penniless state upon arrival. Not only had they been forced to work in the woods, thereby neglecting their seeding, but the situation had been aggravated in Chesham by that "ennemi dangereux," Pierre Vaillant. Vaillant had assured settlers that there was no need to seek jobs in the fall because the government would come to their assistance. Chartier suggested that those who had no future prospects in the colony should be assisted to leave, while the sick should be aided immediately, and the fifty or so families in less dire straits should be given work on local roads.[67] As a result, the government set aside $2,000 for relief. The needy colonists received $869 in cash, while $788 in potatoes, oats, barley, and buckwheat seed was distributed in April and May, and transportation and administrative expenses absorbed the remainder of the grant. Repayment was to be in the form of road work. The whole affair was kept scrupulously secret because the government did not wish to encourage demands from other areas, or ridicule of its troubled project.[68]

Chicoyne, who played a secondary role in the relief operation, had, not surprisingly, become very unpopular by this time. Though his pecuniary interests in the colony may well have been to its benefit, and though his transactions were probably within the strict definition of the law, he had set himself up as a ready-made scapegoat for anyone with a grievance. Even the local priests became critical.[69] Finally, in May 1877, the government allowed Chicoyne's appointment as repatriation agent to expire. The colony's status as repatriation centre thereby officially ended, having, it appears, considerably exceeded its $60,000 budget.[70]

As table 19 demonstrates, the short-term results were quite impressive, with a total of 1604 new settlers arriving in the area. However the results in terms of repatriation were disappointing, because only 782 of the colonists were from the United States.[71] Predictably, the majority of these were from mill towns in Massachusetts, though a few came from as far away as Minnesota and Michigan. Gagnon himself admitted to a Massachusetts board of inquiry in 1881 that no more than 600 families had moved back to any part of Quebec, and that about half of these had subsequently returned to New England.[72]

The disappointing response to the repatriation project should have been predictable, given that the French Canadians had gone to New England in the first place to escape the rigours and uncertainties of marginal farms.[73] Furthermore, there was considerable opposition from within the Franco-American community itself. In 1875 Gagnon wrote that those newspapers supporting the project faced criticism and financial loss. Only three were willing to take this risk.[74] A second source of resistance was the Franco-American merchants and professionals, who were uneasy at the prospect of losing their clientele. More surprisingly, dissenting voices could also be heard among New England's French-speaking clergy. None seem to have gone beyond a tacit approval, while two or three actually denounced the project.[75] The *Pionnier* commented sardonically that the expensive churches being built in New England motivated the curés towards discouraging repatriation: "le désir de briller, d'éclipser les Canadiens du pays natal, la vaine gloriale, en un mot, ainsi que l'intérêt peronnel, y jouent un grand rôle."[76] Finally, to the

Table 19
Origins of Colonists in Ditton, Chesham, and
Emberton Townships

	16 April 1875	31 Oct. 1876
Quebec inhabitants	116	932
Europeans	132	138
Repatriated Canadians	75	857
Totals	323	1927

Source: *Annuaire*, 1896–99, 290, 398, 406.

further disgust of the *Pionnier*, Manitoba was a more attractive site
than Quebec to many of the repatriating French Canadians.[77] Most
of those who did move to La Patrie appear to have returned to their
adopted homeland with the renewal of economic prosperity in 1879.
In the final analysis, the entire repatriation scheme only served to
injure the French Canadians of New England because it reinforced
the hostility of American nativists, sensitive to any resistance to their
great cultural melting pot.[78]

As for the other colonists who took advantage of the government
subsidies, the only Europeans were four families from France and
three from Belgium. In fact some of the English and Norwegian
families introduced to Ditton by J.H. Pope and his Compton Colonization Society clearly took advantage of the sudden demand for
land by selling their farms and moving elsewhere. From 124 in 1875,
the number of Europeans in the township declined to 99 in 1876.
As shown in table 20, most settlers moved to the colony from within
Quebec itself, the majority from the Eastern Townships, and, surprisingly enough, quite a number from the pioneer Lac Saint-Jean–
Saguenay region. In addition, the recession hit Canadian cities almost as soon as it did those in America, so that forty-seven of the
colonist families were from the urban centres of Montreal, Quebec,
Trois-Rivières, Sherbrooke, and Coaticook.[79]

The Franco-Americans were not alone in deserting their holdings
once they had collected the government loan. After the public funds
dried up in 1877, the two principal sources of income became the
sale of railway ties and ship's knees, but the first would disappear
once construction of the International was complete, and the prospects for a local lumber industry could not have been promising in
townships where the BALC, Pope, and Sawyer, owned over twenty-
three thousand acres, and licensees held cutting rights to fifty square
miles of timber leases.[80] To make matters worse, the end of the
decade brought a succession of crop failures. In 1879 Father Chartier

Table 20
Regional Origins of Quebec Colonists Registered under the Repatriation Act

	Ditton	Chesham	Emberton	Total
Eastern Townships	89	212	114	415
Montréal – Québec – Trois-Rivières (cities)	30	32	59	121
Lac Saint-Jean – Saguenay	64	13	–	77
Other	68	80	64	212
Totals	251	337	237	825

Source: Québec, État des comptes publics, 1876, 136–53.

reported that frosts had prevented the colonists from growing enough food for their own subsistence. Conditions were such that some would have to leave the colony. In 1880 he wrote that the population had been diminished by frozen crops and lack of winter employment. In fact, according to the curé, Ditton's population experienced a drastic drop from 900 in 1879 to 570 in 1880. Still he remained optimistic. The unsuitable ones who had forced themselves into the colony were gone for good, but most of those departees who had kept their farms would return.[81]

Few of the departing colonists ever did return, as the government found out when it attempted to recoup the $60,320 reportedly invested in the colony's improvement.[82] The mayor of Ditton stated that many of those who had originally claimed lots had come only for this "loan" and had subsequently disappeared. An 1885 meeting of Ditton, Chesham, and Emberton colonists claimed that 223 of the repatriation lots had been abandoned. Anyone wishing to take over one of the neglected lots would be saddled with a $140 debt for the "improvements," as well as the regular crown land price of sixty cents per acre. Furthermore, these homesteads were far from being a bargain, for the houses were frequently located either in swamps, on stony ground, or where there was no water. In some cases the improvements made valued only $60, though the government had invested the full $140. Even those lots which once had been promising were by 1884 grown up in brush, with their buildings in ruins.[83] Finally, in 1898, the Department of Crown Lands was forced to admit that none of the loans would be repaid, and it cancelled all sums owed for improvements on the repatriation lots.[84]

Though few of the repatriation colonists remained on their holdings, the money invested in the project was not entirely wasted. Upon collecting the subsidies for improving their assigned lots, many of the settlers may simply have moved to nearby land outside the reserve to avoid repayment. Whatever the reason, the population of Ditton, Chesham, and Emberton did not decline after the project ended, but rose slightly from 1927 in 1877 to 2112 in 1880. By 1881 each occupant reported an average of 176 bushels of grain and root crops, a respectable harvest when compared with the 153 bushels for the average resident of the upper St Francis district as a whole. There were three churches (two with curés), five schools, five post offices, ten sawmills, two flour mills, five forges, five stores, one hotel, three well-organized municipalities, and sixty-five miles of roads, including one to the railway station at Scotstown.[85] Though many of these developments were not a direct result of the repatriation programme, all of them must have been stimulated by the funds which poured into the area through that project.

But the settling of three obscure townships was a far cry from the benefits which its proponents had boasted the repatriation programme would bring. Once it had exhausted the scheme's political potential, the government arrived at the conclusion that this was not the most profitable way to invest its severely limited resources, especially when railroad expenditures were pushing it dangerously into debt.[86] Aside from a small colony in Temiscouata Township, the whole repatriation idea was dropped after 1877.[87] Furthermore, with an employment crisis in Canadian cities, the province was actually forced to stop encouraging large numbers of francophones to return from the United States – only those who could support themselves would be welcome.[88] By the 1880s many French-Canadian nationalists began to rationalize the exodus as part of their providential mission to "conquer" New England.[89] When pressure to subsidize repatriation to the Lac Saint-Jean region emerged in the later 1890s, it was Laurier's federal government which made the only response.[90] Indeed, after the La Patrie project, no Quebec administration became directly involved in colonization schemes of any kind throughout the remainder of the century.

In launching the repatriation project the Quebec government was apparently motivated by the rather unrealistic dream that the province's isolated and mountainous crown land could be made as attractive as the American mill towns, not only to French Canadians in Quebec, but in New England as well. In the case of La Patrie the problem was not so much that the colony was isolated, for the railway helped to alleviate that problem, but the upper St Francis district was high and rugged terrain, where the valleys themselves were afflicted by a short growing season. Despite the physical shortcomings, a considerable number of francophones did remain in the area. More might have stayed on the cleared lots had Chicoyne chosen the sites with greater care, assuming that better crown land was available, but it was probably inevitable that even serious colonists would move to avoid repaying their $140 loan. It made more sense to invest some of that money in higher quality land held by private interests, than to reimburse the government.[91]

Doomed to failure or not, given Quebec's obsession with its departing population, it is hardly surprising that an attempt was made to repatriate the exiles who finally seemed willing to return. And what choice was there but to turn to colonization when the province's own factories were laying off workers? If the project attracted some of Quebec's own unemployed labourers, it was because they had nowhere else to turn in an age when social welfare assistance was severely limited. Indeed, government grants were necessary to attract people to the frontier during economic recessions because the lumber companies would not be providing a dependable outside source of income. To a certain degree, then, the Quebec state was subsidizing a reserve pool of industrial labour, a pool which included some of the temporarily unemployed from New England mill towns.[92]

Such may not have been the aim of the bourgeois-nationalist promoters of the project, but they were certainly not blinded by pure idealism. The assembly voted funds without opposition, but without any great outbursts of enthusiasm.[93] The draftsman, Siméon Le Sage, was skeptical from the first about the practicality of repatriation. He certainly favoured colonization as one means of keeping French Canadians in Quebec, but his biographer calls him a pragmatic as opposed to a doctrinaire "apôtre de la colonisation" because he also supported industrialization.[94] Ferdinand Gagnon was clearly committed to repatriation at this time, but he was, after all, a paid agent of the government, and he soon became a vocal supporter of American naturalization.[95] Finally, Jérôme-Adolphe Chicoyne was the person most actively involved in, and most devoted to, the colony. As we shall see, there can be no doubting his moral conviction in promoting colonization throughout the remainder of his life. He seems to have managed La Patrie almost as a paternal despot, placing a great deal of emphasis upon religious and patriotic ideals within the community. But he too had a personal investment in the colony. It offered not simply prestige and authority, but a chance for capital investment as well. To all concerned, then, including the settlers themselves, the repatriation project promised certain immediate and concrete benefits. This is not to deny that French-Canadian nationalism imbued with conservative Catholic ideals was a primary motivating force, but it does remove La Patrie from the realm of romantic agrarian visionaries.

CHAPTER NINE

Forest Exploitation and Colonization: The Return of European Land Companies

To invite people to subscribe money for Empire Settlement Schemes, from which they get nothing themselves, will never carry far. The sources of such generosity are easily choked by the sands of difficulty and dispute.

Stephen Leacock, *My Discovery of the West*

If the federal government's resort to colonization companies in the Prairies followed the disappointment of "the Repatriation Movement and of racial and/or group settlements," much the same can be said of Quebec.[1] Most of the eastern province's involvement with free-enterprise agencies also post-dated disillusionment with the state-subsidized efforts studied in previous chapters. The BALC may not have been an encouraging precedent to reintroduce private settlement agencies into the upper St Francis district, but neither Conservative nor Liberal provincial regimes could resist a scheme which promised relief from the administration of large tracts of land and financial profits as well. Furthermore, a crucial safeguard to the public interest had been included in the 1859 legislation which established the mechanism for reservation of blocks of crown land by private corporations. Land titles would issue directly to settlers themselves, after they had fulfilled the standard residency requirements, and the reserve would expire within ten years. Only lots judged unfit for agriculture would become the property of the companies, presumably to exploit as sources of timber.[2] In short, colonization companies appeared to be tailor-made for a province embarrassed by the contradiction between its ideological commitment to frontier population expansion and its financial dependency upon the capitalistic exploitation of timber. The only problem was that those companies based in Britain would obviously aim to introduce British immigrants, but the French-Canadian politicians no doubt realized how slim were the chances that a significant number of Anglo-Protestants would settle in such a marginal area.

This possibility was especially unlikely by the time rail access to the timber resource attracted foreign capitalists. During the late 1870s and early 1880s, better opportunities for the would-be settler lay in western Canada, but at least the upper St Francis district could take some advantage of the attention being paid to the Prairie West by overseas investors. As principal promoter of the struggling International Railway, it was very much in J.H. Pope's interest to use his influence at the head of the Department of Agriculture to deflect a small part of that attention to his own constituency. The drawback for Pope was that these companies would, theoretically at least, compete with the lumber monopolists for supplies of raw material; however, their reserves would be located to the east of C.S. Clark and Company's principal area of operation. Here a struggle would ensue with the powerful G.B. Hall Company, a struggle which would ultimately make the provincial administration regret its involvement with the colonization companies.

The most important post-Confederation land companies to operate in the upper St Francis district were the Glasgow Canadian Land and Trust Company (incorporated in 1873), the Dominion of Canada Land and Colonization Company (incorporated in 1880), and the Compagnie de Colonisation et de Crédit des Cantons de l'Est (incorporated in 1881). Their headquarters were in Glasgow, London, and Nantes, respectively. The background of most of the investors is impossible to identify, given the paucity of surviving company records, but the founders essentially represented merchant and professional capital, with some industrial and land-based wealth thrown in for good measure. As the second or railway phase of European industrialization drew to a close, attention shifted increasingly to overseas investment outlets.[3] This was particularly true of Scotland where the mainstay textile and iron industries were on the decline by the 1870s, and the rising shipbuilding and steel industries were not yet organized to tap the large amount of loanable funds available. Here the investment trust was pioneered as a device to exploit the savings of the *petite bourgeoisie* for investment.[4] Whereas these institutions deployed investors' money over a range of ventures, mostly in North America, companies were also formed to invest in particular and specific undertakings, generally connected with land, railways, and mines.[5] French investment, which began in Quebec after 1880, was also largely resource oriented – particularly in the agriculture-based sector. In contrast to their British counterparts, the French appear to have consciously focused on enterprises that would complement their national economy.[6]

The French colonization companies, with their potential to provide lumber for the home market as well as to expand the French-language frontier, nicely suited such an imperialist strategy. Ironically, when the first two such endeavours were launched in the Beauce and Matapedia districts in 1871 and 1872, respectively, they came up against the restrictions of France's emigration policy.[7] But this did not prevent the exploitation of Franco-Catholic zeal in order to impose the Nantes-based colonization company on the upper St Francis district, as we shall see. As for the British-based enterprises, those in western Canada may have been motivated by a combination of "philanthropy and rapacity," to use Leacock's phrase, but their counterparts in the upper St Francis district demonstrated precious little of the former quality, as we shall also see.

THE GLASGOW CANADIAN LAND AND TRUST COMPANY

The Scottish overseas investment craze originated in 1873 as a response to the exceptionally low prices for securities on the depressed New York stock exchange.[8] Although the more industrialized Glasgow was much less active than Edinburgh or Dundee in the launching of such joint-stock ventures, the Glasgow Canadian Land and Trust Company was founded that very year by four Glasgow merchants (including its president, Robert Fraser), one Edinburgh merchant, one Glasgow solicitor, and a Lanark County farmer named John Scott – the company's first manager.[9] Thomas Coats, the prominent Paisley thread manufacturer, would acquire a major interest in 1875.[10] As owner of the largest firm in British manufacturing industry, Coats obviously did not fit the investment pattern we have described; however, he was in the process of extending his textile operation into New England rather than diversifying into new local industrial endeavours. Coats was also a committed Home-Rule Liberal, not a sentimental imperialist, but the Glasgow Canadian Company's original prospectus made no mention of assisted emigration or colonization.[11] The declared aim was to acquire real estate anywhere in Canada, the United States, or elsewhere for the purpose of exploiting minerals and timber, carrying on a general trade, and lending money based upon mortgages.[12]

Such ambitions were, however, strictly limited by its act of incorporation. The company could acquire a maximum of only 50,000 acres in each of Quebec and Manitoba, in addition to mining properties which could be exploited anywhere in Canada.[13] Under such controlled conditions, and in view of the company's failure to develop any mines, the projection of 25,000 shares at ten pounds each would prove to be completely unrealistic. No more than 3340 shares would ever be issued. But if the Glasgow Canadian Company was restricted in one sense, it enjoyed a special privilege in another. Contrary to the rules of the 1859 legislation, it became indirectly eligible for an outright land purchase rather than a temporary reserve. An arrangement was worked out with the Compton Colonization Society whereby it effectively turned over much of its 12,195 acre crown land reserve by claiming as resident settlers those names provided by the company.[14] To take as an example range three, lot six, of Marston Township, Martha M. Scott (probably the manager's wife) is listed in the crown land files as having paid the first instalment in April 1873, and the second in August 1874. A year later the lot was transferred to the new manager, Aeneas McMaster, who proceeded to pay the three remaining instalments by June 1878.[15] The letters patent were issued the following September, and McMaster finally transferred the lot, along with all others in his name, to the company in November 1879.[16] As we shall see, there was at least a pretence made that the required acreage had been cleared and cabins erected. Nevertheless, the government grant of 8043 acres in Marston, Ditton, and Hampden clearly flouted both the spirit and the letter of crown land regulations.

The Glasgow Canadian Company did not confine its activities to public land, for much of the region's timber-producing territory was in the hands of private owners. In the fall of 1873 Scott paid $24,650 to several absentee proprietors as well as to the BALC for seven lots in Newport and sixty-one lots in Clinton, at the southern tip of Lake Megantic.[17] Logs from the company's Marston and Clinton holdings were destined to be floated down the Chaudière to the Quebec market, but the company had been designed to do more than sell unmilled timber.[18] In anticipation of the arrival of the International Railway, it paid the BALC and two speculators $16,460 for 3060 acres alongside the Salmon River on both sides of the Lingwick-Hampden border.[19] Thus was born the future municipality of Scotstown (1887 acres), on the very site where the BALC had failed completely some thirty-five years earlier to establish the pioneer colonization centre of Victoria. The Sherbrooke-based land company had, as recently as 1872, sold nearly the entire township of Lingwick to the C.S. Clark lumber company, but the Scotstown mill site commanded the Glasgow Canadian Company's upriver timber sources in Hampden and Ditton townships. Presumably to serve as a transshipment site for the American lumber market, the company's final purchase was a five-and-a-half acre lot (from J.H. Pope) alongside the Grand Trunk Railway in Lennoxville.[20]

Scott wasted little time in commencing development of the Victoria Falls mill site. As early as May 1874 some two hundred men, including sixty Scots immigrants, were employed building a dam (at a cost of $6 to $9 thousand), clearing land, and preparing lumber for buildings.[21] By the fall of 1875 two hundred acres had been cleared and a portable steam sawmill had produced enough lumber to build three two-storey structures – an office/store, a boarding-house, and a hotel – as well as fourteen family dwellings, a blacksmith shop, and a large barn.[22] During the first year of operations three to four million feet of spruce and pine logs had been driven into the mill pond to await construction of the large sawmill. Unfortunately for the company, international demand for lumber, which had been rising steadily over the previous several years, suddenly plummeted in 1874.[23] To make matters worse, construction of the International proceeded at a snail's pace, stalling at the village of Robinson after the summer of 1875.

Stricken with panic, the Glasgow Canadian directors fired Scott, officially on the grounds of mismanaging the company's funds, though the action also provided an escape from his exorbitant contract.[24] It then decided to postpone construction of the Scotstown sawmill. The log booms would consequently have to be cleared at a loss.[25] C.S. Clark's monopoly of the Salmon – upper St Francis River network had been granted a reprieve.

The colonization company's relations with its American contractor, Isaac Pinkham, soon turned sour as well, resulting in his court claim of $1899 during the winter of 1875. Defence witnesses voiced suspicions that it was Pinkham, a contractor for Clark as well as Scott, who had cut the company's boom, presumably hoping that its logs would be carried to Brompton Falls by the spring break-up. The company also claimed that Pinkham's piers had been too short and light to hold the log booms during spring flood conditions, and that the houses built for colonists in Marston had needed an additional investment. The court found that Pinkham was owed only $276, but in two additional cases the Glasgow Canadian Company was condemned to pay $375 in additional wages to James Scott, who had temporarily replaced his father as manager, and $3480 (with Pinkham) to a local merchant.[26]

If these cases were not a serious financial burden, they were certainly symptoms of the company's troubled status. In 1875 pressure from the French-Canadian colonists in Marston and the repatriation colony in Ditton resulted in the confiscation of twenty-three and a half company lots. The new manager, Aeneas McMaster, protested that the government had failed to build the promised access road into Ditton. In his words, "these lands were cancelled for the benefit of those holding certain creeds and belonging to a certain nationality, who easily get all their roads and other conveniences granted them."[27] Most of the Ditton lots were subsequently restored, with a commitment that those already occupied by the repatriation colony would be compensated for elsewhere.[28] As for the Marston lots, they too were returned owing to the favourable report of the inspector of crown land agencies, John Hume. He found that, contrary to agent Wright's assertion, the company had begun to chop trees on three of its confiscated lots, while a house had been built and an acre of underbrush slashed on the fourth. Father J.B.A. Cousineau of Piopolis had supported the illegal possession of the latter lot by a French-Canadian colonist on the grounds that there was only "une espece de chantier" on it. Hume rejected this charge as well as the priest's claim that all the company's houses "ne sont guère bonne que pour des enfants," being only five feet high between floor and ceiling. Six feet one and a half inches was the average height in the thirteen houses Hume had inspected, though he failed to mention that alterations had been done prior to his tour. To be fair to the company, it had not skimped in contracting the construction of its sixteen houses, for it paid Pinkham seventy dollars for each, plus seventy-nine dollars for plaster and lime.[29]

Father Cousineau had also charged that the company had instituted a leasehold system, whereas it actually promised to hand titles over to the colonists once they paid the government price (through labour for the company, if they wished) of sixty cents per acre, plus the fifteen dollars advanced for each acre cleared. As Hume insisted, the terms seem to have been reasonable even though the logs would be a clear profit to the company, and it was no doubt too demanding to expect colonization of each crown lot to begin within the first two years. But the inspector neglected to point out the crucial fact that the Glasgow Canadian enterprise did not hold the land as a temporary reserve. Location tickets had been issued to its individual members, with the result that the company would acquire full title to the land once the settlement conditions had been fulfilled. Given the choice of proceeding to strip each lot of its marketable timber, which would be perfectly legal, or encouraging colonists to reimburse the investment in their lots, it is not difficult to imagine which course the company would follow. In effect, then, the so-called settlers must have simply been labourers living in company cabins only so long as it took them to log its land. Furthermore, it appears that the company did not attempt to establish individuals even temporarily on all the lots it logged, for in 1877 the commissioner of crown lands rejected its request to forego duties on timber cut by "settlers" on lots they did not occupy.[30]

The inevitable result of the Glasgow Canadian Company's privileged status was described as early as 1877 by twenty-nine-year-old George Robertson, who claimed to have lived in two of the Marston cabins. He testified that all the cabins had been "pretty habitable nice houses" until travellers to and from the Lake Megantic settlements had begun to seek overnight shelter in them, both for themselves and their horses. After Hume's visit, individuals even used the cabins as cow stables and as sources of wood to make furniture.[31]

The company was still susceptible to cancellation of its location tickets, but any incentive to colonize the crown holdings ended in May 1878, when the Department of Crown Lands accepted the local agent's informal statement that settlement conditions had been fulfilled.[32] Eleven years later, as we saw in chapter 5, the municipality of Marston South protested to the government that the company's lots, most of which fronted the public road, were blocking the community's expansion. The clearings were completely overgrown, and those buildings which had not collapsed were worthless. Because the company refused to sell the land in quantities that colonists could afford, the councillors wanted the province to buy it back, and then make it available to local individuals.[33] This was a vain hope, for the Montagu Paper Company of Massachusetts eventually acquired the Marston property in 1894.[34]

The only other land sold by the Glasgow Canadian Company prior to liquidation was some building lots in Scotstown, the railroad lot in Lennoxville, 1500 acres in Hampden, and most of the Clinton Township property.[35] Its attitude to colonization in Clinton was even less positive than in Marston, since McMaster objected strenuously to paying taxes for a road which would accommodate the Nantes-based colonization company's settlers in neighbouring Woburn: "This matter of taking advantage of the law to force us to provide roads for a Jesuit Settlement from Old France is iniquitous, and every objection should be made to the injustice."[36] The Glasgow Canadian Company was clearly operating just as any lumber company would, except that it was not eligible to lease timber berths from the crown.

Whether he was expressing anger over the International Railway's skirting of his company's Marston lots, or whether he anticipated additional favours from the Liberal administration which had so obligingly granted the company its land titles in 1878, McMaster became an outspoken critic of the powerful local MP. A libel suit (later dropped) ensued after McMaster published a letter concerning Pope's seizure of a local minister's goods and chattels:

The bag that has been so often gorged with spoils taken from honest people will have to disgorge some of its ill-gotten gain in the shape of damages and costs. I claim it is the duty of every honest man in the county who detests arrogance and oppression, dishonesty and duplicity, and who loves liberty of thought and conscience to stand forth and assist in defending Rev. Mr. McDonald from a persecution which the dishonorable pursuer backed by tricks of law seems to delight to engage in.[37]

If McMaster's political stance was motivated by strategic considerations, it backfired because the provincial Tories were soon returned to power. The Conservative press reported with more than a little satisfaction in 1880 that all Compton County sawmills were working to capacity except the one in Scotstown:

This certainly does not speak very flatteringly for the business capacity of the agent of The Glasgow Canadian Land and Trust Company. You are entitled to great credit, Mr. Editor, for the masterly and incontrovertible manner in which you have defended Hon. Mr. Pope from the dastardly insinuations and false statements made by this unscrupulous and ambitious resident of Scotstown.[38]

One might have expected the Glasgow Canadian Company to be in a reasonably good position by 1879, with the international market on the road to recovery, a large sawmill on a good railway connection, and no further obligations to the government.[39] Yet the company never seems to have made a profit. There are no surviving financial records on which to base such a judgement, but its shares never became a marketable commodity. Their book value did not move from the original ten pounds even though their number remained strictly limited. Only twenty-four individuals, including heirs, ever were associated with the Glasgow Canadian Company, and most held their interests right up to the liquidation of the company. The only significant movement, apart from Scott's sale of his 700 shares after he was fired, was President Fraser's divestiture of 950 units to two Glasgow bankers in 1878. The suspicion that this transfer represented the equivalent of collateral in return for financial assistance is strengthened by the fact that the shares were returned to Fraser's widow in 1896, shortly before the company effectively ceased operations.[40]

The final evidence for the Glasgow Canadian Company's poor financial record comes from the solicitor in charge of liquidation. He reported that the company had paid no dividends for some time prior to the 1897 decision to voluntarily wind up its affairs, and that it "has not had a successful business career owing mainly to the difficulty experienced in disposing of its lands and properties and the timber grown thereon."[41] Even though the property was advertised frequently in Canadian newspapers, six years were to pass before an offer would be made. The land and buildings were valued at the original investment figure of $125,500, but in 1903 the company accepted with alacrity the offer of only $30,815.[42] For this sum, Montreal's Great Northern Lumber Company acquired the Scotstown property and 7075 acres in additional land, as well as various credits such as a $3500 mortgage against a local sawmill operator. The price allowed shareholders (there were no other creditors) only nine and a half shillings on the pound.[43]

It appears that to make a profit the Glasgow Canadian Company would have had to acquire more timber resources to supply its Scotstown mill, which had absorbed more than $25,000 for the dam and plant alone, not to mention the $30,000 invested in the International Railway. With some two-thirds of its lumber-producing property out of the mill's reach on the Lake Megantic–Chaudière drainage network, the company found itself having to rely on local customers at a time when small steam sawmills were proliferating throughout the district.[44] The margin of profit on sawing lumber purchased from others, particularly in an environment dominated by the Clark and Hall companies, would presumably never repay the company's investment in the Scotstown infrastructure. Certainly it never made a profit from the sale of either its town or its rural lots.[45] Unfamiliar with the North American environment, the Scottish investors simply failed to realize just how worthless marginal agricultural land would be once its timber had been removed. Thus the company was stuck paying taxes ($5,300 between 1897 and 1904) on unmarketable land for which it had either paid a high price to speculators or on which it had invested in improvements for the crown.[46] In sum, it was forced to compete on the one hand with monopolistic lumber firms which had access to large supplies of timber at nominal rents, and, on the other, with local farmers and small-scale mill operators who were burdened with relatively little overhead. The Glasgow Company operation would become economically viable only in 1903 when purchased at a cut-rate price by a company which would consolidate it with the Scotstown Mills, also in liquidation at that time.[47]

THE DOMINION OF CANADA
LAND AND COLONIZATION
COMPANY

The completion of the International Railway and the recovery of the lumber market in the late 1870s set the stage for the introduction of a second British-based colonization company to the Lake Megantic area. The lack of company records makes it impossible to identify stockholders, but the Dominion of Canada Land and Colonization Company, launched in 1880, appears to have had a more impressive financial base than its Glasgow counterpart. Two of the directors were Lord Dunmore, world adventurer and lord-in-waiting to Queen Victoria, and a Lieutenant-Colonel or Major-General Synge.[48]

The Dominion Company's driving force was Francis Stockwell, background unknown, who applied on behalf of several English capitalists for an ambitious 300,000-acre purchase with cash in eastern Compton and southern Beauce counties. Their proclaimed objectives were to settle British immigrants on farms and to breed cattle for export to foreign markets.[49] The Legislative Assembly's standing committee on agriculture, immigration and colonization recommended that the proposal be rejected, but the government did offer a 100,000-acre reserve. Its conditions would require that at least forty families be settled the first year, sixty the second, and fifty each of the third and fourth years. As usual, the letters patent would be issued directly to the settlers, upon recommendation by Stockwell. The company agreed to these terms, with the added advantage that 5000 acres would be patented in its own name once 500 acres had been cleared and $1000 invested in buildings. Altogether, the Dominion Company received much the largest reserve of any of the province's colonization companies – 99,609 acres of which 79,032 acres were located in the Eastern Townships and the remainder in the Matapedia area. Of this amount, 1,390 acres, found to be already occupied by squatters, were subtracted from the reserve.[50]

By the time it was officially incorporated under the presidency of Lord Dunmore, who visited the area in 1883, the Dominion Company had radically modified and enlarged its list of goals.[51] The export of beef was no longer specifically mentioned, but the company was to engage "in all the different branches of industry in the country, such as warehouses, factories, dwelling houses, stores, wharves, and such other premises, buildings, machinery, and plant. And to make such roads, tramways, canals or other works of a like or similar nature as may be necessary."[52] Though the company did not admit it, the most important "branch of industry" would of course be the manufacturing of lumber. Furthermore, its plan to use the latest steam technology to pull trees out by the roots and process lumber in portable mills was designed to minimize the amount of local labour and capital investment required.[53] The Dominion Company's interest in timber soon led to a direct conflict with the major monopolist in the Lake Megantic area. Stockwell tried to prevent the licence holder, G.B. Hall of Montmorency Falls, from cutting on his company's reserve by taking a writ of injunction before the Superior Court in Sherbrooke. He contended that the reserve fell under the protection of a new regulation, passed in 1880, which declared that timber licensees had to wind up their operations each May on any crown lots for which location tickets had been issued during the previous year. Hall and Company replied that the legislation did not apply to reserves, thus they had the right to continue cutting on each lot until full legal title had been ratified. To add moral strength to their case, they presented testimony from local Catholic priests to the effect that clearings made by the Dominion Company were unfit for settlement, that only one of its houses was habitable, and that the quantity of lumber cut was greatly in excess of what was needed for building houses.[54]

Fearing the precedent that a victory for the Dominion Company would set, Eugène-E. Taché, assistant commissioner of crown lands, testified in favour of Hall.[55] He pointed out that, like all licence holders, the Hall Company had been assured that it could operate within its designated limits until 1889, even though cutting permits were subject to yearly renewals. Furthermore, no colonization society formed after 1869 had been allowed to infringe upon the timber berths, by which he presumably meant that the societies could take logs only from the portion of each lot cleared for cultivation. Neither of these two points were particularly germane, because of the 1880 regulation. The key question was whether or not a colonization company's reserve could be considered the equivalent of a location ticket held by an actual settler. Taché argued that it could not, and he concluded that "in future timber berths situate within the subdivided portions of this Province would not be worth buying should they be exposed at any moment to be enveloped in some colonization scheme and there [sic] area thereby reduced by 100,000 acres at a time."[56] With such inexplicit legislation, the case could have gone either way.

In fact, Stockwell lost the first time, but managed to win before a court of appeal.[57]

The next problem he faced was the forty-four squatting families on the 5000-acre special reserve in Whitton. Mostly French Canadians, they refused to accept terms offered by the English colonization company. Their attitude was clearly articulated by Jacques Picard, MLA for Richmond-Wolfe:

Après tant de sacrifices et tant de dévouement de la part de ces vieux et vaillants pionniers ... n'était-il pas raisonnable que les fils de tous ces vieux défricheurs de bois n'eussent, sinon la préférence, au moins le privilège, et l'espoir surtout, de pouvoir un jour s'établir eux aussi, sur une terre de gouvernement, à côté et dans le voisinage de leurs bons vieux parents.[58]

The Department of Crown Lands tried without success to convince the company to accept land elsewhere in place of that already occupied. It then instructed Stockwell that attempts must be made to keep the squatters on their lots, but if anyone were to be evicted, he would have to be paid for the improvements.[59] Ironically, by taking up the squatters' cause, the nationalist clergymen and politicians dealt the Dominion Company a trump card which it played to full advantage.[60] In June 1882 Stockwell conceded that the squatters could stay on company land, where they would be dealt with on more liberal terms than the immigrants, but only on condition that they be considered part of the two hundred families the company was obliged to settle.[61] He had not counted, however, upon the determination of the squatters, for they failed to reach an agreement before the 30 June deadline set by the government. The colonists' obstinacy appears to have been encouraged by the local priest – in fact the bishop of Sherbrooke himself refused to intercede on the company's behalf.[62]

To force a settlement, Stockwell finally took legal action against several colonists, demanding that they abandon their land or pay $250 in damages. Father Philémon Brassard of Saint-Romain-de-Winslow begged the government to intervene, saying that the squatters were willing to pay for their land, but not to the Dominion Company. The Department of Crown Lands replied that its hands were tied, and suggested that Stockwell's terms be accepted. The curé was assured that, when the colonists paid the company, the department would issue the letters patent directly to them. But the French Canadians remained distrustful, and Father Brassard asked for a government inspection, charging that the land company had brought only beggars who were living at its expense.[63]

The priest may have been exaggerating, but government bush ranger P.W. Nagle found that the company had done nothing in Spalding and Ditchfield, and not enough in Whitton. In the latter township, 560 acres had been cut over, 340 acres partly cleared, and 270 acres made ready for crops. There were thirty-one houses, fifteen of which were occupied by immigrant families, and five by single men. Most of the men worked on company roads, but only about four miles had been completed. Not surprisingly, however, a sizeable quantity of timber had been cut. Stockwell protested that there were over forty settlers, and that Nagle had been misled because more than one family lived in some of the fifteen houses in order to be close to the road work. He claimed that, after submitting his report, Nagle had conceded to him privately that the company did have its full quota of settlers for the year.[64]

The Department of Crown Lands must have been impressed by Stockwell's defence, for a couple of months later it sent another agent, O.B. Kemp, to report on the company's operations. Kemp's first act was to attend a meeting between the company's representatives and the squatters. He counselled the latter to accept the company's terms "in spite of several obnoxious conditions" such as the reservation of mineral rights, mill sites, and fisheries.[65] Most of the squatters followed Kemp's advice, paying only sixty cents per acre where the company's own settlers were charged five dollars per acre, but he reported that if he had inspected the company lots before the meeting, he would have told them to stick to their original position.[66] He found that, without the squatters, the company did not have the required number of settlers for the year. Furthermore, they had not been brought directly from Britain, as the Dominion Company had promised, but had been lured away from their original destinations after their arrival in Quebec.

Kemp argued that the whole operation was more a speculative than an agricultural one because the prospectus claimed that the settler would be able to pay for his lot from the sale of timber, whereas the law stated that until letters patent were issued, timber could only be used for buildings, fences, and firewood. The crown lands agent was not entirely right in this assertion, for ever since 1873 colonists who had made two payments and fulfilled the other settlement conditions could obtain permits to market the timber on their lots.[67] His second point was a more damaging one – a great deal of work had been done, and an immense amount of timber taken, on lots unfit for settlement. Kemp therefore advised the department to insist upon the expired deadline it had set for the company to reach an agreement with the squatters. In this way, the squatters need not be counted as company settlers, legally enabling the government to cancel the whole reserve.

This recommendation was not heeded, and 1883 found the Dominion Company still struggling for existence. It was becoming increasingly unpopular, however, and Conservative MLA Jacques Picard launched a bitter attack against it in the Legislative Assembly on 19 February. He charged that former Premier Joseph-Adolphe Chapleau (who had failed to deliver Picard a promised seat in the Legislative Council), must have bowed to outside pressure when he made the arrangement because much of the Eastern Townships and Matapedia land was near railways and therefore valuable.[68] William Sawyer of Compton rose to the defence of the company, claiming that it had built a number of good houses and new roads, made extensive clearings, and that it had not sold any wood. But Sawyer was alone in his stand. The Quebec City resident, George Irvine, obviously spoke for the Hall lumber company when he proclaimed that the Dominion Company was simply using colonization as a pretext to sell timber. He charged that the colonists were actually being paid to stay on their lots, and, like Picard, he felt that the terms of the contract should be executed to the letter. Even the commissioner of crown lands, W.W. Lynch, and his predecessor, E.J. Flynn, admitted that the results were not what they should have been, and that they too had lost confidence in colonization companies. Lynch confessed to having been swayed by the prestige and influence of Lord Dunmore and other members of the organization: "On devait avoir des engins spéciaux pour faire le défrichement. Tout devait marcher comme par enchantement et la forêt devait en peu de temps faire place à de riants chalets élévés au milieu de fermes superbement cultivés. C'était un pays de cocagne que l'on devait avoir, ni plus ni moins." Finally, Premier Joseph-Alfred Mousseau promised that no more large concessions would be made. He believed that putting an intermediary between the government and the colonists was prejudicial to the interests of the latter.[69]

Despite this near unanimity of opinion, the government continued to act with extreme caution, perhaps because of the company's readiness to resort to the courts. In April of the same year (1883), P.W. Nagle submitted still another harsh report. He emphasized that the old country settlers "keep going and coming and shifting about in such a manner that one hardly knows where to find them from one month to another."[70] But once again the department decided to check into Nagle's findings. Contradictory reports were filed by two inspectors in June, the French Canadian supporting Nagle and the English Canadian defending the company.[71]

But whether or not the details of Nagle's report were correct, it was quite apparent that the Dominion Company had not lived up to expectations. In July it decided to follow the BALC tactic of sacrificing part of its claim in return for cancellation of the remaining debt. The government was asked to reclaim all but the Whitton, Spalding, Ditchfield, and Louise tracts, leaving 55,381 acres. To that date, the company had paid $36,000 plus interest, while the cost for the diminished reserve was only $33,228. It asked that the difference between the two sums be refunded, and that the number of families required be reduced to 111. This would mean that the quota had already been reached.[72]

The government reacted favourably to this proposal, but it insisted upon several modifications. The number of acres was more strictly limited – 22,550 for purely settlement purposes, plus the 5000-acre block for the company itself. Also the squatters were not to be considered as inhabiting the company's reserve, and ninety more families had to be settled within the next three years. Licences for lumber companies would not be renewed for the three-year period, but neither the Dominion Company nor its settlers were to be allowed to cut outside their clearing areas. Finally, the government would refund $8217.[73]

The position of the Dominion Land Company appeared secure for the time being, but the collapse of the timber market in 1884 completely ruined it. A year later Nagle reported that "the settlers have done nothing of themselves except to occupy the lots and shift about from time to time."[74] The company, which had sold its portable steam mills and all its lumber, seemed to be at a standstill. In 1886 Nagle found that many of its settlers had left the country, or moved to other lots which they occupied as squatters. He recommended cancellation of the entire reserve because it had become a nuisance to lumbermen and future settlers.[75] A local resident claimed that most of the company's efforts were a dead loss: its settlers, tiring of the hard work, soon left, and the houses were either burned down or taken away piece by piece.[76]

Even though the Dominion Company had paid $30,000 to the government and invested $50,000 in clearing operations, it disappeared from the scene quickly once its decline set in. It had no private holdings to dispose of, having relied upon portable steam sawmills rather than investing in a village centre for manufacturing lumber. In contrast to its counterparts from Glasgow and (as we shall see) Nantes, the Dominion Company's holdings were simply not advantageously located for exploitation by a local mill site. It made some sense for the Glasgow Canadian Company and the Compagnie de Colonisation et de Crédit des Cantons de l'Est to erect large mills on the International Railway at Scotstown and at the town of Lake Megantic, respectively, because a good proportion of their logs could be floated to these sites for processing and shipment. But much of the Dominion Company's reserve was drained by the Chaudière River downstream from the railway crossing at the outlet of Lake Megantic. From Spalding and Gayhurst (38,243 acres) the only feasible shipping route was via the distant Grand Trunk Railway near Lévis. Difficult though they were to move through such a rough terrain, portable mills would meet the requirements of the Whitton reserve (20,590 acres), with its close proximity to the International Railway.[77]

Stockwell had presumably been aware from the start of the geographical limitations to his company's lumber production. He may well have anticipated an active land market because much of the reserve lay within reasonable railway access for agricultural produce, an advantage not enjoyed by any previous colonization projects in the upper St Francis district. If such was the strategy, Stockwell had failed to realize that most of the arable land would have been claimed well before the appearance of his company. Consequently, the so-called settlers of the Dominion Land Company, like those of its Glasgow-based counterpart, remained essentially labourers who shifted from lot to lot in their logging operations. Even if the company's original intention had not been simply to skim off profits from each lot, this was in effect what it was doing until caught by the lumber crash of the mid-1880s.

LA COMPAGNIE DE COLONISATION ET DE CRÉDIT DES CANTONS DE L'EST

The third major land company to operate in the Eastern Townships was established in 1881, two years before the Quebec government publicly announced its disillusionment with the privately sponsored settlement projects. If the British colonization companies quickly became political embarrassments, a company originating in France was a nationalist's dream come true, particularly when it was financed by clerico-conservative capital, as we shall see. The founding of the Nantes-based colonization company was no small coup on the part of Jérôme-Adolphe Chicoyne, in light of the failure of its two highly publicized French predecessors, mentioned above. But 1880 brought a dramatic renewal of economic interest in Quebec from a country which had traditionally disposed of nearly all its capital exports within western and central Europe. Furthermore, in campaigning for French investment in his project, Chicoyne appealed emotionally to those who dreamed of France's glorious imperial and Catholic past. While still employed as the province's repatriation agent, he had suggested to Gustave Bossanges, the powerful Paris agent of the Allan Steamship Line, that he imitate the English practice of directing capital to Canada to be invested at 8 per cent interest. The result would be, in Chicoyne's view, a strengthening of "l'élément français" in the Eastern Townships, while liberating large numbers of colonists from the grip of usurers charging 12 to 20 per cent interest. Bossanges remained indifferent to the idea, but Chicoyne's big chance came in 1880 when he was sent to Europe as representative of the Société de Colonisation de Sherbrooke.[78] Mgr Antoine Racine had founded the society as a response to the threat of British colonization companies operating in the region, and Chicoyne's assignment was to attract French and Belgian settlers to its reserve in mountainous Woburn Township, on the Maine border south of Lake Megantic.[79]

Once in France, Chicoyne directed his attention to a more ambitious scheme. He went directly to Paris where he met G. Mollat, lawyer and director of the conservative newspaper, *L'Espérance du Peuple*. Mollat took Chicoyne to his home in Nantes where he was introduced to Adolphe Bécigneul, a notary, and to Bécigneul's wealthy uncle, Eugène-Marie Peigné. A missionary of the Immaculate Conception order and heir to a fortune from his grain merchant father, Peigné was the perfect candidate for Chicoyne's settlement scheme. Hoping to find a worthy cause to support, he invited the persuasive Canadian to describe his project on a pilgrimage to Lourdes. By the end of the trip Peigné had agreed to advance the $20,000 needed to launch a colonization company. The only condition was that his nephew, Eugène Bécigneul, accompany Chicoyne to Canada to help manage the company's affairs.[80]

Having received the Pope's blessing in June 1881, Chicoyne's project was incorporated with the distinctly unromantic name of the "Compagnie de Colonisation et de Crédit des Cantons de l'Est." Chicoyne's reasoning was that, given the Anglo-Protestants' dominance in the Eastern Townships, it was necessary to avoid "tout ce qui serais de nature de froisser [leur] susceptibilité."[81] As director-general, Chicoyne was in charge of local operations, while major decisions were supposed to be ratified by at least two of three annually elected *censeurs*. The first three incumbents were Abbé Peigné, Adolphe Bécigneul, and Raphaël de Bouay de La Bégassière, a Nantes landowner and ex-captain of the papal Zouaves, but company headquarters was to be in Sherbrooke making it necessary that a majority of the administrators be Townships residents.[82]

Practical control may have rested on the western side of the Atlantic, but Chicoyne's main target for investment funds would remain the clerico-conservative élite of France. The company's prospectus was explicit: "Ses actionnaires français appartiennent exclusivement à la bonne école et représentent par leurs idées, par leurs principes, la vieille France d'autrefois, cette France chrétienne dont nous sommes si justement glorieux d'être issus."[83] The first share issue numbered 177 at 500 francs ($100) each. The company planned eventually to divide its capital into two classes of $100,000. Class B funds would be used to lend money to colonists, farmers, and others at a moderate rate of interest, as well as to acquire privately owned land of low value. This land would in turn be sold to colonists who would occupy it as tenants until their rents had paid for it.[84] Although steps were taken towards implementing this banking and real estate scheme, as we shall see, it was never actually brought into operation.

The class A funds were destined for a colony in Woburn Township. To begin with, Chicoyne planned to pay three dollars an acre for the only block not reclaimed by the crown in 1880 – the 4628 acres owned by Lemuel Pope, a cousin of John Henry Pope.[85] To this block, called the *Domaine*, would be added 20,000 acres of crown lands available at sixty cents an acre. Once the land was purchased, a sawmill would be built in Woburn, at the site of the future village of Channay. (The name was adopted from the home of Chicoyne's French ancestors.) One tenth of each government lot would be cleared, and the wood sent to the sawmill. A farm would be established on the meadowland, where the wild hay could be cut. Lots would be sold to colonists at a price covering company expenses, later fixed at the low rate of seventy-five cents an acre. Up to half the value of the clearings made by the colonists would be lent to them, and they would obtain title to the land when the debt was repaid at 6 per cent interest. All commercial wood, except that used for heat and buildings, would be reserved by the company. Nothing would be done for the moment on the *Domaine*, because no settlement duties were required there. Until the Channay mill was built, logs would be floated down the Arnold River to the southern tip of Lake Megantic. From there they could be boomed to the northern end of the lake to the sawmills at the terminus of the International Railroad at Agnès–Lake Megantic. The expenses would be considerable:

To purchase the *Domaine* (4628 acres)	64,020 francs
To purchase 200 government lots	60,000 francs
To clear the government lots	100,000 francs
To build a sawmill at Channay	20,000 francs
To establish the farm	30,000 francs
Divers	25,980 francs
	300,000 francs ($60,000)

Chicoyne nevertheless promised that there would be a $36,000 profit just from selling the wood accumulated in the clearing operations.[86]

He did not, furthermore, plan to confine his activities to Woburn. Having purchased Lemuel Pope's land, he took steps towards acquiring most of the BALC's 11,200 acres in his former theatre of operations, Ditton Township. To make the Ditton tract more attractive to the Nantes investors, Chicoyne had exploited the desire of the Trappist monks at Meilleray, near Nantes, to found a new home in Canada should government taxation force them out of France. By choosing Ditton, Chicoyne claimed, they would prevent the establishment of "une colonie anglaise ou protestante."[87] When the Trappists did acquire 800 acres from the land company, Chicoyne used the same argument in reverse: "Il me fait peine de songer que les anglais et les protestants s'enricheront par les sueurs des Pères Trappistes."[88] He did not, however, forget to guard his company's interest, for he suggested that the remaining Ditton land not be purchased until it became certain that the new monastery would be built. After two years of effort by three of his priests and an investment of $8000, the superior was disappointed to find on his visit that the area was not at all suitable for the order's purposes. Chicoyne was left to liquidate the property at a considerable loss to the financially straitened monastery.[89] Needless to say, he dropped his own plans for investing in Ditton, focusing instead upon Woburn where he reserved an additional 9449 acres from the crown.[90]

Having acquired sufficient land, Chicoyne's next step was to ensure that his enterprise would be given plenty of favourable publicity. He took over the editorship of Sherbrooke's *Le Pionnier*, presumably to maintain political support as much as to attract local investment capital. Unfortunately his plan to have Abbé Peigné send him "un bon breton" as his replacement backfired when the person in question quickly deserted to the enemy *Progrès* camp.[91] A second measure designed to stimulate government assistance was the remodelling of Mgr Racine's colonization society into a subsidiary of the Nantais company, with the bishop remaining president and Abbé Peigné becoming vice-president. Though technically limited to promoting "les intérets religieux de la future paroisse de Saint-Augustin," the society was eligible for a colonization road subsidy, thereby contributing materially to the colonization company.[92]

By the autumn of 1881 Chicoyne had spent Peigné's $20,000 without beginning any actual clearing or construction operations. He asked that the value of shares be multiplied two and a half times to $50,000, adding that a local promotion would only introduce the anglophone population into the enterprise. To persistent French complaints about having to take all the financial risks, Chicoyne retorted that he would have to travel outside the Eastern Townships to avoid the English-speaking market.[93] Comfortable in the realization that the Nantes directors were already too deeply involved to let him down, Chicoyne never did find the time for such a campaign.

In November the Nantes officers obligingly launched a campaign to sell more shares. Their circular, sent to the diocesan clergy as well as to select friends, copied the chauvinistic example set by Chicoyne:

Le but que nous nous proposons est d'enlever au protestantisme le monopole de la colonisation des immenses forêts vierges du Bas Canada ...

Deux siècles d'occupation anglaise et de pression persécutrice n'ont pu altérer ni la pureté de la foi, ni l'amour de la mère-patrie chez ces familles généreuses et fidèles ...

... ces admirables enfants de l'antique royaume de France veulent demeurer catholiques et franco-canadiens. Ils tournent vers nous leurs mains suppliantes et le regard de leur espérance.

Jacques Cartier et les colons qui le suivirent étaient en majeure partie des Bretons, c'est à la fidèle et catholique Bretagne de venir en aide à leur descendants.

But material considerations were not entirely neglected, for rocky Woburn Township was transformed into a country with "trois cent mille stères de bois propres au commerce," "les prairies si vastes et si fécondes," and "une rivière dont les flots roulent d'or, du cuivre et de l'étain."[94] Perhaps the fact that Quebeckers would have difficulty recognizing the area thus described had as much to do with Chicoyne's request that the circular remain in France as did his expressed fear of an Anglo-Protestant backlash.[95]

Chicoyne interpreted the new share issue as giving him a free hand not only to implement his programme but to broaden its scope.

Having decided to build a sawmill at the town of Lake Megantic rather than at Channay, Chicoyne invested $1780 in 37 acres of town property. Twelve acres were to be used for the mill, and 25 for speculation. Chicoyne added 106 acres at the mouth of the Arnold River to serve as a station for the steamboat which would haul the company's log booms to the Lake Megantic mill.[96] After contracting to supply over two million feet of wood, he started to erect a building which was to be no ordinary sawmill. Boasting a granite foundation and stone pillars, it measured 75 by 60 feet, and was flanked by two annexes of 30 by 40 feet. With the steam engine and circular saw alone, it would cost $13,500. In addition, a variety of other saws were to be installed to make use of all the wood cut in clearing operations. The building would also house a flour mill at an added expense of $5,000.[97] Unfortunately, future developments were to prove that such a large outlay of capital was unwarranted.

In December 1881, President Charles Paumier began to worry about the declining French market for timber, but Chicoyne assured him that Central and South American demand was more than adequate.[98] When Paumier and Abbé Peigné again expressed concern in March, Chicoyne reassured them: "Je vois dans cette Compagnie une institution toute providentielle qui, avec le temps, va répondre à un grand besoin dans nos Cantons de l'Est."[99]

As for colonization itself, Chicoyne was even more confident. By March 1882, he had still not bothered to draw up a plan, yet he actually discouraged the French administrators from recruiting emigrants on the grounds that those who arrived on their own initiative would be more committed and less demanding.[100] Chicoyne was no doubt recalling his La Patrie experience, and furthermore his true goal was to attract French Canadians, rather than potentially troublesome French immigrants. Predicting confidently that people would flood in once the project was completed, he nonetheless had promised to start advertising as soon as the government had extended its road beyond Channay to the crown lots where the first arrivals would be settled. Meanwhile, the Société de Colonisation de Sherbrooke transferred 2,000 acres of its crown reserve to the company to serve as pasture for a Swiss cheese factory at Channay. The factory would in turn provide a market for the Woburn colonists' milk. Chicoyne also planned to build a small sawmill at Channay for the use of the settlers.[101]

At the same time, he finally took steps to launch the financial part of the enterprise. When the town of Coaticook's Société de Construction (a community trust company) was liquidated, Chicoyne and several of his Sherbrooke colleagues bought all the shares for $1,700. They planned to resell them to the local clergy and French Canadians as shares in class B of the company's operations.[102] For the immediate future Chicoyne would have to remain preoccupied with the Lake Megantic operations; he had not sold any class A shares in Quebec, and he again needed more money. The company had only $6,637 on hand to meet obligations of $12,300, and Chicoyne predicted that by 30 June 1883 he would need to spend an additional $39,254.[103] The French directors replied, however, that shares were not selling well in France, no doubt because of the lack of dividends from the first year's operations. Chicoyne had promised immediate profits, but delays in getting the wood to Lake Megantic, and in constructing the mill and its railway branch, meant that returns had been slow in coming.[104] Finally, in November, Chicoyne announced that a 2.5 per cent dividend would be paid, but, in order to continue immediate operations, $10,000 would be needed to cut wood, $3,000 for the Channay colony, and $2,000 for mill operations. Chicoyne still opposed taking a loan – he wanted the French officials to sell 150 more shares – but in December he was forced to borrow $2,000 at 7 per cent interest. By that time he had doubled his estimate to $20,000 for cutting and floating operations, but France sent only $4,000, saying that $8,000 more would be available in the spring.[105]

The company's finances were clearly in a dangerous position, but this was not Chicoyne's only headache, for the government had begun to exert pressure on it to start colonizing. Because nationalist deputies were crying for strict measures against Lord Dunmore's Dominion Land Company, the Department of Crown Lands could not be overly lenient towards the Nantais operation.[106] Chicoyne's excuse for his company's neglect was that the government had not completed its road to the crown land reserve before the previous autumn. He emphasized that real progress had been made on the company's privately purchased farm and village properties and stressed that Mgr Racine would not collaborate with a group of speculators. The minister of crown lands replied that he was not satisfied with Chicoyne's excuses, but, because the bishop was as-sociated with the project, he would grant a twelve-month delay.[107]

Chicoyne's desperate demands for money persisted throughout the winter. Money was needed for more clearing, for cattle, for advances to the colonists, for payment of the government instalment, and for the Lake Megantic mill. Even though it did not augur well for the year's earnings, Chicoyne had to respond to government pressure and the lack of financial resources by restricting logging to concentrate upon establishing the colony.[108]

During the next few months he repeatedly reassured his nervous French partners, boasting that he could count on allies among the English-speaking deputies to "adoucir les rigueurs administratives," and promising that the government would never take back lands where colonization had been initiated.[109] Even if some of the property were to be seized, the company's down payment would be returned. Finally, the colony would always have the private *Domaine*, which included the best agricultural land, and which could supply the sawmill for a good ten years. As for local financial support, Chicoyne promised to begin offering the class B shares to the general public at the first opportunity. It would be impossible, however, for him to sell class A shares because his Eastern Townships compatriots had invested all they could afford in class B, and he still did not have time to travel to the rest of the province.[110]

If the shareholders were reassured, their relief was short-lived; in mid-summer Chicoyne recommended that the meadowland of the valuable *Domaine* be sold to settlers immediately because there was not enough money to develop it. This was the one piece of land to which the company held clear title, but Chicoyne rationalized that its sale would attract a more prosperous class of settlers, thereby aiding the projected cheese factory and guarding against charges of speculation.[111] Such philanthropy clearly did not appeal to the French directors, and in August they summoned Chicoyne to submit a detailed report in person.[112]

When he arrived in Nantes, Chicoyne learned that the former editor of *Le Pionnier* had been forwarding copies of the rival *Progrès de l'Est*.[113] The latter newspaper had indeed been critical of the whole operation. It reported that the wood market was flooded, that employees were complaining about their salaries, and that the company was threatening to sue the man who had installed the Moulins nantais machines. It also carried on its long-standing personal vendetta with Chicoyne, of whom it stated:

Ceux qui savent comment il a conduit les travaux du gouvernement dans les cantons du rapatriement, savent aussi que M. Chicoine est un homme de jugement sur et solide, muri par une longue expérience dans l'art de faire de l'argent, d'un désintéressement à tout épreuve et ne travaillent que pour la plus grande gloire de la religion et l'avancement du Canada français! Les profits sont peut-être lents à venir, mais les riches capitalistes qui lui ont confié leurs milliers de francs, doivent s'attendre à recueillir ces mérites spirituels plutôt que de l'or, eux qui ont entrepris ces grands travaux en vue de la conversion des "sauvages" du Canada! Lorsqu'il a dévotement baisé les mains de l'abbé de Belle-Fontaine, avant de reprendre la route du pays lors de son premier voyage, M. Chicoyne a dû leur faire comprendre par cet acte d'humilité et de piété qu'à l'example du Divin Maître, son royaume n'est point de ce monde![114]

In spite of the damaging attacks, Chicoyne was again able to dispel the directors' fears.[115] He returned to Quebec without additional money, but at least he again had moral support. On the home front, he faced the annoyance of a second Bécigneul son, who boasted that he had been sent to spy on Chicoyne, but affairs had finally taken a turn for the better.[116] In December 1883, Chicoyne declared a profit of $6,363, which meant that the company could offer a 5 per cent dividend. Furthermore, colonization had progressed well enough to satisfy the government, and the company store in Lake Megantic had proven to be profitable.[117]

To further reassure the French investors, Chicoyne fused the class B shares with class A, which meant that his Sherbrooke colleagues had become investors in the mill and colonization operations. This may have strengthened French confidence, but it failed to bring much extra capital into the company. In spite of the declared profit, Chicoyne again began to issue appeals for money ($10,000) from France. He rationalized that because the Quebec public had been led to believe that he had gone to Nantes to prevent the French shareholders from dropping the enterprise, a campaign to sell shares within the province would only reinforce this opinion and weaken the company's position. Whether the French directors believed this rather flimsy excuse or not, they obligingly sent $5,000 in January.[118]

In truth, the company had reason to maintain its confidence in Chicoyne. During the winter of 1883-84, over four million feet of timber was cut, the mill operated smoothly, colonists began to buy the *Domaine* lots, and a group of Swiss immigrants arrived with machinery for manufacturing cheese.[119] When the log drive of four million feet of spruce, and a million feet of pine and cedar began on schedule in April, the company's financial embarrassments finally appeared to be over.[120] But disaster lay just around the corner.

In May Chicoyne announced a "Krach" in the New York market – the European commercial crisis had finally reached America.[121] The price of wood dropped quickly, and, although Chicoyne managed to maintain the budget at an equilibrium, most of the profits came from the store.[122] Rather than reduce operations to cut costs, the indefatigable Chicoyne decided to focus more intensively on colonization until the end of the recession. Although no company up to that point had made a profit in the Eastern Townships from selling land to colonists, Chicoyne acquired 2,200 more acres from the government to start a second company farm called Toutes-Joies in honour of the youth and labour circle directed by Abbé Peigné in Nantes.[123] The Department of Crown Lands, which was beginning to learn from experience, laid down stringent conditions. Within two years the company would have to build a Swiss Gruyère cheese factory, as well as instruct at least six Quebec students in the manufacturing process. Within three years, 5 per cent of the land was to be under cultivation (10 per cent within five years).[124]

Though selling land to poor colonists would never generate much capital, Chicoyne's colonization and land speculation projects did proceed smoothly. The Sherbrooke committee's annual report of 25 November recorded that the *Domaine* farm had been rented to Swiss colonists who were operating butter and cheese factories on a small scale; several other *Domaine* lots had been sold to French Canadians; colonization of the government lots in Woburn had been a success, with good crops harvested; the value of the property at the southern tip of Lake Megantic had increased with the construction of a government quay; and the Lake Megantic town lots were also becoming more and more valuable. Finally, the store at Lake Megantic had brought a 17 per cent profit in the previous eleven months. The report concluded that with $3,418 on hand (a figure that was soon to become a subject of controversy), the company could proceed at a slow pace without further shares being sold. However, more money would be required if the company were to hold its lumber until prices were restored.[125]

Winter logging and sawmill operations would obviously not be extensive, so Chicoyne was granted a six months' leave of absence. He took advantage of this opportunity to acquire a federal grant through J.H. Pope, ostensibly to pay his expenses to Switzerland where he was to recruit more cheese-making immigrants.[126] But Chicoyne's primary motive for going to Europe was to rescue the company from stagnation by convincing Abbé Peigné to embark on another share-selling programme. This, remarkably enough, he had little trouble doing – $50,000 was to be invested by one of Peigné's rich connections alone.[127] It appeared certain that the company would easily ride out the recession, but Chicoyne seemed to be jinxed. At the last minute, his Sherbrooke colleagues pulled the rug out from under him by submitting a special report which accused him of having purposefully placed the company in a dangerous financial position by withdrawing all the funds before he had left for Europe.

Chicoyne argued that the treasury had actually been empty when the Sherbrooke committee had submitted its 25 November report, but the other members had insisted on proceeding without further shares being sold. Whether they wished to sabotage Chicoyne's sales campaign, or simply to cover up the mistake they had made with the November report, as Chicoyne himself suggested in his reconstruction of events, their March report had a disastrous effect upon the prospects for selling shares in France. Chicoyne reported to his wife: "Le rapport du 'bureau' canadien est arrivé comme un obus prussien parmi ces têtes françaises si spirituelles, à idées si généreuses, mais en même temps il faut le dire, si légères et si facilement échauffées."[128] The Nantes committee decided to advertise its shares anyway, but to little avail.[129]

Chicoyne bitterly denounced his "propres compagnons d'armes" for their maladroit intervention at the moment when he was about to "monter à l'assaut des actionnaires dans le but si noble de sauver une entreprise bonne et solide en elle-même et si utile à notre patrie."[130] He was partly to blame himself, however, because he had signed the overly optimistic November report. Autocrat that he was, Chicoyne appears not to have taken the committee seriously and to have decided to rescue the company on his own accord by selling shares in France.

This reversal was the last straw for the exasperated Chicoyne. Claiming that the company did not have enough capital to continue operations, he counselled Abbé Peigné to liquidate it at the first favourable opportunity. He warned that if his advice were not followed, "il devra y avoir un crac épouvantable avant longtemps."[131] Instead, Adolphe Bécigneul was sent to Lake Megantic with $2,800 to try to salvage the enterprise.[132] In effect, he replaced Chicoyne as manager, who wrote to his wife in April, "je pense que notre Compagnie va tourner en affaire de famille. M. Peigné va s'en emparer et la faire conduire par ses neveux. Tant mieux."[133] In July, Chicoyne officially resigned as director general. To charges that he was abandoning the company in its hour of need, he replied that he had been eased out by Peigné and Bécigneul.[134] Chicoyne's final recommendation to the company was to abandon the first crown land grant (9,449 acres). In this way not only could it avoid the reputation of being an obstacle to colonization, but the money reimbursed could be invested in the 1884 Toutes-Joies grant (2,200 acres). By December, Chicoyne had resigned completely from the administration.[135]

Still the company struggled on. In July 1886, it issued a report claiming that twenty acres of the Toutes-Joies farm had been cleared, and that thirty of its ninety-eight other lots were occupied. The report blamed the slow progress on the oversized Lake Megantic mill, which manufactured too much lumber in a time of crisis, thereby diverting money destined for colonization in Woburn. Wishing to return to its original purpose, colonization, the company asked the government for permission to retain the Toutes-Joies farm and twenty-four improved lots. It wanted the money it had paid towards the other lots to be credited towards those it retained. In harmony with its expressed desire to concentrate upon colonization alone, the company sold its Lake Megantic mill for $12,000, little more than half its cost, to an entrepreneur from Portland, Maine.[136]

Quebec granted the company's request, but two more years passed with little being accomplished.[137] Crown inspector Nagle reported that colonization was progressing at a snail's pace: "Where parties have left or went to the States, others have taken their places, and a few who were absent have returned to reside." In Channay, the company still owned a store and operated a good sawmill in connection with a grist-mill, but it had failed to establish the cheese factory, or to improve the Ferme Toutes-Joies. Nagle recommended that the company at once abandon claim to all lots not settled, including Toutes-Joies. He even felt that, in the interest of the settlers, the company might have to liquidate itself in the near future.[138]

Refusing to give in, the Nantes directors made still another desperate effort to salvage the enterprise. After expensive materials were imported from Europe to build the cheese factory, Bécigneul convinced the government to issue land titles in the name of the company, rather than in the names of the settlers. This would enable him to force the settlers to pay for the improvements made. In return, Bécigneul promised to expand the clearing operations, to lend cows to the colonists, and to establish butter and cheese factories.[139] The company eked out an existence for another five years, never managing to overcome the debts incurred during the optimistic days of Chicoyne's administration. In 1892, the elderly but persistent Peigné suggested that he might reconstitute a colonization company with his sixth of the liquidated assets. He even declared himself willing to become the curé of Woburn, an offer that Mgr Racine wisely declined.[140] In the end, nothing came of the whole face-saving device, for the company finally breathed its last in 1893.[141]

Like the other colonization enterprises, the Nantais company was a complete financial failure. It had, however, come close to success, and even though its $60,000 investment was overshadowed by that of the other two colonization companies, it did benefit the area in which it operated. The opening of Woburn Township to settlement

was no great accomplishment, but a major industry had been introduced into the pioneer centre of Lake Megantic, a town which would
grow to 2,500 people by 1901.[142]

Motivation is less easy to judge. Abbé Peigné and his coterie were
clearly genuinely committed to French Catholic rural expansion,
although they probably did not realize how little financial profit
could be made from such an enterprise in late nineteenth-century
Quebec. As for Chicoyne, there was certainly an element of oppor-
tunism in his readiness to play upon the theme of an abandoned
French Canada, importuned by the powerful Anglo-Protestant majority yet remaining a faithful daughter of ancien régime France.
Still, there is no reason to doubt his commitment to the cause of
French-Canadian colonization, if only because it was the basis of his
public career. Chicoyne would spend the remainder of his active life
supporting the agrarian cause through journalism and politics.[143]

But Chicoyne's agrarianism had nothing to do with the failure of
the Compagnie Nantais, and his investment in the Lake Megantic
mill was certainly a more entrepreneurial move than was the Woburn
cheese factory which appealed to the government and the French
directors. Whereas the latter fell into disrepair, the sawmill's new
owner invested an additional $24,000 in the plant in 1890, thereby
multiplying production five-fold to 100,000 feet per day.[144] Indeed,
timber would have been a more logical cash staple than would milk
for the colonists in this most isolated of the region's townships.

The Quebec government's problems with the Dominion Land
Company in the early 1880s ensured that no more land reserves
would be made available for colonization companies. Their failure
to attract settlers and their unpopularity with French-Canadian nationalists were damaging enough, but probably more important was
the threat presented to monopolistic timber companies by Stockwell's
court victory. A colonization company might contribute far more
investment capital per acre than would a lumber firm, but political
pressures dictated that no government would consent to a land reserve in the knowledge that it was thereby cancelling a logging licence
within that reserve.

The inability of the colonization companies to stimulate much land
settlement is not difficult to explain. They monopolized the timber
taken in the clearing operations, and the soil and topography of any
crown lands remaining by this time would certainly not have been
suited to a market-oriented agricultural economy. Even the raising
of cattle for beef was becoming less and less viable as western pro-

duction steadily increased during the 1880s. Though he was referring to the Prairies of the 1930s, Stephen Leacock understood the
dilemma faced by colonization projects which could not depend
upon a staple export in the age of industrial capitalism:

The ideal settlement raises its own food and eats it; catches its own fish and
cooks it; cuts its own lumber and builds its houses with it. It cooks, bakes,
boils, cans, ferments, sews, stitches, paints; it carpenters, it blacksmiths, – it
pushes self-sufficiency as far as ever it can till the points where it meets the
needs for machine products from outside. These grudgingly it must buy,
with things which, grudgingly, it will sell.[145]

Because there was no chance that a non-utopian colonization company would have been able to exercise the centralized authority
contemplated by Leacock, a saleable commodity would inevitably
have to be found.[146] In the upper St Francis district that commodity
was timber but the rub was that the colonization companies, not their
settlers, controlled the harvesting, manufacturing, and marketing of
this product. Company members may have been touched to varying
degrees by the sense of idealistic imperialism which Leacock felt was
essential to the success of their "Valley of Hope," but they were first
and foremost capitalist enterprises whose chief raison d'être was to
make a profit for their shareholders.[147] Furthermore, the paternalistic
imperialism of a Lord Dunmore, even with the impressive financial
backing of his company, resulted in a much less valuable addition
to the local economy than did the operations of the strictly business-
oriented Glasgow company. Indeed, the Nantes company's main
legacy lay not in the realm of agricultural expansion, despite its
sincere efforts, but in its contribution to the commercial-industrial
centre at Lake Megantic. And, as far as the local settlers were concerned, any benefits to be gained from the patriotism of the French
company's directors was simply cancelled out by their concomitant
conservative agrarianism for it meant that they would never consider
establishing a lumber co-operative to encourage settler participation.
After half a century of experimentation, the futility of grandiose
colonization projects must have become obvious to the bourgeois-
nationalist spokesmen and politicians, yet they would remain frus-
tratingly blind to the necessity of settler access to the timber resource,
and even to the contribution of small indigenous capitalists to the
maintenance of a local population base.

Conclusion

The act of uprooting oneself and moving to a frontier of settlement has generally been interpreted as a declaration of independence, as a step towards controlling one's own destiny. According to Turner's thesis, the freedom-loving United States is a product of just this process on a national scale. On the upper St Francis frontier, however, the settlers' destinies were deeply influenced by forces and institutions beyond their control. Hebridean crofters and French-Canadian habitants did not appear in the district simply by chance. As individuals and families, they exercised a certain degree of free will in making their decision to locate there, but, on a practical level, they were obliged by economic circumstances to seek new homes where a minimal capital investment would be required. They were therefore susceptible to the enticement of inexpensive land or easy payment terms presented through various programmes organized by state, church, and private entreprise. And, on a less tangible level, the agents of colonization did not fail to play upon the settlers' deep-seated desire to possess their own land and maintain their traditional family ties and community structures. This the colonists were successful in doing, but within tightly circumscribed limits which kept them perpetually on the margin of impoverishment.

State, church, and capital, in their various guises, each made a major impact upon the colonists' destinies in the upper St Francis district, but these institutions certainly did not always operate in unison or harmony with each other. To the representatives of the British government during the first half of the nineteenth century, emigration to Lower Canada promised relief for landlords and ratepayers, as well as stronger imperial ties in a disaffected but strategically important colony. To the French-Canadian nationalist élite, operating through both church and state, the colonization movement offered a foothold in the Anglo-Protestant townships and diversion of the ever-increasing exodus to New England's mill towns. Metropolis and colony clearly had conflicting political and ideological goals, with the British American Land Company becoming one of the grievances leading to the Rebellion of 1837. Britain's retirement from the contest came in 1848 with the advent of responsible government and the inauguration of the Eastern Townships colonization-roads project. After Confederation the Catholic Church and the provincial administration could openly demonstrate their religio-nationalist zeal by establishing Zouave and repatriation colonies and by encouraging a group of French religio-imperialists to invest in the upper St Francis district.

The province devoted $10,280 to the Lambton Road, $22,400 to the free-grants colonization roads prior to 1850, an additional $76,000 to the district's colonization roads prior to Confederation, $12,600 to district colonization societies between 1869 and 1875, and over $60,000 to the repatriation colony during the next three years.[1] If the annual colonization road subsidy for the post-Confederation period were included, it would be safe to estimate that the province spent upwards of $200,000 on direct promotion of settlement in the upper St Francis district between the 1840s and the 1890s. Furthermore, it granted double that amount to the International Railway, not to mention its subsidization of the Quebec Central which ran along the western periphery of the district. The constant complaints of the clerico-nationalists to the contrary, as far as grants are concerned the state was not lacking in generosity towards the colonization movement. Furthermore, it encouraged European colonization companies to invest an additional $150,000 during the 1870s and 1880s. Perhaps there was little the provincial authorities could do to reverse the damage caused by the imperial government when it imposed the British American Land Company on the district. Municipal taxation eventually did force the company to alienate most of its timber lands at a low price. The problem was that they were sold to an even more parasitical monopoly as far as the local settlers were concerned – the C.S. Clark lumber company. Apologists for the provincial government could argue that a dependable revenue source was needed to facilitate public investment in colonization projects, including roads, but the value of such assistance tends to pale when one considers that Clark and Company would float away $115,000 in timber during a single rather unexceptional winter.

Given that the scales were so heavily weighted against the colonist, there is a germ of truth to the theory that the colonization movement was essentially a nationalist-capitalist coalition for the exploitation of a dependent class of settlers. But there was, nevertheless, a basic conflict between the forces of French-Canadian nationalism and those of large-scale, English-language capitalism. Admittedly, John Henry Pope could use his political influence to acquire a provincial colonization subsidy for his railroad, and Jérôme-Adolphe Chicoyne could call on Pope's Department of Agriculture to grant him a passage to Europe for the purpose of promoting French-Catholic colonization, but this was part of a political game of mutual trade-offs. There was no strong or even implicit alliance between these two Conservatives as far as colonization was concerned, for Chicoyne wanted as little as possible to do with English-Protestant capital and Pope was far from enthusiastic about French-Canadian settlement in his constituency. In 1864, for example, he complained to Galt that colonizing priests were receiving local colonization road subsidies which he wished to be directed to a road into Ditton Township were he was surreptitiously operating a gold mine:

all I can say is that I leave this matter in your hands if the people of this county are to be entirely at the mercy of Catholic clergy (not of this county) but near Montreal. It will make more effort to wake them up to the absurd and degrading position in which we are placed ... it has remained for Mr. Chappa [sic] to place those Devils over me in the representation of this county.[2]

As the hard-nosed, successful capitalist on the one hand, and the rather idealistic nationalist on the other, Pope and Chicoyne epitomize the basic conflicting forces on the upper St Francis frontier. In the legislature Pope was originally dubbed the "log-roller" for his parochialism, and, even as Macdonald's right-hand man, he never became known for his eloquence.[3] An opposition member of Parliament said of his Compton colleague in 1888: "There are few men who can sit here with a solid countenance, and answer to all attacks and questions that 'there ain't nothing to it' better than my honourable friend."[4] Chicoyne, on the other hand, may have entered politics relatively late in life, but he apparently became known as the "Nestor" of Quebec's Legislative Assembly.[5] Chicoyne appears to have turned to politics almost as an admission of failure in the business world, and when someone offered him a share in the profits if he would intervene with Pope to obtain a survey contract for the Saint-Boniface area of Manitoba, he was indignant: "L'influence que je possède auprès de l'Hon. J.H. Pope résulte de la confiance que mes compatriotes veulent bien reposer en moi et je ne veux me servir de cette influence qu'en faveur des intérêts publics."[6] Pope himself demonstrated none of these scruples. Even though he complained that "reason, comfort and one's family and pecuniary interest rebel against the sacrifices one must make by remaining in Politics,"[7] he was able to have the rules bent or ignored to insure profitability for his lumber and railway operations, not to mention the Ditton gold mine which officially did not even exist. His "pecuniary interests" remained healthy enough to allow him to bequeath $115,000 in cash to his children and grandchildren, $11,000 to three local Protestant institutions, and extensive properties in Eaton, Ditton, and Winslow to his son, in addition to an unspecified residue for his widow.[8]

The dichotomy between Pope and Chicoyne must not be carried too far, however. Chicoyne's nationalism did not preclude capitalist ambitions, as his conflict of interest at La Patrie and his construction of a major sawmill operation at Lake Megantic would testify, and the Loyalist-descended Pope was a nationalist in his own right – witness his opposition to Sanborn and Galt's annexationism in 1849, his officership in the militia, and his pivotal role in western expansion.[9] Both Chicoyne and Pope were of relatively humble rural origins, though Chicoyne certainly attained a superior education, and both played prominent roles in the realm of agriculture – Chicoyne as a journalist, speaker, and organizer, Pope as a federal minister and major breeder of imported livestock.[10] Although it is true that Pope was a partner in two large-scale manufacturing firms, the C. S. Clark lumber company and the Paton woollen mills, in both cases the original entrepreneurial initiative and much of the control came from outside the region. Pope also invested in the Eastern Townships Bank and two Sherbrooke utilities, but, like the other "agricultural capitalists" who dominated the region, his main business interests were linked to the land in one way or another – whether as a farmer, lumberman, mine owner, or railway promoter.[11]

Chicoyne's background was not that of a businessman, but his ambitions were not so different from those of Pope. Indeed, one could argue that Chicoyne's colonization projects were as entrepreneurial as anything attempted by Pope, with the possible exception of the latter's railway adventure which was, after all, largely funded with taxpayers' money. A good exposition of Chicoyne's socio-economic philosophy can be found in the report he drafted in 1893 for the Legislative Assembly's special committee to examine the causes for migration from the countryside. While bemoaning the growth of cities and the evolution towards a highly specialized and integrated economy, Chicoyne realized that Quebec farmers had no choice but to adapt. His report therefore stressed the importance of improved agricultural techniques, a more practical system of education, farm credit, and increased sensitivity to the market. Colonization was relegated to a secondary position.[12]

Chicoyne's appeal to French-Catholic nationalism served a useful purpose, up to a point, but it was a shaky rock on which to establish the foundations of a capitalist empire. Perhaps the greatest handicap it imposed was to direct investment towards an economically marginal district simply because it lay within Quebec, a compunction the region's English-speaking capitalists certainly did not feel bound by.[13] But whether the explanation for Chicoyne's failure as a colonizing entrepreneur is rooted in a lack of business acumen, the poor economic opportunities offered by a district whose limited resources had already been largely monopolized by English-speaking capitalists, an extraordinary share of bad luck, or some combination of all three of these factors, he clearly felt no contradiction between his nationalist ideology and his capitalist ambitions. Towards the end of his career, Chicoyne began to promote agricultural co-operatives as a form of rural self-defence, but he never appears to have conceived of an agri-forestry economy which would have accepted the inevitability of subsistence-style agriculture on marginal frontiers.[14] In fact, his 1893 legislative report recommended that distinctions be made between arable land and that suited only for mines and timber.

As middle-class North Americans, Chicoyne and his nationalist colleagues were not about to promote a radical, mixed-economy model which would have weakened the dominance of industrial capitalism in the forest industry. Yet, to a degree that is difficult to measure because of its largely illegal nature, that model was implemented by the colonists on their own initiative or on that of the local sawmill operators and merchants.[15] Whether the distinction made by contemporary authorities, as well as later historians, between "true" and "false" colonists is a valid one or not is difficult to judge, as is the extent to which lumber companies entered employees' names as land claimants to gain cheap and guaranteed access to timber. No doubt some individuals acted as transient parasites on the large timber limits, but the land-granting system gave them little encouragement to do otherwise, and certainly most long-term residents in the upper St Francis district relied upon some level of income from the forest. This, then, was the hidden economy of Quebec's colonization zones, an economy never encouraged by government, yet one which it had to tolerate on an unofficial basis to keep colonists on their homesteads. If the result was disastrous in terms of managing the exploitation of the forest, the fault can hardly be laid at the doors of the settlers who, after all, gained only a fraction of the spoils that they and their offspring should by rights have been entitled to.

Appendixes

Appendix A
Sales of Privately Held Lots in Lingwick Township, 1807–66, with price per acre in parentheses (BALC purchases in italics)

William Vondenvelden Grant, 1807

Range	Lot	1st Sale	2nd Sale	3rd Sale	4th Sale	5th Sale	6th Sale
5	5	?	1810(b) (—)	1817 (—)	1818(b) ($0.50)	1860 ($0.80)	
	7	?	1834(a) ($0.22)	*1835(b)* (*$0.76*)	*1835(c)* ($1.00)		*1835(c)* (*$1.00*)
	8	?	1810(a) ($0.65)	1813 ($0.06)	1834(a) ($0.20)	1835(a)? ($0.20)	*1835(b)* (*$0.76*)
6	10	1821 ($0.21)	1808(c) ($0.59)	1833(a) ($0.24)	1834(a) ($0.20)	1835(b) ($0.76)	
	5	?	*1835(d)* (*$1.00*)	1813 ($0.06)	1834(a) ($0.46)	1834(b) ($0.60)	*1835(c)* (*$1.00*)
	6	?	1835(a) ($0.20)	1834(d) ($0.20)	1834(f) ($0.40)	1835(a) ($0.20)	*1835(b)* (*$0.76*)
7	8	?	1810(a) ($0.65)	1833 ($0.24)	1835(a) ($0.20)	*1835(b)* (*$0.76*)	
	9	?	1808(a) ($0.50)	1833 ($0.24)	1834(a) ($0.20)	*1835(b)* (*$0.76*)	
	5	?	1808(c) ($0.59)	1834(a) ($0.20)	1834(a) ($0.40)	1835(a) ($0.20)	*1835(b)* (*$0.76*)
	7	?	1808(c) ($0.59)	1813 ($0.06)	1834(f) ($0.40)	*1835(b)* (*$0.76*)	*1835(c)* (*$1.00*)
	8	?	1808(b) ($0.42)	*1834(a)* (*$0.76*)	1834(a) ($0.46)	1835(a) ($0.20)	
	10	?	1810(a) ($0.65)	1834(f) ($0.20)	1834(a) ($0.46)	1834(b) ($0.60)	
	11	1819(b) ($0.22)	*1834(c)* (*$0.60*)				
	12	1819(b) ($0.22)	*1834(c)* (*$0.60*)				
	14	?	1808(b) ($0.42)	1834(e) ($0.20)	1834(f) ($0.40)	1834(a) ($0.20)	*1835(b)* (*$0.76*)
	15	?	1808(c) ($0.59)	1833 ($0.24)	1835(a) ($0.20)	1835(b) ($0.76)	
	17	?	1810(a) ($0.65)	1813 ($0.06)	1834(a) ($0.46)	1834(b) ($0.60)	*1835(c)* (*$1.00*)
	18	?	1808(c) ($0.59)	1833 ($0.24)	1835(a) ($0.20)	*1835(b)* (*$0.76*)	
8	2	?	1835(a) ($0.09)	*1835(b)* (*$0.76*)	1834(f) ($0.40)	1835(a) ($0.09)	
	3	?	1808(a) ($0.50)	1834(d) ($0.20)	1835(a) ($0.09)	*1835(b)* (*$0.76*)	
	5	?	1808(c) ($0.59)	1833 ($0.24)	1834(b) ($0.60)	1835(a) ($0.20)	*1835(b)* (*$0.76*)
	6	?	1810(a) ($0.65)	1834(a) ($0.46)	1834(b) ($0.60)	1835(a) ($0.09)	*1835(b)* (*$0.76*)
	7	?	1810(½)(a) ($0.65)	1834(a) ($0.46)			
			1808(½)(c) ($0.59)	1833 ($0.24)			
	9	?	1810(b) (—)	1817 (—)	1818(b) ($0.50)	1860 ($0.80)	

Grp	No.								
8	10	?			1808(b) ($0.42)	1834(e) ($0.20)	1834(f) ($0.40)	1835(a) ($0.09)	*1835(b)* *($0.76)*
	12	?			1810(a) ($0.65)	1813 ($0.06)	*1835(c)* *($1.00)*	*1835(b)* *($0.76)*	
	13	?			1835(a) ($0.09)	*1835(b)* *($0.76)*	1835(a) ($0.09)	*1835(b)* *($0.76)*	
	14	?			1808(c) ($0.59)	1833 ($0.24)	1835(a) ($0.09)	*1835(b)* *($0.76)*	
	16	?	1821	($0.21)	*1835(d)* *($1.00)*	*1835(b)* *($0.76)*	*1835(b)* *($0.76)*	*1860* *($0.80)*	
	17	?			1808(b) ($0.42)	1834(e) ($0.20)	1834(f) ($0.40)	1835(a) ($0.08)	*1835(b)* *($0.76)*
9	1	?			1808(b) ($0.42)	1834(e) ($0.20)	1834(f) ($0.40)	1835(a) ($0.08)	*1835(b)* *($0.76)*
	3	?			1808(c) ($0.59)	1833 ($0.24)	1834(f) ($0.40)	*1835(b)* *($0.76)*	
	4	?		($0.21)	1835(a) ($0.08)	*1835(b)* *($0.76)*	1834(f) ($0.40)	*1835(b)* *($0.08)*	
	6	?			1810(a) ($0.65)	1818(a) –	1835(a) ($0.08)	*1860* *($0.80)*	
	7	?			1835(a) ($0.08)	*1835(b)* *($0.76)*	1818(b) ($0.50)	*1835(b)* *($0.08)*	
	8	?			1808(b) ($0.42)	1834(e) ($0.20)	1834(f) ($0.40)	1835(a) ($0.08)	*1835(b)* *($0.76)*
	10	?			1808(b) ($0.42)	1834(e) ($0.20)	1834(f) ($0.40)	1835(a) ($0.08)	*1835(b)* *($0.76)*
	11	?			1808(a) ($0.50)	1834(d) ($0.20)	1834(f) ($0.40)	1835(a) ($0.08)	*1835(b)* *($0.76)*
	13	?			1808(b) ($0.42)	1834(e) ($0.20)	1834(f) ($0.40)	*1835(b)* *($0.76)*	
	14	?			1834(d) ($0.20)	1834(f) ($0.40)	1835(a) ($0.08)	*1835(b)* *($0.08)*	
	15	?		($0.21)	1810(b) –	1817 –	*1835(b)* ($0.50)	*1860* *($0.80)*	
	17	?			1808(b) ($0.42)	1834(e) ($0.20)	1834(f) ($0.40)	1835(a) ($0.08)	*1835(b)* *($0.76)*
	18	?			1808(c) ($0.59)	1833 ($0.24)	1835(a) ($0.18)	*1835(b)* *($0.76)*	
10	1	?	1821	($0.21)	*1835(d)* *($1.00)*	*1835(b)* *($0.76)*	1818(b) ($0.50)	*1860* *($0.80)*	
	2	?			1835(a) ($0.18)	1817 –	1834(f) ($0.40)	1835(a) ($0.18)	
	4	?			1810(b) –	1834(e) ($0.20)	1834(f) ($0.40)	1835(a) ($0.18)	
	5	?			1808(b) ($0.42)	1834(d) ($0.20)	1835(a) ($0.50)	*1835(b)* *($0.18)*	
	6	?			1808(a) ($0.50)	1833(a) ($0.24)	1835(a) ($0.18)	*1835(b)* *($0.76)*	
	8	?			1808(c) ($0.59)	1818(a) –	1835(b) ($0.18)	*1835(b)* *($0.76)*	
	9	?			1810(a) ($0.65)	*1835(b)* *($0.76)*	1818(b) ($0.50)		
	11	?			1835(a) ($0.18)	1833 ($0.24)	*1835(b)* *($0.76)*		
	12	?			1808(c) ($0.59)	1818(b) –	*1860* *($0.76)*	*1835(b)* *($0.76)*	
	13	?			1810(a) ($0.65)	1818(a) –	*1860* *($0.80)*	*1860* *($0.80)*	
	15	?			1808(b) ($0.42)	1834(e) ($0.20)	1834(f) ($0.40)	1835(a) ($0.18)	*1835(b)* *($0.76)*
	16	?			1810(a) ($0.65)	1813 ($0.06)	*1835(c)* *($1.00)*	1835(a) ($0.18)	

Appendix A (cont'd)

Range	Lot	1st Sale	2nd Sale	3rd Sale	4th Sale	5th Sale	6th Sale
11	18	?	1808(b) *($0.42)*	1834(e) *($0.20)*	1834(f) *($0.40)*	1835(a) *($0.18)*	1835(b) *($0.76)*
	13	?	1810(b) –	1817 –	1818(b) *($0.50)*	1860 *($0.80)*	
	14	?	1835(a) *($0.20)*	1835(b) *($0.76)*	1835(c) *($1.00)*		
	16	?	1810(a) *($0.65)*	1813 *($0.06)*			
	17	1819 *($0.22)*	*1834(c)* *($0.60)*				

French-Canadian Militia Grants (patented 1840–42) (location tickets issued in 1825)

Range	Lot	1st Sale	2nd Sale	3rd Sale	4th Sale	5th Sale	6th Sale
10	½SW19	?	*1866* *($0.60)*				
11	½NW18	1837(b) *($0.20)*					
	½SE18	1837(a) *($0.20)*					
	½NW19	1836(a) *($0.20)*	*1866* *($0.60)*				
	½SE19	1836(b) *($0.20)*	1839(a) *($0.30)*	1859 *($1.00)*			

Source: Sherbrooke Registry Office, Lingwick Township.

Note: Vondenvelden and Pennoyer were both land surveyors.

Key

1807 William Vondenvelden acquires each of his associates' 1200-acre blocks for $4.45.

1808(a) Jesse Pennoyer (Compton) to William Shearer (Barnet, Vt.); $200 of this $500 sale went to W. Vondenvelden. (Shearer willed this land to two daughters and two sons in 1817.

1808(b) Jesse Pennoyer (Compton) to Thomas Clark (Barnet Tp., Vt.)

1808(c) Jesse Pennoyer to Daniel Smith (Newhampton Tp., N.H.); $420 of this $1600 sale went to W. Vondenvelden; 2700-acre sale includes 400 acres outside Lingwick.

1810(a) Jesse Pennoyer (Compton) to Gordon and Hazen Lawrence (Meredith, N.H.); 3100-acre sale includes 400 acres outside Lingwick.

1810(b) Jesse Pennoyer (Compton) to David Tilton (Shipton Tp.)

1813 Gordon Lawrence (Shipton Tp.) to Ezekiel Hart (Trois-Rivières), sheriff's sale; includes r.5, l.18, a crown lot.

1817 David Tilton (Shipton Tp.) to C.F.H. Goodhue

1818(a) Gorden Lawrence (Shipton Tp.) to C.F.H. Goodhue (Orford Tp.)

1818(b)   C.F.H. Goodhue (Orford Tp.) to Bainbridge, Bainbridge & Brown (London). Includes r.4,l.5 (should be r.5,l.5). r.5,l.5), r.5,l.6, crown lot. This sale is complicated by the fact that Widow Vondenvelden sued for Jesse Pennoyer's land in 1817, which led to a sheriff's sale in 1819 when Goodhue purchased lots for $0.21 per acre which had already been purchased two years earlier. In 1831 he sold the same lots to Bainbridge et al. for $2.00 per acre, though he had already done so for $0.50 per acre in 1818.

1819   Francis Cottrell (Baie St Antoine), sheriff's sale (Widow Vondenvelden v. J. Pennoyer)

1821   Aaron Allen (William Henry) sheriff's sale (Widow Vondenvelden v. J. Pennoyer)

1833   Daniel Smith, Jr (Meredith, N.H.) to C.F.H. Goodhue (Ascot Tp.); 2835-acre sale includes 400 acres outside Lingwick. Presumably to ensure that the title to all the lots he had purchased were clear, Goodhue in Oct. 1833 paid William Vondenvelden, Jr, $400 for all the lots originally granted by the crown in 1807. This included lots in the hands of other parties, but it is doubtful that either Vondenvelden or Goodhue actually claimed these.

1834(a)   Hazen Lawrence (Stanstead Tp.) and Noah Lawrence (Meredith, N.H.) to Alexander Kilborn (Stanstead Tp.). Note that r.6, l.8 and r.7, l.10 and 17, had already been purchased by Ezekiel Hart at a sheriff's sale in 1813. Consequently in 1835 Hart successfully challenged Samuel Hatt's ownership of these three lots. In fact these lots were not included in Hatt's 1835 seizure of Goodhue's Lingwick lands (see 1835(a)). In 1847 Noah Lawrence (Meredith, N.H.) sold for $2000 (to Warren Lowell and James Bell, both of N.H.) half interest in all but two of the Lingwick lots (plus five and a half others) his father had originally acquired in 1810, even though these lots had long since been alienated by him and his family. In 1851 Lowell (Meredith, N.H.) sold his supposed half interest for $800 to John P. Small (Meredith, N.H.).

1834(b)   Alexander Kilborn (Stanstead) to G.J. Goodhue (Ascot Tp.)

1834(c)   Francis Cottrell (Baie St Antoine) to BALC

1834(d)   William Shearer and others (Barnet, Vt.) to Simeon M. Dennison (Shipton)

1834(e)   Widow and son Thomas Clark and others (Barnet, Vt.) to Simeon M. Dennison (Shipton). This sale was repeated between Thomas C. Clark (Peacham, Vt.) and S.M. Dennison (Shipton Tp.) in 1839 at 10¢ per acre.

1834(f)   Simeon M. Dennison (Shipton Tp.) to G.J. Goodhue (Orford Tp.)

1835(a)   Hon. Samuel Hatt (Chambly) by sheriff's sale, Hatt v. G.J. Goodhue (Sherbrooke Village). Note four sale prices for four sets of lots.

1835(b)   Hon. Samuel Hatt (Chambly) to BALC; 11,000-acre sale includes 1000 acres in Bury, 2000 acres in Stoke, and 400 acres in Shipton.

1835(c)   Ezekiel Hart (Trois-Rivières) to BALC

1835(d)   Aaron Allan (William Henry) to BALC

1836(a)   Jean Montminy (St Charles, Bellechasse County) to James Hastings Kerr (Quebec)

1836(b)   Féréol Terrien (St Nicolas) to André Bezeau (St Nicolas)

1837(a)   Jean Chabot (St Charles, Rivière Boyer) to James Hastings Kerr (Quebec)

1837(b)   Bazile Chabot (St Césaire) to James Hastings Kerr (Quebec)

1839(a)   André Bezeau (St Nicolas) to Henry Lemesurier, Esq. (Quebec); includes 200 acres in Acton Tp.

1859   Trustees to estate of Lemesurier, Filstone & Co. (Quebec) to Thomas, John, and Anthony Mason (Quebec)

1860   Trustees to the bankrupt estate of the late firm of Bainbridges & Brown (London) to BALC

1866   Son and widow of James Hastings Kerr (Quebec) to BALC

Appendix B
Timber Production on the Crown Limits of the Eastern Townships.
(St Francis Agency (1855–69) and the St Francis and Arthabaska Agencies (1868–81)[1].
Including Ratio to Province of Canada (1855–66)/Quebec (1866–81)

Winter	Licence Area (sq. mi.)	%	Saw-Logs				Crown Revenue (all timber)	%
			White Pine	%	Spruce	%		
1855–56	825	(2.6)	52,372	(7.0)	7,806	(7.2)	9,060	(3.2)
1856–57	–		88,689	(9.1)	36,500	(27.4)	12,326	(4.3)
1857–58	–		53,738	(8.0)	73,228	(44.7)	9,475	(4.7)
1858–59	–		57,501	(5.5)	78,364	(25.9)	10,079	(3.6)
1859–60	1,614	(5.9)	47,603	(3.7)	128,721	(38.8)	17,059	(5.0)
1860–61	1,270	(4.8)	34,652	(2.9)	79,373	(20.0)	9,256	(2.7)
1861–62	1,165	(4.4)	25,201	(2.7)	45,169	(16.2)	8,283	(2.9)
1862–63	1,319	(4.4)	48,029	(4.4)	62,194	(20.4)	12,042	(3.6)
1863–64	1,283	(4.0)	42,910	(3.3)	61,810	(20.3)	11,441	(3.2)
1864–65	–		–		–		–	
1865–66	1,209	(3.5)	34,258	(2.0)	66,425	(22.3)	7,989	(2.2)
1866–67[2]	1,110	(6.2)	24,786	(2.2)	66,166	(17.8)	6,983	(3.6)
1867–68	992	–	37,878	(2.6)	37,488	(9.2)	8,262	(2.5)
1868–69	220	(0.7)	16,573	(1.1)	23,428	(6.1)	9,285	(2.6)
1869–70	602	(1.9)	28,349	(1.9)	64,360	(14.4)	9,638	(2.4)
1870–71	608	(1.5)	9,296	(0.6)	54,577	(14.8)	5,600	(1.3)
1871–72	1,248	(2.8)	16,003	(1.7)	27,547	(6.3)	9,239	(1.8)
1872–73	1,002	(2.1)	21,568	(1.0)	122,864	(13.8)	12,229	(2.3)
1873–74	871	(1.9)	32,855	(1.4)	213,831	(19.4)	18,654	(3.5)
1874–75	784	(1.7)	61,159	(4.2)	25,880	(4.3)	10,653	(2.8)
1875–76	506	(1.1)	8,097	(0.7)	69,130	(8.8)	8,430	(2.2)

1876–77	–		–		–		–
1877–78	835	(2.0)	14,546	(1.4)	52,785	(6.6)	7,916	(2.5)
1878–79	770	(1.6)	2,594	(0.2)	67,939	(10.4)	7,643	(2.2)
1879–80	889	(1.9)	10,566	(0.6)	101,447	(8.4)	12,588	(2.3)
1880–81	703	(1.4)	5,308	(0.2)	101,349	(7.9)	11,766	(1.8)

Source: 1855–58 *JLAC,* 1857–59, Apps., reports of CCL.

1858–64 *SPPC,* 1861–65, reports of CCL.

1865–66 *SPC,* 1867–68, no. 6, report of CCL.

1866–76, 1877–81 *SPQ,* 1868–83, reports of CCL.

1 After Confederation a large portion of the C.S. Clark and Company limits was located in the Chaudière Agency, but this agency is not included here because much of it lay outside the Eastern Townships region, oriented towards Quebec City, not Sherbrooke and the Grand Trunk Railway. Furthermore, the company's activities would leave a greater mark on the smaller St Francis and Arthabaska Agencies.

2 Starts fiscal year system (July 1 to June 30), that is, the report for the fiscal year ending 30 June 1868 is for winter of 1866–67. See Hardy *et al., L'exploitation forestière,* 20; Gaudreau, *L'Exploitation,* 42–44. From this date on, the records list not fees and duties owed the government but only revenue actually collected.

Appendix C
Finances of the Colonization Societies Active in Marston Township, 1869–75, in dollars

Society[1]	1869–70		1870–71		1871–72		1872–73		1873–74		1874–75	
	Subscription	Grant	Subscription	Grant	Subscription	Grant	Subscription	Grant	Subscription	Grant	Subscription	Grant
Montréal-Ouest no 1	–	–	300	300	300	300	300	300	–	–	600	600
Montréal-Ouest no 2	–	–	–	–	150	150	150	150	–	–	150	150
Montréal-Ouest no 3	–	–	–	–	150	150	150	150	150	150	150	150
Montréal-Centre no 1	–	–	–	–	265	265	310	300	150	150	–	–
Montréal-Centre no 2	–	–	–	–	150	150	155	150	150	150	600	600
Montréal-Centre no 3	–	–	–	–	150	150	138	138	150	150	150	150
Montréal-Est no 1	–	–	–	–	130	130	200	200	250	250	300	300
Montréal-Est no 2	–	–	–	–	–	–	257	257	225	188	150	150
Quebec West no 1	–	–	655	477	300	300	–	–	–	–	–	–
Compton no 1	600	450	600	–	–	–	–	–	–	–	–	–
Sherbrooke no 1	–	–	300	300	–	–	–	–	–	–	–	–

Source: SPQ, 1869–75, Reports of the CCL.

1 Of the Montreal societies only Ouest no 1 and 2, and Centre no 2, held reserves in Marston, but all their resources were pooled in a common association which focused its energies on Marston.

Abbreviations

AAQ	Archives de l'archevêché de Québec
AAS	Archives de l'archevêché de Sherbrooke
AC	Archives of the former Department of Agriculture and Colonization, Province of Quebec, *see* Quebec, Ministère d'Énergie, Mines, et Ressources
AETR	Archives de l'évêché de Trois-Rivières
ANQ-Q	Archives nationales du Québec à Québec
ANQ-S	Archives nationales du Québec à Sherbrooke
ASSH	Archives du séminaire de Saint-Hyacinthe
BALC	British American Land Company
CCL	Commissioner of Crown Lands
CHR	*Canadian Historical Review*
CO	Colonial Office
DCB	*Dictionary of Canadian Biography*
ETHS	Eastern Townships Historical Society (Sherbrooke)
JAC	ASSH, Jérome-Adolphe Chicoyne Papers
JLAC	Canada, Province of, *Journals of the Legislative Assembly*
JLAQ	Quebec, *Journals of the Legislative Assembly*
NA	National Archives of Canada
NMC	National Map Collection
PP	British Parliamentary Papers
PP, IUP	*British Parliamentary Papers*, Irish University Press
RL	Registre de lettres
RHAF	*Revue d'histoire de l'Amérique française*
SL	ANQ-Q, Siméon Le Sage Papers
SPC	Canada, *Sessional Papers*
SPPC	Canada, Province of, *Sessional Papers*
SPQ	Quebec, *Sessional Papers*
SRO	Scottish Record Office

Notes

PREFACE

1 Vicero, "Immigration of French-Canadians to New England," 108, 129, 152–79, 193.
2 See the review of the literature in Massicotte, "Les Études régionales."
3 See Morissonneau, *La Terre promise*; Dussault, *Le Curé Labelle*; and Proulx, *Le Roman du territoire*.
4 See the many articles on the Lac Saint-Jean region by Gérard Bouchard and associates.
5 This interpretation is expressed most clearly in Séguin, *La Conquête du sol*.

CHAPTER ONE

1 The most detailed study of this period is Ouellet, *Lower Canada*.
2 The political developments of the 1840s are discussed at length in Monet, *The Last Cannon Shot*.
3 Creighton, *Empire of the St. Lawrence*.
4 Young, *George-Étienne Cartier*.
5 Though its argument is somewhat dated and exaggerated, the most trenchant statement on the ideological impact of ultramontanism remains Brunet, "Trois dominantes de la pensée canadienne-française."
6 *JLAC*, VIII (1849), app. 2.
7 Lavoie, "Les mouvements migratoires des Canadiens," 78.
8 The most detailed treatment of the political background to the Association des Townships is in Parent, *Deux efforts de colonisation française*.

9 The best treatment of this subject is Proulx, *Le Roman du territoire*.

10 Gérin-Lajoie, *Jean Rivard*, 264.

11 Ibid., 150, 194.

12 Morissonneau, *La Terre promise*, 124.

13 *Le Pionnier* (Sherbrooke), 17 Nov. 1876 (my emphasis). *Le Pionnier*'s enthusiasm for large-scale industry would cool noticeably during the ensuing depression years, which were disastrous for Sherbrooke. See McKercher, "The French-Canadian Press in Sherbrooke."

14 Morissonneau, *La Terre promise*, 135. For Ontario, see Jones, *History of Agriculture in Ontario*, 299–300. For an intriguing theory on the politico-cultural ramifications, see Wynn, "Notes on Society and Environment in Old Ontario," 58–60.

15 The best study on Labelle is Dussault, *Le Curé Labelle*.

16 Morissonneau, *La Terre promise*, 72.

17 See Little, "Watching the Frontier," 93–111.

18 See Little, "The Catholic Church and French-Canadian Colonization."

19 On the struggle against absentee proprietors in the Bois-Francs, see Little, "Colonization and Municipal Reform."

20 Little, "Watching the Frontier," 98, 103, 105–6.

21 *Le Pionnier* (Sherbrooke), 16 Oct. 1890. For an indication of how dramatic the "invasion" process could be, see Bellavance, *Un village en mutation*. On the topic in general, see Ross, "Ethnic Relations and Social Structure."

22 On the *modus vivendi* worked out between anglophones and francophones in the constituency of Richmond-Wolfe, see Sevigny, "Le capitalisme et la politique dans une région québécoise de colonisation," chap. 7.

23 Hamelin and Roby, *Histoire économique*, 163–64. This statement is repeated in Linteau, Durocher, and Robert, *Quebec*, 109, and Trofimenkoff, *The Dream of Nation*, 135–36.

24 Quebec's provincial governments certainly did not neglect the promotion of industrialization, which actually developed at a pace close to that of Ontario; see Marcel Hamelin, *Les Premières Années du parlementarisme québécois*; Ryan, *The Clergy and Economic Growth*, 34.

25 Tobias, "Canada's Subjugation of the Plains Cree."

26 Levitt, *Henri Bourassa*, 61–63.

27 Hodgins, "Unconventional Priest of the North," 128–29, 131.

28 Hodgins, Benidickson, and Gillis, "Ontario and Quebec Experiments in Forest Reserves," 31.

29 Gaudreau, *L'Exploitation des forêts publiques au Québec*, 39.

30 Vanay, "Colonisation et monopole forestier," 41–56.

31 Gaunitz, "Local History as a Means of Understanding Economic Development," 15, and, "Resource Exploitation on the North-Swedish Timber Frontier," 137–38; Raumolin, "The Impact of the Forest Sector," 396, 404.

32 See Jean, *Agriculture et développement*. But Mario Lalancette does suggest that the seigneurs of La Malbaie encouraged an agri-forestry economy by granting large concessions (up to 1000 arpents) in the interior; see Lalancette, "Essai sur la répartition de la propriété foncière à la Malbaie," 76.

33 Lower, *Settlement*, 29, 52, 64, 66.

34 Hamelin, *Les Premières Années*, 238–39.

35 My emphasis. Cross, "Dark Druidical Groves," 54. A fairer assessment of the settlers' attitude towards trees can be found in Ball, "Technology of Settlement," 82.

36 McCalla, "Forest Products and Upper Canadian Development."

37 Lower, *Settlement*, 67; but see Gillis, "Ottawa Lumber Barons"; Gillis and Roach, "Early European and North American Forestry," 212–13.

38 Roach, "Farm woodlots," 202.

39 Raumolin, "Impact of the Forest Sector," 396–98, 415.

40 See, for example, Séguin, *La Conquête du sol*, 50; Hamelin and Roby, *Histoire économique*, 225–26; Roach, "Farm woodlots," 207.

41 Bouchard, "Co-intégration et reproduction," 22–24. Another positive account of the combination of lumbering with farming activities can be found in Wynn, *Timber Colony*, 72–78, 82–84.

42 Gaudreau, "Le rapport agriculture-forêt."

43 Séguin has come much closer to this interpretation in his recent book written with René Hardy; see chap. 5 of *Forêt et société*.

44 Nelles, *Politics of Development*, 45.

45 An insightful study on the conservative English-Canadian version of this myth is Fraser, "Like Eden in Her Summer Dress."

46 Rock, "Agrarian Propaganda," 214–18.

47 Marx, *Machine in the Garden*, 126–30.

48 Gérin-Lajoie, *Jean Rivard*, 209–11, 249–51. His biographer states of the early colonization promoter, Father Calixte Marquis, that: "il voit dans l'éducation des jeunes gens de la campagne le remède principal aux maux qui nuisent à la colonisation"; Morin, "La pensée colonisatrice," 110.

49 Gérin-Lajoie, *Jean Rivard*, 250. For the arguments of western promoters, see Smith, *Virgin Land*, chap. 16.

50 On the admirable success of French-Canadian farmers in Kansas, see McQuillan, "Farm Size and Work Ethic"; for a more general over-

view of French-Canadian migration to the Midwest, see McQuillan, "French-Canadian Communities in the American Upper Midwest."

51 Cross, "Dark Druidical Groves," 49. The depth of the élite's hostility towards logging is amply illustrated in Wynn, "'Deplorably Dark and Demoralized Lumberers'?" and his "Notes on Society," 55–56.

52 Savard, *Master of the River*, 62–63. In *La Terre promise*, 113, Morissonneau goes still further by arguing that even the colonists "appartient fondamentalement à la galerie nomade et doit être enlevé du portrait de famille agricole."

53 Dussault, *Le Curé Labelle*, 110.

54 Linteau, Durocher, and Robert, *Quebec*, 221.

55 See Little, "Colonization," and Cross, "'The Laws Are Like Cobwebs.'"

56 Dussault, *Le Curé Labelle*, 273–74.

57 For a detailed study of the American system, see Hurst, *Law and Economic Growth*.

58 Raumolin, "Impact of the Forest Sector," 397, 422.

59 For a detailed study of Picard's political and financial careers see Sevigny, "Le capitalisme."

60 Gaunitz, "Local History," 57–58.

61 Nova Scotia is an exception, for here forestry land was alienated in thousands of small grants, and monopolists failed to gain a foothold. See Robertson, "Trees, Treaties and the Timing of Settlement."

62 According to Normand Séguin, this is the definition first applied by Robert Hirsch in 1967 (*La Conquête*, 30). For a useful sociological discussion on the persistence of the agricultural-logging economy in one Laurentian community, see Fortin, "Socio-Cultural Changes."

63 Gérard Bouchard tends to present a more positive interpretation. See Bouchard, "Co-intégration," and "Introduction."

64 Séguin's thesis is outlined in the introduction to *La Conquête*.

65 For a full discussion of the geology of the Eastern Townships, see Blanchard, *Le Centre du Canada français*, 181–232.

66 Bouchette, *A Topographical Description*, 362–66.

67 AC, Vieux dossiers, Correspondance, no. 3343 (O.C. 3715), Remarks on the Megantic and St Francis Territories and Lambton Road, 26 April 1848.

68 *Description of the Surveyed Townships and Explored Territories of the Province of Quebec* (Quebec, 1889), 201–2.

69 The Megantic Fish and Game Corporation was chartered in 1887. See *Guide to the Megantic, Spider, and Upper Dead River Regions of Quebec and Maine* (Boston: Heber Bishop, 1888).

70 Lajoie, *Agricultural Lands*, fig. 9, and Quebec–South Part, Soil Capability for Agriculture (insert map).

71 Gagnon, "La colonisation aux confins de l'Estrie," 23; Blanchard, *Le Centre*, 237; Kesteman, "Une bourgeoisie," 107.

72 Kesteman, *Histoire de Lac-Mégantic*, 48.

73 Pruitt, "Self-Sufficiency and the Agricultural Economy," 345, 347.

74 Ouellet (*Lower Canada*, 124–25) claims that the traditional diet was 13 minots (1 minot = 1.1 bushel) of wheat or the equivalent of over two pounds of bread a day (Pruitt, "Self-Sufficency," 343), and Greer (*Peasant, Lord and Merchant*, 34–36, 206) claims that the average adult of the upper Richelieu consumed about 15 minots of wheat and potatoes per year. On seed requirements, see Bitterman, "Middle River: The Social Structure of Agriculture," 198.

75 These consumption figures are from Lewis and McInnis, "Agricultural Output and Efficiency in Lower Canada, 1851." They estimate that draft horses consumed 53.7 bushels of oats and 1 ½ tons of hay per year, and colts somewhat less than half that amount.

76 Gaffield, *Language, Schooling*, 80.

77 Jones, *History of Agriculture*, 297. During the early sixties, settlers on the Hastings Road in Ontario's Canadian Shield reacted to the threat of crop failures and fluctuating prices by increasingly diversifying their crops; Parson, "The Colonization of the Southern Canadian Shield," 270–72.

78 P.W. Gates, *The Farmer's Age*, 173.

79 Grant, *Highland Folk Ways*; Jones, *History of Agriculture*, 218–20.

80 Minville, *L'Agriculture* 1: 496.

81 Bateman, "The 'Marketable Surplus,'" 354. This estimate is similar to that made for the Quebec of 1871. Lewis and McInnis, "Agricultural Output," F-2.

82 The 1891 *Census Reports* record a value of $83,340 in factory butter production for the Eastern Townships but none for Compton County where most of the upper St Francis townships were located.

83 McCalla, "Forest Products," 186.

84 During the winter of 1857–58 a government inspector found 272 hands in twenty of the thirty-three camps which reported manpower. ANQ-Q, Terres et Forêts, Correspondance générale, Statement no. 9/58, logs cut by C.S. Clark and Co., James R. McDonald, 7 April 1858.

85 Lewis and McInnis, "Agricultural Output," A-4, F-2.

86 Gaffield, *Language, Schooling*, 80.

87 The farm was leased for $400 a year, with the terms including a stipulation that at least half the hay and grain be fed to livestock on the property so that the manure could be applied to the soil. No wood was to be cut, except for fuel for the house. ANQ-S, E.P. Felton file, 3 March 1859, no. 41; 26 Aug. 1859, no. 149; 18 Nov. 1865, no. 170.

88 The Canadian Meat and Produce Company operated the second largest factory in Sherbrooke, purchasing 400 head of local cattle in the month of October 1875 alone. Kesteman, "Une Bourgeoisie," 187–88.

89 Breen, *The Canadian Prairie West*, 18, 28, 111–12.

90 Kesteman, "Une Bourgeoisie," 213–14. Home production in fertile Compton Township remained steady at one-third the level of Winslow during the same period; Little, "Social and Economic Development," 105, 111.

91 Grant and Inwood, "How Urban was Cloth Manufacture in 1870?" 10, 17.

92 See Little, "The Social and Economic Development," 103, 109. On the family life cycle, see Greer, *Peasant, Lord, and Merchant*, 23, 71–81.

93 In 1861 Clark and Company valued its raw material at $1.00 per hundred board feet for pine and $0.50 per hundred board feet for spruce. According to the conversion table officially adopted by the province in 1888, a twelve-foot log producing one hundred board feet, was fifteen inches in diameter. Gaudreau, *L'Exploitation*, 29.

94 Hamelin and Roby, *Histoire économique*, 270. It is clear that more ashes were processed in 1871 than in 1861, a reflection of the land clearing undertaken by the newly founded colonization societies, but the census statistics are too confused to make much sense of.

95 ANQ-Q, E21, Terres et Forêts, Correspondance générale, Return of timber cut by C.S. Clark and Co. during the season of 1857–58. A search through notary files of the district failed to turn up a single contract between Clark and a subcontractor. This is a sharp contrast to the St Maurice Valley; see Gauthier, "La sous-traitance et l'exploitation forestière," 59–67.

96 Blanchard, *Le Centre*, 293. Christian Pouyez and Yolande Lavoie challenge Blanchard's similar hypothesis for the Saguenay–Lac Saint-Jean region in *Les Saguenayens*, 159, 164.

97 See Hardy and Séguin, *Forêt et société*; Séguin, *La Conquête du sol*; Gaffield, *Language, Schooling*; and Craig, "Agriculture and the Lumberman's Frontier."

98 See Lapointe, *Historique de St. Vital de Lambton*, 100–3, 110.

99 Linteau, Durocher, and Robert, *Quebec*, 147–48.

100 Chayanov, *Theory of Peasant Economy*; Lenin, *Capitalism and Agriculture*.

101 Pilon-Lé, "La différenciation de la paysannerie montréalaise," 50.

102 Cole Harris's variation on the frontier thesis applies only to the first colonization movement when land was plentiful and external mar-

kets essentially inaccessible; see Harris, "The Simplification of Europe Overseas," 469–83.

103 Cross, "Dark Druidical Groves," 28.

104 Osborne, "Frontier settlement in eastern Ontario," 29.

105 For a good analysis of Frank and his neo-Marxist critics, see Goodman and Redclift, *From Peasant to Proletarian*, 29–43.

106 Bouchard, "Co-intégration," 12.

107 Bouchard comes closest to this concept, which he borrows from Alain Touraine, in an article published in 1979 where he speculates upon the fundamental disarticulation between the externally controlled economy and the internal socio-cultural system. Bouchard, "Un Essai d'anthropologie régionale," 120–23.

CHAPTER TWO

1 See for example Karr, *The Canada Land Company*, Johnston, "Immigration" and "Stratford and Goderich," and Saunders, "The New Brunswick and Nova Scotia Land Company."

2 Skelton, *Life and Times*; Norman Macdonald, *Canada*; Cowan, *British Emigration*; Goldring, "British Colonists"; Rudin, "Land Ownership"; Kesteman, "Une Bourgeoisie," 437–56.

3 For a brief account of the company's role in developing its Roxton Township lands, see Little, "The Catholic Church," 157–59.

4 Saunders, "The New Brunswick and Nova Scotia Land Company," 62–64; and Karr, *The Canada Land Company*, 25.

5 See Macdonald, *Canada*, 286–89; and Little, "Imperialism and Colonization," 517–18.

6 NA, MG11, CO 387, Aylmer Papers, vol. 7, 18–20, Aylmer to Goderich, Quebec, 13 April 1832; see also pp. 85–86, Aylmer to Goderich, Quebec, 18 March 1833; p. 96, 24 April 1833; vol. 8, 45, Aylmer to Peter McGill, Quebec, 28 July 1832; Little, "Imperialism and Colonization," 532.

7 Cited in Macdonald, *Canada*, 294. Because of "severe illness" Galt had resigned by 1833. *Information Respecting the Eastern Townships ...* , 4.

8 NA, CO 387, Aylmer Papers, vol. 2, 77, no. 180, Goderich to Aylmer, Downing St, 7 March 1833.

9 NA, RG1 L3L, Land Records, Compton County – General, 24356, Peter McGill to Aylmer, Quebec, 5 Dec. 1832.

10 NA, CO 387, Aylmer Papers, vol. 2, 140, no. 40, E.G. Stanley to Aylmer, Downing St., 4 Jan. 1834; NA, MG24 154, BALC Papers, Correspondence 1835–89, I, 336–41, crown's charges against the BALC, Court of King's Bench, District of Sherbrooke, 26 Feb. 1841. Mac-

donald, *Canada*, 295, claims that the price for the St Francis Tract was £74,992.

11 Goldring, "British Colonists," 194–95. The BALC paid 4*s*. per acre for 9,000 acres of clergy reserves in Bury, Newport, Westbury, and Lingwick townships. NA, Land Records, Compton County – General, 24540, 24547, 24555, 25727.

12 NA, BALC Papers, I, 121, Instructions from Court of Directors to Commissioner in Canada, 27 Jan. 1834; V, Letterbook, 1834–36.

13 Goldring, "British Colonists," 195. Despite the company's financial crisis in the late thirties, by 1853 it reportedly had acquired 176,000 acres beyond its original purchase in crown and clergy reserves, and 228,000 acres in private transactions. NA, BALC Papers, Correspondence 1835–89, 381, Charles Bischoff's Report, 28 Nov. 1853.

14 NA, BALC Papers, I, 109–10, Instructions 27 Jan. 1834.

15 NA, CO 387, Aylmer Papers, vol. 2, 296, no. 2, C. Grant to Lord Aylmer, Downing St, 23 April 1835; ANQ-Q, E21, Terres et Forêts, BALC, art. 1866, Charles Buller to John Fraser, 1 Oct. 1838. The N.B. and N.S. Land Company had to finance all its own improvements; Saunders, "The New Brunswick and Nova Scotia Land Company," 96.

16 *Information Respecting the Eastern Townships*; NA, BALC Papers, V, 1036, Samuel Brooks to Moffatt and McGill, 25 June 1835. The government had a few years earlier constructed a road from Lennoxville through Dudswell, Weedon, and Ham, but its supervisor of surveyors reported in 1836 that it "is already nearly impassable even as a bridle way." ANQ-Q, E21, Terres et Forêts, BALC, Capt. R. Hayne to Stephen Walcott, Quebec, 3 Feb. 1836.

17 *Second Report of the Proprietors of the British American Land Company*, 8. The company later claimed that it had spent £64,490 for its Sherbrooke properties; NA, RG4 A1, S Series, 1838, vol. 538, 180.

18 *Information*, 1842.

19 NA, BALC Papers, I, 118, Instructions, 1834.

20 Langelier, *List of Lands Granted by the Crown*, 315, 345.

21 For a brief history of the original granting system in operation, see Little, "Samuel Gale," *DCB* VI: 268–70.

22 Details on company transactions with speculators can be found in NA, BALC Papers, V, 995–96, Samuel Brooks to Moffatt and McGill, 9 April 1835; 999–1000, 16 April 1835; 1042, Samuel Brooks to William Lord of Shipton, 8 July 1835; 1042, Samuel Brooks to Calvin May of St Armand, 8 July 1835; 1042, Samuel Brooks to Moffatt and McGill, 9 July 1835.

23 NA, Land Records, Bury Township, 89424–41; 94923–28. Lieutenant Abraham Steele finally succeeded in obtaining letters patent to 500 acres despite the company's claim that its settlers had improved

some of this land. NA, Land Records, Compton County – General, 24606–9, John Fraser to Chief Secretary, Sherbrooke, 17 Dec. 1840. See also ANQ-Q, Terres et Forêts, BALC, A.C. Webster to John Davidson, Sherbrooke, 12 Dec. 1836.

24 NA, CO 387, Aylmer Papers, vol. 6, no. 70, Aylmer to Lord Glenelg, Quebec, 6 July 1835.

25 ANQ-Q, Terres et Forêts, art. 1866, BALC, Capt. R. Hayne to Stephen Walcott, Quebec, 3 Feb. 1836.

26 NA, BALC Papers, V, 944, John Moore to Moffatt and McGill, 30 Oct. 1834.

27 ANQ-Q, Terres et Forêts, BALC, Hayne to Walcott, 3 Feb. 1836.

28 NA, BALC Papers, I, 118, Instructions, 1834; Hoekstra and Ross, "The Craig and Gosford Roads," 54.

29 The company presumably did not take advantage of the St Francis River below Richmond because of obstructions by rapids and falls and because of the low swampy land at the river's mouth.

30 Moore noted that settlers selected home sites which offered shelter and water rather than building along the road front; NA, BALC Papers, V, 1050–53, John Moore to Moffatt and McGill, Sherbrooke, 17 [no month] 1835.

31 Ibid., 1087, Samuel Brooks to Moffatt and McGill, 7 Dec. 1835.

32 NA, MG11, CO 384/39 (1835), 11, A.C. Buchanan to Lord Aylmer, Quebec, 12 Dec. 1834; 384/41 (1836), 396, Buchanan's Report on Emigration, 12 Dec. 1835.

33 NA, BALC Papers, V, 1048, Samuel Brooks to Moffatt and McGill, 23 July 1835; 1049, 30 July 1835; 1070, 24 Sept. 1835. Numbers remained low in August; see 1058, 13 Aug. 1835; 1059, 17 Aug. 1835; 1060, 18 Aug. 1835. Buchanan's charge that the company was hiring only Americans (i.e., Townships residents) for road work was clearly unjustified; CO 384/41 (1836), 399.

34 NA, BALC Papers, V, 1018, Samuel Brooks to Guy C. Colclough, 1 June 1835; 1014, Samuel Brooks to Moffatt and McGill, 28 May 1835.

35 Information Respecting the Eastern Townships, part 2, 3.

36 NA, BALC Papers, V, 1048, Samuel Brooks to Moffatt and McGill, 23 July 1835.

37 NA, CO 384/41 (1836), 47, A.C. Buchanan to Sir Geo. Grey, Tyrone, 20 May 1836.

38 Ibid., 399, Extract from Buchanan's Weekly Report, week ending July 25 1836.

39 Ibid., 401, A.C. Buchanan to Geo. Moffatt, Quebec, 29 July 1835; Pentland, Labour and Capital, 58, 110. Buchanan may have been presuming that some of the pauper settlers would eventually acquire

farms since such was the assumption of Colonial Secretary George Grey, upon whose strategy that of Buchanan was closely modelled. See L. F. Gates, *Land Policies*, 271.

40 The results of a similar experiment in Upper Canada had been disappointing; L.F. Gates, *Land Policies*, 181.

41 NA, CO 384/41 (1836), 401–2, Pott. Gill [sic] to A.C. Buchanan, Montreal, 19 Aug. 1835.

42 Ibid. Without citing a source, Skelton (39) states that there would be only three annual instalments after the initial down payment of 20 per cent. The directors' 1834 instructions did state that titles should be granted as soon as possible so that purchasers would acquire a strong interest in their land and gain the right to vote. The company could secure what was left of the debt by having the settler sign a bond and mortgage. NA, BALC Papers, I, 120, Instructions, 1834.

43 Ibid., 120–22. In sharp contrast, when the N.B. and N.S. Land Company began its operations in 1835, it promised an advance on the passage fare, a log house, and five acres cleared, as well as supplies at moderate prices, the provision of medical assistance, and, of course, employment on company projects; Saunders, "The New Brunswick and Nova Scotia Land Company," 67.

44 Cowan, *British Emigration*, 205–6; W. Cameron, "The Petworth Emigration Committee," 233, 238.

45 The negotiations with the Canada Company were cancelled when rebellion broke out in 1837; West Sussex Record Office, Petworth Emigration Committee Papers, R. Ellice to Sir C. Burrell, 16 Jan. [1836]; Nathaniel Gould to Brydone, n.d.; T. Sockett to T.M. Jones, 16 March 1835; T.M. Jones to T. Sockett, 10 March 1835. The Petworth references are from notes kindly provided by Dr Philip Goldring of Parks Canada, Historic Sites. See also Cowan, *British Emigration*, 205–6; Cameron, "The Petworth Emigration Committee," 233.

46 West Sussex Record Office, Petworth Papers, J.M. Brydone to T. Sockett, 25 Jan. 1836. BALC inspector, Charles Bischoff, would pay the Eastern Townships the same backhanded compliment: "I cannot speak of the effects of the long winter but so far as I saw I should prefer the Eastern to the Western [Upper Canada] as a Gentleman's Residence." NA, BALC, Correspondence 1835–89, 394, Charles Bischoff's Report, 28 Nov. 1853.

47 West Sussex Record Office, Petworth Papers, J.M. Brydone to N. Gould, 1 Feb. 1836; H. Bruyères to J.M. Brydone, 19 Feb. 1836; J.M. Drydone to T. Sockett, 12 Oct. 1838.

48 Cowan, *British Emigration*, 206.

49 Brooks purchased 20,070 pounds of pork (costing $1405) and 700 bushels of wheat. He had planned to purchase another 16,000 to 20,000 pounds of pork and 1000 bushels of wheat, but the commis-

sioners vetoed the former, and a shortage of barrels and milling capacity precluded the latter. NA, BALC Papers, V, 1096, Samuel Brooks to Moffatt and McGill, 9 Jan. 1836; 1100, 25 Jan. 1836; 1101, 1 Feb. 1836; 1102, 4 Feb. 1836; 1102, 5 Feb. 1836; 1104–5, 11 Feb. 1836.

50 PP, 1837 (132), XLII, 17, Buchanan's Report for 1836, Quebec, 12 Dec. 1836.

51 Ibid., 32, W. Wigget Chute to A.C. Buchanan, Pickenham Hall, Brandon, Norfolk, 28 April 1836.

52 Ibid., 26, Buchanan's Report for 1836; 39, A.C. Buchanan to A.C. Webster, Quebec, 20 May 1836; 34–35, Alexander R.C. Dillars, Wonston Rectory, Whitechurch, Hants, to A.C. Buchanan, 2 June 1836; A.C. Buchanan to Dallas [sic], Quebec, 15 Aug. 1836; 20 Oct. 1836.

53 Ibid., 17, Buchanan's Report for 1836. The possibility of reaching the Eastern Townships by May, and thereby planting a crop the first year of settlement, was one of the advantages offered by the BALC over Upper Canada and the midwestern states; *Second Report to the Proprietors*, 13.

54 Mack, *A Letter from the Eastern Townships*, 20.

55 PP, 1837 (132), XLII, 41–42, A.C. Webster to A.C. Buchanan, Sherbrooke, 13 Nov. 1836; 27–28, Extracts from Buchanan to Governor-in-Chief; Skelton, *Life and Times*, 40. Buchanan calculated that a total of 9600 immigrants settled in Lower Canada and 13,000 in Upper Canada, PP, 1837 (132) XLII, 23, Buchanan's Report for 1836. The company expanded the number of colonists to 300 families in its 1837 promotional pamphlet, *Lower Canada, Lands for Sale in the Eastern Townships* (London, Jan. 1837). Local historian Leonard S. Channell reports only 100 to 200 individuals and thirty houses at the Victoria village site itself; *History of Compton*, 33. The Shipton newcomer W.G. Mack wrote in 1836 that 50 German families had settled at Salmon River; *A Letter*, 20.

56 NA, BALC Papers, I, 135–7, Extracts from Dispatch, 22 April 1837. The Victoria dam was 180 to 200 feet wide and bolted to the rocks on either side.

57 Channell, *History of Compton*, 33–34.

58 The roadway included five bridges, and it was to be twenty-two feet wide, raised four feet in the centre, and cleared an additional twenty feet on the sides. ANQ-Q, Terres et Forêts, BALC, Moffatt and McGill to W.B. Felton, Montreal, 15 Jan. 1836; NA, S Series, 1838, vol. 549, 68–69, John Fraser to C. Buller, Que., 22 Sept. 1838. The government was reluctant to recognize the validity of the extra expenditure owing to a lack of company vouchers. ANQ-Q, Terres et Forêts, BALC, T.L. Goldie to John Fraser, Montreal, 11 April 1839.

59 NA, BALC Papers, I, 133–35, Extracts from dispatch, 14 Feb. 1837.

60 Ibid., 134, 140, 22 April 1837; NA, S Series, 1838, vol. 538, 178, John Fraser to Earl of Durham, Quebec, 12 June 1838.

61 Goldring, "British Colonists," 192. *Annuaire de Séminaire Saint-Charles-Borromée*, 1891–92, 30–31; the company would later exaggerate the rate of desertions, for though there were no English-born residents in Lingwick Township by 1844, the census records 472 in Bury.

62 NA, S Series, 1838, vol. 538, 179–80.

63 PP, IUP, Emigration Series, III (1841), 219, H.P. Bruyères to Sir George Grey, 27 Aug. 1838; NA, BALC Correspondence 1835–89, 254–6, Henry P. Bruyères to Sir Geo. Grey, 8 Nov. 1838.

64 See Hunter, *Making of the Crofting Community*, chap. 1–3; Gray, *Highland Economy*.

65 NA, BALC Papers, V, 886, Samuel Brooks to Moffatt and McGill, 2 July 1834; 1009-10, 21 May 1835; 1016, 25 May 1835; 1027, 15 May 1835; 1040, 29 June 1835; 1046, 16 July 1835. In 1835 McDougall outbid the BALC agent for 6040 acres in Westbury; ibid., 1043, 9 July 1835.

66 NA, CO 384/44, 161, Col. McDougall to Lord Glenelg, 10 April 1837.

67 NA, CO 384/74, 352–70, D. McDougall to Lord Stanley, 21 Sept. 1843.

68 NA, CO 384/44, 153–67. For Buchanan's much less ambitious and less generous scheme, which would not have included the BALC, see CO 384/42, 97–108, Report of A.C. Buchanan, Colonial Office, 7 March 1837.

69 PP, IUP, Emigration Series, XIX, 387–88, Report on Applicability of Emigration to Relief of Distress in the Highlands, 29 July 1837.

70 NA, CO 384/50, 288–91, John Bowie to Sir George Grey, Edinburgh, 5 Jan. 1838.

71 NA, CO 384/45, 29–31, Elliot to James Stephen, 2 Feb. 1838; 166–67, 26 March 1838; 268, Elliot's First Annual Report on Emigration to Lord Glenelg, 28 April 1838; CO 384/50, 291, Draft Reply, 28 Feb. [1838]. Colonel McDougall had strongly supported the distress committees' proposal; ibid., vol. 45, 130–31, McDougall to Lord Glenelg, London, 19 March 1838; 133, Answer, 29 March 1838.

72 Buchanan claimed that the families would settle in "Brampton" (presumably Brompton Township, near Sherbrooke), but provincial surveyor Russell reported that "Scotch Highlanders" had been established in Lingwick in November 1838; PP, IUP, Emigration Series, XX, 38–39, Buchanan's Annual Report for 1838, Quebec 20 Jan. 1839; NA, MG11, CO 42/258, 71, Andrew Russell to Commissioners of Crown Lands, Quebec, 19 March 1839. The island's proprietor, Mackenzie of Seaforth, was one of only two who took advantage of the Glasgow relief committee's limited offer to subsidize emigration; PP, IUP, Emigration Series, III, 48–49, 62. No other departures from

Stornoway, the principal town in Lewis are recorded back to 1831 where the list begins; ibid., 42–44.

73 Ibid., III, 124, 174. See also the lengthy excerpt from the Inverness *Herald* of 1838 in B. Epps, "Immigrant File."

74 The agent is quoted in Donald Macdonald, *Lewis*, 166.

75 Cited in *The Record*, 21 Oct. 1988, 5.

76 *Annuaire*, 1891–92, 30–31; NA, S Series, 1838, vol. 538, 180. For road work projected in the spring, see NA, MG24 A27, Durham Papers, sect. V, vol. 1, 381–3, John Fraser to Durham, Quebec, 12 June 1838.

77 The Gould mill was under construction in 1842; *Information*.

78 Ibid.; ANQ-Q, Terres et Forêts, BALC, John Fraser to C. Buller, Quebec, 22 Sept. 1838. After his tour of inspection in the spring of 1839, provincial surveyor Andrew Russell was full of praise for the quality of the road work; NA, MG11, CO 42/258, 69–73, Andrew Russell to Commissioners of Crown Lands, Quebec, 19 March 1839.

79 NA, S Series, 1838, vol. 538, 179–80.

80 NA, BALC Papers, Correspondence 1835–89, 254–56, Henry P. Bruyères to Sir George Grey, 8 Nov. 1838; 258–59, George Grey to H.P. Bruyères, 10 Sept. [sic] 1838; 264, 28 Nov. 1838.

81 Ibid., III, 277, John Fraser to Major T.L. Goldie, Montreal, 4 April 1839.

82 Ibid., 277–80; NA, S Series, 1838, vol. 538, 180–82.

83 PP, IUP, Emigration Series, III, 222–3, H.P. Bruyères to Duke of Argyle, the Rt. Hon. the Marquis of Northampton and the deputation from Mull District, London, 13 April 1839.

84 NA, BALC Papers, Correspondence 1835–89, 277, John Fraser to Major T.L. Goldie, Montreal, 4 April 1839; NA, S Series, 1838, vol. 538, 180–82.

85 The 1842 and 1844 Census Reports record fourteen and eleven Catholics, respectively, in Lingwick, while in 1846 the missionary priest reported fifteen poor and miserable Catholic families; *Annuaire*, 1891–92, 31. The 1851 census lists none.

86 Channell, *History of Compton*, 257. N. Macdonald, *Canada*, 297–98, gives a brief and confused account of the first Scottish settlement in the St Francis Tract.

87 NA, MG11, CO 42/258, 71, Andrew Russell to Commissioners of Crown Lands, Quebec, 19 March 1839.

88 *Montreal Gazette*, 16 Nov. 1841.

89 Cited in D. Macdonald, *Lewis*, 166.

90 See Saunders, "The New Brunswick and Nova Scotia Land Company," 71, 195–207. The two Hebridean colonies established in western Canada in the late 1880s also had contrasting results; see Stuart, "The Scottish Crofter Colony."

91 NA, CO 384/61, 38–40, T.F. Elliot, R. Torrens, and E. Villiers to Lord John Russell, 21 April 1840. The 1841 emigration file of the Colonial Office papers contains an undated memorial from J.C. Orchard of Grantown, Invernessshire, outlining a project to establish 10,000 Highland families in the wilds of Lower Canada where they would contribute towards "neutralizing the French population in their resistance to British authority." In contrast to Colonel McDougall's scheme, Orchard recommended that the settlers be required to repay all expenses to the government. CO 384/67, 290–93, Plan of Emigration ... by J.C. Orchard.

92 NA, BALC Papers, Correspondence 1835–89, 310, John Fraser to Rt. Hon. Charles Poulett Thomson, 9 March 1840.

93 Skelton, *Life and Times*, 41–42; Goldring, "British Colonists," 200; Cowan, *British Emigration*, 125.

94 NA, CO 384/61, 39–40, Elliot, Torrens, and Villiers to Russell, 21 April 1840; NA, BALC Papers, Correspondence 1835–89, I, 361.

95 See Goldring, "British Colonists," 200–1 for an account of the negotiations.

96 See the correspondence in NA, CO 384/67, 43–56, 83–92.

97 *Montreal Gazette*, 5 Oct. 1841 (advertisement dated 26 May 1841); *Information*, 1842.

98 Skelton, *Life and Times*, 43.

99 *Montreal Gazette*, 5 Oct. 1841. John MacIver, who sailed with his family aboard the "Lady Hood," was from Lower Barvas, on the coast north of Uig. Whyte, *A Dictionary of Scottish Emigrants*, no. 6965.

100 The majority on board the "Charles," 233 passengers, had disembarked at Sydney, Nova Scotia, where the second major North American colony of Lewismen was developing. The arrivals at Quebec included 84 men, 50 women, and 89 children under fourteen years of age. PP, IUP, Emigration Series, XXI, 261.

101 Cowan, *British Emigration*, 137.

102 *Montreal Gazette*, 16 Nov. 1841.

103 St Andrew's Society of Montreal, Minute Book, I, 20 Sept. 1841; Mackenzie, *History of the Highland Clearances*, 148–49.

104 *Montreal Gazette*, 5 Oct. 1841; St Andrew's Society, Minute Book, I, 4 Feb. 1852. The Sherbrooke Emigration Society had been established in January 1841, and some of its members contributed uncultivated lots to encourage immigration; McCord Museum, Hale Papers, G.F. Bowen to Edward Hale, Sherbrooke, 19 Jan. 1841.

105 *Montreal Gazette*, 16 Nov. 1841.

106 United Church Archives, *Home and Foreign Missionary Record for the Church of Scotland* 1838–43, 192 [1842], "Canada-Salmon-River." This collection contains only photocopies of pages relating to Canada. Front pages with dates are frequently missing.

107 NA, S Series, 1842, no. 3191, 20395, 22 Dec. 1842.

108 PP, IUP, Emigration Series, XXII, 10.

109 Most of the 79 listed as Canadian-born in Lingwick would have been Scots children.

110 *Montreal Gazette*, 16 Nov. 1841; United Church Archives, *The Home and Foreign Missionary Record of the Free Church of Scotland*. (1843–50), Edinburgh, Oct. 1846, 507.

111 See, for example, NA, BALC Papers, IX, Land Contracts, 1970, Samuel Mills, 27 June 1843.

112 Ibid., Correspondence 1835–89, 386, Report of Charles Bischoff, 28 Nov. 1853.

113 Skelton, *Life and Times*, 52.

114 NA, BALC Papers, IX, Land Contracts, 1973, George Downes, 20 July 1846. I have no proof that George Downes arrived in 1836, but the payment of back interest proves that he had occupied the property before 1846; 1836 was the year of the English group immigration to the St Francis Tract; and, according to the 1851 census, Downes had a daughter born in England in 1835 and a son born in Canada in 1839.

115 Johnston, "Immigration," 210–11, 202–22.

116 Skelton, *Life and Times*, 52–53.

117 NA, BALC Papers, XII, Reports and Accounts, 1861–1910, 2611–31.

118 Channell, *History of Compton*, 252.

119 Quoted in *Sherbrooke Daily Record*, 16 March 1957, 34; see Channell, *History of Compton*, 242–43, 248–49, 252–55, for other examples of English settlers.

120 Charles Bischoff reported in 1853 that all the original Highland settlers but one family had left the village of Gould. NA, BALC Correspondence, 1835–89, 396, Bischoff's Report, 28 Nov. 1853. Channell estimates that about twenty families made the move (*History of Compton*, 268), while a report issued by Catholic missionary priests in 1851 (*Le Canadien emigrant*) claimed that forty Scots families had moved from company lands in Weedon to Winslow.

121 United Church Archives, *Home and Foreign Missionary Record of the Free Church of Scotland*, Dec. 1844; NA, RG7 G14, Governor General's Correspondence, 9266, John Fraser to J.M. Higginson, London, Canada West, 4 Sept. 1845.

122 Skelton, *Life and Times*, 49–50.

123 ANQ-Q, E21, Terres et Forêts, art. 1890, Registre de Correspondance de T. Boutillier, Bureau de l'Inspecteur des Agences, Saint-Hyacinthe, 57, T. Boutillier to J.G. Robertson, 19 June 1854; 183, T. Boutillier to B. Garneau and J.B. Coulombe, 21 Sept. 1854; 213, T. Boutillier to J.G. Robertson, 7 Oct. 1854.

124 See Rudin, "The Transformation of the Eastern Townships."

125 *JLAC*, XVII (1859), app. 19, C.O. Closter to A.C. Buchanan, Quebec,

27 Dec. 1858; *SPPC*, XVIII (1860), no. 18, 24–25, Report by C.O. Closter, Quebec, Dec. 1859; Loken, *From Fjord to Frontier*, 18–19.

126 NA, BALC Papers, Correspondence 1835–89, 419–20, John S. Cummins to R.W. Heneker, Bury 15 Aug. 1859.

127 Ibid., 421–22.

128 Ibid., 447–50, John S. Cummins to My Dear Sir, Cork, 13 March 1860.

129 Ibid., 451–52, Henry Wiggins to My Dear Sir, Eglinton, Derry, 14 March 1860.

130 Ibid., 475–76, J.S. Cummins to A.H. Brown, Esq., Cork, 30 May 1860; London, 20 June 1860; 482, J.S. Cummins to R.W. Heneker, Sherbrooke, 2 Oct. 1860.

131 In 1869, Heneker himself went to England to promote emigration to the Townships, but his efforts were directed towards labourers for Sherbrooke and the local farms; *Le Pionnier*, 14 May 1869.

132 NA, BALC Papers, I, 1–3, R.W. Heneker to Douglas Brymner, Ottawa, 25 Feb. 1887.

133 The location of the BALC's lands in Weedon was still not officially fixed in 1860. The company claimed the first three ranges, which lay between Lingwick and the St Francis River, but the government refused to agree to any lots on which squatters had settled. NA, BALC Correspondence 1835–89, 436, Mr. Russell to R. Heneker, Crown Lands Department, 27 Jan. 1860; 442–43, 6 Feb. 1860; 445, 20 Feb. 1860.

134 Ibid., 396–97, Charles Bischoff's Report; Skelton, *Life and Times*, 53.

135 Rudin, "Land Ownership," 32; Cowan, *British Emigration*, 139. In two separate transactions in 1873 and 1875 the company also made major sales to William Little of New York: Newport, 54 lots; Auckland, 29 ½ lots; Ditton, 59 lots; Bury, 29 lots; Dudswell, 52 lots; Lingwick, 37 ½ lots; Weedon, 3 lots. All this land had returned to the BALC by 1878. Cookshire Registry Office, Reg. B, vol. 7, 668–72, no. 4255; vol 8, 505–8, no. 4710.

136 Saunders, "The New Brunswick and Nova Scotia Land Company," 180.

137 While Rudin claims that the entrepreneurial ambitions of the three successive BALC commissioners were constantly being reined in by the London court of directors, Kesteman is critical of the commissioners as well. See Rudin, "Land Ownership and Urban Growth," 28–37; Kesteman, "Une Bourgeoisie," 438, 447–48. For the Canada Company's similar policy, see Karr, *The Canada Land Company*, 40–41, 73–75.

138 The "industrial" land held from sale in Sherbrooke represented far more than a few acres of river frontage, with the result that the city's

working class lived in conditions even more crowded than the worst areas of Montreal; see Kesteman, "La condition urbaine."

CHAPTER THREE

1 Goldring, "British Colonists," 182–85.
2 Kingston entrepreneurs had a similar attitude about the development of their Canadian Shield frontier; see Osborne, "Frontier settlement," 215, 218.
3 For a brief history of the firm, see Price, *Introduction*, 47–52.
4 Young, "James Bell Forsyth," *DCB* IX: 273.
5 ANQ-Q, Terres et Forêts, Megantic Land Company (1838–39), J. Bell Forsyth to My Dear Sir (Private), Quebec, 22 March 1839.
6 Young, "Forsyth," 273.
7 L. Dechêne, "William Price," *DCB* IX: 639–40.
8 Dechêne, "Price," 639; Cowan, *British Emigration*, 136.
9 Roy, *Juges*, 229.
10 ANQ-Q, Terres et Forêts, Megantic Land Company, Memorandum of a proposed Arrangement. The official upset price for crown land in two Megantic Townships not included in the Megantic Tract, Thetford and Tring, was only three shillings per acre.
11 NA, BALC Papers, Correspondence 1835–89, 206, Walcott to J.B. Forsyth, 12 April 1836; 207, J.B. Forsyth to T.F. Elliot, Quebec, 8 Oct. 1836.
12 Ibid., 210, Prospectus, Quebec and Megantic Land Company, 23 April 1838.
13 The names listed on p. 211 are J. Gibb, J. Dean, H. Caldwell, J.H. Kerr, J. McLeod, D. Burnet, C. McCallum, Pierre Pelletier, William Phillips, H. Pemberton, W. Petry, J. Leaycraft, J.M. Fraser, J.B. Forsyth, and R.H. Gairdner. Price's name is missing. Henry Caldwell's father, John, had lost the south-shore seigneury of Lauzon to the state in 1834 because of over investment in the timber industry, but the family continued to own valuable properties in the Québec-Lévis area; Roy, *Histoire de la Seigneurie de Lauzon* V: 148–49, 412, 477, 521–22. James Hastings Kerr was a land agent and owner of 21,000 acres in Lower Canada; *Appendix (B) to the Report of the Affairs of British North America from the Earl of Durham (Minutes of Evidence)* (1839), 55–61. Pierre Pelletier was a Quebec merchant; Bervin, "Aperçu sur le commerce," 547. James Gibb was a Quebec timber contractor; Dechêne, "Price," 640. James Dean and J.W. Leaycraft have been identified as executives of the Quebec Chamber of Commerce; Ouellet, *Histoire de la Chambre de Commerce*, 99, 103.
14 NA, BALC Papers, Correspondence 1835–89, 211–12, Prospectus.

15 On Merritt, see Talman, "William Hamilton Merritt," *DCB* IX: 544–48; and on Stayner, see Little, "Colonization and Municipal Reform," 115. Stayner's name was misprinted as T."H." and the same probably occurred for "E." Hagerman. Christopher Hagerman was a prominent member of Upper Canada's Family Compact. On Bell, see Pentland, *Labour and Capital*, 39. The other major shareholders included the three commissioners plus H.J. Caldwell, William Phillips, C. McCallum, J.H. Kerr, James McKenzie, and William Chapman. For a complete list of all shareholders, see NA, BALC Papers, Correspondence 1835–89, 217–20.

16 NA, BALC Papers, Correspondence 1835–89, 199, Forsyth, Price, and Gairdner to Charles Buller, Quebec, 16 June 1838; 210, Prospectus.

17 Ibid., 199, Forsyth, Price, and Gairdner to Buller.

18 ANQ-Q, Terres et Forêts, Megantic Land Company, Thos. E.M. Turton to James Bell Forsyth, Quebec, 30 July 1838.

19 The colonization road was originally to be called the Durham Road and the colony Lambton; ibid., J. Bell Forsyth to My Dear Sir, Private, Saturday.

20 NA, BALC Papers, Correspondence 1835–89, 225–27, Forsyth and Gairdner to Andrew Russell, Quebec, 10 Aug. 1838.

21 The unsurveyed townships of Stuart and Neilson were presumably named in honour of Chief Justice James Stuart and John Neilson, two prominent members of Durham's Special Council. Gairdner had to be content with an unsurveyed location near the source of the Chaudière which ultimately was named Gayhurst. Russell's two other projected but unsurveyed townships, Shenley and Dorset, were left with these names.

22 NA, BALC Papers, Correspondence 1835–89, 228, Forsyth and Gairdner to Russell, Quebec, 10 Aug. 1838.

23 Ibid., 233, Andrew Russell to Commissioners of the Megantic Land Company, Tring, 11 Oct. 1838.

24 ANQ-Q, Terres et Forêts, Megantic Land Company, Thos. Turton to Forsyth *et al.*, Quebec, 19 Oct. 1838.

25 Pay lists are scattered throughout the Megantic Land Company papers in the ANQ at Quebec.

26 ANQ-Q, Terres et Forêts, Megantic Land Company, Joseph Bouchette to Commissioner of Crown Lands, Quebec, 12 Dec. 1839.

27 Ibid., J. Bell Forsyth to T.L. Goldie, Quebec, 23 March 1839.

28 Ibid., Andrew Russell to the Commissioners of the Quebec and Megantic Land Company, Quebec, 23 March 1839.

29 Ibid., J.B. Forsyth to T.L. Goldie, Quebec, 23 March 1839; ANQ-Q, Terres et Forêts, "Terres de la Couronne: Administration générale, 1827–99," art. 1865, Cantons en générale 1827–84, J. Bell Forsyth to My Dear Sir (Private), Quebec, 22 March 1839.

237 Notes to pages 72–75

30 NA, BALC Papers, Correspondence 1835–89, 281–82, John Davidson
    to Major Goldie (Private), 6 April 1839.
31 ANQ-Q, Terres et Forêts, Megantic Land Company, Walter Har-
    grave's Report on the origen [sic], progress, and present state of the
    Lambton Road ... , 19 Feb. 1842.
32 Ibid., J. Bell Forsyth and R.H. Gairdner to Sir, Quebec, 11 Sept.
    1839. As early as February the commissioners had expressed their
    hesitation to purchase the Megantic Tract "unless offered at such a
    price as we think improbable." As an alternative they recommended
    that a special unpaid board of commissioners be established to place
    one hundred families alongside the road as quickly as possible. NA,
    RG7 G14, Governor General's Correspondence, vol. 6, 2366, J.B.
    Forsyth, William Price and R.H. Gairdner to T.L. Goldie, Quebec,
    11 Feb. 1839.
33 Ibid., Hargrave's Report.
34 NA, CO 384/61, 38, T.F. Elliot, R. Torrens, and E.E. Villiers to Lord
    John Russell, 21 April 1842. For a good description of the essentially
    laissez-faire emigration policies of the Colonial Office and Land
    Board in the 1840s, see Shepperson, *British Emigration*, 201–15.
35 NA, CO 384/61, 56, T.F. Elliot, R. Torrens, and E.E. Villiers to Lord
    John Russell, 21 April 1842.
36 Ibid., 39.
37 Ibid., CO 384/52, 276, William Lloyd, to My Lord, rec'd 7 Feb. 1839.
38 Ibid., 274.
39 Ibid.
40 Ibid., CO 384/61, 41, Elliot *et al.* to Russell, 21 April 1840. The Land
    Board was clearly inspired by the proposal of Wakefield and Edward
    Ellice through the British North American Colonial Association to
    launch large-scale public works on their Beauharnois seigneury;
    Ibid., 40–41, Elliot *et al.* to Russell, 21 April 1840. For a brief history
    of the association and Wakefield's behind-the-scenes influence, see
    Macdonell, "Gibbon Wakefield and Canada."
41 NA, CO 384/61, 586, A.B. Hawke, Emigrant Office, Toronto, 13 Sept.
    1839.
42 Ibid., 583–84, Sydenham to Lord Russell, Montreal, 14 Jan. 1841;
    590, 26 Jan. 1841.
43 Ibid., 66–67, Elliot, Torrens, and Villiers to J. Stephen, 2 July 1840;
    L.F. Gates, *Land Policies*, 260–62.
44 NA, CO 384/61, 590, Sydenham to Lord Russell, Montreal, 26 Jan.
    1841.
45 NA, RG4 C1, Provincial Secretary's Correspondence, Canada East,
    1840–41, vol. 44, no. 707, 2797–98, Memorial of the Emigration As-
    sociation of the District of St Francis, now the Territorial district of
    Sherbrooke, to Lord Sydenham, 12 May 1841.

46 Ibid., 2799–81. The petition was signed only by William Morris as president. A retired military officer and relatively recent immigrant to the Eastern Townships, Morris was a landowner, justice of the peace, and a lieutenant-colonel of the militia who had commanded the volunteers of the Sherbrooke district during the rebellion; ibid., no. 61, 262–64, Memorial of Morris to Lord Sydenham enclosed in William Morris to Chief Secretary, Lennoxville, 23 March 1841.

47 ANQ-Q, Terres et Forêts, "Terres de la Couronne: Administration générale, 1827–99," art. 1863, William Hargrave's Report, 19 Feb. 1842.

48 Ibid.

49 £208 was spent on the four bridges. Hargrave noted that, in addition to the new causeways in Tring, stones and small stumps had been removed.

50 NA, RG1 E5, Records Put By, 1839–67, vol. 13, 158, Walter Hargrave to John Davidson, Lambton Road, 18 Oct. 1842.

51 Rapport sur les missions du diocèse de Québec, July 1845, no. 6, 151–54, quoted in Lapointe, Historique de St. Vital, 26.

52 NA, Provincial Secretary's Correspondence, 1846, no. 1229, 6711–20.

53 Ibid., 6721, Civil Secretary to Ls. Ed. Bois, curé of Saint-François Beauce, 14 May 1846.

54 NA, Provincial Secretary's Correspondence, 1850, no. 1160, Petition presented by L. Provancher and others, Tring, 22 April 1850.

55 JLAC, x (1851), app. V, Report of the Special Committee appointed to enquire into the causes which prevent or retard the settlement of the Eastern Townships, appendix, testimony of Rev. N. Nazaire A. Leclerc.

56 Quoted in Lapointe, Historique de St. Vital, 34.

57 NA, Civil Secretary's Correspondence, 1851, no. 1353, Petition presented by N. Leclerc and others, Lambton, 10 June 1851.

58 ANQ-Q, Terres et Forêts, art. 1890, Registre de Correspondance de T. Boutillier, Bureau de l'Inspecteur des Agences, Saint-Hyacinthe, 204, T. Boutillier to Dr. Labrecque at Lambton, 2 Oct. 1854; 228, 23 Oct. 1854; 249, 17 Nov. 1854.

59 See Little, "Colonization and Municipal Reform."

CHAPTER FOUR

1 One minor exception was the 1844 decision to offer free fifty-acre grants along the new section of the Gosford Road in isolated Ham South and Wolfestown. A small number of British families (most of whom had Irish-sounding names) settled briefly in the two townships. AC, Vieux dossiers, Correspondance, 1851, no. 2982, T. Bouthillier to J. Felton, Montreal, 20 Jan. 1844; J.S. Sanborn to J.H.

Price, Toronto, 10 June 1851; Langelier, *Liste des Terrains*, 1084–85, 1100–1.

2 See Monet, "French-Canadian Nationalism."

3 Little, "The Catholic Church," 149–50.

4 *Le Canadien* (Québec), 22 Oct. 1847, 11 Feb. 1848.

5 Ibid., 16 Feb. 1848.

6 Ibid., 22 Oct. 1847.

7 *Le Journal de Québec*, 7 March 1848.

8 *L'Avenir* (Montréal), 4 March 1848. The original model was founded in Malbaie in 1847. Le Roux, "La colonisation du Saguenay," 69.

9 *Les Mélanges religieux*, 21 March 1848. Quoted in L. Pouliot, "L'Institut Canadien," 66.

10 *Le Journal de Québec*, 1 April 1848.

11 Ibid., 30 March 1848.

12 Monet, *The Last Cannon Shot*, 294; *L'Avenir* (Montréal), 15 April 1848, 19 April 1848.

13 *La Minerve* (Montréal), 6 April 1848.

14 Pouliot, *Monseigneur Bourget* III: 46. Augustin-Norbert Morin, a member of the Baldwin–La Fontaine administration, was offered the first vice-presidency but he turned it down at the last minute. Pouliot feels that Morin did so because his presence on the executive committee with Papineau could have been interpreted as a split in the La Fontaine party; Pouliot, "L'Institut Canadien," 69–70. The new society was also considered a threat to the influence of the Saint-Jean-Baptiste Society founded by Ludger Duvernay, editor of *La Minerve*. Bernard, *Les Rouges*, 45.

15 R.E. Caron was first vice-president of the Association des Townships, and honorary president of the Institut Canadien; J.B.A. Chartier was archival secretary for both organizations; J.M. Hudon was the corresponding secretary for the association and a vice-president of the Institut Canadien; F. Eventurel was the treasurer of both organizations; and E. Chinic was the assistant treasurer of the association and a vice-president of the Institut Canadien. *Le Journal de Québec*, 15 April 1848, 20 April 1848.

16 Elgin's concerns are expressed in his correspondence with Lord Grey in the fall of 1847 and spring of 1848; Doughty, ed., *The Elgin-Grey Papers* I.

17 Ibid., 145–46, Elgin to Grey, Montreal, 26 April 1848.

18 Ibid., 138, Grey to Elgin, 14 April 1848; Piva, "Continuity and Crisis," 191–92. No mention of the amount was made in Grey's dispatch, but the province had claimed £20,000. See the Executive Council's resolution of 17 March 1848 in Doughty, *The Elgin-Grey Papers* I: 136.

19 See the third-last paragraph of the provincial government's official reply to the Association des Townships. A rough handwritten draft of both the Association des Townships' petition and the government's reply is deposited in NA, RG4 C1, Civil Secretary's Correspondence, vol. 229, no. 1871, 66–150. For printed drafts of the two documents see *JLAC*, VIII (1849), app. 2; and of the government's reply only, see Doughty, *the Elgin-Grey Papers* IV, app. 7, 1361–72; *The Pilot* (Montreal), 17 June 1848, in AC, Correspondance, 1848, no. 3343. Michael Piva's detailed study appears to assume that the grant was simply meant to ease the province's debt burden, since he makes no mention of the colonization issue; see his "Continuity and Crisis," 192–93.

20 Doughty, *the Elgin-Grey Papers* I: 145–46, Elgin to Grey, Montreal, 26 April 1848.

21 Ibid., 194–92, Elgin to Grey, Montreal, 29 June 1848. Father O'Reilly too made use of the loyalty question to further his project. He proclaimed: "Que la croix du clocher brille dans chaque township maintenant inculte, depuis les voisines colonies américaines jusqu'au fleuve. Et que l'Angélus du soir se répète d'échos en échos depuis le Lac Mégantic jusqu'à Québec d'un côté, et jusqu'à Saint-Hyacinthe de l'autre: et nous aurons fait un premier pas pour sauver le Canada." *Le Journal de Québec*, 18 Nov. 1848. That Lord Elgin had some reason to doubt the loyalty of the English-speaking Townships residents would be proven by the wave of annexationist sentiment which swept through the region the following year.

22 Doughty, *The Elgin-Grey Papers*, I: 194, Lettre pastorale de Monseigneur l'Évêque de Montréal pour encourager l'Association des Établissements Canadiens des Townships, 17 June 1848.

23 *Le Journal de Québec*, 20 June 1848; *L'Avenir* (Montréal), 28 June 1848; Parent, *Deux Efforts*, 71–72.

24 A commissioned report on the district was submitted on April 26. AC, Correspondance, 1848, no. 3343, Remarks on the Megantic and St Francis Territories and Lambton Road, 26 April 1848.

25 *JLAC*, VIII (1849), app. 2, Bourget to Elgin, Montreal, 14 June 1848; R.B. Sullivan to Bourget, 29 June 1848. The same reduction was decreed for the two new colonization roads begun in Canada West; L.F. Gates, *Land Policies*, 274.

26 To guard against the danger of speculators taking advantage of the low crown land prices, resident agents would have to continue to enforce settlement conditions.

27 See, for example, Skelton, *Life and Times*, 12; Innis, *Economic History*, 138; and Robert Hill's introduction to Sellar, *The Tragedy of Quebec*, xvii.

28 For details see Little, "The Catholic Church," 156–59; and Parent, *Deux Efforts*, 60–82.

29 *Annuaire*, 1889–90, 485; Ouellet, *Economic and Social History*, 511–12.

30 *Le Journal de Québec*, 15 July 1848.

31 *Mandements* III: 523, Circulaire addressée au clergé du Diocèse de Québec, par l'Association du District de Québec pour l'Établissement des Canadiens-Français dans les Townships du Bas-Canada, 11 Aug. 1848.

32 Fauteux, *Patriotes*, 88; AC, Correspondance, 1848, no. 5226, Rapport générale et statistique de l'état des chemins et établissements sous la surintendance de J.O. Arcand ..., Ham Township, 24 Dec. 1848.

33 *JLAC*, VIII (1849), app. 2, Arcand to Elgin, 24 July 1848.

34 Ibid., N.H. Baird to Thomas H. Begley, 31 July 1848; Begley to Arcand, 20 Oct. 1848.

35 Ibid., Arcand to Begley, 8 Jan. 1849; AC, Correspondance, 1848, no. 5226, Rapport générale, 24 Dec. 1848.

36 *JLAC*, VIII (1849), app. 2, Taché to Lord Elgin, 22 Jan. 1849; Begley to Arcand, 9 Feb. 1849.

37 Arcand himself had paid fifty shillings ($10) for his journey of forty-five miles with a small portmanteau. AC, Correspondance, 1848, no. 5226, Rapport générale, 24 Dec. 1848.

38 *Le Journal de Québec*, 19 Aug. 1848, 9 Sept. 1848.

39 NA, Civil Secretary's Correspondence, 1848, no. 1871, Petition of Association du District de Qué., 5 Oct. 1848.

40 ANQ-Q, Terres et Forêts, art. 1865, Terres de la Couronne: Administration général, 1827–99, Arcand to T. Bouthilier [also spelled Boutillier], Ham, 16 Sept. 1848.

41 AC, Correspondance, 1849, no. 3583, Arcand to T. Bouthilier, Lac Aylmer, Garthby, 6 Oct. 1849.

42 Ibid., 1848, no. 5226, Rapport générale, 24 Dec. 1848; 1849, no. 146, Arcand to Bouthilier, Montreal, 15 Jan. 1849; no. 147, Arcand to Bouthilier, Saint-Michel-d'Yamaska, 11 Jan. 1849.

43 Ibid., 1849, no. 558, Arcand to Bouthilier, Ham Township, 16 Feb. 1849; no. 688, Arcand to Bouthilier, Montreal, 28 Feb. 1849.

44 Ibid., 1848, no. 5226, Rapport générale, 24 Dec. 1848.

45 Ibid., 1849, no. 569, Arcand to Bouthilier, Ham Township, 16 Feb. 1849.

46 *Annuaire*, 1889–90, 496–97.

47 AC, Correspondance 1849, no. 1179, Arcand to Bouthilier, Dudswell, 27 March 1849; no. 1959, Arcand to Bouthilier, Malmaison, Garthby, 18 May 1849.

48 Ibid., 1848, no. 5226, Rapport générale, 24 Dec. 1848.

49 See Macdonald, *Canada: Immigration*, 17; Parker, "Colonization Roads," 33–34. Other historians have placed more emphasis on the

government's desire to extend the settlement frontier; see Spragge, "Colonization Roads"; Murray, "Agricultural Settlement," 178–86; Miller, *Straight Lines*; Parson, "The Colonization," 263–66; Wynn, "Notes on Society," 54–58.

50 Arcand reported 105 settlers in Wotton, 17 in Ham South and "une vingtaine" in Stratford; AC, 1850, no. 298, Rapport générale ... pour l'année ... 1849, Garthby, 5 Jan. 1850.

51 Archives de l'évêché de Nicolet, Saint-Grégoire-le-Grand, 1787–1943, C. Marquis to Charles-Félix Cazeau, Saint-Grégoire, 3 Nov. 1848. Reference kindly provided by Wendie Nelson. Father O'Reilly claimed that the Saint-Grégoire claimants were "all substantial farmers, or the sons of wealthy parents." NA RG7 G20, Governor General's Secretary, XLVII, 5104, O'Reilly to My Lord [Elgin], 11 Nov. 1848. Between 1844 and 1849, 175 people, including eight families, were reported to have migrated from the parish to the United States. Morin, "Calixte Marquis," 42.

52 AC, Correspondance, 1850, no. 298, Rapport générale ... 1849, 5 Jan. 1850.

53 Ibid., no. 501, Arcand to Bouthilier, Saint-Olivier du Lac Aylmer, Malmaison, 11 March 1850.

54 The costs included a 200-foot bridge and numerous causeways up to 1000 feet in length. Ibid., 1850, no. 1066, Arcand to Jean Lanvegin, Malmaison, 22 July 1850; no. 1453, Report ... Arcand, Garthby, 12 Oct. 1850. Much of the information that follows is from Arcand's report of 12 Oct. 1850.

55 *Annuaire*, 1889–90, no. 15, 487; O'Bready, *Histoire de Wotton*, 71; Morin, "Calixte Marquis," 43; *Le Journal de Québec*, 14 Nov. 1848, 18 Nov. 1848; Canada, Manuscript Census, 1851–52, Stratford and Garthby Townships.

56 AC, Correspondance, 1850, no. 502, Arcand to Bouthilier, Saint-Olivier du Lac Aylmer, 21 March 1850. This clearing rate comes close to the maximum of one acre per month for each adult male pioneer estimated in Russell, "Forest into Farmland," 330, 334.

57 *Annuaire*, 1887–88, no. 13, 298; 1889–90, no. 15, 498, 503.

58 AC, Correspondance, 1850, no. 1453, Report ... Arcand, 12 Oct. 1850.

59 Ibid., 1851, no. 686, W.L. Felton to J.H. Price, Sherbrooke, 14 July 1851.

60 The average Stratford family harvested twenty bushels of grain and seventy bushels of potatoes and turnips; Canada, Manuscript Census, 1851–52, Garthby and Stratford Townships. Colonist production in Papineau's Ottawa Valley seigneury of Petite Nation in 1831 and 1842 was equally low. Food had to be imported at various times in the 1830s and 1840s. Baribeau, *La Seigneurie*, 82–101.

61 AC, Correspondance, 1852, no. 544, Arcand to Jean Lanvegin, Lac Aylmer, 12 April 1852.

62 François Bégin to Mgr Turgeon, 11 April 1852; cited in *Annuaire*, 1889–90, no. 15, 500–1.

63 *Stanstead Journal*, 6 May 1852.

64 AAQ, RL, XXIII, 425, Turgeon to F. Bégin, 7 April 1852.

65 *Le Journal de Québec*, 15 Aug. 1848, 29 Aug. 1848, 5 Sept. 1848, 31 Oct. 1848; NA, governor General's Secretary, XLVII, 5104, O'Reilly to My Lord [Elgin], 14 Nov. 1848.

66 AAQ, RL, XXIII, 451, Turgeon to Bégin, 28 April 1852.

67 *Annuaire*, 1889–90, no. 15, 490, 503; AC, Correspondance, 1852, no. 808, Arcand to Jean Langevin, Lac Aylmer, 24 May 1852.

68 NA, RG1 E1, Minute Books (1841–67), State Book N, 342, 2 July 1853.

69 ANQ-Q Terres et Forêts, art. 1890, Registre de correspondance de T. Bouthilier, 256, Bouthilier to J.G. Robertson, 24 Nov. 1854; 270, Bouthilier to J. Coulombe, 5 Dec. 1854; 326, Bouthilier to W.L. Felton, 10 Feb. 1855; 437, Bouthilier to J.T. LeBel, 17 Aug. 1855; 439, Bouthilier to J.B. Coulombe and Eucher Arcand, 17 Aug. 1855; *JLAC*, XIII (1854–5), app. NNN.

70 Quoted in Morin, "La pensée colonisatrice," 82.

71 ANQ-Q, Terres et Forêts [unidentified photocopy], J.T. Le Bel to Joseph Cauchon, Malmaison, Garthby, 28 March 1856.

72 AC, Correspondance, 1856, no. 1420/266, J.T. Le Bel to Jos. Cauchon, Malmaison, Lac Aylmer, 9 Feb. 1856; 1871, no. 4333, Charles Lemire to J.O. Beaubien, S.S. Anges de Ham, 1 Aug. 1871.

73 AC, Orders-in-Council (Branche Est), no. 974, Petition to Quebec Legislative Assembly, received 28 Nov. 1871; Report of Executive Council, approved 4 March 1872; List of Promissory Notes and Accounts in favour of the Commissioner of Crown Lands, Ant. Gagnon, Agent, Arthabaskaville, 4 July 1870. In 1877 the Garthby colonists were once again short of seed grain; ANQ-Q, E25, Agriculture et Travaux Publics, Correspondances reçues, no. 962, J. Picard to C.B. de Boucherville, Wotton, 23 April 1877.

74 AC, Correspondance, 1869, no. 4333, Memo: Department of Crown Lands; J.T. Le Bel to J.O. Beaubien, Wotton, 3 June 1869; John Hume to Commissioner of Crown Lands, 25 Nov. 1871; *Annuaire*, 1889–90, no. 15, 505–7.

75 See Langelier, *Liste des terrains concédés*.

76 On the province's financial status, see Piva, "Continuity and Crisis," 192–93.

77 Macdonald, *Canada: Immigration*, 16. Even in Wotton, the best of the townships involved, the settlers soon fell into debt with, and depen-

dency upon, the local merchants; see Sevigny, "Le Capitalisme et la politique."

78 AC, Correspondance, 1850, no. 1453, Report ... Arcand, 12 Oct. 1850.

79 Macdonald, *Canada Immigration*, 24.

80 See Greer, *Peasant, Lord, and Merchant*; Johnson, "New Thoughts"; Henretta, "Families and Farms."

81 This was the strong feeling of the Hastings colonization road agent; Parson, "The Colonization," 272.

82 Piva, "Continuity and Crisis," 206.

CHAPTER FIVE

1 Nelles, *Politics of Development*, 41.

2 Gillis and Roach, *Lost Initiatives*, 17.

3 A recent detailed account of the changing crown forest regulations is to be found in Gaudreau, *L'Exploitation*, 11–39. See also Bouffard, *Traité du Domaine*, chap. 3.

4 See, for example *JLAC*, 1857, app. 25, Report of the CCL; 1863, app. 8.

5 In the early nineteenth century, pine in Barford Township supposedly girthed fifteen feet; Lower, *North American Assault*, 16. For a history of the early timber industry in the Eastern Townships, see Booth, "Changing Forest Utilization Patterns."

6 ANQ-Q, Terres et Forêts, E21, Coupe du Bois 1838–94, D. McLean to John Davidson, New Ireland, 16 Nov. 1838. See also ibid., G.L. Marler to Sir, Nicolet, 17 April 1841.

7 NA, BALC Papers, vol. 5, Letterbook 1834–36, 956, Samuel Brooks to Moffat and McGill, 11 Dec. 1834; *Bangor Daily Whig & Courier*, 7 June 1860. During the mid-1860s the land company was exporting about one million feet of spruce and pine lumber per year; ANQ-Q, Terres et Forêts, Correspondance générale, G.J. Nagle to R.W. Heneker, Saint-Hyacinthe, 15 Dec. 1866.

8 Lower, *North American Assault*, 96–97, 105–8. Timber entrepreneurs had been anxious to purchase company holdings, including the Township of Garthby, in 1835. BALC Papers, vol. 5, 1043, Samuel Brooks to Moffatt and McGill, 9 July 1835; 1062, 24 Aug. 1835.

9 ANQ-Q, Terres et Forêts, Correspondance générale, Bazile Lupien to John Rolph, Lake Aylmer, 11 June 1853; B. Lupien to Honourable Sir, Lake Aylmer, 11 June 1853; Adolphus Aylmer to B. Lupien, Melbourne, 24 June 1853; Pierce and Flowers to B. Lupien, Lake Aylmer, 1 July 1853; W. Brough to B. Lupien, Montreal, 18 June 1853; John McCormick, Quebec, 28 June 1853.

10 Wood, *History of Lumbering*, 200, 212, 219–20.

11 *Maine Farmer*, 27 Oct. 1853. Benjamin Dyer, also of Bangor, applied for cutting rights in Wotton, Ham South, Garthby, Stratford, Winslow, and Whitton, but his name does not appear again. ANQ-Q, Terres et Forêts, Correspondance générale, B. Lupien to CCL, Lake Aylmer, 3 Sept. 1853. Unfortunately, I have been unable to uncover any information in local histories concerning Clark's background.

12 ANQ-Q, Terres et Forêts, Correspondance générale, J.H. Pope to Clark, Brown & Co., Lake St Francis, 30 April 1854; *JLAC*, 1857, app. 25, sub-app. o; *Sherbrooke Gazette*, 1854 (cited in *Sherbrooke Daily Record*, 16 March 1957 (supplement), 122).

13 Hamelin and Roby, *Histoire économique*, 218. In spite of their own statistics Hamelin and Roby (p. 219) write: "En 1860, la Mauricie est le deuxième grand centre forestier du Québec." Not only was a much higher percentage of Eastern Townships timber land in private hands, thus escaping the crown timber reports, but, as we shall see, the consistent undervaluation of timber cut by C.S. Clark and Company throws the accuracy of such statistics into serious doubt. The best that can be said for the annual reports is that they provide a rough indication of trends over time, provided we assume that the ratio of logs not reported remained somewhat constant each year. On the ratio of timber cut on private lands in Quebec, see Gaudreau, *L'Exploitation*, 67–70.

14 Baker Library, Harvard University, R.G. Dun Collection, Canada, Vol. 3, 229, 1 Aug. 1857.

15 Clark paid £108 in ground rents and £505 in duties on lumber cut, of a total of £1812 collected in the agency. *JLAC*, 1857, app. 25, sub-app. o. Clark and Company's Eastern Townships licences were distributed as follows (in square miles): three in Coleraine, 25 sq. mi., 10 sq. mi., 19 sq. mi.; Winslow, 12, 13, 25, 25; Stratford, 20, 20, 15, 16; Garthby, 10; Lambton, 25; Adstock, 25, 15; Price, 25; Ditton, 25, 25; Hampden, 25, 25; Weedon, 10. By 1859, it had berths in sixteen townships as well as licences for clergy reserves in five others. ANQ-Q, Terres et Forêts, Lettres envoyées, art. 857, 88, Andrew Russell to G.J. Nagle, Toronto, 26 Aug. 1858; art. 858, 8, P.M. Vankoughnet to G.J. Nagle, Toronto, 19 Aug. 1859. Clark's early partners were Warren Brown and William H. McCrillis of Portland and Bangor, respectively; Richmond Registry Office, Reg. B. vol. 1, 161, no. 172.

16 The company was reported by a timber inspector to have paid Pierce and Flowers either £15,000 or £30,000. ANQ-Q, Terres et Forêts, Correspondance générale, Report of Inspection of Lumbering Operations in Eastern Townships, V. Larue, Saint-Charles, 23 June 1854.

See also ibid., C.S. Clark to S.V. Larue, Sherbrooke, 4 May 1855, and Report of Cyprien Blanchet, 22 May 1854.

17 Ibid., Sale and Transfer from Messrs. C.S. Clark and Co. and Thomas Howe to David Davidson and Ferdinand McCulloch, Esqs. in trust, 23 Nov. 1855.

18 Defebaugh, *History of the Lumber Industry* 1:108.

19 *Canadian Times* (Sherbrooke), 18 Jan. 1855; cited in *Sherbrooke Daily Record*, 16 March 1957, 147.

20 The 1861 census states that there were 150 employees. The best descriptions of the mill are in *Sherbrooke Daily Record*, 16 March 1957, 147; *The Canada Directory*, 71; ANQ-Q, Terres et Forêts, Correspondance générale, Memo [no date, etc.]; *Eastern Townships Gazeteer*, 57. The mill's production compares favourably with that of the "huge, steam-powered mills" of Saint John, N.B., by 1860; Judd, "Lumbering," 58.

21 ANQ-Q, Terres et Forêts, Correspondance générale, Sale and Transfer from Clark and Howe to Davidson and McCullough, 23 Nov. 1855.

22 Canada, Manuscript Census, Brompton Township, 1861. Two million feet of the boards were spruce, worth $13,000.

23 Value added = value produced − (cost of raw materials + 6/100 value produced). See Kesteman, "Une Bourgeoisie," 164–65, 757. The salary is based on the $32,000 reported for a workforce of 140 in 1871.

24 Howe had technically purchased all the company's property for £40,000 in October, 1854. Richmond Registry Office, Reg. B, vol. 1, 161, no. 172; 163, no. 173. Dun's records noted that the company was "short of money" as early as January 1855; Baker Library, R.G. Dun, Maine, vol. 22, 117, W.H. McCrillis. See also entries for July 1855, Feb. 1856, Aug. 1856, and Jan. 1857.

25 ANQ-Q, Terres et Forêts, Correspondance générale, Sale and Transfer from Clark and Howe to Davidson and McCulloch, 23 Nov. 1855.

26 *First Annual Statement of Trade and Commerce of Chicago*, 1858, 38; cited in Price, *Introduction to the Social History*, 65.

27 Dun did not note the transfer until 1861 (Baker Library, R.G. Dun Collection, Canada, vol. 3, 229, 20 March 1861). Pope was to pay $17,074 to the Bank of Montreal and $11,926 to the City Bank; Richmond Registry Office, Reg. B, vol. 3, 54, no. 830. No satisfactory biography of Pope exists, and his personal papers have apparently been destroyed, but we do know that he was involved in the Eastern Townships Bank, the Paton Manufacturing Company of Sherbrooke, the Sherbrooke Water Power Company, and Sher-

brooke Gas and Water Company, as well as in local railroads and copper and gold mines; Channell, *History of Compton*, 156–57.

28 Richmond Registry Office, Reg. B, vol. 6, 247, no. 171; 268, no. 188.

29 Dun's investigators consistently reported that Clark and Company were a good credit risk because they always paid local debts; Baker Library, R.G. Dun, Canada, vol. 3, 229, 15 March 1858, 2 July 1858, 25 March 1859, 6 Aug. 1859, and 6 Aug. 1860.

30 Rudin, "Naissance et déclin," 170–71. The avoidance of an official partnership also limited legal liability, as demonstrated by the failure of George Craigin to prove in the courts that Clark had effectively been part owner of the company during the sixties. ANQ-S, Queen's Bench, St Francis, 1868, no. 212, George Cragin *v.* J.H. Pope et al., testimony of J.H. Pope, 24 Nov. 1869; testimony of Thomas Bennett, 26 Feb. 1872; Plumitif, vol. 8, 1872–74, 33, Judgement – 11 June 1872. No partnership with Pope was ever filed in the registry office. ANQ-S, E.P. Felton notary file, 31 March 1879, no. 362, D. Thomas to C.P. Cleveland, Richmond, 12 March 1879; C.P. Cleveland to D. Thomas (telegram), Sherbrooke, 13 March 1887.

31 Lower, *North American Assault*, 130, 134, 150; *SPC*, XXIII (1864), no. 25; *Eastern Townships Gazeteer*, 57. Portland shippers would also fail to recoup their pre-war business; Smith, *History of Lumbering*, 145.

32 The notary files (G.H. Napier, D.M. Thomas, J.A. Archambault, William Richie, J.I. Mackie, E.P. Felton) and Richmond Registry Office record forty purchases between 26 Feb. 1866 and 23 Oct. 1875, all but two occuring in the 1870s. Most of the lots were located in Windsor and Stoke and the majority were sold by businessmen and other town dwellers rather than by local farmers.

33 The land purchased was distributed as follows: Bury 1,949 acres; Lingwick, 27,859 (with 182 added later); Newport, 12,500; Stoke, 24, 975; Windsor, 7,000; Weedon, 15,050; Auckland, 6,500; Clifton, 4,000. ANQ-S, D.M. Thomas file, 1 March 1872, no. 4509A; Cookshire Registry Office, Reg. B, vol. 2, 132, no. 818. Sherbrooke's *Le Pionnier* (1 March 1872), a strong advocate of French-Canadian colonization in the Eastern Townships, declared that this transaction would not hurt the cause because the land involved was not fertile.

34 The deed for one transaction, amounting to $7,120.60, specifies 4,790 acres, but the lots listed for Dudswell, Westbury, and Lingwick add up to 6,101 acres. Cookshire Registry Office, Reg. B, vol. 2, 556–60, no. 1095; ANQ-S, D.M. Thomas file, 4 Nov. 1872, no. 4795; ANQ-S, E.P. Felton file, 3 Sept. 1872, no. 215; Richmond Registry Office, Reg. B, vol. 8, 219.

35 *SPQ*, 1875, Report of CCL, no. 2, x; Lower, *North American Assault*, 150.

36 ANQ-Q, Terres et Forêts, Correspondance générale, 1874, no. 168,
William Farwell to CCL, Robinson, 10 Jan. 1874. These townships
were part of the Chaudière watershed and appear to have been dif-
ficult to protect. During the winter of 1869–70, Breakey & Co. of
Quebec had cut 4,500 pine logs in trespass; ibid., 1870, no. 1583,
William Farwell to CCL, Robinson, 18 April 1870.

37 The term was for one year at the interest rate of 9 per cent; Cookshire Registry Office, Reg. B, vol. 4, 661–4, no. 2423. A marginal
note indicates that the mortgage was still outstanding on 18 March
1884.

38 The Ditton Township purchasers, in two separate transactions, were
Pope and Horace Sawyer, Eaton Township lumber merchant, sawmill operator, and a sometime business associate of Pope; ANQ-S, J.I.
Mackie file, 29 April 1875, no. 1208; 25 Nov. 1875, no. 1382A; 25
Nov. 1875, no. 1382B. The conclusion that many of the protestors
were employees, and perhaps also colonist-suppliers of timber, is
based on the amounts involved, as well as on names and places of
residence. One of the more frequent protestors was Thomas Bennett, the company scaler – a total of $1,802 in nine separate actions.
Another was Pope himself – $11,400 in three actions starting in
1878. Aside from these protests, the file of E.P. Felton, n.p., includes
a total of forty-two by the end of the decade, amounting to $8,036.

39 Gravel, *Sainte Praxède de Brompton*, 33.

40 Cookshire Registry Office, Reg. B, vol. 5, 683–8, no. 3077.

41 Ibid., vol. 7, 725–38.

42 ANQ-S, E.P. Felton file, 11 March 1878, no. 354.

43 Ibid., 1 April 1878, no. 464.

44 *Portland Board of Trade Journal*, Feb. 1898, 295; Bacon, *Portland*, 74;
Smith, *History of Lumbering*, 146. At the same time Clark had to
mortgage 1306 acres in Weedon to Lennoxville flour merchants who
were owed $1,593; ANQ-S, E.P. Felton file, 7 Feb. 1879, no. 141.

45 ANQ-S, E.P. Felton file, 20 June 1879, no. 667. The transaction was
technically a sale, but its conditions made it in fact a mortgage.

46 Bacon, *Portland*, 74. The mortgage of the company to the E.T. Bank
was transferred to Seth W. Milliken in 1884; Cookshire Registry Office, Reg. B, vol. 5, 683–88, no. 3077.

47 Lower, *North American Assault*, 150. See the production table in Gaudreau, "L'Exploitation," 6.

48 The purchase also included the ten acres in Stoke Township, directly
across from the Brompton mill, thereby freeing Clark's dam from
any restrictions by the land company (see note 60). Cookshire Registry Office, Reg. B, vol. 9, 301–5, no. 5119.

49 Ibid., 308–12, no. 5123.

50 ANQ-Q, Terres et Forêts, Correspondance générale, 1880, no. 5799,
   W.F. Milliken, 30 Sept. 1880, meeting at office of Brook, Camirand,
   and Hurd in Sherbrooke on 20 Oct. re estate of late C.S. Clark
   [cover of document only]. Gravel claims the death was in 1882.
51 Gravel, *Sainte Praxède de Brompton*, 11–12.
52 For its trespassing, see for example ANQ-S, Queen's Bench, Cragin *v.*
   Pope et al.; 1868, no. 282, Charles King *v.* J.H. Pope et al.
53 ANQ-Q, Terres et Forêts, Lettres envoyées, art. 855, 479–80, W. McD.
   Dawson to C.S. Clark & Co., Sherbrooke, 16 June 1855.
54 ANQ-S, E.P. Felton file, 17, Oct. 1855, no. 49–50.
55 ANQ-S, Queen's Bench, Cragin *v.* Pope et al., testimony of J.H. Pope,
   24 Nov. 1869. The exact date of take-over is unknown, but, up to
   1865 at least, Holyokes cut almost as much timber as Clark did in
   Garthby Township. AC, Correspondance, 1866, no. 10645/784, Return of Timber Dues, Garthby, 1854–65.
56 ANQ-S, E.P. Felton file, 13 Nov. 1858, no. 150. The dumping into
   rivers of any mill refuse except sawdust had been prohibited since
   1843, but in 1851 legislation exempted the St Lawrence, Ottawa, and
   "any other River or Rivulet wherein Salmon, Pickerel, Black Bass or
   Perch do not abound." McLaren, "The Tribulations of Antoine
   Ratté," 213–14, 240. A fish ladder for migrating Atlantic salmon had
   been added to the Brompton Falls dam in 1858, but the Clark Company continued to dump its sawdust in the river. Allard, "Préservation ou développement," 94, 105–7. The federal government failed
   to take effective action against river pollution by sawmills until after
   the turn of the century; see Gillis, "Rivers of Sawdust," 84–103.
57 *JLAC*, 10 March 1858, 58; 22 April, 301; 28 April, 360. A similar
   petition from Edward Hale and others of Orford (16 April 1858,
   250) added a second proviso: "the protection of the different descriptions of fish which pass by the said dam."
58 Ibid., 28 April 1858, 361; 3 May, 397.
59 Ibid., 3 July 1858, 790; 12 July, 832; 24 July, 908. The only major
   limitation to Clark's domination of the river was imposed by the
   BALC which allowed Clark's dam to adjoin its Stoke lot on condition
   that all of the Brompton lot not required for mill operations be relinquished, and that Clark's use of the water-power be restricted to
   the sawmill, leaving the remainder for the land company. ANQ-S, D.
   Thomas file, acte de dépôt, 9 Dec. 1874, no. 5510.
60 ANQ-S, E.P. Felton file, 31 March 1879, no. 362; 10 May 1880, no.
   364.
61 The main purpose of these dams was to impound water for the
   sluicing and driving of logs during the spring. Booth, *Les Cantons*,
   41.

62 NA, RG4 C1, Civil Secretary's Correspondence (Incoming), no. 1947 (vol. 442), Petition des Habitants de Weedon, Garthby, Stratford, Winslow, etc., Stratford, 7 June 1858; *JLAC*, 21 June 1858, 722.

63 The government failed in its 1859 attempt to pass legislation permitting mill owners to flood neighbouring lands and pay damages or compensation. Benidickson, "Private Rights," 369.

64 ANQ-Q, E25, Agriculture et Travaux Publics, Correspondance reçues, no. 962, J. Picard to C.B. de Boucherville, Wotton, 23 April 1877; Terres et Forêts, Lettres envoyées, art. 870, 10, E.E. Taché to Louis N. Labrecque, Quebec, 3 May 1879.

65 In the Temiscouata district, seigneurs tightly controlled colonization as a potential impediment to the lumber industry. Willis, "Urbanization," 138–39. For a discussion of conflict in the Mauricie, see Hardy and Séguin, *Forêt et société*, 152–56.

66 Gaudreau, *L'Exploitation*, 34–36; ANQ-Q, Terres et Forêts, Lettres envoyées, art. 855, 165, Wm. McD. Dawson to B. Lupien, 29 July 1853. An amendment passed in 1859 mentioned the permit, but it had been dropped once again by 1868. Finally, in 1872 the government introduced a bill to allow colonists who had paid two instalments and fulfilled settlement conditions to obtain a timber permit, but the licensee was supposed to hold preference of purchase. Gaudreau, *L'Exploitation*, 37–38.

67 ANQ-Q, Terres et Forêts, Lettres envoyées, art. 857, 67, A. Russell to G.J. Nagle, Toronto, 20 Aug. 1858. See also Hodgetts, *Pioneer Public Service*, 139.

68 *JLAC*, 1862, app. 1, Report of John Hume.

69 ANQ-Q, Terres et Forêts, Correspondance générale, J.T. Le Bel to Joseph Cauchon, Malmaison, Garthby, 28 March 1856.

70 Ibid., Antoine Roy to Monsieur le secrétaire provincial, Lambton, 10 Nov. 1856. Enclosed is the petition of three "habitants de Lambton," Saint-Vital, 10 Nov. 1856.

71 Ibid., Ls. Labrecque to L.V. Sicotte, Lambton, 2 March 1858.

72 Ibid. (attached), D.R. to Sicotte (private), Toronto, 22 [...] 1858; Lettres envoyées, art. 856, 512, L.V. Sicotte to Ls. Labrecque, 31 March 1858. Ross's support may have been made easier by the fact that Clark's mill lay outside his Beauce constituency.

73 ANQ-Q, Terres et Forêts, Correspondance générale, Ls. Labrecque to L.V. Sicotte, Lambton, 7 Oct. 1858.

74 Ibid., Lettres envoyées, art. 857, 179, Andrew Russell to Ls. Labrecque, Toronto, 19 Oct. 1858.

75 Ibid., art. 858, 433, P.M. Vankoughnet to G.J. Nagle, Toronto, 29 March 1859. The onus appears to have been on the agent not to renew licences for lots sold to individuals. In 1880 legislation finally

gave timber companies only until the following May to wind up operations on any lot claimed by a settler since the timber licence had been renewed. Québec, Legislative Assembly, *Débats*, 1890, II, 476–80.

76 ANQ-Q, Terres et Forêts, Correspondance générale, John Bignell to Andrew Russell, Lambton, 26 May 1859.

77 Dallaire's five lots, claimed between 1850 and 1857, had been specifically removed from Clark's licence in December 1858; ibid., Clark's licence for Aylmer, 12 Dec. 1858. Dallaire claimed a sixth lot which the Crown Land Office apparently had no record of; ibid., G.J. Nagle to P.M. Vankoughnet, Saint-Hyacinthe, 28 May 1859.

78 Ibid., Michel Godette to G.J. Nagle, Lambton, 13 May 1859.

79 Ibid., C.S. Clark & Co., Brompton Falls, 26 April 1859.

80 Ibid., G.J. Nagle to Michel Godette, Saint-Hyacinthe, 4 May 1859.

81 Ibid., G.J. Nagle to P.M. Vankoughnet, 28 May 1859.

82 Ibid.

83 Ibid., Duval and Taschereau to P. Vankoughnet, Québec, 12 May 1859.

84 Ibid., Telegraph, J.H. Pope to G.J. Nagle, Sherbrooke, 9 May 1859. Dallaire's lawyers claimed that the company's men were the aggressors. Seventy-five had succeeded "avec des armes et des haches et des barres de fer à chasser les gardiens et prendre possession du bois." Nagle felt the story was apocryphal. Ibid., Duval and Taschereau to Vankoughnet, 12 May 1859; Nagle to Vankoughnet, Saint-Hyacinthe, 28 May 1859; G.J. Nagle to J.H. Pope, Saint-Hyacinthe, 9 May 1859.

85 NA, Civil Secretary's Correspondence (Incoming), vol. 478, no. 1067, Affidavit of Mayor of Aylmer Township.

86 ANQ-Q, Terres et Forêts, Correspondance générale, 1869, no. 366, Affidavit, Romain Dallaire, Saint-Vital, 30 August 1868. The commissioner of crown lands was inclined to blame Blanchet, the lately dismissed Beauce agent, for "stirring up this trouble as he is known to have been himself a speculator in crown lands." Ibid., Note on cover of Nagle to Vankoughnet, Saint-Hyacinthe, 28 May 1859.

87 NA, Civil Secretary's Correspondence (Incoming), vol. 478, no. 1067, Affidavit of mayor of Aylmer, 5 May 1860.

88 Ibid., Petition of Inhabitants of Aylmer and Lambton to Governor General Head, 25 April 1860; Draft reply to Mayor Michel Tanguay, Que., 3 July 1860; D. Morin to Chas. Alleyn, 28 July 1860, 10 April 1862.

89 ANQ-Q, Terres et Forêts, Correspondance générale, Petition of Colons des Townships de Lambton, Price, Aylmer, and Gayhurst, 7 May 1860.

90 Ibid., Petition of Mayors of Municipalities of Beauce, 1 May 1862. Repeated in 1863; Lettres envoyées, art. 860, 307–8, A. Russell to G.J. Nagle, Quebec, 31 July 1862; 446, A. Russell to G.J. Nagle, Quebec, 7 Nov. 1862.

91 Ibid., art. 859, 491, A. Russell to G.J. Nagle, Quebec, 9 Nov. 1861.

92 Ibid., Correspondance générale, W. Farwell to A. Russell, Robinson, 10 Sept. 1863.

93 Ibid., G.J. Nagle to W. McD. Dawson, Saint-Hyacinthe, 13 March 1857.

94 ANQ-Q, Terres et Forêts, Correspondance générale, G.J. Nagle to A. Russell, Saint-Hyacinthe, 26 Sept. 1863. On the added difficulty of clearing land where timber had been removed, see Ball, "The Technology of Settlement," 58–65.

95 Ibid., Lettres envoyées, art. 860, Circular by A. Campbell, Quebec, 17 June 1864.

96 Ibid., art. 862, 419, A. Russell to G.J. Nagle, Quebec, 8 June 1865.

97 Ibid., art. 859, 226–27, P.M. Partridge to G.J. Nagle, Quebec, 9 April 1861; art. 860, 165–66, A. Russell to G.J. Nagle, Quebec, 26 April 1862; art. 866, 242, E.E. Taché to W. Farwell, Quebec, 4 June 1872.

98 Ibid., art. 860, 224, A. Russell to J.F. Bérubé, 29 Jan. 1864; 482, A. Russell to G.J. Nagle, Quebec, 29 July 1864; art. 862, 37, A. Russell to G.J. Nagle, Quebec, 9 Sept. 1864.

99 Ibid., Correspondance générale, 1869, no. 366, Affidavit of Charles Gagnon, Price farmer [mayor of Lambton], 25 Aug. 1868; Affidavit of François Blais, Lambton farmer, Saint-Vital, 30 Aug. 1868.

100 Perhaps the provincial government did not feel so obliged to protect Ditton and Hampden because their reserves were held by largely inactive English-speaking colonization societies. ANQ-Q, Terres et Forêts, Correspondance générale, 1872, no. 2854–5, 26 Aug. 1872; no. 2891, L. Pope to CCL, Robinson, 17 Aug. 1872; no. 3274, W. Farwell to CCL, Robinson, 28 Sept. 1872; Cover, 7 Oct. 1872.

101 Ibid., 1873, no. 193, J.I. Mackie to CCL, Cookshire, 13 Jan. 1873.

102 Ibid., no. 264, F. Paquette to CCL, Paquetteville, 18 Jan. 1873.

103 Ibid., 1874, no. 358, John Hume to CCL, Quebec, 27 Jan. 1874.

104 Ibid., no. 5208, John Hume to CCL, Quebec, 24 Nov. 1874.

105 Ibid., Lettres envoyées, art. 867, 133, P. Fortin to crown timber agents (confidential instructions), Quebec, 28 Feb. 1874. See, for example, the cases mentioned in ibid., art. 868, 303, E.E. Taché to W. Farwell, Quebec, 22 March 1876.

106 Gaudreau ("L'Exploitation," 15) suggests that the vertical saws of the large mills became less efficient as the size of the logs decreased. After 1875 water-driven sawmills were seldom built. Lower, *North*

American Assault, 48. Small mills were also appearing closer to the sources of timber in Maine during the 1870s; see Smith, *A History of Lumbering*, 108.

107 *Sherbrooke Daily Record*, 21 March 1959; Mayhew, *History of Canterbury*, 36–38.

108 *Sherbrooke Gazette*, 19 Nov. 1880. The Quebec Central reached Weedon in 1875, Thetford Mines in 1878, and the Lévis and Kennebec running to Quebec City by 1881. Booth, *Railways* ii: 105.

109 Canada, *Census Reports*, 1871, 1881. Note that in 1880–81 four times as many logs were sawed in Compton County as were reported cut on crown lands throughout the St Francis and Arthabaska agencies.

110 During the 1880s Rufus Pope and W.B. Ives, MP for Richmond-Wolfe, established the Cookshire Mill Company (with exports to South America of 50 million feet worth $650,000 by the mid-1890s), the Scotstown Lumber Company, the Salmon River Pulp Company also of Scotstown, and the Royal Paper Mills of East Angus. Channel, *History of Compton*, 46, 131–32.

111 ANQ-Q, E4, Secrétariat provincial, Correspondance générale, Municipalités, art. 884, no. 481, petition dated Dec. 1877.

112 ANQ-Q, Terres et Forêts, art. 940, Inspectors' reports, Winslow, 1885.

113 Gravel, *Sainte Praxède de Brompton*, 56. The first chemical pulp mill in Canada had been put into operation a short distance downriver at Windsor Mills in 1866. Booth, *Les Cantons*, 65. The Brompton Pulp and Paper Company held reserves of 287,000 acres in the Eastern Townships and Maine, and enjoyed the exclusive right to store and float logs on 132 square miles of lakes and 151 miles of streams and brooks, not to mention the St Francis itself above Brompton Falls. Brouillette, "L'industrie," 179–80; MacKenzie, "The History of Man's Utilization," 62–65.

114 NA, BALC Papers, vol. 12, Reports and Accounts, 1861–1910, 2409, Commissioner's Report to Henry Paull, Sherbrooke, 25 Jan. 1897. The rise of the pulp and paper industry had the same effect in the Mauricie; see Hardy and Séguin, *Forêt et société*, 155–56.

115 ANQ-Q, Terres et Forêts, Correspondance générale, Report of inspection of lumbering operations in Eastern Townships, V. Larue, Saint-Charles, 23 June 1854.

116 Ibid., J.H. Pope to Clark, Brown & Co., Lake St Francis, 30 April 1854.

117 ANQ-S, Queen's Bench, Cragin *v.* Pope et al, testimony of Richard Charles Porter, 15 Sept. 1871.

118 ANQ-Q, Terres et Forêts, Correspondance générale, S.V. Larue to W. McD. Dawson, St Charles, 12 June 1854. Perhaps Larue was not aware that the Brompton mill was already in operation. Clark had

obtained permission to delay payment of dues on the grounds that the timber would be sawed in the province; ibid., W. McD. Dawson to C.S. Clark, Quebec, 9 May 1854.

119 Ibid., 1874, no. 5208, John Hume to CCL, Quebec, 24 Nov. 1874. Graeme Wynn claims that New Brunswick's early "deputy surveyors," working under considerably greater handicaps, did act as an effective check against those attempting to cheat the government. Wynn, "Administration in Adversity."

120 ANQ-Q, Terres et Forêts, Correspondance générale, G.J. Nagle to Geo. F. Austin, Saint-Hyacinthe, 9 March 1857. Attached to 3167/61, Nagle to Austin, 9 April 1861.

121 Ibid., G.J. Nagle to C.S. Clark & Co., Saint-Hyacinthe, 9 April 1857.

122 Ibid., Statement no. 9/58, Logs cut by C.S. Clark & Co., James R. McDonald, 7 April 1858.

123 Ibid., Return of timber cut by C.S. Clark Co. during the season 1857–58.

124 Ibid., Statement of logs cut in Nagle Agency, 1857–58, 4 Sept. 1858.

125 Ibid., Memorandum, P.M. Vankoughnet, Quebec, 26 Sept. 1861; J.H. Pope to P.M. Vankoughnet, Quebec, 23 March 1861 (private). Pope would later claim that two million feet reported by government agents in Black Creek in 1856–57, when rescaled by himself and an experienced assistant, produced not more than *300,000* feet of sawlogs; ibid., Affidavit of Washington Lunt of Sherbrooke, 19 June 1865. Even a government wood ranger would swear that thousands of Clark's logs were small and worthless from dry rot, and that he had seen hundreds floated over the dam at Brompton Falls; ibid., Affidavit of Michel Gaudette of Weedon, 8 June 1865. This was presumably the Michel "Godette" who had served the company's interests against Dallaire in 1859.

126 Ibid., G.J. Nagle to A. Russell, Saint-Hyacinthe, 5 March 1861.

127 Ibid., Memorandum respecting claim of Messrs. C.S. Clark & Co. ... by P.M. Partridge, [n.d.].

128 Ibid., Memorandum, P.M. Vankoughnet, Quebec, 26 Sept. 1861; see also Lettres envoyées, art. 859, 484, A. Russell to G.J. Nagle, Quebec, 6 Nov. 1861.

129 Ibid., Correspondance générale, P.M. Vankoughnet, Quebec, 18 March 1862.

130 Ibid., J.H. Pope, Brompton Falls, 17 March 1862. A.T. Galt upheld Pope's claim; ibid., A.T. Galt to A. Russell, 25 Feb. 1862.

131 Ibid., Lettres envoyées, art. 865, 338, E.E. Taché to G.J. Nagle, Quebec, 24 Nov. 1869; 263, G.A. Bourgeois to G.J. Nagle and 5 others, Quebec, 17 June 1869; Correspondance générale, 1869, no. 3104, G.J. Nagle to E.E. Taché, Saint-Hyacinthe, 12 Oct. 1869.

132 These lots were restored to the Clark licence in the fall of 1869; ibid., Lettres envoyées, art. 865, 299, E.E. Taché to G.J. Nagle, Quebec, 25 Sept. 1869.

133 Pope's case also mentioned the repayment of unspecified fees for logs cut in Weedon which had proven to be on BALC land. Ibid., Correspondance générale, 1869, no. 3796, J.H. Pope to G.J. Nagle, Cookshire, 3 Dec. 1869. After Pope had been forced to pay the land company $2000 for this trespass in 1865, he had had the audacity to claim compensation for the full amount from the government; ibid., J.H. Pope to Campbell, Brompton Falls, 20 April 1865; 22 May 1865.

134 Ibid., 1869, no. 3796, E.E.T. pour le commissaire, 9 Dec. 1869; ibid., Lettres envoyées, art. 865, 361, E.E. Taché to G.J. Nagle, Quebec, 10 Jan. 1870.

135 Ibid., Lettres envoyées, art. 866, 4, E.E. Taché to J.H. Pope, Quebec, 17 August 1870. In 1871 Taché reiterated to the timber agent that dues would have to be paid on all logs, irrespective of quality; ibid., 123, E.E. Taché to W. Farwell, Quebec, 7 July 1871.

136 Ibid., 13–16, E.E. Taché to J.H. Pope, Quebec, 5 Sept. 1870.

137 There are only a few earlier instances in which the Crown Lands Office came close to using coercion. The Clark and Company licences were supposedly not renewed for the 1857–58 season because Nagle was not satisfied with the accuracy of the returns for the preceding season; ibid., art. 857, 115–17, P.M. Vankoughnet to C.S. Clark & Co., Toronto, 8 Sept. 1858. However, they cut on all the limits that winter in any case. For the 1859–60 and 1860–61 seasons, the licences for Winslow, Adstock, and Price were forfeited for non-payment of outstanding dues, but once again the company ignored the government's action. In 1862 all was forgiven and the $439 in trespass fees (for 21,526 logs) was removed; ibid., art. 860, 395, A. Russell to G.J. Nagle, Quebec, 27 Sept. 1862.

138 Ibid., 64–65, E.E. Taché to W. Farwell, Quebec, 11 Jan. 1871; E.E. Taché to J.H. Pope and C.S. Clark & Co., Quebec, 11 Jan. 1871.

139 Ibid., 76, E.E. Taché to W. Farwell, Quebec, 4 Feb. 1871.

140 Hamelin, Les Premières Années, 189–90.

141 ANQ-Q, Terres et Forêts, Lettres envoyées, art. 869, 1, E.E. Taché, Circular to crown timber agents, Quebec, 7 Feb. 1877.

142 Ibid., art. 867, 98, E.E. Taché to W. Farwell, Quebec, 10 Feb. 1874; 133, P. Fortin to crown timber agents (confidential instructions), Quebec, 28 Feb. 1874.

143 Hodgetts, Pioneer Public Service, 141.

144 Cross, "Lumber Community," 312. The best description of the centralization process in a British North American context is Wynn, Timber Colony, chaps. 5 and 6.

145 See Gillis, "Ottawa lumber barons," 14; and Wall, "Nineteenth-century Land Use," 235–39.

CHAPTER SIX

1 Ouellet, *Economic and Social History*, 490.
2 Silver, *The French-Canadian Idea*, 237.
3 Dussault, *Le Curé Labelle*, see especially chap. 2; Morissonneau, *La Terre promise*, 54; Proulx, *Le Roman du territoire*.
4 Dussault underestimates the crucial ideological role played by the French-Canadian exodus (*Le Curé Labelle*, 170, 332), and Morissonneau greatly exaggerates the pull of the northern frontier.
5 T.S. Provost, *La Bourse et la vie* (Joliette: Imprimerie du Collège de Joliette, 1883), 166; quoted in Morissonneau, "La Colonisation équivoque," 45.
6 *L'Ordre*, 3 April 1867; quoted in Morin, "La pensée colonisatrice," 95.
7 Hamelin, *Les Premières Années*, 96, 98ff, 206.
8 For details, see Little, "The Peaceable Conquest," 326–29. For a brief description of a comparable plan promoted by Father Calixte Marquis in 1867, see Morin, "La pensée colonisatrice," 95–98.
9 *SPQ*, IV (1870), app. 10, Report of Abbé Chartier; Reports of the CCL in V (1871), VI (1872), VIII (1874), IX (1875); AC, Section Ouest, adj. 4472, Report by John Hume, 10 March 1876.
10 AETR, Collection Abbé Edmond Moreau, Moreau to Mgr Laflèche, Montreal, 27 March 1871. For a brief description of Moreau, see Hardy, *Les Zouaves*, 95–96.
11 One of the first enterprises was a company organized to supply fresh fish to the Boston Market; Channell, *History of Compton*, 271, 279–80; NA, MG30 H17, J.P. Jones, "History of Lake Megantic, 1760-1921" (non-paginated). A.C. Taschereau of Sainte-Marie de Beauce began cutting timber at Lake Megantic in the 1830s. NA, BALC Papers, vol. 5, Letterbook 1834–36, 1021, Samuel Brooks to Moffatt and McGill, 4 June 1835; 1025, 15 June 1835.
12 Channell, *History of Compton*, 280.
13 AC, Section Ouest, adj. 4792, R.W. Heneker to P. Garneau, Sherbrooke, 10 July 1877; Nelles, *Politics of Development*, 20–21.
14 AC, Section Ouest, adj. 4117. The Reciprocity Mining Company had paid all crown instalments after purchasing its sixteen location tickets in 1865 from Arthur Rankin of Essex County, England. Sherbrooke Registry Office, Reg. B, vol. 18, 474, no. 347; AC, Livre des recettes, Marston. I found no record of their cancellation by the government, but it disqualified their purchase at a sheriff's sale in 1873 on these

grounds. Cookshire Registry Office, Reg. B, vol. 3, 256, no. 1445; AC, Section Ouest, adj. 4516, Report of W.F. Collins on Petition of R.D. Morkill, 10 Nov. 1875. A third group from Montreal actually opened a gold mine in 1865, but it seems to have acquired a relatively small number of lots; AC, Section Ouest, adj. 4279.

15 ANQ-Q, Agriculture et Travaux Publics, Correspondances reçues, no. 2174, William Farwell to G.A. Bourgeois, Robinson, 10 Nov. 1868.

16 Ibid., Registres de Lettres envoyées, art. 636, vol. 5, S. Le Sage to Lemuel Pope, 17 Sept. 1870; vol. 7, 650, E. Moreau to W. Sawyer, 1 Sept. 1871; art. 637, vol. 8, 308, E. Moreau to Donald Beaton, 28 Sept. 1871; Le Pionnier, 27 May 1870.

17 SPQ, V (1871), 252.

18 AETR, Collection Abbé Edmond Moreau, Moreau to Laflèche, Montreal, 27 March 1871. Marston was in the Diocese of Trois-Rivières, but apparently Laflèche had no one to spare because Montreal provided a priest on a temporary basis; ibid., 4 April 1871.

19 AAS, Parish Papers, Saint-Zenon-de-Piopolis, A.A. Gagnon to Mgr. Antoine of Sherbrooke "Notes sur St. Zenon de Piopolis ...," [n.d.]; L'Union des Cantons de l'Est (Arthabaskaville), 22 June 1871; Le Journal des Trois-Rivières, 1 June 1871; Archives du Séminaire de Québec, Fonds Viger-Verreau 34, no. 376, chem. vi, 30–2, Union Allet, Séance de 15 mars 1871 (reference kindly provided by René Hardy).

20 As the title suggests, this is the thesis of Hardy, Les Zouaves, une stratégie du clergé québécois au XIXᵉ siècle.

21 Mgr Bourget had presented each member of the sixth detachment with a relic of St Zenon. On his cult see Hardy, Les Zouaves, 183. The original seven Zouave settlers were reported to be Odilon Martel, Damien Leclerc, Ulric Moreau (Canon Moreau's brother), Louis Blanchard, Clovis Fortier, Arthur Penny, and M. Blais. AAS, "Notes sur St. Zenon de Piopolis." A list of Zouave land claimants in 1873 adds Elzéar Cloutier, Alfred Gaumont, William Hamer, Arthur Champagne, and Charles Langlois, but includes only three of the original seven names. Presbytère de Piopolis, Livre de caisse du 19 avril 1871 au 17 avril 1873. Of the nine of these individuals listed in Elio Lodolini's study on the Canadian Zouaves, the four youngest were born between 1848 and 1851, and only two (one of whom may have been a student at the time of recruitment) are listed as farmers. (Both were presumably living on their fathers' land though they were in their late twenties by 1869.) Three had been students; two, landed proprietors; one, a carpenter; and one, a potter. Lodolini, Les Volontaires, 99–140. The Zouave colonists' lack of experience is stressed in Le Constitutionnel (Trois-Rivières), 14 Aug. 1871.

22 SPQ, VI (1872), General Report of the Commissioner of Agriculture

and Public Works, app. 2; Piopolis, Livre de caisse; AAM, "Diocèse de Trois-Rivières," 295.104, Mgr. Laflèche to Mgr Bourget, Trois-Rivières, 25 July 1873.

23 *Le Nouveau Monde* (Montréal), 19 June 1873.

24 With the Montreal Colonization Society unable to provide immediate aid in November, the Zouaves turned to their own organization, the Union Allet. *Bulletin de l'Union Allet,* 25 Nov. 1873.

25 ANQ-Q, Terres et Forêts, Lettres envoyées, art. 866, 267, E.E. Taché to William Farwell, Que., 20 Aug. 1872; Correspondance générale, 1876, no. 1965, Charles Patton to CCL, Robinson, 17 May 1876. For a brief biography of Hall, see Andrée Désilets's article in *DCB* X.

26 This article, published 25 Nov. 1873, is reprinted in Drolet, *Zouaviana,* 118–19.

27 Drolet, *Zouaviana,* 120. ANQ-Q, Terres et Forêts, Lettres envoyées, art. 867, 51, E.E. Taché to W.J. McAdams, Que., 14 Jan. 1874.

28 ANQ-Q, Terres et Forêts, Lettres envoyées, art. 870, 270, E.E. Taché to Abbé J.B.A. Cousineau, Que., 22 March 1880. There was an over-land market for ship's knees from Piopolis; ANQ-Q, Agriculture et Travaux Publics, Correspondances reçues, no. 33597, L. Pope to E. Moreau, Robinson, 24 Jan. 1876.

29 *SPQ,* Reports of the Commissioner of Agriculture and Public Works in VIII (1874), 2, and IX (1875), 280–81.

30 *Bulletin de l'Union Allet,* 25 Oct. 1874, 8.

31 Ibid., 25 Oct. 1875, 24 March 1876; AAS, Rapports sur les Paroisses et Missions, Saint-Zenon-de-Piopolis, 1876–80.

32 *Le Journal des Trois-Rivières,* 4 Oct. 1875; *L'Union des Cantons de l'Est* (Arthabaskaville), 7 Oct. 1875. The *Bulletin de l'Union Allet* on 25 Oct. 1875 inflated these statistics somewhat. As we shall see, it is doubtful if either school was in effective operation.

33 AETR, Collection Abbé Edmond Moreau, Moreau to Mgr Laflèche, 11 Sept. 1871.

34 AC, Section Ouest, adj. 4472.

35 Ibid., Register Book, Section Ouest, 1871–72, NO. 3835, E. Moreau to E. Taché, 17 June 1871.

36 Ibid., J. Hume to CCL, 31 Oct. 1871; W. Farwell to J. Hume, 30 Oct. 1871.

37 Ibid., Compton Colonization Society Resolution, 20 March 1871; C. Patton to P.E. Gendreau, 24 April 1871, 10 June 1871; J.B. Champagne to L. Pope, 30 Oct. 1871; L. Pope to J. Hume, 30 Oct. 1871.

38 *Le Pionnier* (Sherbrooke), 19 Feb. 1872.

39 AC, Section Ouest, adj. 4279, John Hume to CCL, Leeds, 12 Aug. 1872.

40 Unidentified newsclipping in NA, MG29, Fonds LaRocque, Cahiers de coupures de journaux, 214.

41 AC, Section Ouest, adj. 4279 and 4472.

42 This biographical sketch is based on information from the manuscript census, Marston and Whitton Townships, 1871, and ANQ-S,
Queen's Bench, St Francis District, no. 837\ McMinn v. Bradford, returned and filed 18 June 1872. McMinn was also co-owner of a
heavily mortgaged store in Gould. Cookshire Registry Office, Reg. B,
vol. 4, 128–29, no. 1975; 184–85, no. 2024.

43 There appears to be no historical study of the Protestant Defence
Alliance, which had sprung from a dispute between Protestant and
Catholic missionaries at the Oka Indian Reserve near Montreal. The
only other branch to appear in the Townships was in Sherbrooke.
See *Le Progrès* (Sherbrooke), 4 Feb. 1876, 11 Feb. 1876; *Le Pionnier*
(Sherbrooke), 4, Feb. 1876.

44 *Daily Witness* (Montreal), 27 Jan. 1876.

45 Ibid.

46 Ibid., 21 Feb. 1876. It is unlikely that McMinn was the author of this
letter for he was a known Liberal supporter. ANQ-S, St Francis District, Sessions of the Peace and Magistrate's Court, Queen v. Aeneas
McMaster, affidavit James R. Woodward, 2 March 1880.

47 Hume also investigated cancellations in neighbouring townships, but
found that they were all warranted. Except where indicated otherwise, the following information from his report is found in AC, Section Ouest, adj. 4472.

48 Hamelin and Roby, *Histoire économique*, 175.

49 Wright's report is in AC, Section Ouest, adj. 4430.

50 ANQ-Q, SL, Correspondance, I, 427, Le Sage to O'Neil, 28 May 1873.

51 Fourteen location tickets were restored, Ryan was reimbursed, and
McMinn was exonerated from compensating Beaudoin. AC, Section
Ouest, adj. 4474.

52 NA, Jones, "History of Lake Megantic," II, part I; Channell, *History of
Compton*, 280.

53 See the municipality's lengthy protest of 7 Oct. 1889 in AAS, Parish
Papers, Saint-Zenon-de-Piopolis, Session of Municipal Council of
Marston South.

54 The Scots protested that they had opened a school near the company lots shortly before hearing of the municipal division. ANQ-Q,
E13, Education, Lettres expédiées, vol. 49, 820, G. Ouimet to Ant.
Grenier, 19 Nov. 1879; Lettres reçues, 1879, no. 1097, Petition to G.
Ouimet, Piopolis, 21 June 1879; no. 2877, Ant. Gagnon to G. Ouimet, Piopolis, 13 Nov. 1879; Ant. Grenier to G. Ouimet, Piopolis,
22 April 1880.

55 Ibid., Lettres reçues, 1877, no. 2878, J.B.A. Cousineau to G. Ouimet,
Piopolis, 20 Aug. 1877; 11 Sept. 1877; 1878, no. 638, Marston syn-

dics to G. Ouimet, 2 April 1878; J.B.A. Cousineau to G. Ouimet, Piopolis, 11 May 1878; 30 Dec. 1878.

56 As late as 1881, there is no record of Marston South's residents having paid school taxes, but the government grant, which was supposed to be equivalent to each district's assessment, equalled $41.42 for the 1880–81 school year. The only other funds directed to the parish's schools up to this point were $20.00 in 1878–79 and $10.00 in 1880–81 as supplementary grants for poor municipalities. See the reports of the Superintendent of Public Instruction in *SPQ*, XIII (1879), 284; XIV (1880), 177, 264; XV (1881–82), 287.

57 Presbytère de Piopolis, "Cahier de délibérations," 1876, 1877, 1879; "Originaux depuis 1874 à nos jours," Mgr Racine to J.B.A. Cousineau, Sherbrooke, 15 Jan. 1881.

58 *Sherbrooke News*, 24 Sept. 1877, found in NA, J.P. Jones, "History of Lake Megantic." The traveller was not impressed with the condition of the Bury and Megantic Road, though it had apparently taken all of the county's colonization roads grant ($3634) to complete it for all-season travel in 1876. ANQ-Q, Agriculture et Travaux Publics, Registres de lettres envoyées, art. 643, vol. 26, no. 14746, 218–19, J.O. Fontaine to W. Sawyer, 27 July 1876; art. 646, vol. 35, 673, J.O. Fontaine to P. Brassard, 7 July 1880.

59 "Saint-Zenon de Piopolis," *Le Messager de Saint-Michel de Sherbrooke*, 26 March 1933.

60 The range of parish delinquents was fourteen to nineteen, but most of these appear to have lived outside Marston, for when the figure of sixteen was broken down in 1878, Marston had only one delinquent and Ditchfield, where a colony of French-speaking Protestants had been established, had fourteen. AAS, Rapports sur les Paroisses et Missions, Saint-Zenon-de-Piopolis, 1879, 1880.

61 Frédéric Boucher de Grosbois was a Piopolis merchant who planned to open a sawmill in 1874. Cookshire Registry office, Reg. E, Partnership Book, vol. 1, no. 12; AC, Section Ouest, adj. 4379, F.B. de Grosbois to Hon. Monsieur, Piopolis, 10 Nov. 1874; Certif. of J.B. Cousineau, Piopolis, 17 Jan. 1875. According to Channel (*History of Compton*, 281) the only remaining Zouave veteran in 1896, Odilon Martel, "prospered and owns several farms." For a brief outline of each Zouave's progress in the colony see "Saint-Zenon de Piopolis," *Le Messager de Saint-Michel de Sherbrooke*, 22 Jan. 1933.

62 Channell, *History of Compton*, 281.

63 Unidentified newsclipping, "Un Colon," 18 July 1876, in NA, MG29, Fonds La Rocque, Cahiers de coupures de journaux, 131; *Bulletin de l'Union Allet*, 16 June 1877.

64 For an overview, see Little, "Watching the Frontier Disappear."

65 Fellman, "Rehearsal for the Civil War."
66 Ibid., 297–98, 301.
67 My thanks to Professor Margaret Bennett of the School of Scottish Studies, University of Edinburgh, who provided this song and its translation by her mother, Margaret Bennett of the Isle of Skye.
68 See MacKay, *By Trench and Trail*.
69 Martial law was imposed on the district as a result of Scots defiance. See Rudin, "The Megantic Outlaw."
70 MacKay, "The End of the Trail," in *By Trench and Trail*, 71. The demoralized Highlanders had not resisted exile at mid-century, but they did strike out against their landlords during the 1880s; see Hunter, *Making of the Crofting Community*.

CHAPTER SEVEN

1   On the history of these railroads, see Hamelin, *Les Premières Années*, 96–101; Booth, *Railways*.
2   See Angus, "The Politics of the Short Line."
3   *Le Pionnier* (Sherbrooke), 17 April 1868, 10 July 1868, 21 July 1868. In October, Pope's home municipality of Eaton Township engaged a surveyor to trace a railroad route from Lennoxville to Cookshire, and in May 1869 the local council voted to take $4,000 in the company's shares. *Stanstead Journal*, 3 Dec. 1868; Cookshire, Municipality of the Township of Eaton, Minute Book – ByLaws – Procès verbaux, 1855–72, 3 May 1869, 104–6; 5 July 1869, 195.
4   Kesteman speculates that the primary objective was to "ouvrir une région forestière quasi-inviolée"; "Une Bourgeoisie," 516.
5   Quebec, *Statutes*, 1869, 32 Vict., c. 52, 57, 58.
6   Ibid., c. 58. The municipalities of Bury, Lingwick, Dudswell, and Weedon submitted petitions protesting the incorporation of the Sherbrooke, Eastern Townships, and Kennebec Company. ANQ-Q, Secrétariat Provincial, Correspondance général, Municipalités, art. 873, no. 332–33, 20 Feb. 1869; no. 341, 22 Feb. 1869. It is difficult to understand why the latter two townships raised objections, for they would be directly served by the project in question. As we shall see, in April they would offer monetary support.
7   Hamelin, *Les Premières Années*, 105; Skelton, *Life and Times*, 85, 207.
8   Hamelin, *Les Premières Années*, 106, 193–94; Booth, *Railways*, I: 28–29; McCord Museum, Sanborn Papers, folio VI, E. Raymond to J. Sanborn, Boston, 19 Oct. 1872.
9   *Le Pionnier* (Sherbrooke), 29 Jan. 1869.
10 For his criticisms of the BALC, *see* ibid., 28 Aug. 1867.
11 Ibid., 21 May 1869, 28 May 1869, 4 June 1869, 14 Jan. 1870.

12 McCord Museum, Sanborn Papers, folio IV, J. Sanborn to Nancy, Ottawa, 11 June 1869.

13 Quebec, *Statutes*, 1869, 32 Vict., c. 52, The only MLA on the St Francis company's board of directors was C.H. Pozer of Beauce. While Compton's Conservative MLA James G. Ross denied that he opposed Pope's project, *Le Pionnier* (1 Sept. 1871) attributed his electoral defeat to that cause. Ross was replaced by Pope's close ally, William Sawyer of Eaton Township.

14 Young, *Promoters and Politicians*, 25.

15 *Le Pionnier* (Sherbrooke), 28 May 1869. Lambton, Stratford, and Garthby defeated their subsidy proposals; ibid., 20 Aug. 1869.

16 Quebec, *Statutes*, 1869, 32 Vict., c. 57, 58. Rather than taking the risk of investing directly in their projects, railway promoters would purchase the debentures floated by municipalities. Kesteman, "Une Bourgeoisie," 528–29.

17 *Le Pionnier* (Sherbrooke), 11 Feb. 1870. The full subsidy was offered in the case where one of the two companies completed fifteen continuous miles of construction. Quebec, *Statutes*, 1869, 32 Vict., c. 52.

18 Details on the Maine connection can be found in Omer Lavallée, "International of Maine," chap. 2, kindly loaned by the author. See also Angus, "The Politics of the Short Line," 11–13.

19 Rudin, "The Transformation," 34; "Naissance et déclin," 170–71.

20 There is no evidence that Wolfe County ever voted on a subsidy for the Sherbrooke-Kennebec line, though county votes appear to have been the norm on the north shore. See Young, *Promoters and Politicians*, 63–66.

21 *Le Pionnier* (Sherbrooke), 22 April 1870. The Quebec Railway Act of 1869 authorized each municipality subscribing over $20,000 to name an ex-officio director; Young, *Promoters and Politicians*, 23.

22 *Le Pionnier* (Sherbrooke), 10 June 1870.

23 Ibid., 1 July 1870. The Compton County minutes record that no returns were received from Sherbrooke and Hereford, but this must simply mean that their mayors were absent from the council meeting which followed that referendum; Channell, *History of Compton*, 60.

24 *Le Pionnier* (Sherbrooke), 22 July 1870.

25 Ibid., 7 Oct. 1870. The vote was six to four, with the representatives from North and South Winslow, Clifton, and Auckland absent. Channell, *History of Compton*, 60–61.

26 Ibid., 30 Dec. 1870, 11 Feb. 1871. The affirmative votes were from Eaton, Newport, Westbury, Bury, Lingwick, South Winslow, Whitton, and Sherbrooke; the negative from Ascot, Orford, Compton, Clifton, Hereford, North Winslow, and Auckland. The Sherbrooke majority was from 80 to 90 votes out of 428. ANQ-S, Queen's Bench,

St Francis District, no. 685, Attorney General *v.* Compton County (1870); ANQ-Q, Secrétariat Provincial, Correspondance générale, Municipalités, art. 874, no. 1146.

27 *Le Pionnier* (Sherbrooke), 17 Feb. 1871.

28 See by-law 37 in ANQ-Q, Secrétariat Provincial, Correspondance générale, Municipalités, art. 874, no. 1146.

29 ANQ-S, Queen's Bench, St Francis District, no. 685, Attorney General *v.* Compton County (1870).

30 *Le Pionnier* (Sherbrooke), 23 Dec. 1870, 13 Jan. 1871; ANQ-Q, Secrétariat Provincial, Correspondance générale, Municipalités, art. 875, no. 1480.

31 *JLAQ*, IV (1870), 21, 32, 45, 85; Quebec, *Statutes*, 1871, 34 Vict., c. 30. Clifton residents asked to separate from Compton as well, but those in most other townships, including some from Sherbrooke and Ascot, submitted petitions opposing alteration of the county's boundaries. *JLAQ*, IV (1870), 22, 26, 48, 64, 77; ANQ-Q, Secrétariat Provincial, Correspondance générale, Municipalités, art. 874–75.

32 *Le Pionnier* (Sherbrooke), 5 Jan. 1872, 2 Feb. 1872.

33 Ibid., 19 Feb. 1872.

34 Hamelin, *Les Premières Années*, 193; *Le Pionnier* (Sherbrooke), 11 July 1873, 6 Aug. 1875.

35 Quebec, *Statutes*, 1872, 35 Vict., c. 23; *Le Pionnier* (Sherbrooke), 29 Dec. 1871. There was some question about the value of the wood. McCord Museum, Sanborn Papers, folio v, J.G. Robertson to Sanborn, Quebec, 20 Nov. 1871; G. Irvine to J.H. Pope, Quebec, 9 Dec. 1871; J.H. Pope to J. Sanborn, Ottawa, 14 Dec. 1871; W. Sawyer to J. Sanborn, Quebec, 23 Dec. 1872.

36 McCord Museum, Sanborn Papers, folio v, A.T. Galt to J. Sanborn, Montreal, 25 Oct. 1871, 15 Dec. 1871 (private); 15 Jan. 1872; *Stanstead Journal*, 2 Nov. 1871.

37 *Le Pionnier* (Sherbrooke), 20 Dec. 1872; McCord Museum, Sanborn Papers, folio VI, Estimate of Work Done & Materials furnished by Brooks, Ryan & Co., 1 March 1872. The engineer's "General specification of works" can be found in ibid., folio VII.

38 Quebec, *Statutes*, 1872, 35 Vict., c. 22. Only $50,000 had been subscribed by individuals as of November 1871; *Stanstead Journal*, 2 Nov. 1871.

39 McCord Museum, Sanborn Papers, folio VI, J.H. Pope to J. Sanborn, Ottawa, 28 March 1873; J.H. Pope to A. Brooks, Ottawa, 28 March 1873. Sherbrooke was more co-operative than Compton Township; *Le Pionnier* (Sherbrooke), 7 March 1873.

40 ANQ-S, Queen's Bench, St Francis, No. 977, A. Brooks et al. *v.* Compton County, Declaration filed 12 April 1873.

41 McCord Museum, Sanborn Papers, J.H. Pope to J. Sanborn, 24 June 1873.

42 Lavallée, "International of Maine," chap. 2; *Stanstead Journal*, 12 March 1874, 13 Aug. 1874; *Le Pionnier* (Sherbrooke), 11 Sept. 1874. In December 1874 Pope mortgaged 700 acres in Eaton Township as security for a $10,000 loan from the Trust and Loan Company of Canada, located in Montreal. The mortgage was discharged four years later. Cookshire Registry Office, Register B, vol. 4, 347, no. 2146.

43 Hamelin, *Les Premières Années*, 203–4.

44 Ibid., 254. The International subsidy represented two-thirds of a full subsidy on twenty-seven miles (i.e. $72,000), less 5 per cent on account of provincial bonds being negotiated at 95 per cent; ANQ-Q, Agriculture et Travaux Publics, Registres de Lettres envoyées, art. 641, vol. 20, no. 11749, 459, S. Le Sage to W. Sawyer, 25 Feb. 1875. *Le Pionnier* (Sherbrooke), 16 July 1875.

45 Young. *Promoters and Politicians*, 82–83, 86; Rumilly, *Histoire II*: 25–27.

46 *Sherbrooke News*, 2 Dec. 1875.

47 On the Bélangers, see Kesteman, "*Le Progrès*."

48 *Sherbrooke News*, 16 Dec. 1875; *L'Union des Cantons de l'Est* (Arthabaskaville), 3 Jan. 1875. Picard's party loyalty and his sympathy for north-shore colonization ultimately softened his criticism of the government. See Sevigny, "Le capitalisme," 129–33.

49 *Le Pionnier* (Sherbrooke), 10 Dec. 1875. See also *Sherbrooke News*, 9 Dec. 1875; and *Le Progrès* (Sherbrooke), 11 Dec. 1875.

50 *Sherbrooke News*, 16 Dec. 1875. See also *Le Progrès* (Sherbrooke), 17 Dec. 1875; and Young, *Promoters and Politicians*, 84.

51 *Le Progrès* (Sherbrooke), 4 Feb. 1876, 11 Feb. 1876.

52 See Little, "Lucius Seth Huntington," *DCB* XI: 437–39.

53 Channell, *History of Compton*, 158; *Sherbrooke News*, 28 Sept. 1876. Hamelin claims that all work ceased on the north shore; *Les Premières Années*, 262.

54 Quebec, *Statutes*, 1877, 40 Vict., c. 3; *Sherbrooke News*, 7 Dec. 1876; *Le Progrès* (Sherbrooke), 7 Dec. 1876.

55 *Sherbrooke News*, 7 Dec. 1876. Both the *News* and *Le Progrès* ceased publication in April 1878 when their co-owner, Louis-Charles Bélanger, decided to run as an independent Liberal candidate; see *Le Progrès* (Sherbrooke), 18 April 1878; Kesteman, "*Le Progrès*," 141–44, 162–69. In 1878 the remaining $2,000 per mile for the final sections of the railroads was again divided in half and granted for the mileage completed since 1876; Quebec, *Statutes*, 1878, 41 Vict., c. 2.

56 *SPQ*, XXII (1889), no. 166, A. McMaster to F. Langelier, Scotstown, 13 May 1878; *Le Pionnier* (Sherbrooke), 30 Nov. 1877; *Stanstead Journal*, 17 Jan. 1878.

57 ANQ-Q, Agriculture et Travaux Publics, Registres des Lettres reçues, no. 166, International to W. Sawyer, Quebec, 30 Sept. 1879.

58 Channell, *History of Compton*, 62; *SPQ*, XXII (1889), no. 7, Report of Commissioner of Public Works, app. 3-C. The details of the railway's financing are misinterpreted in P.B. Waite's short biography of Pope in *DCB* XI: 707.

59 Channell, *History of Compton*, 62; these words of Pope's biographer, C.H. Mackintosh, are cited on p. 158.

60 G. Stephen to J.A. Macdonald, 30 Jan. 1889; quoted in Angus, "The Politics of the Short Line," 113.

61 Ibid., 112–13.

62 The quotation is from Skelton, *The Day*, 55

63 Channell, *History of Compton*, 60.

64 Hamelin and Roby, *Histoire économique*, 131.

65 Stornoway, Winslow South Municipal Assessment Records, 144, Amounts paid to C.A. Bailey to apply to Railroad Taxes.

66 Channell, *History of Compton*, 59–60, 108–9, 120, 246, 269. The Liberal opposition charged that W.B. Ives, Pope's son-in-law and MP for Richmond-Wolfe, was also closely linked to the International; Angus "The Politics of the Short Line," 109. Ives would be the chief force behind construction of the Hereford Railway through Compton County during the late 1880s. Channell, *History of Compton*, 44, 46, 62–63. On the role of the local notables in railroad construction, see Kesteman, "Une Bourgeoisie," 543–50.

67 Hamelin, *Les Premières Années*, 162, 236–37.

68 Perron, "Genèse des activités laitières," 118–20, 124, 139.

CHAPTER EIGHT

1 Quoted in Belisle, *Histoire*, 340.

2 *SPQ*, VI (1872), 350, 355.

3 Le Sage was the chief administrator of the province's colonization programme from 1869 to 1888. For a detailed study of his career, see Trépanier, *Siméon Le Sage*.

4 ASSH, JAC, Correspondance générale, 1858–74, P.E. Gendreau to Chicoine, 20 Dec. 1872; *SPQ*, VII (1873–74), 305.

5 Vicero, "Immigration," 208–9, 232; Le Blanc, "Regional Competition," 114.

6 *SPC*, VI (1873), 66; *Annuaire*, 1896–99, 282.

7 *Annuaire*, 1896–99, 276.

8 ASSH, JAC, Correspondance générale, 1858–74, P.E. Gendreau to Chicoine, 20 Dec. 1872; ANQ-Q, Travaux Publics, Lettres envoyées, XVI, no. 9314, Le Sage to Gendreau, 10 Nov. 1873; ANQ-Q, SL, Correspondance, II, 174, Le Sage to J.C. Taché, 27 Feb. 1875; Hamelin, *Les Premières Années*, 181–82; Trépanier, *Siméon Le Sage*, 164–66.

9 *Annuaire*, 1896–99, 283–84; Hamelin, *Les Premières Années*, 181.

10 Hamelin, *Les Premières Années*, 180; Macdonald, *Canada, Immigration*, 96. After 1870, Quebec had attempted to attract French-speaking immigrants from Europe but with little success. France and Germany (for Alsace-Lorraine) charged stiff fees for permission to solicit emigrants, and local opposition was encountered in Belgium. In addition, most of the francophones who did move to Quebec soon grew discontented and left. *SPQ*, VI (1872), ix-x, xiii, 299–306, 341–42; VII (1873–74), 178, 304. For more details see Hamelin, *Les Premières Années*, 170–81; and Trépanier, *Siméon Le Sage*, 125–63.

11 *SPQ*, IX (1875), 12; ANQ-Q, SL, Correspondance, II, 229, Le Sage to O'Neill, 2 July 1875.

12 His name was spelled Chicoine until 1879 when he changed it to the form apparently used by his ancestors in France. ANQ-Q, Travaux Publics, Lettres envoyées, IX, no. 5283, Le Sage to Barnard, 7 March 1872; XIII, no. 7316, Le Sage to Chicoine, 24 Jan. 1873.

13 For a description of this college at the time of Chicoyne's attendance, see Savard, *Jules-Paul Tardivel*, 15–19.

14 Auclair, *Figures canadiennes* II: 189.

15 ASSH, JAC, Correspondance générale, 1882–96, Order appointing Chicoyne as chief emigration agent for Montreal, 27 June 1873.

16 See ASSH, JAC, V, Mémoires, 31 July 1876. This autobiographical sketch is based on these memoirs.

17 *SPQ*, IX (1875), 12.

18 Chaput, "Some Rapatriement Dilemmas," 401; Belisle, *Livre d'or*, 155; Vicero, "Immigration," 268.

19 ANQ-Q, Travaux Publics, Lettres envoyées, IX, no. 11983, Le Sage to Chicoine, 7 April 1875; Belisle, *Histoire de la presse*, 97.

20 ASSH, JAC, Correspondance générale, 1875, Gendron to Chicoine, 8 May 1875. In March Gendron had asked $90 per lot for sixteen lots, with five acres cleared and sowed on each. ANQ-Q, Travaux Publics, Lettres reçues, no. 29577, Gendron to Le Sage, 6 March 1875.

21 ASSH, JAC, Correspondance générale, 1875, Gendron to Chicoine, 8 May 1875; RL, I, Chicoine to Rev. Monsieur, 14 May 1875.

22 ASSH, JAC, Correspondance générale, 1875, Le Sage to Chicoine, April 1875; ANQ-Q, Travaux Publics, Lettres envoyées, XXI, no.

11983, Le Sage to Chicoine, 7 April 1875; JAC, RL, I, Report to Colonization Bureau, 30 April 1875.

23 Belisle, *Histoire*, 99; ASSH, JAC, RL, I, Chicoine to Le Sage, 14 May 1875.

24 ASSH, JAC, RL, I, Chicoine to Le Sage, 22 May 1875.

25 Belisle, *Histoire*, 100. The *Pionnier* reported a killing frost in the Sherbrooke area on 11 June. For other press reports in 1875, see Kesteman, *Documents*, 22.

26 JAC, RL, I, Chicoine to Le Sage, 24 June 1875, 1 July 1875, 13 July 1875, 19 July 1875, 31 July 1875.

27 *Daily Witness* (Montreal), 12 Jan. 1876. Even the Conservative Sherbrooke *Gazette* denounced Pope's speech favouring the repatriation project; *Le Pionnier* (Sherbrooke), 22 Feb. 1878. Pope was probably motivated by the necessity to develop some of the 4210 acres he had acquired from the crown as settlement lots in Ditton. His real aim was to monopolize the potential gold deposits, but he had paid only sixty cents an acre rather than the usual two dollars for mineral-bearing land. Most of the Norwegian and English settlers he attracted in 1869 had quickly left, and we have seen that the subsidy acquired under the Colonization Societies Act brought no greater success. AC, Section Ouest, adj. 4792; *Le Pionnier* (Sherbrooke), 28 Aug. 1868, 22 March 1879; *Annuaire*, 1896–99, 255–59; Chartier, "La colonie," 407–9.

28 ASSH, JAC, RL, I, Chicoine to H.G. Malhiot, 25 Sept. 1875.

29 AC, Section Ouest, adj. 4472, Report by John Hume, 10 March 1876.

30 *Daily Witness* (Montreal), 27 Jan. 1876.

31 Ibid., 29 Jan. 1876.

32 ASSH, JAC, RL, I, Chicoine to Gagnon, 24 Aug. 1875; Chicoine to P. Garneau, 1 July 1875; Chicoine to Le Sage, 1 July 1875.

33 Ibid., Chicoine to Le Sage, 18 Aug. 1875; cited in Belisle, *Histoire*, 106; ASSH, JAC, RL, I, Chicoine to Gagnon, 28 Sept. 1875.

34 ASSH, JAC, RL, I, Chicoine to Le Sage, 19 May 1875, 25 May 1875.

35 *Le Progrès* (Sherbrooke), 17 Dec., 1875.

36 *SPQ* IX (1875): 14.

37 ASSH, JAC, RL, Chicoine to Gagnon, 28 Sept. 1875. This site had become the centre of the Bagot colonization society's activities in 1873, when a Catholic chapel was built there, prompting a Franco-American to move his hotel (which included the post office, store, and weekly stagecoach) from the nearby English-speaking hamlet of West Ditton. Abbé Gendreau of Cookshire erected a sawmill at the new site shortly afterward. *Le Pionnier* (Sherbrooke), 12 April 1872, 10 April 1879; *Annuaire*, 1896–99, 275.

38 ASSH, JAC, RL, Chicoine to Tellier, 11 Oct. 1875.

39 Ibid., Chicoine to P.A. Gendreau, 3 May 1877.

40 Ibid., Chicoine to Ernest Gagnon, 14 Oct. 1876.

41 Ibid., Chicoine to P. Garneau, 13 July 1875; ANQ-Q, Travaux Publics, Lettres envoyées, XXIII, no. 13194, Le Sage to Racine, 21 Sept. 1875; Chartier, "La colonie du rapatriement," 47–48.

42 In 1873, for example, Chicoyne had been involved in the opening of a French ribbon factory in Saint-Hyacinthe. ANQ-Q, Travaux Publics, Lettres reçues, no. 19278, Chicoyne to Le Sage, 21 Dec. 1872; no. 19797 1/2, 19 Feb. 1873.

43 ASSH, JAC, RL, Chicoine to Louis Coté, 31 Oct. 1876.

44 Ibid., Chicoine to Le Sage, 10 Oct. 1875, 11 Nov. 1875; Chicoine to P. Garneau, 30 Aug. 1876; ANQ-Q, Travaux Publics, Lettres envoyées, XXI, no. 11966, Le Sage to Gagnon, 6 April 1875; XXIII, no. 13203, Le Sage to Chicoine, 22 Sept. 1875.

45 Le Pionnier (Sherbrooke), 26 Aug. 1876; ASSH, JAC, Correspondance générale, 1876, Chicoine to C. Boucher de Boucherville, 29 April 1876; Stanstead Journal, 9 March 1876. Prior to this, the trees cut in the clearing operation had simply been burned. État des comptes publics, 157–58.

46 ASSH, JAC, RL, Chicoine to J.A. Chapleau, 31 Oct. 1876.

47 ASSH, JAC, Correspondance générale, 1876, F.X. Larose to 'Monsieur,' 10 April 1876.

48 Le Pionnier (Sherbrooke), 8 Dec. 1876.

49 Le Progrès (Sherbrooke), 24 Aug. 1877. Rivals for government patronage, as well as for subscriptions, Sherbrooke's two French-language newspapers, though both Conservative supporters, were to be found on opposite sides of almost any local issue. The Progrès finally joined the Mercier camp after the hanging of Riel; see Kesteman, "Le Progrès."

50 SPQ, IX (1875), 16; Le Progrès (Sherbrooke), 7 Jan. 1876.

51 Le Progrès (Sherbrooke), 7 Jan. 1876. These reports did not fail to reach Le Sage. ANQ-Q, Travaux Publics, Lettres envoyées, XXIV, no. 13721, Le Sage to Chicoine, 18 dec. 1875; ASSH, JAC, RL, Chicoine to Gagnon, 4 Jan. 1876.

52 ETHS, Fonds Victor Chartier, Mgr A. Racine to V. Chartier, 27 April 1876, 28 April 1876.

53 Le Pionnier (Sherbrooke), 9 May 1879. Pierre-U. Vaillant was born in Assomption county in 1830. He taught French in Vermont and Illinois, worked as a carpenter for three years in Fall River, Massachusetts, became correspondent for the Protecteur Canadien and the Etendard national, and helped to found the Echo du Canada. In 1873

he moved to Chesham where he operated a sawmill, only to return to the United States and journalism in 1881. Belisle, *Histoire*, 301.

54 Gérin-Lajoie, *Jean Rivard*, 150. This analogy was made by the *Pionnier* itself (31 Aug. 1877).

55 ASSH, JAC, RL, Chicoine to Gagnon, 24 May 1876; ETHS, Fonds Chartier, Mgr A. Racine to V. Chartier, 2 April 1876.

56 ASSH, JAC, RL, Chicoine to Vaillant, 11 May 1876; ETHS, Fonds Chartier, F. Bilodeau to Chartier, 10 Aug. 1876; Chesham petition, 15 Oct. 1876. Bishop Racine was not content to concede the final victory to Vaillant, for in 1878 he recommended that the post office change hands and name; ETHS, Fonds Chartier, Racine to Chartier, 31 Oct. 1878.

57 See *Le Progrès* (Sherbrooke), 20 April 1877, 28 June 1877, 21 Sept. 1877, 5 Oct. 1877.

58 ASSH, JAC, RL, Chicoine to Gagnon, 12 May 1876.

59 Ibid., Chicoine to Gagnon, 24 May 1876.

60 *Le Pionnier* (Sherbrooke), 23 June 1876; *Notre-Dame-des-Bois de 1877 à 1952 (Programme souvenir)* (Sherbrooke, 1952), 25, 27, 31, 37; ETHS, Fonds Chartier, Notre-Dame-des-Bois, Notes, n.d.

61 ANQ-Q, Travaux Publics, Lettres reçues 1876, no. 35752, Gagnon to Le Sage, 13 July 1876.

62 *Le Progrès* (Sherbrooke), 27 Oct. 1876.

63 ASSH, JAC, RL, Chicoine to Le Sage, 20 Dec. 1876.

64 ETHS, Fonds Chartier, Chartier to Boucherville, 19 Dec. 1876.

65 ASSH, JAC, RL, Chicoine to Le Sage, 12 Jan. 1877.

66 *Le Progrès* (Sherbrooke), 26 Jan. 1877; ASSH, JAC, Correspondance générale, 1876–79, 37 Emberton colonists to C.B. de Boucherville, n.d.; ETHS, Fonds Chartier, Le Sage to V. Chartier, 20 Jan. 1877.

67 ASSH, JAC, RL, Chicoine to Le Sage, 20 Dec. 1876; ETHS, Fonds Chartier, Chartier to Le Sage, 24 Jan. 1877.

68 ETHS, Fonds Chartier, Chartier to J.O. Fontaine, 30 June 1877; J.O. Fontaine to Chartier, 21 Feb. 1877, 11 April 1877, 20 April 1877, 26 April 1877; Le Sage to Chartier, 20 Jan. 1877. In addition, the Diocese of Sherbrooke contributed $265. AAS, Parish Papers, Saint-Pierre La Patrie, no. 7, "Sommes payées à divers colons nécessiteux de Chesham, Ditton, et Emberton depuis le commencement de l'hiver."

69 ASSH, JAC, Correspondance générale, 1876, Elisée Noël to Chicoine, 3 Nov. 1876.

70 Ibid., J.A. Chapleau to Chicoine, 13 Oct. 1876; ASSH, JAC, RL, Chicoine to Fontaine, 7 May 1877. *Le Pionnier* (17 Aug. 1877) claimed that $80,000 had been invested in the project, with $28,000 devoted

to clearing land and building roads. Gagnon himself spent $5000 in New England. Trépanier, *Siméon Le Sage*, 166.

71 Gilles Paquet's figure, based on Canadian *Sessional Papers*, is 960. Paquet, "L'émigration," 339.

72 Vicero, "Immigration," 234. This was a drastic drop from the 3000 repatriating families Gagnon reported in 1876. *État des comptes publics*, 154. The 1881 *Census Reports* record only 181 American-born in the three townships, though it must be remembered that most of the parents and some of the children would have been born in Canada.

73 See, for example, Hareven and Langenbach, *Amoskeag*, 18, 59, 66.

74 Belisle, *Histoire*, 98.

75 ANQ-Q, Travaux Publics, Lettres envoyées, XXII, no. 12500, Le Sage to Gagnon, 30 June 1875; *SPQ*, IX (1875), 365.

76 *Le Pionnier* (Sherbrooke), 13 March 1874. See also the editions of 9 Jan. 1874, 13 Feb. 1874, and 20 Feb. 1874; and Vicero, "Immigration," 234.

77 *Le Pionnier* (Sherbrooke), 10 Jan. 1879. On repatriation to Manitoba, see Painchaud, "Le Manitoba," chap. 1.

78 See Vicero, "Immigration," 357; P. Anctil, "Chinese" and "L'identité."

79 *Le Pionnier* (Sherbrooke), 29 Oct. 1875, 23 Dec. 1875; Hamelin and Roby, *Histoire économique*, 195. Three of the major industries in Sherbrooke were forced to close their doors in 1876, causing an exodus of 500 people that year; *Stanstead Journal*, 27 July 1876; *Annual Reports from Different Departments of the city of Sherbrooke for the Year ending 31st December, 1890*, 5. Coaticook was hit even more severely by the recession: *Le Pionnier* (Sherbrooke), 23 Dec. 1875; Gravel, *Histoire de Coaticook*, 88.

80 *Le Pionnier* (Sherbrooke), 8 Feb. 1878; AC, Section Ouest, adj. 4792; ANQ-S, J.I. Mackie file, no. 1208, 1382 A&B; ASSH, JAC, RL, I, Chicoine to Peigné, 16 Nov. 1880.

81 *SPQ*, XIV (1880), 400. AAS, Rapports sur les paroisses, Saint-Pierre-la-Patrie, 1879, 1880. Chartier's figure may have been inaccurate, since the 1880–81 *Census Reports* record 898 inhabitants for Ditton.

82 AC, adj. 4839, Memo. by W.E. Collins, 20 Jan. 1881.

83 AC, Order in Council 1108, Report of Ditton, Chesham, and Emberton committees, 16 Feb. 1885; P.L.N. Prévost to Commissioner, 5 Aug. 1884; Nagle to Taché, 31 Aug. 1886. A watchman had to be hired as early as 1877 to prevent the dismantling of the houses. ETHS, Fonds Chartier, Fontaine to Chartier, 27 Oct. 1877.

84 AC, O.C. 1244, Rapport d'un Comité de l'Hon. Conseil Exécutif, 16 Nov. 1898.

85 *Le Pionnier* (Sherbrooke), 30 May 1879.

86 The 1875–76 provincial budget included only $58,569 for coloniza-
tion roads, and $57,200 for agricultural promotion. *État des comptes
publics*, 16, 118, 129, 134.

87 ANQ-Q, Travaux Publics, Lettres envoyées, XXVIII, 252, Magnon to
Gagnon, 13 March 1877.

88 ANQ-Q, SL, Correspondance, II, 438, Le Sage to Gagnon, 1 Jan. 1877.
Gagnon continued to receive a small grant from the Quebec government until January 1880. Trépanier, *Siméon Le Sage*, 166.

89 Le Blanc, "The Francophone 'Conquest,'" 288–310; Roby, "Les Canadiens français," 3–22.

90 Le Blanc, "Colonisation et rapatriement." The only provincial money
spent on repatriation during the 1880s and 1890s was $341 from
1880 to 1883 and $6,443 from 1888 to 1891. Trépanier, *Siméon Le
Sage*, 167. Ottawa and Quebec supplied limited support to repatriation again in the 1930s. Le Blanc, "Regional Competition," 118.

91 Much of the land in the area was still owned by speculators. ETHS,
Fonds Chartier, Chartier to commissioner of agriculture and public
works [summer 1877]; Chartier to superintendent of public instruc-
tion, 21 Oct. 1878.

92 Many French Canadians moved back and forth across the border
throughout their active lives; see Anctil, "La Franco-Américanie,"
32–34.

93 Quebec, Assemblée nationale, *Débats de l'Assemblée Législative, 1874–
75* (Québec, Journal des Débats, 1976), 202–5, 207–8, 277–78, 304.

94 Trépanier, *Siméon Le Sage*, 123–24.

95 Le Blanc, "Regional Competition," 122.

CHAPTER NINE

1 Macdonald, *Canada. Immigration*, 235. See also Lalonde, "Colonization Companies."

2 *JLAC*, XVII (1859), app. 17; *SPPC*, XVIII (1860), no. 12.

3 Hobsbawm, *The Pelican History of Britain* III: 118–19.

4 Among the shareholders of the Glasgow Canadian Land and Trust
Company were four unmarried women, two clerks, a blacksmith, a
veterinary surgeon, a house decorator, a saddler, an engineer, and
an accountant; see various lists of shareholders in SRO, BT2/472,
Board of Trade, Dissolved Company File, Glasgow Canadian Land
and Trust Company (hereafter Board of Trade File).

5 Dickson, *Scottish Capitalism*, 249–5; Lenman, *Economic History*, 192–
93; Cottrell, *British Overseas Investment*, 28, 37.

6 Cottrell, *British Overseas Investment*, 47. For a good survey, see M.
Quinn, "Les Capitaux français," 546–63.

7 See Quinn, "Les Capitaux français," 538–43; Montpetit, *Colonie française*.

8 Jackson, *The Enterprising Scot*, 297.

9 R.H. Campbell (*The Scots Abroad*, 20) claims that Robert Fleming's Scottish American Trust, also launched in 1873, was the pioneer effort.

10 SRO, Board of Trade File.

11 On Coats, see Campbell, *Scotland*, 177–81; Checkland and Checkland, *Industry and Ethos*, 29; Dickson, *Scottish Capitalism*, 184, 249. Beginning in the late 1890s, the Coats family would make major investments in western American mining operations. Jackson, *The Enterprising Scot*, 192–93.

12 SRO, Board of Trade File, Memorandum of Association.

13 SRO, CS 243/2884, Court of Session File, Glasgow Canadian Land and Trust Company (hereafter Court of Session File), Act of Incorporation.

14 *SPQ*, XXII (1889), 3. For a list of the colonization society's reserved lots, see AC, Branche Ouest, O.C. 940.

15 See AC, Marston, no. 13831 in each of the following: Livre des recettes: Dossier général du Canton; Registry of Assignments, West Section.

16 Langelier, *Liste des terrains concédés*, 346; Cookshire Registry Office, Register B vol. 9, 225–27, no. 5066.

17 Cookshire Registry Office, Register B, vol. 3, 383, no. 1558; 442, no. 1608; 443, no. 1609; 445, no. 1610; 459, no. 1624; 544, no. 1685.

18 AC, Register Book, West Section, adj. 4472, Report of John Hume, Leeds, 10 March 1876 (hereafter Hume Report), A. McMaster to J. Hume, Scotstown, 12 Feb. 1876.

19 Cookshire Registry Office, Reg. B, vol. 3, 136–37, no. 1349; 302, no. 1485; 583, no. 1713.

20 Ibid., 167–70, no. 1375; 170–74, no. 1376.

21 The two figures of costs were cited by witnesses in a court case; ANQ-S, Queen's Bench, St Francis District, no. 661, Isaac N. Pinkham *v.* Glasgow Canadian Land and Trust Company (hereafter Pinkham case) (writ deposited 21 Dec. 1875). *SPQ*, VII (1873–74), vii, 307; VIII (1874), app. 23 to Report of CCL; *Le Pionnier* (Sherbrooke), 16 May 1873.

22 ANQ-S, Pinkham case; and no. 558, James Scott *v.* Glasgow Canadian Land and Trust Company (hereafter Scott case) (writ deposited 30 Sept. 1875).

23 Lower, *North American Assault*, 150.

24 ANQ-S, Scott case, Alexander Robertson to R.N. Hall, Glasgow, 4 May 1875. Scott had contracted for £1000 sterling the first year, with half

to be paid in company shares; £750 cash and £250 in shares the second year; and £1000 cash and 5 per cent of dividends each subsequent year. His permanent replacement, Aeneas McMaster of New Edinburgh near Ottawa, would be paid only$1000 per year. Ibid., Deposition of John Scott, 25 Nov. 1875, and A. McMaster, 26 Jan. 1876.

25 Ibid., Alexander Robertson to James Scott, Glasgow, 8 July 1875.

26 Ibid., Plumitif, vol. 9, 246; vol. 10, p. 337, no. 199; 384, 16 June 1877.

27 AC, Hume Report, A. McMaster to John Hume, Scotstown, 12 Feb. 1876. McMaster was correct in assuming that the pressure to cancel the Ditton lots came from the manager of the repatriation colony. ASSH, JAC, Letterbooks, I, Chicoyne to H.G. Malhiot, La Patrie, 25 Sept. 1875 (confidential).

28 AC, Register Book, West Section, no. 3427, McMaster to Commissioner, 5 Sept. 1876; SPQ, XXII (1889), no. 166, 13, McMaster to Langelier, Scotstown, 13 May 1878. Hume complained that repatriation agent Chicoyne had directed settlers to the second range "even before the sixty days after cancellation had expired." AC, Hume Report.

29 AC, Hume Report. McMaster himself testified in court that at least one of the contractor's houses had originally been only five feet two inches to the ceiling, but that he had directed his foreman to lower its floor, as well as to improve the quality of several others. ANQ-S, Pinkham case, writ and declaration, 21 Dec. 1875; defendant's plea, 7 March 1876; defendant's testimony, 29 Nov. 1876.

30 ANQ-Q, Terres et Forêts, Lettres envoyées, art. 869, 98, E.E. Taché to W. Sawyer, Quebec, 22 May 1877. This decision was reversed by the Liberal administration in 1878. SPQ, XXII (1889), no. 166, 18, F. Langelier, CCL, 18 May 1878. For an interesting, autobiographical account by the son of one of the Scots immigrants employed by the company, see Sherman, History of the Families, 26–28.

31 ANQ-S, Pinkham case, George Robertson, 28 March 1877.

32 SPQ, XXII (1889), no. 166, 22, C. Patton to A. McMaster, Robinson, 23 May 1878.

33 AAS, Parish Papers, Saint-Zenon-de-Piopolis, Session of Municipal Council of Marston South, 7 Oct. 1889.

34 Channell, History of Compton, 280.

35 SRO, Court of Session File, Detailed Balance Sheet at 31 Dec. 1902. Forty-two of the Clinton lots were sold to the Montagu Paper Company for $21,796 in 1890. Cookshire Registry Office, Register B, vol. 23, 601, no. 12529. The town lots were generally sold at $100 for an acre.

36 ASSH, JAC, Correspondance générale, 1877–87, A. McMaster to
    Charles H. Cunningham, Scotstown, 17 May 1881.
37 *Weekly Examiner* (Sherbrooke), 17 Oct. 1879, clipping found in ANQ-S,
    Queen's Bench, St Francis, no. 36, J.H. Pope *v.* A. McMaster.
38 *Sherbrooke Gazette*, 26 Nov. 1880. The *Stanstead Journal* (25 Nov.
    1880) and *Le Pionnier* (25 Nov. 1880) were also critical of McMaster.
39 Lower, *North American Assault*, 150. The mill was built in 1877, the
    year the railroad arrived; ANQ-S, Pinkham case, testimony of C.H.
    Parker, millwright, 13 Jan. 1877.
40 SRO, Board of Trade File, Summary of Capital and Shares, 1873–96.
41 SRO, Court of Session File, Petition to Lords of Council and Session
    for Supervision Order, 25 Aug. 1903; A. Robertson to Sir (Notice of
    Extraordinary Meeting), Glasgow, 6 Nov. 1897; Board of Trade File,
    Special Resolution passed 17 Nov. 1897, confirmed 8 Dec. 1897.
42 SRO, Court of Session File, Abstract of Liquidators' Accounts,
    17 Nov. 1897–25 June 1904.
43 Ibid., Sales approval, 22 Sept. 1903.
44 As early as 1877 McMaster had offered to purchase all logs which
    could be supplied by the repatriation colonists in Ditton; ASSH, JAC,
    Letterbooks, I, Chicoyne to Le Sage, La Patrie, 12 Jan. 1877.
45 Apart from the price paid for Scotstown's land, dam, and mill, the
    Glasgow Canadian Company invested over $45,000 in developing
    the town but sold only $16,500 in building lots as well as collecting
    approximately $750 per year for rents; SRO, Court of Session File,
    Detailed balance sheet at 31 Dec. 1897; Report and Expenditure,
    13 Dec. 1897–30 Oct. 1902.
46 SRO, Court of Session File, Abstract of accounts of liquidators from
    31 Dec. 1897 to 26 Oct. 1904.
47 Ibid., James B. Scott to Alexander Robertson, Montreal, 28 July
    1903. Michie (*Money, Mania*, 154–60) claims that most of the joint-
    stock overseas investments were unprofitable, but Jackson (*The Enter-
    prising Scot*, 310–12) suggests that the final answer awaits the de-
    tailed study of individual companies.
48 *Dictionary of National Biography*, Supplement (Jan. 1901 – Dec. 1911),
    I: 665–66; NA, Jones, "History of Lake Megantic," 1881–82, uniden-
    tified newspaper clipping; 1882.
49 It was also in 1880 that Scottish investment began in American cattle
    companies. Jackson, *The Entreprising Scot*, 298.
50 AC, Branche Ouest, O.C. 1044, Report of CCL, 30 March 1881; *JLAQ*,
    XIV (1880), 351. The standing committee reluctantly supported this
    arrangement, but insisted that the conditions should be carried out
    to the letter, and that no more reserves should be made until the
    results of this one became known; *JLAQ*, XIV (1880), 350.

51 NA, Jones, "History of Lake Megantic," 1882.

52 AC, Branche Ouest, O.C. 1044, O.B. Kemp's Report, 26 Oct. 1882.

53 Details on the high hopes entertained for this machine can be found in NA, Jones, "History of Lake Megantic," II, part 1: 1875.

54 AC, Branche Ouest, O.C. 1044, E.E. Taché to E.J. Flynn, 19 Dec. 1881.

55 The Dominion Company seems to have had more support from Agriculture and Public Works, for Taché's counterpart in that department, L.S. Le Sage, actually asked to become a member of the board. ANQ-Q, SL, Correspondance, III, 43, Le Sage to F.W. Stockwell, 27 Dec. 1882. The request is surprising, not only for the conflict of interest it would have entailed, but also because Le Sage was a French-Canadian nationalist. See Trépanier, *Siméon Le Sage*.

56 AC, Branche Ouest, O.C. 1044, Memorandum on the difficulty.

57 Québec, *Débats*, 19 Feb. 1883, 454.

58 Ibid., 19 Feb. 1883, 435–36.

59 AC, Branche Ouest, O.C. 1044, E.J. Flynn to F. Stockwell, 30 July 1881.

60 Unidentified newspaper clipping in NA, Jones, "History of Lake Megantic," II, part 1.

61 AC, Branche Ouest, O.C. 1044, O.B. Kemp's Report, 26 Oct. 1882.

62 Ibid., Stockwell to W.W. Lynch, 3 Oct. 1882.

63 Ibid., P. Brassard to E.E. Taché, 5 Aug. 1882; Taché to Brassard, 14 Aug. 1882.

64 Ibid., P.W. Nagle to E.E. Taché, 30 Aug. 1882; Stockwell to Lynch, 19 Oct. 1882.

65 Ibid., O.B. Kemp's Report, 26 Oct. 1882. Further conditions specified that the settler had to build and maintain, at his own expense, all ditches and fences between his and the company's lands; he was not able to require "découvert" of company acreage adjoining his; he could sell no wood from his lot until letters patent were issued; and instalments had to be paid without fail every year; if they were sixty days overdue, the company could reclaim the property. See *Le Pionnier* (Sherbrooke), 17 May 1883, and deeds recorded in the Cookshire Registry Office.

66 See Cookshire Registry Office, Register B, vol. 12, 720–21, no. 6989; vol. 13, 28–29, no. 7017.

67 Quebec, *Statutes*, 1873, 36 Vict., c. 8.

68 Sévigny, "Le capitalisme et la politique," 157, 161–62.

69 Québec, *Débats*, 19 Feb. 1883, 431, 443–44, 447, 450, 452, 458.

70 AC, Branche Ouest, O.C. 1044, Nagle to Taché, 11 May 1883.

71 Ibid., A.B. Filion to Lynch, 27 June 1883; J. Lloyd to Lord Dunmore, 20 June 1883.

72 Ibid., H.B. Brown to Lynch, 5 July 1883.

73 Ibid., O.C. 1072, Report of a Commission of the Honourable the Executive Council, 15 Oct. 1883.

74 Ibid., O.C. 1044, Nagle to Taché, 9 Feb. 1885.

75 Ibid., Nagle to Taché, 6 Dec. 1886, 15 Dec. 1886.

76 NA, Jones, "History of Lake Megantic."

77 Ibid., 1882.

78 ASSH, JAC, RL, I, Chicoyne to Bossanges, 1 Sept. 1877; Chicoyne to Melayer Masselin, 2 April 1879.

79 Lavallée, "Monseigneur Antoine Racine," 38; ASSH, JAC, RL, I, Chicoyne to Taché, 30 Dec. 1882.

80 La Compagnie de Colonisation et de Crédit des Cantons de l'Est, *Notice sur son but et son organisation*, 11–12; Cauchon, *Lac Mégantic*, 3.

81 ASSH, JAC, RL, I, Chicoyne to Peigné, 12 Dec. 1880; Compagnie, *Notice*, 13.

82 The minimum number of shares for a *censeur* was ten, and, for an administrator, five. According to Compagnie, *Notice*, 31, 36, the first board of administration was composed as follows: Charles Paumier (president), former notary in Nantes; J.A. Chicoyne (vice-president), Sherbrooke lawyer; G. Mollat, Nantes Lawyer, director of *l'Espérance du Peuple*; Adolphe Langlais, "arbitre de commerce" in Nantes; Jacques Picard, Wotton notary and merchant, MLA for Richmond-Wolfe; H.C. Cabana, Sherbrooke lawyer, ex-mayor, and publisher of *Le Pionnier*; Elisée Noël, Sherbrooke notary and provincial colonization agent; William Murray, Sherbrooke businessman and vice-president of the company that owned *Le Pionnier*; Eugène Bécigneul (assistant director).

83 Quoted in Cauchon, *Lac Mégantic*, 5.

84 Compagnie, *Notice*, 12, 26, 29.

85 A road builder and land speculator, Lemuel Pope had clearly received preferential treatment because bush ranger Nagle had reported that "I have not found nor do I know of a single instance where proprietors or parties holding land in Woburn have occupied the land or complied with the land or Government regulations as to settlement duties, etc." AC, Section Ouest, adj. 4866, extract from P.W. Nagle's report dated 29 Sept. 1880, located in memo by W.E. Collins, 19 Jan. 1881.

86 ASSH, JAC, RL, I, Chicoyne to Peigné, 16 Nov. 1880; II, "Mémoire sur les affaires de la Compagnie de Colonisation et de Crédit des Cantons de l'Est," 6 May 1882.

87 ASSH, JAC, RL, I, Chicoyne to Peigné, 16 Nov. 1880.

88 Ibid., 12 Dec. 1880.

89 Ibid., Correspondance, Abbé Eugène to Cher Monsieur, 4 Jan. 1883, 1 March 1883; RL, II, Chicoyne to Abbé V. Rousselot, 23 May 1883.

The Meilleray Trappists later founded a chapter at Lake of Two Mountains; Chartier, "La colonie," 329.

90 ASSH, JAC, RL, I, Chicoyne to Peigné, 14 April 1881.

91 Ibid., 31 March 1881; *Le Pionnier* (Sherbrooke), 12 Jan. 1882.

92 ASSH, JAC, RL, I, Chicoyne to Peigné, 24 March 1881; II, 5 May 1881.

93 Quinn, "Les capitaux," 544; ASSH, JAC, RL, II, Chicoyne to Peigné, 31 Oct. 1884; Chicoyne to Charles Paumier, 24 Nov. 1881; Chicoyne to A. Langlais, 28 March 1882.

94 Quoted in Cauchon, *Lac Mégantic,* 5–7.

95 ASSH, JAC, RL, II, Chicoyne to Paumier, 21 Dec. 1881.

96 Ibid., Chicoyne to Paumier, 16 Nov. 1881; Compagnie, *Notice,* 22.

97 ASSH, JAC, RL, II, Chicoyne to Paumier, 24 Nov. 1881; "Notice et mémoire sur les *Moulins nantais* en construction au Lac Mégantic," 31 Dec. 1881; Kesteman, *Histoire de Lac-Mégantic,* 59.

98 Ibid., Chicoyne to Paumier, 21 Dec. 1881, 27 Dec. 1881.

99 Ibid., 28 March 1882.

100 Ibid., 2 March 1882, 28 March 1882, 6 April 1882.

101 Ibid., Chicoyne to Abbé H.O. Chalifoux, 2 March 1882; "Mémoire sur les affaires," 6 May 1882.

102 Ibid., "Mémoire sur la classe B," 4 Aug. 1882.

103 Ibid., "Mémoire sur les affaires," Chicoyne to A. Langlais, 22 Aug. 1882.

The list of expenses was as follows:

Clearing and seeding the *Domaine*	$ 300
Construction of the Moulins nantais in Lake Megantic	$5,000
Operation of the Moulins nantais	$5,500
Owed to various people	$1,500
	$12,300

104 Ibid., Chicoyne to Paumier, 6 Nov. 1882.

105 Ibid., 23 Nov. 1882, 4 Dec. 1882, 23 Dec. 1882, 6 Jan. 1883.

106 Ibid., 25 Feb. 1883.

107 Ibid., Chicoyne to Taché, 30 Dec. 1882; Chicoyne to Paumier, 20 Jan. 1883.

108 Ibid., Chicoyne to Langlais, 21 Jan. 1883; Chicoyne to Paumier, 27 Jan. 1883.

109 Ibid., Chicoyne to Paumier, 25 Feb. 1883.

110 Ibid., 6 March 1883, 5 March 1883.

111 Ibid., 22 July 1883.

112 Ibid., 15 July 1883; Chicoyne to Peigné, 6 July 1883; Chicoyne to Paumier, 31 Aug. 1883.

113 ASSH, JAC, Voyages en Europe: 1877–85, Chicoyne to Caroline, 11 Oct. 1883.

114 *Le Progrès de l'Est,* (Sherbrooke) 15 Sept. 1883.

115 ASSH, JAC, Voyages, Chicoyne to Caroline, 6 Oct. 1883.
116 ASSH, JAC, RL, II, Chicoyne to Peigné, 10 April 1884. Ignoring Abbé Peigné's objections, Chicoyne shipped the first Bécigneul son, Eugène, to Channay where he would be out of the way; ibid., Chicoyne to Paumier, 24 Jan. 1884.
117 ASSH, JAC, RL, II, Chicoyne to Paumier, 6 Dec. 1883; Chicoyne to Langlais, 23 Dec. 1883.
118 Ibid., Chicoyne to Paumier, 13 Dec. 1883, 3 Jan. 1884, 6 Jan. 1884, 24 Jan. 1884.
119 Ibid., 13 Feb. 1884, 24 Feb. 1884, 20 March 1884, 19 April 1884.
120 Ibid., Chicoyne to Rumery, Birnie and Co., 18 April 1884.
121 Ibid., Chicoyne to Paumier, 15 May 1884, 30 May 1884.
122 Ibid., 16 Nov. 1884. On 22 November 1884 the statement of profits was as follows:

Store	$3,162
Sale of lots at Lake Megantic	$ 427
Mill	$ 959

123 Ibid., 16 Nov. 1884; Chicoyne to Cher Monsieur, 26 Sept. 1884; Cauchon, *Lac Mégantic*, 13–14.
124 AC, Branche Ouest, O.C. 1082, "On the application of the Eastern Townships Colonization and Credit Company," 4 Nov. 1884.
125 ASSH, JAC, RL, II, "La Compagnie de ... . Exposé de la Situation."
126 Ibid., Chicoyne to Paumier, 30 Nov. 1884; 7 Nov. 1884; Chicoyne to Pope, 7 Jan. 1885.
127 Ibid., Voyages, Chicoyne to Caroline, 20 Feb. 1885.
128 Ibid., Chicoyne to Caroline, 6 March 1885.
129 Ibid., 11 March 1885, 24 March 1885, 1 April 1885.
130 Ibid., 6 March 1885.
131 Ibid., 24 March 1885, 1 April 1885.
132 Ibid., 7 April 1885.
133 Ibid., 9 April 1885.
134 Ibid., RL, II, Chicoyne to Messieurs les Administrateurs, 23 June 1885, 3 July 1885; Chicoyne to Cher Monsieur, 14 Aug. 1885.
135 Ibid., Chicoyne to administrators, 10 Nov. 1885; Chicoyne to G. Mollat, 30 Dec. 1885.
136 AC, Register Book, West Section, 1887, no. 4553, Report of la Compagnie de Colonisation des Cantons de l'Est, 6 July 1886; *Le Progrès de l'Est* (Sherbrooke), 3 Sept. 1886.
137 AC, Section Ouest, adj. 5681, Nagle to Taché, 31 Dec. 1886.
138 Ibid., 30 June 1888. The parish reports do indicate a slow growth in Woburn's population: 1884, 58; 1886, 90; 1887, 97; 1888, 134; 1889, 160; 1890, 164; 1891, 187. AAS, Rapports des Paroisses, Saint-Augustin de Woburn.

139 *Le Pionnier* (Sherbrooke), 21 Oct. 1887, 21 June 1888; AC, Section Ouest, adj. 5681, Bécigneul to Taché, 5 Sept. 1889.

140 AAS, Parish Papers, Sainte-Agnès-de-Lac-Mégantic, Peigné to Racine, 18 Aug. 1892; RL, I, no. 879, 605, Racine to Peigné, 30 Aug. 1892.

141 *Le Pionnier* (Sherbrooke), 17 March 1893.

142 Judging from the parish reports, Channay was much like the other French-Canadian pioneer communities in the area, though slightly poorer. AAS, Rapports des Paroisses, Saint-Augustin de Woburn, 1884–91.

143 Chicoyne was director and editor of *Le Pionnier* from 1886 to 1901, and director from 1886 to at least 1896 of *La Colonisation*, a review destined for a European audience. In 1890, he drafted a project to promote immigration and repatriation to the Canadian North-West. After serving as mayor of Lake Megantic and Sherbrooke, he became MLA for Wolfe in 1892, remaining in the assembly until his career was cut short by paralysis in 1904. See Little, "Peaceable Conquest," 471–72; Deschênes, "Jérôme-Adolphe Chicoyne," 159–60.

144 Kesteman, *Histoire*, 60.

145 Leacock, *My Discovery of the West*, 234.

146 On the utopianism of certain Prairie settlement projects, see Rasporich, "Utopian Ideals."

147 This point is emphasized by Jackson, *The Enterprising Scot*, 314.

CONCLUSION

1 *JLAQ*, I (1867–68), app. 12; Little, "Peaceable Conquest," 328, app. 1. The assertions of Ontario's colonization-roads historians to the contrary, only a small part of Canada East's $726,305 share of the colonization roads budget was spent in older, settled parishes (see Spragge, "Colonization Roads," 1; and Parker, "Colonization Roads," 35–36).

2 NA, Alexander T. Galt Papers, MG27 I D8, Correspondence, 1858–91, J.H. Pope to Galt, 29 July 1864.

3 Channell, *History of Compton*, 161.

4 Quoted in Myers, *A History of Canadian Wealth*, 303.

5 Auclair, *Figures canadiennes* II: 189, 191.

6 ASSH, JAC, Correspondance générale, 1905–6, L.P. de Courval to Chicoyne, Piopolis, 18 Sept. 1885; Arthabaskaville, 17 Oct. 1885; Chicoyne to Courval, Sherbrooke, 20 Sept. 1885.

7 McCord Museum, Sanborn Papers, folio VI, J.H. Pope to J. Sanborn, Ottawa, 14 Oct. 1872.

8 Cookshire Registry Office, Register B, vol. 22, 579–83, no. 11959.

9 See Waite, "John Henry Pope," and Breen, *The Canadian Prairie West*, 18–19.

10 While at La Patrie, for example, Chicoyne was a provincial officer in the Cercles agricoles organization; ANQ-Q, Travaux Publics, no. 394, Chicoyne to Monsieur Barnard, 10 Feb. 1877.

11 Kesteman sees the dominance of this type of capitalism in the Eastern Townships as the chief explanation for the region's lack of industrial investment; "Une Bourgeoisie," 558–59, 585–91, 615–16, 652, 717–21.

12 *JLAQ*, XXVII (1893), app. 1.

13 Kesteman, "Une Bourgeoisie," 555, 586–91. Ronald Rudin makes a similar argument for the limitations to growth of Quebec's French-Canadian banks; see his *Banking en français*, 147.

14 Deschênes, "Jérome-Adolphe Chicoyne," 159–68.

15 Normand Séguin describes how the authorities turned a blind eye for a number of years while the Hébertville colonists cut timber on mountain lots for which a single settlement-lot instalment had been made; *La Conquête*, 132–36. Séguin claims that the wood was for fuel and construction, but another historian suggests that commerce was also involved. St-Hilaire, "La Structuration foncière," 141.

Bibliography

The bibliography is organized into five sections: manuscript sources, printed primary sources, maps, newspapers, and secondary sources. All abbreviated references cited in the notes are given in full here.

MANUSCRIPT SOURCES

ARCHIVES DE L'ARCHEVÊCHÉ DE MONTRÉAL (AAM)
Diocèse de Trois-Rivières 295.104

ARCHIVES DE L'ARCHEVÊCHÉ DE QUÉBEC (AAQ)
Registre de lettres, vol. 1–25 (1816–52)

ARCHIVES DE L'ARCHEVÊCHÉ DE SHERBROOKE (AAS)
Parish papers, Saint-Zenon-de-Piopolis
Rapports des paroisses et missions: Saint-Augustin-de-Woburn, Saint-Pierre-La-Patrie, Saint-Zenon-de-Piopolis

ARCHIVES DE L'ÉVÊCHÉ DE NICOLET
Saint-Grégoire-le-Grand, 1787–1943

ARCHIVES DE L'ÉVÊCHÉ DE TROIS-RIVIÈRES (AETR)
Collection Abbé Edmond Moreau

ARCHIVES DU SÉMINAIRE DE QUÉBEC
Fonds Viger-Verreau, 34

ARCHIVES DU SÉMINAIRE DE SAINT-HYACINTHE (ASSH)
Fonds Jérôme-Adolphe Chicoyne

ARCHIVES NATIONALES DU QUÉBEC À QUÉBEC (ANQ-Q)
Fonds Agriculture et Travaux publics (E25)
    Correspondances reçues, 1867–80
    Registres de lettres envoyées, 1867–80

Fonds Éducation (E13)
    Lettres expédiées, 1870–80
    Lettres reçues, 1870–80
Fonds Secrétariat Provincial (E4)
    Correspondance générale, Municipalités, 1867–80
Fonds Siméon Le Sage (PO149)
    Cahiers de correspondances
Fonds Terres et Forêts (E21)
    British American Land Company (BALC)
    Correspondance générale, 1846–80
    Coupe du Bois, 1828–95
    Inspectors' reports, Winslow Township, 1885
    Megantic Land Company, 1838–39
    Registre de correspondance de T. Boutillier, Bureau de l'inspecteur
        des agences, Saint-Hyacinthe, 1854–55
    Section Bois et Forêts, Lettres envoyées, 1851–80
    Sociétés de Colonisation
    Terres de la Couronne: Administration générale, 1827–99

ARCHIVES NATIONALES DU QUÉBEC À SHERBROOKE (ANQ-S)
    Court of Queen's Bench, District of St Francis, 1836–80
    Notary Files of J.A. Archambault, E.P. Felton, J.I. Mackie, G.H. Napier,
        William Ritchie, and D.M. Thomas
    Sessions of the Peace and Magistrate's Court

BAKER LIBRARY, HARVARD UNIVERSITY, CAMBRIDGE, MASS.
    R.G. Dun Collection

COOKSHIRE TOWN HALL
    Municipality of the Township of Eaton, Minute Book–By Laws–Procès
    verbals, 1855–72

EASTERN TOWNSHIPS HISTORICAL SOCIETY, SHERBROOKE,
QUEBEC (ETHS)
    Fonds Victor Chartier

MCCORD MUSEUM, MCGILL UNIVERSITY, MONTREAL
    Hale Papers
    Sanborn Papers

NATIONAL ARCHIVES OF CANADA (NA)
    British American Land Company Papers (MG24 154)
        Correspondence, 1835–89
        Early transcripts and corporate records
        Letterbook, 1834–36

Record of deeds, 1835–66
Land contracts
Special reports, 1886–1904
Reports and accounts, 1861–1910
Canada, Manuscript Census, 1851–81
Civil Secretary's Correspondence–Incoming (s Series), 1838 (RG4 A1)
Civil/Provincial Secretary's Correspondence–Incoming, Canada East, 1839–67 (RG4 C1)
Civil Secretary's Correspondence–Outgoing, 1852–67 (RG4 C2)
Colonial Office Papers
  Aylmer Papers (CO387)
  Emigration (CO384)
  Q Series (MG11, CO42)
Durham Papers (MG24 A27)
Executive Council, Records Put By, 1839–67 (RG1 E5)
Executive Council, Minute Books (1841–67) (RG1 E1)
Alexander T. Galt Papers, Correspondence: 1858–91 (MG27 ID8)
Governor General's Correspondence, 1845–47 (RG7 G14)
Governor General's Secretary, 1848 (RG7 G20)
J.P. Jones, "History of Lake Megantic, 1760–1921" (non-paginated manuscript, with newsclippings and notes) (MG30 H17)
Land Records, Lower Canada: Bury Township; Compton County – General; Lingwick Township (RG1 L3L)
Fonds La Rocque (MG29 C89)

PRESBYTÈRE DE PIOPOLIS, QUÉBEC
Cahier de délibérations, 1875–80
Livre de caisse, 19 avril 1871–17 avril 1873
Originaux depuis 1874 à nos jours

PUBLIC RECORD OFFICE, LONDON, ENGLAND
Colonial Office Papers (NA copies consulted, see above)

QUÉBEC, MINISTÈRE D'ÉNERGIE, MINES, ET RESSOURCES
(Archives of the former Ministère de l'Agriculture et de la Colonisation, AC)
Adjudications, Section Ouest, Winslow and Marston Townships, 1850–80
Dossier générale du canton, Marston (12050/1921)
Livre des recettes, Marston
Orders-in-Council (Branche Ouest), 1867–80
Register Book, West Section
Registry of assignments, West Section, Marston
Vieux dossiers, Correspondance, 1848–80

ST ANDREW'S SOCIETY OF MONTREAL
Minute Book, 1

SCOTTISH RECORD OFFICE, EDINBURGH (SRO)
Board of Trade, Dissolved Company File (BT2/472)
Court of Session File (CS243/2884)

SHERBROOKE, RICHMOND, AND COOKSHIRE REGISTRY OFFICES
Registers of Land Transactions

STORNOWAY MUNICIPAL OFFICE
Winslow South Municipal Assessment Records

WEST SUSSEX RECORD OFFICE, CHICHESTER, ENGLAND
Petworth Emigration Committee Papers

PRINTED PRIMARY SOURCES

Annuaire de Séminaire Saint-Charles Borromée. Sherbrooke, 1887–92.
Appendix (B) to the Report of the Affairs of British North America from the Earl of Durham (Minutes of Evidence). (1839).
British Parliamentary Papers. Emigration Series. Shannon, Ire.: Irish University Press, 1968–71.
Canada. *Census Reports*, 1871, 1881.
The Canada Directory. Montreal: John Lovell, 1857.
Canada, Province of. *Census Reports*, 1851, 1861.
– *Journals of the Legislative Assembly*, 1841–59.
– *Sessional Papers*, 1860–66.
Compagnie de Colonisation et de Crédit des Cantons de l'Est. *Notice sur son but et son organisation*. Sherbrooke: Imprimerie du Pionnier, 1881.
Doughty, Sir Arthur G., ed. *The Elgin–Grey Papers, 1846–1852*, 4 vols. Ottawa: King's Printer, 1937.
Eastern Townships Gazeteer. St Jean: Smith and Company, 1867.
Gérin-Lajoie, Antoine. *Jean Rivard*. Trans. Vida Bruce. Toronto: McClelland and Stewart, 1977.
Great Britain. *Parliamentary Papers*, 1837 (132) XLII, 15–43, Annual Report from the Agent for Emigration in Canada for 1836.
Guide to the Megantic, Spider, and Upper Dead River Regions of Quebec and Maine. Boston: Heber Bishop, 1888.
Information Respecting the Eastern Townships. London: W.J. Ruffy, 1833.
Information Respecting the Eastern Townships. Quebec: Emigrant Agency Office of the British American Land Company, 1842.
[Langelier, Jean-Chrysostome.] *List of Lands Granted by the Crown in the Province of Québec*. Quebec: Queen's Printer, 1891.
Lower Canada, Lands for Sale in the Eastern Townships. London, Jan. 1837.
Mack, W.G. *A Letter from the Eastern Townships of Lower Canada*. Glasgow: David Robertson, 1837 (copy at Metropolitan Toronto Library).

MacKay, Angus (Oscar Dhu). *By Trench and Trail*. Seattle and Vancouver: MacKay Printing and Publishing Co., 1918.
– *Donald Morrison, The Canadian Outlaw: A Tale of the Scottish Pioneers*, n.p., 1892.
Mandements, lettres pastorales et circulaires des évêques de Québec. III. Québec: A. Coté, 1888. Edition arranged by H. Têtu and Abbé C.O. Gagnon.
Poisson, Adolphe. *Sous les Pins*. Montréal: Librairie Beauchemin, 1902.
Québec. *Débats de la Législature provinciale*, 1879–90.
– *Débats de l'Assemblée législative*, 1874–75. Québec: Journal de Débats, 1976.
– *États des comptes publics*, 1876.
– *Journals of the Legislative Assembly*, 1867–92.
– *Sessional Papers*, 1869–90.
– *Statutes*, 1869–79.
The Report of the Earl of Durham, 2nd ed. London: Methuen and Company, 1905.
Savard, Félix-Antoine. *Master of the River*. Trans. Richard Howard. Montreal: Harvest House, 1976.
Second Report to the Proprietors of the British American Land Company. London, [1836].
Sherbrooke. *Annual Reports from Different Departments of the City of Sherbrooke for the Year ending 31st December 1890*. Sherbrooke: 1891.

MAPS

Blaiklock, F.W. "Plan of the Survey of the Residue of the Township of Marston, 1862." Québec, Énergie, Mines, et Ressources, Service Arpentage, Canton M13B.
"Frontenac, s.d., Section de la carte: canton Marston, Qué." ANQ-Q, NC 82-5-3, D-320.
Gray, O.W. *Map of the District of St. Francis, Canada East. From Surveys ... under the direction of O.W. Gray, Topographical Engr*. Published by Putnam and Gray; D.E. Slack, Publishing agent, 1863. NA, NMC, H2/307/1863.
Pennoyer, Joseph. "Plan of the Township of Lingwick as surveyed by order of the British American Land Company in 1836.7.8&9 by Jos Pennoyer, P.L.S." Office of the BALC, Sherbrooke, 28 Nov. 1860. Québec, Énergie, Mines, et Ressources, Service Arpentage, L22A.
Pennoyer, Joseph, and R. Oughtred. "Plan of the Township of Lingwick as surveyed at sundry times from 1836 to 1866 ... for the British American Land Company by Joseph Pennoyer and R. Oughtred, Provincial Land Surveyors." Québec, Énergie, Mines, et Ressources, Service Arpentage, L22.
"Plan of an Exploratory Road Line from the U.S. Boundary ... to the Megantic Road, Sept. 1861." Québec, Énergie, Mines, et Ressources, Service Arpentage, ch. 29.

Russell, Andrew. *Map of Part of the Eastern Townships of Lower Canada Exhibiting Colonization Roads, 1861*. Quebec: Department of Crown Lands, 1861. NA, NMC, VI/307/1861.

[–] *The Megantic and St. Francis Territories.* NA, NMC, H2/307/[1836].

[–] *Roads and Settlements made by the British American Land Company in the townships of Eaton, Bury and Lingwick, 1838*. Québec, Énergie, Mines, et Ressources, Service Arpentage, Chemin S.B.

– "Sketch to accompany 'Report on the Works performed under the direction of the British American Land Company'." ANQ-Q, carte B-307.

NEWSPAPERS

L'Avenir (Montréal). 1848.

Bangor Daily Whig and Courier. 7 June 1860.

Bulletin de l'Union Allet (Montréal). 1873–81.

Le Canadien (Québec). 1847–48.

Le Constitutionnel (Trois-Rivières). 1871.

Daily Witness (Montreal). 1870–76.

Home and Foreign Missionary Record for the Church of Scotland. 1838–43 (United Church Archives, Victoria University, University of Toronto).

The Home and Foreign Missionary Record of the Free Church of Scotland. 1843–50 (United Church Archives).

Le Journal de Québec. 1847–49.

Le Journal des Trois-Rivières. 1871–72, 1875.

Maine Farmer. 1853, 1855.

La Minerve (Montréal). 1848.

Montreal Gazette. 1816–36.

Le Nouveau Monde (Montréal). 1870–73.

Le Pionnier (Sherbrooke). 1866–93.

Portland Board of Trade Journal. February 1898.

Le Progrès (Sherbrooke). 1874–78, 1883–89.

The Sherbrooke Daily Record. 16 March 1957 (supplement), 21 March 1959.

Sherbrooke Gazette, 1851–63.

Sherbrooke News. 1874–78.

Stanstead Journal. 1845–90.

L'Union des Cantons de l'Est (Arthabaskaville). 1866–82.

SECONDARY SOURCES

Allard, Yolande. "Préservation ou Développement: Le cas du saumon atlantique et de la Rivière Saint-François avant 1900." MA thesis, Bishop's University, 1988.

Anctil, P. "'Chinese of the Eastern States,' 1881." *Recherches sociographiques* XXII (1981): 125–31.

– "La Franco-Américanie ou le Québec d'en Bas." In *Du continent perdu à l'archipel retrouvé: Le Québec et l'Amérique française*, edited by Dean R. Louder and Eric Waddell. Québec: Les Presses de l'université Laval, 1983.

– "L'identité de l'immigrant québécois en Nouvelle-Angleterre; Le rapport Wright de 1882." *Recherches sociographiques* XXII (1981): 331–60.

Angus, Murray E. "The Politics of the Short Line." MA thesis, University of New Brunswick, 1958.

Auclair, Elie J. *Figures canadiennes*. II. Montréal: Éditions Albert Lévesque, 1933.

Bacon, Geo. F. *Portland: Its Representative Business Men and Its Points of Interest*. Newark, N.J.: Glenwood Publishing Co., 1891.

Ball, Norman Roger. "The Technology of Settlement and Land Clearing in Upper Canada Prior to 1840." PHD thesis, University of Toronto, 1979.

Baribeau, Claude. *La Seigneurie de la Petite-Nation, 1801–1854: Le rôle économique et sociale du seigneur*. Hull: Éditions Asticou, 1983.

Bateman, F. "The 'Marketable Surplus' in Northern Dairy Farming: New Evidence by Size of Farm in 1860." *Agricultural History* LII (1978): 345–63.

Belisle, Alexandre. *Histoire de la presse franco-américaine*. Worcester: Ateliers Typographiques de l'Opinion Publique, 1911.

– *Livre d'or des Franco-Américains de Worcester, Massachusetts*. Worcester: La Compagnie de publication Belisle, 1920.

Bellavance, Marcel. *Un Village en mutation: Compton, Québec, 1880–1920*. Ottawa: Parks Canada, 1982.

Benidickson, J. "Private Rights and Public Purposes in the Lakes, Rivers, and Streams of Ontario, 1870–1930." In *Essays in the History of Canadian Law*, vol. II, edited by David H. Flaherty. Toronto: University of Toronto Press, 1983.

Bernard, Jean-Paul. *Les Rouges, libéralisme et anticléricalisme au milieu du XIXe siècle*. Montréal: Les Presses de l'Université du Québec, 1971.

Bervin, G. "Aperçu sur le commerce et le crédit à Québec, 1820–1830." *RHAF* XXXVI (1983): 527–51.

Bitterman, Rusty. "Middle River: The Social Structure of Agriculture in a Nineteenth-Century Cape Breton Community." MA thesis, University of New Brunswick, 1985.

Blanchard, Raoul. *Le Centre du Canada français*. Montréal: Librairie Beauchemin Limitée, 1947.

Booth, John Derek. *Les Cantons de la Saint-François/Townships of the St. Francis*. Montréal: McCord Museum, McGill University, 1984.

– "Changing Forest Utilization Patterns in the Eastern Townships of Quebec, 1800 to 1850." PHD thesis, McGill University, 1972.

– *Railways of Southern Quebec.* 2 vols. Toronto: Railfare, 1982–85.

Bouchard, G. "Co-intégration et reproduction de la société rurale; pour un modèle saguenayen de la marginalité." Unpublished essay kindly provided by the author.

– "Introduction à l'étude de la société saguenayenne aux XIXe et XXe siècles." *RHAF* XXX (1977): 3–27.

– "Un Essai d'anthropologie régionale: L'histoire sociale du Saguenay aux XIXe et XXe siècles." *Annales: économies, sociétés, civilisations* XXXIV (1979): 106–25.

Bouchette, Joseph. *A Topographical Dictionary of Lower Canada.* London: W. Faden: 1815.

Bouffard, Jean. *Traité du Domaine.* 1921; repr. Québec: Presses de l'université Laval, 1977.

Breen, David H. *The Canadian Prairie West and the Ranching Frontier 1874–1924.* Toronto: University of Toronto Press, 1983.

Brouillette, B. "L'Industrie des pâtes et du papier." In *La Forêt.* Montréal: Éditions Fides, 1944.

Brunet, M. "Trois dominantes de la pensée canadienne-française: l'agriculturisme, l'anti-étatisme et le messianisme." In *La Présence anglaise et les Canadiens.* Montréal: Beauchemin, 1958.

Cameron, Rondo E. *France and the Economic Development of Europe, 1800–1914.* Princeton, N.J.: Princeton University Press, 1961.

Cameron, W. "The Petworth Emigration Committee: Lord Egremont's Assisted Emigration from Sussex to Upper Canada, 1832–1837." *Ontario History* LXV (1973): 231–45.

Campbell, R.H. "Scotland." In *The Scots Abroad: Labour, Capital, Enterprise, 1750–1914,* edited by R.A. Cage. London: Croom Helm, 1985.

– *Scotland since 1707; The Rise of an Industrial Society.* Edinburgh: John Donald Publishers, 1985.

Cauchon, Alphonse. *Lac Mégantic: la compagnie Nantaise, le chemin de fer, 1879–1936.* Sherbrooke: Imprimerie Le Messager, 1936.

Channell, Leonard S. *History of Compton County.* Cookshire: L.S. Channell, 1896.

Chaput, D. "Some Rapatriement Dilemmas." *CHR* XLIX (1968): 400–12.

Chartier, C. Edmond. "La colonie du rapatriement." *Revue canadienne* XIII (1914): 319–28, 406–15; XIV (1914): 40–50, 321–31; XV (1915): 351–61; XVI (1915): 227–36, 364–80.

Chayanov, A.V. *The Theory of Peasant Economy.* Edited by Daniel Thorner, Basile Kerblay, and R.E.F. Smith. Homewood, Ill.: Richard D. Irwin, 1966.

Checkland, Sydney, and Olive Checkland. *Industry and Ethos: Scotland 1832–1914.* London: Edward Arnold, 1984.

Cottrell, P.L. *British Overseas Investments in the Nineteenth Century.* London: Macmillan, 1975.

Cowan, Helen I. *British Emigration to British North America: The First Hundred Years*. Toronto: University of Toronto Press, 1961.

Craig, B. "Agriculture and the Lumberman's Frontier in the Upper St John Valley, 1800–70." *Journal of Forest History* XXXII, 3 (1988): 125–37.

Creighton, D.G. *The Empire of the St. Lawrence*. Toronto: Macmillan, 1956.

Cross, Michael. "The Dark Druidical Groves. The Lumber Community and the Commercial Frontier in British North America, to 1854." PHD thesis, University of Toronto, 1968.

– "The Laws Are Like Cobwebs.: Popular Resistance to Authority in Mid-Nineteenth Century British North America." In *Law in a Colonial Society: The Nova Scotia Experience*, edited by P.B. Waite et al. [Toronto: Carswell], 1984.

– "The Lumber Community of Upper Canada, 1815–1867." In *Canadian History before Confederation: Essays and Interpretations*, edited by J.M. Bumsted. Georgetown: Irwin-Dorsey, 1972.

Dechêne, L. "William Price." *DCB* IX.

Defebaugh, James Elliott. *History of the Lumber Industry of America*. I. Chicago: The American Lumberman, 1906.

Deschênes, G. "Jérôme-Adolphe Chicoyne (1844–1910)." *Coopérative et développement* XV, 2 (1982/83): 153–66; XVI, 1 (1983): 159–68.

Désilets, A. "George Benson Hall." *DCB* X.

Dickson, Tony. *Scottish Capitalism. Class, State and Nation from before the Union to the Present*. London: Lawrence and Wishart, 1980.

Dictionary of Canadian Biography. Edited by G.W. Brown et al. 11 vols to date. Toronto: University of Toronto Press, 1965– .

Dictionary of National Biography. Supplement, I. London: Oxford University Press, 1920; repr. 1963.

Drolet, Gustave A. *Zouaviana*. Montréal: Eusèbe Senécal et fils, 1893.

Dussault, Gabriel. *Le Curé Labelle: Messianisme, utopie, et colonisation au Québec, 1850–1900*. Montréal: Hurtubise HMH, 1983.

Elliott, Bruce S. *Irish Immigrants in the Canadas: A New Approach*. Kingston and Montreal: McGill-Queen's University Press, 1988.

Epps, B. "Immigrant File: When the First Scots Came from Lewis." *The Record* (Sherbrooke), 21 Oct. 1988.

Fauteux, Aegidius. *Patriotes de 1837–1838*. Montréal: Les Éditions des Dix, 1950.

Fellman, M. "Rehearsal for the Civil War: Antislavery and Proslavery at the Fighting Point in Kansas, 1854–1856." In *Antislavery Reconsidered: New Perspectives on the Abolitionists*, edited by Lewis Perry and Michael Fellman. Baton Rouge and London: Louisiana State University Press, 1979.

Fortin, G. "Socio-Cultural Changes in an Agricultural Parish." In *French-Canadian Society*, edited by Marcel Rioux and Yves Martin. Toronto: McClelland and Stewart, 1964.

Fraser, Robert. "Like Eden in Her Summer Dress: Gentry, Economy and

Society, Upper Canada, 1812–1840." PHD thesis, University of Toronto, 1979.

Gaffield, Chad. *Language, Schooling, and Cultural Conflict. The Origins of the French-Language Controversy in Ontario.* Kingston and Montreal: McGill-Queen's University Press, 1987.

Gates, Lillian F. *Land Policies of Upper Canada.* Toronto: University of Toronto Press, 1968.

Gates, Paul W. *The Farmer's Age: Agriculture 1815–1860.* White Plains, New York: M.E. Sharpe, 1960.

Gaudreau, Guy. "Le Rapport agriculture-forêt au Québec." *RHAF* xxx (1979): 67–78.

– *L'Exploitation des forêts publiques au Québec, 1842–1905*, Québec: Institut québécois de Recherche sur la Culture, 1986.

Gaunitz, S. "Local History as a Means of Understanding Economic Development: A Study of the Timber Frontier in Northern Sweden during the Industrialization Period." *Economy and History* xxii, 1(1979): 38–62.

– Resource Exploitation on the North-Swedish Timber Frontier in the 19th and Beginning of the 20th Centuries." In *History of Sustained Yield Forestry: A Symposium*, edited by Harold K. Steen. Santa Cruz: Forest History Society, 1984.

Gauthier, B. "La Sous-traitance et l'exploitation forestière en Mauricie (1850–1875)." *Material History Bulletin* xiii (autumn 1981): 59–67.

Gillis, R. Peter. "The Ottawa Lumber Barons and the Conservation Movement, 1881–1914." *Journal of Canadian Studies* ix (Feb. 1974): 14–30.

– "Rivers of Sawdust: The Battle over Industrial Pollution in Canada, 1865–1903." *Journal of Canadian Studies* xxi (spring 1986): 84–103.

– and Thomas R. Roach. "Early European and North American Forestry in Canada: The Ontario Example, 1890–1914." In *History of Sustained-Yield Forestry: A Symposium*, edited by Harold K. Steen. Santa Cruz: Forest History Society, 1984.

– *Lost initiatives. Canada's Forest Industries, Forest Policy and Forest Conservation*, New York: Greenwood Press, 1986.

Goldring, Philip. "British Colonists and Imperial Interests in Lower Canada, 1820 to 1841." PHD thesis, University of London, 1978.

Goodman, David and Michael Redclift. *From Peasant to Proletarian. Capitalist Development and Agrarian Transition.* Oxford: Basil Blackwell, 1981.

Grant, I.F. *Highland Folk Ways.* London: Routledge and Kegan Paul, 1980.

Grant, J., and K. Inwood. "How Urban Was Cloth Manufacture in 1870?" Essay presented at a joint session of the annual meetings of the Canadian Economics Association and the Canadian Historical Association, June 1987.

Gravel, Albert. *Histoire de Coaticook.* Sherbrooke: La Tribune, 1925.

– *Sainte Praxède de Brompton (Bromptonville): Cinquante ans de vie paroissiale dans les Cantons de l'Est.* Sherbrooke: Le Progrès de l'Est, 1921.

Gray, Malcolm. *The Highland Economy, 1750–1850*. Edinburgh: Oliver and Boyd, 1957.

Greer, Allan. *Peasant, Lord, and Merchant: Rural Society in Three Quebec Parishes, 1740–1840*. Toronto: University of Toronto Press, 1985.

Hamelin, Jean, and Yves Roby. *Histoire économique du Québec, 1851–1896*. Montréal: Fides, 1971.

Hamelin, Marcel. *Les Premières Années du parlementarisme québécois (1867–1878)*. Québec: Les Presses de l'université Laval, 1974.

Hardy, René. *Les Zouaves: Une stratégie du clergé québécois au XIXᵉ siècle*. Montréal: Boréal Express, 1980.

– and Normand Séguin. *Forêt et société en Mauricie: La formation de la région de Trois-Rivières, 1830–1930*. Montréal: Boréal Express et Musée national de l'Homme, 1984.

Hareven, Tamara, and Randolph Linebaugh. *Amoskeag: Life and Work in an American Factory-City*. New York: Pantheon, Books, 1978.

Harris, R. Cole. "The Simplification of Europe Overseas." *Annals of the Association of American Geographers* LXVII, 4 (1977): 469–83.

Henretta, J.A. "Families and Farms: *Mentalité* in Pre-Industrial America." *William and Mary Quarterly* XXXV (Jan. 1978): 3–32.

Hobsbawm, Eric. *The Pelican History of Britain, III: Industry and Empire*. Markham, Ont.: Penguin Books, 1969, repr. 1980.

Hodgetts, J.E. *Pioneer Public Service: An Administrative History of the United Canadas, 1841–1867*. Toronto: University of Toronto Press, 1955.

Hodgins, B.W. "Unconventional Priest of the North: Charles Paradis, 1848–1926." In *His Own Man: Essays in Honour of Arthur Reginald Marsden Lower*, edited by W.H. Heick and Roger Graham. Montreal and London: McGill-Queen's University Press, 1974.

– J. Benidickson, and P. Gillis. "The Ontario and Quebec Experiments in Forest Reserves, 1883–1930." *Journal of Forest History* XXVI (Jan. 1982): 20–33.

Hoekstra, A.E., and W.G. Ross. "The Craig and Gosford Roads: Early Colonization Routes in the Eastern Townships of Quebec." *Canadian Geographical Journal* LXXIX (Aug. 1969): 52–57.

Hunter, James. *The Making of the Crofting Community*. Edinburgh: John Donald Publishers Ltd., 1976.

Hurst, James William. *Law and Economic Growth: The Legal History of the Lumber Industry in Wisconsin, 1836–1915*. Cambridge, Mass.: Harvard University Press, 1964.

Innis, Mary Q. *An Economic History of Canada*. Toronto: Ryerson, 1935.

Jackson, W. Turrentine. *The Enterprising Scot: Investors in the American West after 1873*. Edinburgh: Edinburgh University Press, 1968.

Jean, Bruno. *Agriculture et développement dans l'Est du Québec*. Sillery: Presses de l'Université du Québec, 1985.

Johnson, L.A. "New Thoughts on an Old Problem, Self-Sufficient Agriculture in Upper Canada." Paper presented to the annual meeting of the Canadian Historical Association, June 1984.

Johnston, H.J. "Immigration to the Five Eastern Townships of the Huron Tract." *Ontario History* LIV (1962): 207–24.

– "Stratford and Goderich in the Days of the Canada Company." *Ontario History* LXIII (1971): 71–85.

Jones, Robert Leslie. *History of Agriculture in Ontario, 1613–1880*. Toronto: University of Toronto Press, 1946.

Judd, R.W. "Lumbering and the Farming Frontier in Aroostook County, Maine, 1840–1880." *Journal of Forest History* XXVIII (April 1984): 56–67.

Karr, Clarence. *The Canada Land Company: The Early Years, An Experiment in Colonization, 1823–1843*. Ontario Historical Society Research Publication no. 3. Ottawa, 1974.

Kesteman, Jean-Pierre. "Une Bourgeoisie et son espace: Industrialisation et développement du capitalisme dans le district de Saint-François (Québec), 1823–1879." PHD thesis, Université du Québec à Montréal, 1985.

– *Documents sur l'histoire des Cantons de l'Est (1871–1880)*. [Sherbrooke: n.d.]

– *Histoire de Lac-Mégantic*. Ville de Lac-Mégantic, 1985.

– "Histoire de Sherbrooke. 1: L'âge de l'eau (1792–1852)." Unpublished typescript kindly loaned by author, 1979.

– La Condition urbaine vue sous l'angle de la conjoncture économique: Sherbrooke, 1875 à 1914." *Urban History Review* XII (June 1983): 11–28.

– *"Le Progrès (1874–1878): Étude d'un journal de Sherbrooke*. Sherbrooke: Groupe de Recherche en Histoire Régionale, Département d'histoire, Université de Sherbrooke, 1979.

Lajoie, Paul G. *Agricultural Lands in Southern Quebec: Distribution, Extent, and Quality*. Ottawa: Soil Research Institute, Agriculture Canada, 1975.

Lalancette, M. "Essai sur la répartition de la propriété foncière à la Malbaie, au pays de Charlevoix." In *Sociétés villageoises et rapports villes-campagnes au Québec et dans la France de l'Ouest, XVIIe-XXe siècles*, edited by François Lebrun et Normand Séguin. Trois-Rivières: Centre de recherche en études québécoises, Université du Québec à Trois-Rivières, 1987.

Lalonde, A.N. "Colonization Companies in the 1880s." *Saskatchewan History* XXIV (1971): 101–14.

Lambert, Richard S., with Paul Ross. *Renewing Nature's Wealth*. Toronto: Ontario Department of Lands and Forests, 1967.

Lapointe, J. Alphonse. *Historique de St. Vital de Lambton, 1848–1948*. n.d., n.p.

Lavallée, J.G. "Monseigneur Antoine Racine, premier évêque de Sherbrooke (1874–1893)." Société canadienne d'histoire de l'Église catholique, *Rapport* XXXIV (1967): 31–41.

Lavallée, Omer. "International of Maine." Typescript kindly loaned by author.

Lavoie, Y. "Les Mouvements migratoires des Canadiens entre leur pays et les États-Unis au XIXe et XXe siècles." In *La population du Québec: études rétrospectives*, edited by Hubert Charbonneau. Montréal: Les Éditions Boréal Express, 1973.

Leacock, Stephen. *My Discovery of the West.* Boston and New York: Hale, Cushman and Flint, 1937.

Leblanc, R.G. "Colonisation et rapatriement au Lac Saint-Jean (1895–1905)." *RHAF* XXXVIII (1985): 379–408.

– "The Francophone 'Conquest' of New England: Geopolitical Conceptions and Imperial Ambition of French-Canadian Nationalists in the Nineteenth Century." *American Review of Canadian Studies* XV, 3 (1985): 288–310.

– "Regional Competition for Franco-American Repatriates, 1870–1930." *Quebec Studies* I, 1 (spring 1983): 110–29.

Lenin, V.I. *Capitalism and Agriculture.* New York: International Publishers, 1946.

Lenman, B. *An Economic History of Modern Scotland.* London: B.T. Botsford Ltd., 1977.

Le Roux, Michèle. "La Colonisation du Saguenay et l'action de l'Association des Comtés de l'Islet et Kamouraska." DÉS, Université de Montréal, 1972.

Levitt, Joseph. *Henri Bourassa and the Golden Calf: The Social Program of the Nationalists of Quebec (1900–1914).* Ottawa: Les Presses de l'Université d'Ottawa, 1972.

Lewis Frank D. and Marvin McInnis. "Agricultural Output and Efficiency in Lower Canada, 1851." Kingston, Ont.: Queen's University, Institute for Economic Research, Discussion Paper No. 451, 1981.

Little, J.I. "The Catholic Church and French-Canadian Colonization of the Eastern Townships, 1821–51." *University of Ottawa Quarterly* LII (1982): 142–65.

– "Colonization and Municipal Reform in Canada East." *Histoire sociale– Social History* XIV (May 1981): 93–121.

– "Imperialism and Colonization in Lower Canada: The Role of William Bowman Felton." *CHR* LXVI (1985): 511–40.

– "Lucius Seth Huntington." *DCB* XI.

– "The Peaceable Conquest: French-Canadian Colonization in the Eastern Townships during the Nineteenth Century." PHD thesis, University of Ottawa, 1976.

– "Samuel Gale." *DCB* VI.

– "The Social and Economic Development of Settlers in Two Quebec Townships, 1851–1870." In *Canadian Papers in Rural History*, vol. 1, edited by Donald Akenson. Gananoque: Langdale Press, 1978.

– "Watching the Frontier Disappear: English-Speaking Reaction to French-Canadian Colonization in the Eastern Townships, 1844–90." *Journal of Canadian Studies.* XV (winter 1980–81): 93–111.

Lodolini, Elio. *Les Volontaires du Canada dans l'Armée pontificale*. Ottawa: National Museum of Man, 1976.

Loken, Gulbrand. *From Fjord to Frontier: A History of the Norwegians in Canada*. Toronto: McClelland and Stewart, 1980.

Lower, A.R.M. *The North American Assault on the Canadian Forest: A History of the Lumber Trade between Canada and the United States* New York: Greenwood Press, 1938.

McCalla, D. "Forest Products and Upper Canadian Development, 1815–46." *CHR* LXVIII (1987): 159–98.

Macdonald, Donald. *Lewis: A History of the Island*. Edinburgh: Gordon Wright Publishing, 1978.

Macdonald, Norman. *Canada, 1763–1841: Immigration and Settlement*. London, New York, Toronto: Longmans, Green and Co., 1939.

– *Canada: Immigration and Colonization, 1841–1903*. Toronto: Macmillan Canada, 1966.

Macdonell, U.N. "Gibbon Wakefield and Canada, Subsequent to the Durham mission, 1839–42." *Queen's Quarterly* XXXII (1924–25): 119–36, 285–304.

MacDougall, Alexander G. "The Presbyterian Church in the Presbytery of Quebec. 1875–1925." MA thesis, McGill University, 1960.

Mackenzie, Alexander. *The History of the Highland Clearances*. Glasgow: Alex. MacLaren and Sons, 1946.

MacKenzie, Frank. "The History of Man's Utilization of the St. Francis River, Quebec." BA thesis, Bishop's University, 1977.

McKercher, Joseph. "The French-Canadian Press in Sherbrooke and Industrial Development, 1861–1881." MA essay, Concordia University, 1976.

McLaren, J.P.S. "The Tribulations of Antoine Ratté: A Case Study of the Environmental Regulation of the Canadian Lumbering Industry in the Nineteenth Century." *University of New Brunswick Law Journal* XXXIII (1984): 203–59.

McQuillan, A.D. "Farm Size and Work Ethic: Measuring the success of immigrant farmers on the American grasslands, 1875–1925." *Journal of Historical Geography* IV (1978): 57–76.

– "French-Canadian Communities in the American Upper Midwest during the Nineteenth Century." *Cahiers de géographie du Québec* XXIII, 58 (1979): 53–72.

Marx, Leo. *The Machine in the Garden: Technology and the Pastoral Ideal in America*. New York: Oxford University Press, 1972.

Massicotte, G. "Les Études régionales." *Recherches sociographiques* XXVI, 1–2 (1985): 155–78.

Mayhew, H. Carl. *History of Canterbury Quebec*. [n.p.], 1970.

Michie, R.C. *Money, Mania and Markets: Investment, Company Formation, and the Stock Exchange in Nineteenth-Century Scotland*. Edinburgh: John Donald, 1981.

Miller, Marilyn. *Straight Lines in Curved Space: Colonization Roads in Eastern Ontario.* Toronto: Ontario Ministry of Culture and Recreation, Heritage Planning Studies 3, [n.d.].

Minville, Esdras. *L'Agriculture* I. Montréal: Fides, [1943].

Monet, Jacques. "French-Canadian Nationalism and the Challenge of Ultramontanism." Canadian Historical Association, *Report*, 1966, 41–55.

– *The Last Cannon Shot: A Study of French-Canadian Nationalism, 1837–1850.* Toronto: University of Toronto Press, 1969.

Montpetit, André-N. *Colonie française de Metgermette.* Québec: Blumhart et Cie., 1874.

Morin, M. "Calixte Marquis, missionnaire colonisateur du canton d'Aston (1850–1867)." *Les Cahiers nicolétains* III, 2 (June 1981): 42–51.

– La Pensée colonisatrice de Calixte Marquis." *Les Cahiers nicolétains* III, 3 (Sept. 1981): 78–112.

Morissonneau, Christian. "La Colonisation équivoque." *Recherches sociographiques* XIX (jan.-avril 1978): 33–43.

– *La Terre promise: Le mythe du Nord québécois.* Montréal: Hurtubise, 1978.

Murray, F.B. "Agricultural Settlement in the Canadian Shield: Ottawa River to Georgian Bay." In *Profiles of a Province*, edited by Edith G. Firth. Toronto: Ontario Historical Society, 1967.

Myers, Gustavus. *A History of Canadian Wealth.* Toronto: James Lorimer and Company, 1975.

Nelles, H.V. *The Politics of Development: Forests, Mines and Hydro-Electric Power in Ontario, 1849–1941.* Toronto: Macmillan of Canada, [1973].

O'Bready, Maurice. *Histoire de Wotton.* Sherbrooke: Le Messager, 1949.

Osborne, B. "Frontier Settlement in Eastern Ontario in the Nineteenth Century: A Study in Changing Perceptions of Land and Opportunity." In *The Frontier: Comparative Studies*, edited by D.H. Miller and J.O. Steffen. North Oklahoma: University of Oklahoma Press, 1977.

Ouellet, Fernand. *Economic and Social History of Quebec 1760–1850: "Structures" and "Conjonctures."* Ottawa: Institute of Canadian Studies, Carleton University, 1980.

– *Histoire de la Chambre de Commerce du Québec, 1809–1959.* Québec: Faculté de Commerce, Université Laval, [n.d.].

– *Lower Canada, 1791–1840: Social Change and Nationalism.* Toronto: McClelland and Stewart, 1980.

Painchaud, Robert. "Le Manitoba et l'immigration canadienne française, 1870–94." MA thesis, University of Ottawa, 1969.

Paquet, G. "L'Émigration des Canadiens français vers la Nouvelle-Angleterre, 1870–1910; prises de vue quantitatives." *Recherches sociographiques* V (1964): 319–70.

Parent, Gilles. *Deux efforts de colonisation française dans les Cantons de l'Est (1848 et 1851).* Sherbrooke: Groupe de Recherche en Histoire Régionale, Département d'histoire, Université de Sherbrooke, 1980.

Parker, K.A. "Colonization Roads and Commercial Policy." *Ontario History* LXVII (1975): 31–38.

Parson, H.E. "The Colonization of the Southern Canadien Shield in Ontario: The Hastings Road." *Ontario History* LXXIX (1987): 263–73.

Pentland, H. Clare. *Labour and Capital in Canada, 1650–1860.* Toronto: James Lorimer and Company, 1981.

Perron, N. "Genèse des activités laitières, 1850–1960." In *Agriculture et colonisation au Québec*, edited by Normand Séguin. Montréal: Boréal Express, 1980.

Pilon-Lé, L. "La Différenciation de la paysannerie montréalaise au XIXe siècle: Le problème et les faits." *Culture* I, 1 (1981): 48–55.

Piva, M.J. "Continuity and Crisis: Francis Hincks and Canadian Economic Policy." *CHR* LXVI (1985): 185–210.

Pouliot, Léon. "L'Institut canadien, Papineau, Mgr. Bourget et la colonisation des Townships." *Nouvelle France* XVI-XX (1961–62): 60–70, 174–81, 261–68.

– *Monseigneur Bourget et son temps.* III. Montréal: Les Éditions Bellarmin, 1972.

Pouyez, Christian, and Yolande Lavoie. *Les Saguenayens.* Sillery: Presses de l'Université du Québec, 1983.

Price, Lynda. *Introduction to the Social History of Scots in Quebec (1780–1840).* Ottawa: National Museums of Canada, 1971.

Proulx, Bernard. *Le Roman du territoire.* Montréal: Les Cahiers du département d'études littéraires, Université du Québec à Montréal, 1987.

Pruitt, B.H. "Self-Sufficiency and the Agricultural Economy of Eighteenth-Century Massachusetts." *William and Mary Quarterly* XLI (1984): 333–64.

Quinn, M. "Les Capitaux français et le Québec, 1855–1900." *RHAF* XXIV (1975): 527–66.

Rasporich, A.W. "Utopian Ideals and Community Settlements in Western Canada: 1880–1914." In *The Canadian West*, edited by Henry C. Klassen. Calgary: University of Calgary Comprint Publishing Company, 1977.

Raumolin, J. "The Formation of the Sustained Yield Forestry System in Finland." Essay presented to the Forest History Group symposium in Portland, Oregon, October 1979.

– "The Impact of the Forest Sector on Economic Development in Finland and Eastern Canada." *Fennia* 163:2 (1985): 395–437.

Roach, T.R. "Farm Woodlots and Pulpwood Exports from Eastern Canada, 1900–1920." In *History of Sustained Yield Forestry: A Symposium*, edited by Harold K. Steen. Santa Cruz: Forest History Society, 1984.

Robertson, B.R. "Trees, Treaties, and the Timing of Settlement: A Comparison of the Lumber Industry in Nova Scotia and New Brunswick, 1784–1867." *Nova Scotia Historical Review* IV, 1 (1984): 37–55.

Roby, Y. "Les Canadiens Français des États-Unis (1860–1900): Dévoyés ou missionnaires." *RHAF* XLI (1987): 3–22.

Rock, Lois M. "The Agrarian Propaganda of Nineteenth Century French Canada." PHD thesis, University of Birmingham, 1979.

Ross, Aileen D. "Ethnic Relations and Social Structure: A Study of the Invasion of French-Speaking Canadians into an English-Canadian District." PHD thesis, University of Chicago, 1950.

Roy, J. Edmond. *Histoire de la Seigneurie de Lauzon.* v. Lévis, 1904.

Roy, Pierre-Georges. *Les Juges de la province de Québec.* Québec: Archives de la province de Québec, 1933.

Rudin, Ronald. *Banking en français: The French Banks of Quebec, 1835–1925.* Toronto, Buffalo, London: University of Toronto Press, 1985.

– "Land Ownership and Urban Growth: The Experience of Two Quebec Towns, 1840–1914." *Urban Historical Review* VIII (Oct. 1979): 23–46.

– "The Megantic Outlaw and His Times: Ethnic Tensions in Quebec in the 1880s." *Canadian Ethnic Studies* XVIII, 1 (1986): 16–31.

– "Naissance et déclin d'une élite locale: la Banque des Cantons de l'Est, 1859–1912." *RHAF* XXXVIII (1984): 165–80.

– "The Transformation of the Eastern Townships of Richard William Heneker, 1855–1902." *Journal of Canadian Studies* XIX (fall 1984): 32–49.

Rumilly, Robert. *Histoire de la province de Québec, II: Le "Coup d'état."* Montréal: Éditions Bernard Valiquette, 1942.

Russell, P. "Forest into Farmland: Upper Canadian Clearing Rates, 1822–1839." *Agricultural History* LVII (1983): 326–39.

Ryan, William F. *The Clergy and Economic Growth in Quebec (1896–1914).* Québec: Les Presses de l'université Laval, 1966.

St-Hilaire, M. "La Structuration foncière en milieu de colonisation agro-forestière: Saint-Fulgence, 1852–1898." *Saguenayensia* XVII, 4 (1985): 138–45.

"Saint-Zenon de Piopolis." *Le Messager de Saint-Michel de Sherbrooke,* 15 jan. 1933 – 23 avril 1933.

Saunders, Ivan J. "The New Brunswick and Nova Scotia Land Company and the Settlement of Stanley, New Brunswick." MA thesis, University of New Brunswick, 1969.

Savard, Pierre. *Jules-Paul Tardivel, la France et les États-Unis.* Québec: Les Presses de l'université Laval, 1967.

Séguin, Normand. *La Conquête du sol au 19ᵉ siècle.* Sillery, Que.: Express, 1977.

Sellar, Robert. *The Tragedy of Québec: The Expulsion of its Protestant Farmers.* 1916; repr. Toronto: University of Toronto Press, 1974.

Sevigny, Daniel. "Le Capitalisme et la politique dans une région québécoise de colonisation: le cas de Jacques Picard à Wotton, 1825–1905." MA thesis, Simon Fraser University, 1982.

Shepperson, W.S. *British Emigration to North America: Projects and Opinions in the Early Victorian Period.* Minneapolis: University of Minnesota Press, 1957.

Sherman, Annie Isabel. *History of the Families Sherman-MacIver, with Stories of People and Places in the Eastern Townships*. Sherbrooke: Page-Sangster, 1971.

Silver, A.I. *The French-Canadian Idea of Confederation, 1864–1900*. Toronto: University of Toronto Press, 1982.

Skelton, O.D. *The Day of Sir Wilfrid Laurier*. Toronto: Glasgow, Brook and Company, 1916.

– *The Life and Times of Sir Alexander Tilloch Galt*. Toronto: Oxford University Press, 1920.

Smith, David C. *A History of Lumbering in Maine, 1861–1960*. Orono: University of Maine Press, 1972.

Smith, Henry Nash. *Virgin Land. The American West as Symbol and Myth*. Cambridge, Mass.: Harvard University Press, 1971.

Spragge, G.W. "Colonization Roads in Canada West, 1850–1867." *Ontario History* XLIX (1957): 1–17.

Stuart. K. "The Scottish Crofter Colony, Saltcoats, 1889–1904." *Saskatchewan History* XXIV (1971): 41–50.

Talman, J.J. "William Hamilton Merritt." *DCB* IX.

Tobias, J.L. "Canada's Subjugation of the Plains Cree, 1879–1885." *CHR* LXIV (1983): 519–48.

Trépanier, Pierre. *Siméon Le Sage, un haut fonctionnaire québécois face aux défis de son temps*. Montréal: Les Éditions Bellarmin, 1979.

Trofimenkoff, Susan. *The Dream of Nation: A Social and Intellectual History of Quebec*. Toronto: Macmillan of Canada, 1982.

Vanay, M. "Colonisation et monopole forestier: Le cas des cantons Biencourt et Auclair durant la crise." *Revue d'histoire du Bas-Saint-Laurent* IX, 2 (1983): 41–56.

Vicero, Ralph Dominic. "Immigration of French-Canadians to New England, 1840–1900: A Geographical Analysis." PHD thesis, University of Wisconsin, 1968.

Waite, P.B. "John Henry Pope." *DCB* XI.

Wall, G. "Nineteenth-century Land Use and Settlement on the Canadian Shield Frontier." In *The Frontier: Comparative Studies*, edited by D.H. Miller and J.O. Steffen. North Oklahoma: University of Oklahoma Press, 1977.

Whyte, Donald. *A Dictionary of Scottish Emigrants to Canada Before Confederation*. Toronto: Ontario Genealogical Society, 1986.

Willis, J. "Urbanization, Colonization and Underdevelopment in the Bas-Saint-Laurent: Fraserville and the Témiscouata in the Late Nineteenth Century." *Cahiers de géographie du Québec* XXVIII (April-Sept. 1984): 125–61.

Wood, Richard G. *A History of Lumbering in Maine 1820–1861*. Orono: University of Maine Press, 1961.

Wynn, Graeme. "Administration in Adversity: The Deputy Surveyors and Control of the New Brunswick Crown Forest before 1844." *Acadiensis* VII (autumn 1977): 49–65.

– "'Deplorably Dark and Demoralized Lumberers'? Rhetoric and Reality in Early Nineteenth-Century New Brunswick." *Journal of Forest History* XXIV (Oct. 1980): 168–87.

– "Notes on Society and Environment in Old Ontario." *Journal of Social History* XIII (1979): 49–65.

– *Timber Colony: A Historical Geography of Early Nineteenth Century New Brunswick.* Toronto, Buffalo, London: University of Toronto Press, 1981.

Young, Brian J. *George-Étienne Cartier, Montreal Bourgeois.* Kingston and Montreal: McGill-Queen's University Press, 1981.

– "James Bell Forsyth." *DCB* IX.

– *Promoters and Politicians: The North-Shore Railways in the Province of Quebec, 1854–85.* Toronto: University of Toronto Press, 1978.

Index